Communism in Transition

Communism in Transition
The End of the Soviet Empires

Amos Yoder

Fully revised and updated edition of
Communist Systems and Challenges

Taylor & Francis

USA	Publishing Office:	Taylor & Francis
		1101 Vermont Avenue, N.W., Suite 200
		Washington, DC 20005-3521
		Tel: (202) 289-2174, Fax: (202) 289-3665
	Distribution Center:	Taylor & Francis Inc.
		1900 Frost Road, Suite 101, Bristol PA 19007-1598
		Tel: (215) 785-5800, Fax: (215) 785-5515
UK		Taylor & Francis Ltd.
		4 John St., London WC1N 2ET
		Tel: 071 405 2237, Fax: 071 831 2035

COMMUNISM IN TRANSITION: The End of the Soviet Empires

1 2 3 4 5 6 7 8 9 0   B R B R   9 8 7 6 5 4 3

This book was set in Times Roman by Taylor & Francis. The editors were Tricia Dewey and Ellen K. Grover; the production supervisor was Peggy M. Rote; and the typesetter was Phoebe Carter. Cover design by Michelle Fleitz. Printing and binding by Braun-Brumfield, Inc.

A CIP catalog record for this book is available from the British Library.

♾ The paper in this publication meets the requirements of the ANSI Standard 239.48-1984 (Permanence of paper).

Library of Congress Cataloging-in-Publication Data

Yoder, Amos.
   Communism in transition: the end of the Soviet Empires / Amos
Yoder.
     p. cm.
   Rev. ed. of: Communist systems and challenges. 1990.
   Includes bibliographical references (p. 261) and index.
   1. Communism—History—20th century.   I. Yoder. Amos.   Communist
systems and challenges.   II. Title.
HX40.Y58   1990
355.43|09 ′04—dc20
                                                       92-37040
                                                               CIP

ISBN 0-8448-1738-4 (case)
ISBN 0-8448-1739-2 (paper)

Contents

Preface

The directions of changes in Communist systems are clearer now than they were in early 1990 when my first book on Communist systems was published. I have made many changes in this new book. However, I believe my original framework of analysis still helps to explain these important events.

Because so much has happened in the last few years, I use primary news sources more than most books on international relations. The on-site reports of officials and reporters were essential for an understanding of the fast developing events during the transition of the Communist societies.

Many people have helped me interpret developments. However, except for my wife, none of them read the draft of this book, so any defects in it are my responsibility.

I would like to thank the following. For background on China, I am in debt to Chinese friends who are better left unnamed. Going back many years, I am indebted to John Holdridge, Edward Rice, and other former colleagues on the China Desk of the Department of State.

For insights into developments in Hungary and Eastern Europe, I am particularly grateful to colleagues at Kossuth University at Debrecen, Hungary. They include Imre Pozsgay, Istvan Hulvely, Ivan Marki, Zoltan Abadi Nagy, Donald and Scila Morse, Richard Alexander, and Kay Sherman. Also Howard Clark in the American Embassy in Budapest provided interesting background material on economic developments.

For information on the Ukraine, I enjoyed my informal conversations with my student, Baran Sandor, and his parents, Dr. and Mrs. Zoltan Sandor. Also, my other students contributed valuable insights into life in Hungary. Lucia Mlynarcyk was very helpful on Czechoslovakia.

I am grateful to Professor Dale Herspring for insights about the Soviet Union and its armed forces, insights which proved to be sound. I also appreciate the background briefings by Frank Foldvary and Jonathan Mayhew of the Department of State.

In Poland, I appreciated the insights of Algis Ivizienis, Susan Bell, and Mr. Guzik of the American consulate. I also appreciated the comments and hospitality of Tadeusza Sendzimira, Wojciech Siekiceko, and Andrzej Wegrznowski, officials of the Huta Sendzimira plant at Krakow, and Sheila Baldwin, Herbert Tull, and Tonica Smith, American assistants, at Nova Huta in Krakow.

In Czechoslovakia Richard Polka and Paul Hacker of the American consulate provided insights into developments in Slovakia and moves toward regional integration in Central Europe.

In East Berlin I benefited from the briefing and material provided by Peter Claussen of the American consulate.

When we toured Eastern Europe and the Soviet Union in 1991 our guides were no longer inhibited by Communist controls. Mira Mison, Bianka, Svetlana, Ludmilla, Helena, Galina, Florin, Ulyana, Ilka, and Angtla gave us firsthand insights into developments in Yugoslavia, Romania, the Soviet Union, Czechoslovakia, Hungary, and East Germany.

The European Community indirectly played a part in the momentous events of 1989 and following, and I appreciate very much the insights and material provided by Guy VanHaeverbeke and Jan Kurlemann of the staff of the European Parliament.

I am grateful that the MacNeil-Lehrer programs and C-Span not only give firsthand coverage of news events, but they frequently bring leaders and experts into my living room to discuss historic events.

Finally, I am especially indebted to my wife, Janet, who has discussed issues with me through the years and who has commented on the draft.

I try to write in simple English, although I use metaphors to be more expressive. The big words that professors use also creep in—it is an occupational disease.

Amos Yoder

Communism in Transition

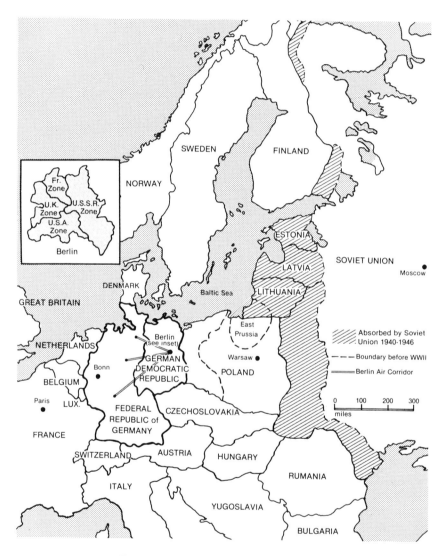

Boundary changes made by the Soviet Union
after World War II

Introduction

Since my first book on Communist[1] systems was published at the beginning of 1990, events in Eastern Europe have continued to take place at breathtaking speed. Although general trends of events were anticipated in that edition, the timing, of course, could not be. The external Soviet empire has ended as Eastern European states have broken away and become democracies.[2] The Warsaw Pact has dissolved. Soviet troops have withdrawn from Czechoslovakia and Hungary and will soon be withdrawn from eastern Germany.

The internal empire of the Soviet Union has also dissolved splitting into a Commonwealth of Independent States (CIS) that are truly sovereign. That loose association, which may not survive, agreed to drastic conventional and nuclear arms reductions and controls that had been accepted by the Soviet Union. Although Russia, along with Ukraine, Belarus, and Kazakhstan, still control nuclear weapons, there is no longer a Soviet superpower, and the danger of a nuclear war between superpowers has vanished.

The Soviet Union also lost its influence in North Korea, China, Vietnam, Cambodia, Cuba, and Laos where it once exercised as much influence as some of the former imperial powers that it attacked in its ideology and propaganda. This worldwide Communist ideological empire has crumbled. Russia in 1992 was preoccupied with trying to establish a viable government in the former Russian Republic and quiet 20 restive nationalities within its boundaries (*Economist* 3/14/92, 59–60).

Russia inherited the United Nations Security Council seat, and it and other members of the CIS are cooperating in the U.N. to address crises in the Middle East and other areas. Wars have dominated twentieth century history, but the positive developments associated with the decline of the Soviet Union promise to be most important.

Events in the former Communist orbit have occurred so rapidly that it is difficult to write about them. Some observers assume that Communism is finished and that it has been decisively defeated in Europe and the Soviet Union. In terms of population, however, three-fourths of the Communist systems were still in existence in 1992. The new developments in the Eastern bloc, and particularly the end of the Soviet empires, demand reassessments of what once were basic assumptions about Communism, democracy, and international politics.

1

This evaluation will cover more than a century, starting with the *Communist Manifesto* of 1848. Lenin used its ideology to exploit the unrest arising from the terrible cost of World War I in Russia to establish the first Communist state. He also established the Comintern to promote a world revolution.

The cold war, which was based on this contest between Communism and democracy, really originated at the close of World War I with the Communist challenge to the capitalist systems outside the Soviet Union. England and France temporarily gave military support to anti-Communist forces, but within a few years the Communist Party consolidated control over the Soviet Union, the world's largest country in area. After World War II the Soviet Union established Communist regimes in Eastern Europe and North Korea. The Stalinist model of political and economic controls was forced on the Eastern European countries and North Korea, which were occupied by Soviet troops.

In 1949 Mao's Communists took control of China, the world's most populous country, and they initially modeled their economic and political system after that of the Soviet Union. During this period the term "cold war" originated and it reached a peak as the United States and other countries under the U.N. flag fought to save South Korea from an invasion by the North. The conflict between the West and Communism was a dominant factor in international politics until the 1989 revolutions.

In 1985 Mikhail Gorbachev began reforming the Soviet Union with the slogans of glasnost (openness) and perestroika (restructuring). In the next five years the pressures released by these policies tore the Soviet Union apart, as minorities in the 15 republics threw off Communist Party controls. Gorbachev's assent allowed the huge empire to break apart without a major war, which was a historic first for a large contiguous empire. This cost him his popularity and his job, and at the end of 1991, a populist type, Boris Yeltsin, took over the job of reforming Russia, the former kingpin of the empire.

In Eastern Europe the people were freed from decades of Communist shackles and the countries began democratic and market reforms. Lenin's statues were toppled by angry demonstrations, and Communism there is no longer a major political force.

Many have written on why the Communist systems failed, and this is important. However, few, if any, have evaluated why the thousands of political experts failed to foresee its failure. I will examine both questions.

Another burning issue is whether the Asian Communist systems will follow the course of the 1989 revolutions in Eastern Europe. China began economic reforms and limited political reforms almost 10 years before those of the Soviet Union. The open door policy that President Nixon began developed into a friendly relationship with the United States. The open door attracted millions of tourists to China, permitted tens of thousands of students to study in the United States and other Western countries, and encouraged thousands of joint ventures with foreign firms.

The Chinese negotiated the peaceful return of Hong Kong from Britain scheduled for 1997. China promised to permit Hong Kong to keep its capitalist system for another 50 years. Chinese leaders reduced the authority of Communist officials in economic enterprises, and China's farmers under the stimulus of local free markets greatly increased food production and more than doubled their income in a decade.

In the spring of 1989, however, China's old Communist leaders ordered repression of demonstrations for democracy led by students. This was covered in detail by the world's news media as a result of the open door policy, and many nations rebuked China for the action. The United States and others imposed limited sanctions. Nevertheless, the Chinese government announced that it intended to continue the openness policy of welcoming foreign investment, while it repressed moves toward democratic reforms. We will look at how the Chinese leaders held on to power and whether there is a basic dynamic in the economic reforms that will bring about democratic reforms.

Changes continue at breakneck speed, and this book attempts to set forth a framework of facts and analysis for perspective on these political earthquakes. The focus is on the following questions: (1) What are basic elements of the Communist ideology that allowed it to dominate half the world? (2) How did the Stalinist model of political and economic controls develop, and why were they discarded? (3) What caused the cold war and the international wars involving Communist systems? (4) Why did thousands of experts fail to anticipate the revolutions beginning in 1989 and their aftermath? (5) What are the implications of these developments?

It is an ambitious survey but it is also a parsimonious one. Focusing on these questions avoids extraneous items such as the philosophy of Marxist theory, details of Communist governments not affecting the changing role of the Communist Party, and history not relevant to major questions.

History, of course, has not yet ended with peace and a victory for democracy and free markets. In 1992 China, Cuba, North Korea, and Vietnam Communists still controlled the governments and they still exerted influenced in other countries, but to a much lesser extent. There was much internal criticism of the new democratic governments in Eastern Europe and a fear persisted of dictators taking over. I will investigate why the prospects for democratic and market reforms appeared hopeful in Eastern Europe, particularly in its northern tier of states.

The great experiments in democratic and market reforms in Eastern Europe have great significance for political scientists and historians. After World War II new schools of scientific social science did not take value systems for granted, and many analysts, including some of the older schools, expected the Communists to be successful in socializing (indoctrinating) their people in Communist values. Some pundits tended to evaluate those systems by such values. The revolutions in Eastern Europe dramatized the failure of the Communist system to sell its values and demonstrated that there was a longing for freedom among the people. The grand experiment to establish democratic and market systems has basic implications for political science.

First I examine the highlights of Communist ideology. Then I look at the collapse of Communism in the Soviet Union and Eastern Europe. Next the subject is Asian and Latin American Communist systems and their challenges to the non-Communist world. I conclude by evaluating the democratic revolutions in the former Soviet Union and in Eastern Europe, their possible effect on other Communist states, why the revolutions surprised Western pundits, and the implications of these events for world peace.

NOTES

1. I capitalize Communism, as most texts do because Communists of many countries supported a standard ideology. In Eastern Europe, particularly, they often acted as a common political party across borders, much more so, for example, than did democrats in Western democracies.

2. The conventional definition of *democracy* is used in this text (see p. 6). This includes the definition used in evaluations of democracies by Freedom House, a nonprofit organization that monitors human rights around the world (Freedom House, 1992).

Chapter 1

Marxism-Leninism

Ideologies affect the actions of leaders, and leaders use ideologies to gain support for policies. Some schools of analysis minimize the importance of ideologies and try to explain politics and foreign policies by concentrating on interests of political groups and countries. This book, however, is based on the belief that ideologies, including the Communist ideology, color leaders' perceptions of the world and of their interests. The Communist ideology has been a powerful tool to promote revolution and allow leaders to control societies. In controlling societies they have tried to indoctrinate or socialize their people to accept their Communist views of society and the world. In this way the ideology attains influence and a momentum that affect both domestic and foreign policies.

Hitler's fascist ideology brought the German nation into World War II. Japan's version of fascism did the same. The Communist ideology, as we will see, was a key factor in promoting the revolution or coup in Russia, the revolution in China, and other wars. It is important, therefore, to understand the main elements of the Communist ideology. But it is also important to define the terms that are used.

DEFINITIONS

Political Terms

There are different dictionaries for ideological and governmental terms, and in order to communicate we must use the same dictionary. Terms are used as weapons of political warfare, and the antagonists attach different meanings to them. There is no judge to determine whose definition of such important words as *democracy* and *Communism* is correct, but if we use the same dictionary, we can understand each other and even communicate across cultures. In this book I use the Western dictionaries that generally define political terms as follows:

Ideology—the integrated assertions, theories, and aims constituting a politico-social program.

Communism (capitalized)—an ideology and a totalitarian form of government based on revolutionary Marxist-Leninism, which interprets history as a class war that eventually results in the establishment of the dictatorship of the proletariat in which one party controls political life and its government owns the means of production. The word *communism* (not capitalized) refers to a social organization in which goods are held in common or to the classless society where the state has withered away as envisaged by Marx as the end result of the historical process after the establishment of the dictatorship of the proletariat.

Democratic—a government in which supreme power is vested in the people and exercised by them directly or indirectly through a system of representation involving periodically held free elections. Communists have called their systems democratic, but the recent revolutions against Communism called for free elections, free speech, freedom to organize an opposition, and other freedoms in a way that made clear the demand for the Western definition of democracy.

Authoritarian—the concentration of political power in a leader or an elite.

Totalitarian—a political regime in which individuals are subordinated to the state, which strictly controls major aspects of life.

Socialist—a social organization based on governmental ownership or control of the means of production and distribution of goods. In Marxist theory the intermediate form of government between capitalism and communism, the dictatorship of the proletariat, is called socialist. The Soviet Union's dictionary, therefore, called its form of government socialist. The Western dictionary, however, called the Soviet Union's government Communist, which means it was totalitarian politically and socialist economically with the Communist ideology as a guide.

Social democracy—a democratic political system with government ownership and control of the economy.

Fascism—a totalitarian form of government dominated by a leader with a nationalistic and racist ideology that regiments the economy but allows private ownership of property.

Ideologies can operate within the framework of governments and economies. The Communist ideology has spawned a certain type of government and economy. In Figure 1-1 governments and economies are shown on a scale to help to define terms and evaluate Communism and other forms of government.

The definitions in Figure 1-1 are those used in the U.S. news media. On the political scale governments could be evaluated according to the degree they allow free elections to be carried out, an opposition to organize, and their citizens to enjoy freedom. Freedom House evaluates governments periodically on a scale of 1 to 7 using such criteria (Freedom House 1989). Political scientists would not agree on precise numbers, but many would agree approximately with the relative position on the scale that Freedom House assigns to various governments.

The Communist news media in the Soviet Union used other definitions and called the Soviet system democratic, claiming it was established and controlled by the working class. As indicted below, that was not correct. At times they called the Western democracies fascist, whereas Western dictionaries put fascism on the totalitarian and opposite end of the scale.

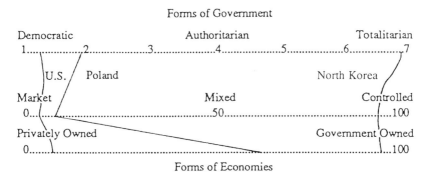

Figure 1-1 A model for comparing governments and economies.

TYPES OF ECONOMY

The economic scales use a scale of 1 to 10. The scale that ranges from "market" to "controlled" indicates a measure of freedom of prices from government control and also freedom from regulations, taxes, licenses, and other forms of control. It would be difficult to give weight to these factors even if full data were available.

The other scale measures ownership, but there are varying degrees of ownership. For example, in China where the government retains ownership farmers have recently been allowed to take long-term leases and even transfer rights to land. This gave the Chinese the incentive to rapidly increase production and incomes. Polish farmers, on the other hand, owned 75 percent of the farmland, but government restrictions on feed, fertilizer, and marketing discouraged food production, and Poland was faced with a severe food shortage (*NYT* 8/10/89, 10). There are no precise ratings of the degree prices are determined by the free market, but I have used IMF reports on price liberalization as a basis for my estimates.

The main purpose of the continuums in Figure 1-1 is to define terms to help analyze the governments and economic systems and not to make a statistical comparison. The figure also illustrates the possibility of a Communist, public-ownership system using market forces to stimulate an economy. Theoretically a government could own enterprises that would operate in a market system. The Chinese Communists and to some extent other Communist countries are beginning to experiment with market forces while retaining government ownership and control of the major sectors of the economy and maintaining the dominant role of the Communist Party. Some of them are also introducing elements of private ownership into the system. The chart does not claim to prove they can be successful, but sets forth a framework to evaluate if market forces might be used with public ownership or control and if this is politically feasible. If the world's economic and political systems were plotted on the chart, it would show that economies of democratic countries are mostly market-oriented and privately owned, and economies of Communist societies are controlled by the government (Freedom House 1988).

The model leaves out an important ideological factor. For example, during most of the 1980s both the Soviet Union and Iran would have been at the totalitarian end of the scale, although one government was atheistic and the other strongly religious. With radically different ideologies, government policies were different. The above definitions and scales, however, compare Communist systems with democratic governments and help to explain economic policies of the revolutions of 1989.

THE COMMUNIST DOCTRINE

Karl Marx's doctrine of Communism is simple and can be quickly understood. He and his friend and close associate, Friedrich Engels, published their explosive ideas in the *Communist Manifesto* more than 100 years ago, and it is still the Communist bible. Some say this publication has been more influential than any other including the Christian Bible. After writing his basic text of Communism, Marx spent most of the rest of his life writing *Das Capital*, which tries to explain the economic basis of history. This is a huge, dull book that many Communists have studied but do not take very seriously.

In the *Communist Manifesto* Marx argued that history involves a continual class struggle based on "economic determinism." For example, the middle class and the commercial class undermined the power of the nobles and the guild masters and established a new and better system, capitalism. Similarly, his theory holds, the laboring class, the proletariat, is undermining the power of the capitalist or bourgeois class, which dominates government and its policies, and the proletariat will establish a new system, which we call Communism (and Communists call socialism). Marx knew what the proletariat wanted without asking them, and he saw them as instruments of class struggle and revolution in a historical process. Governments, he believed, were just committees of the ruling class to exercise control over the proletariat.

Marx saw the above historical process as one based on a struggle over material goods, which he described as dialectical materialism. The struggles, he said, would result in new and higher forms of societies. Philosophers have noted this is related to Hegel's dialectic, which he stated governs history as well as thought. Socrates, Plato, and other philosophers had a similar belief that a better knowledge of the truth comes about by the dialectical process of arguing pro and con—hypothesis and antithesis—to achieve a better understanding or synthesis. Marx's basic belief was that the class struggle over material goods was the driving force of history. He also believed that ideologies grow out of economic factors and provide a superstructure used by the dominant class to control society.

According to Marx, the dynamic of capitalism forces the capitalists to increase production and expand markets, and in doing so they hire more workers.

Thus by increasing the working class they are digging their own grave. He also stated, along the lines of the English economist J. A. Hobson, that because laborers receive minimal wages, under capitalism they cannot buy the total production of the capitalist system. This causes periodic economic crises, he said, so the capitalists, and particularly the banking interests, are forced to find markets abroad, and they invest their surplus profits and capital there. The theory holds that they also exploit these areas for cheap raw materials. Lenin believed World War I was caused by this type of imperialism. Marx and Lenin held that the solution to the world's problems is for the working class, the proletariat, to abolish capitalism and create government ownership of the means of production and a world community of "socialist" nations. Workers would revolt and take control of the government apparatus. "Workers of the world unite. You have nothing to lose but your chains" was Marx's slogan for the Communists.

After the *Communist Manifesto* was published, Marx's supporters divided into two major schools. According to Lenin one political group in Germany sold out to liberal democracy in the late nineteenth and early twentieth centuries because of the benefits this group obtained from a capitalist society. These social democrats believed that they could achieve the Marxist system through democratic procedures. These "revisionists" were bitterly attacked by Lenin's branch of the Communists, the hard-line, revolutionary Communists, or Bolsheviks. Lenin's branch of Communism believed that the Communist Party should be centralized and under the firm control of its leaders. This disciplined party, by seizing political control of the state could speed up the historical process that Marx described in the *Communist Manifesto* (see Appendix 1 for excerpts).

Lenin expanded on Marx's ideas of the dictatorship of the proletariat. His main thesis was that Communists should grab history by the forelock and bring about the overthrow of the capitalist system. For this the Communists needed to organize a tightly controlled, disciplined party ready for violent revolution. Both Marx and Lenin asserted that when the revolutions succeeded in establishing Communism throughout the world, the exploitation of one nation by another would end and there would be peace. At the end of the *Communist Manifesto*, Marx pointed to Germany as the place where the revolution would begin. He and many other Communists believed that the revolution would depend on industrial workers and not the peasants or farmers. However, the revolution occurred first in Russia, which had a very small number of industrial workers, and it also occurred in China, through Mao's organization of the peasants.

When the revolution was being organized, the question of whether workers or peasants should lead the revolution caused disputes among Marxist-Leninists. We will see that Mao organized Chinese peasants to bring about the revolution, but Chinese Communists avoided a theoretical argument by including all the poorer elements of society in the definition of proletariat. After World War I, the Communists claimed that a new form of colonialism, neocolonialism, arose in which capitalists maintained control of countries through investment and trade. They were said to control former colonies by using "national" or local bourgeoisie as their instruments of control.

The Communists also claim that arms races are caused by the profit motive of the munitions makers. Communists have claimed that the arms manufacturers control the governments of the democracies and that they have promoted arms races and wars in order to find markets for armaments (Hunt 1963; Ozinga 1987; *NYT* 1/22/89, 1/23/89, 1/24/89). This basic element of Marxism-Leninism is stated by Mikhail Gorbachev in his book on Perestroika.

> We see how strong the positions of the aggressive and militarist part of the ruling class are in the leading capitalist countries. Their main support comes from the powerful military-industrial complex whose interests are rooted in the very nature of the capitalist system and which extracts huge profits from arms production at the taxpayers' expense. And to make the people believe the money is not being spent in vain, they must be convinced of the existence of an "external enemy" which wishes to encroach upon their well being and "national interests" in general. Hence the reckless and irresponsible power politics (148).

He rejects the inevitability of war and stresses the necessity of getting along with the capitalist system:

> Thirty-odd years ago, the 20th CPSU Congress reached an important conclusion to the effect that a new world war was not inevitable and could be prevented. . . . The very logic of detente was being promoted by the increasing realization that a nuclear war cannot be won. Proceeding from this fact we declared five years ago to the whole world that we shall never be the first to use nuclear weapons. . . . Economic, political and ideological competition between capitalist and socialist countries is inevitable. However, it can and must be kept within the framework of peaceful competition which necessarily envisages cooperation (144–148).

Leading officials of the foreign ministry under Gorbachev reinforced the theoretical basis for détente as follows:

> It is all the more strange to talk about the irreconcilable interests of states with different social systems now that even the class conflicts within capitalist countries largely take place through the achievements of compromise within a mutually accepted legal framework rather than in the form of harsh confrontation. It follows that the Soviet workers' solidarity with their class brothers in the West far from justifies the thesis of global class confrontation. "The myth that the class interests of socialist and developing countries coincide in resisting imperialism does not hold up to criticism at all. The majority of developing countries already adhere to or tend toward the Western model of development and they suffer not so much from capitalism as from a lack of it. (*NYT* 1/7/89, 17, from article in Foreign Ministry's *International Affairs*).

The easily understood criticisms of capitalism have had a strong appeal to workers as well as intellectuals in many countries. Its most influential elements have been those developed by Lenin to provide a program for revolution, particularly in poor and underdeveloped countries. Ho Chi Minh, in an article in the Russian Communist Party newspaper *Pravda* praising Lenin, stated that Lenin gave working people suffering from imperialist oppression "the miraculous weapon to fight for their emancipation—the theories and tactics of Bolshevism." He asserted that Lenin's popularity and doctrine were closely linked to all the successes of the "camp of peace and democracy" that stretched from the Elbe River to the Pacific Ocean and from the Arctic poles to the tropics. On November 3, 1957, he said that the Russian October Revolution "shattered the fetters of imperialism, destroyed its foundation, and inflicted on it a deadly blow. Like a thunderbolt, it has stirred up the Asian peoples from the century-old slumbers. It has opened up for them the revolutionary anti-imperialist era, the era of national liberation" (Fall 1967, 284–285, 326–333).

A modern version of Marxism called the theory of "dependency" appeals to many in Latin America. This theory states that the powerful multinational firms of the United States and other industrial countries have dominated underdeveloped countries in Latin America through large-scale exports and investment. These firms sell their manufactured goods in Latin American countries and develop cheap sources of raw materials there. This theory suggests that the representatives of the multinationals get allies in the government and society of the developing countries to help continue their exploitation of the local economies to prevent them from developing manufactured goods. Closely associated with this theory is the claim that the United States supports military dictatorships in Latin America to maintain economic domination and to develop markets for U.S. military products.

The Communist systems of the current era had the tightly disciplined parties that controlled governments as proposed by Lenin. The Communist parties and governments controlled significant parts of economic and social life. Lenin had no respect for the liberal democratic system as we know it. All good theories and propaganda too have some element of truth in them. Below are pluses and minuses of the Communist ideology discussed in the following chapters. A theory receives a plus if it has proven effective or been accepted by Western observers and a minus if it has not.

PLUSES

1. The Communist theories are simple to understand and persuasive. They were powerful tools for leaders to promote revolution and to justify strict Communist Party controls over society.
2. At the time Marx wrote, workers were exploited by working for low wages. The Communist program called for elementary reforms such as organization of workers, a heavy progressive income tax, free education for all children in public school, and abolition of child labor. These reforms have been adopted by democratic societies.

3. Many economists would agree with Marxists that depressions have been caused by insufficient purchasing power of the people.
4. There were wars for colonial markets in the nineteenth century.
5. The concept of analyzing social systems by class structure is widely used.
6. At least some Marxist systems are relatively egalitarian compared with the difference between rich and poor in many capitalistic societies.
7. The military-industrial complex (a term made popular by President Eisenhower) is politically influential in promoting high military budgets and contributing to the arms race.

The following elements of the ideology have not been confirmed by history and would be graded with a minus by observers who support values of freedom and democracy.

MINUSES

1. Men and women and their leaders have many motives other than economic ones. Material motives are important, but factors such as prestige and sex, as well as ideologies of nationalism and democracy, influence their actions. People with the same economic and class backgrounds will have different ideologies and have developed different types of political systems.
2. The Marxist-Leninist ideology has been used to establish huge bureaucracies and strict controls over societies for the benefit of a Communist elite. As a result, even Communists do not take communism seriously—for example, the prediction of Marx that the state would wither away. The major element of Gorbachev's reforms, as we see in the next chapter, was to try to reduce the Communist Party controls over society and to reduce the huge state bureaucracy.
3. The democratic state is not an instrument of a ruling class. In democracies, in particular, interest groups influence laws and actions of the state. Business groups are influential, but so are labor, farm, professional, church, ethnic, and many other types of interest groups.
4. The Communist economies have not produced as much for consumers as have the capitalist economies. The market economies of the capitalist states have created much higher standards of living. Moreover, Communist economies and not the capitalist economies generally devote the highest proportion of gross national product to armaments.
5. Labor unions in capitalist economies have brought higher wages to the workers. In most Communist countries governments control unions and forbid unions controlled by workers. Government unions do not use strikes and other major pressures to obtain higher wages.
6. Since World War II there have been no periodic and recurring economic depressions in capitalist countries from a lack of workers' purchasing

power as predicted by Marx and Lenin, although there have been more fluctuations in employment and output in capitalist economies than in the controlled Communist economies.

7. Capitalism does not need colonies for prosperity, as illustrated by the rapid economic development of Germany and Japan since World War II. However, there has been a drive by the multinational corporations to find markets and establish plants abroad in industrial and developing countries. The few cases in which they have had strong political influence in a country are featured by socialist and Communist critics of capitalism. These critics do not describe the many cases in which foreign firms have established higher working standards than those of local firms and promoted economic development in developing countries such as South Korea, Taiwan, Singapore, Thailand, the colony of Hong Kong, and many other areas.

8. Colonies existed long before capitalism. Moreover, the Russian Communist system established an imperialistic type of colonial control over Eastern Europe as well as over Mongolia and Afghanistan. I will evaluate oppression by the Soviet Union in Eastern Europe, as well as the revolutions in Eastern Europe that began in 1989.

As suggested above, there is some truth in the Marxist theories, enough to have made them appealing to people and leaders of poorer countries. For example, Marx gave them capitalism and imperialism to blame for their troubles, which made enough good propaganda to divert attention from their own policies, and this was a useful tool for ambitious or corrupt leaders. Nevertheless, Communist systems have collapsed and are being replaced by democratic, market systems. There has been much criticism of the rigid doctrines and policies that controlled life in former Communist countries. We will now look at how domestic and foreign policies of Communist systems were carried out in practice, keeping in mind the pluses and minuses of Communist theory.

Chapter 2

The Stalinist Model and Its Collapse

The Soviet Union was the model for the Communist form of government for other Communist countries, which copied its institutions and followed its lead in foreign policy. After World War II the Soviet Union became the unchallenged leader of the Communist world. This chapter describes and evaluates how Lenin and Stalin established this model, how Stalin built it into a repressive bureaucracy, and finally how Mikhail Gorbachev and Boris Yeltsin ended the 70-year reign of the Communist Party.

THE 1917 REVOLUTION

The Communist revolution led by Lenin in November 1917 was not against the tsar but against the Kerensky government that had overthrown the tsar and was in the process of establishing a democracy in Russia. Communists worshipped Lenin for his leadership in the world's first Communist revolution, and it is revealing to look at Lenin's life and trace how he initiated the Communist system.

Vladimir Ilyich Ulyanov, who later took the revolutionary-style name Lenin, was born in 1870. His father was a minor education official, apparently loyal to the tsarist regime. After his father's death, when Lenin was sixteen, his elder brother, Alexander, became involved in revolutionary activity, was arrested by the tsarist police, and then executed. Lenin was, of course, much affected by his brother's execution and tried to understand him better by studying Marxism. He soon decided to become a professional revolutionary. He was arrested several times and spent a year in jail in St. Petersburg and three years in exile in Siberia. The exile was a restful sojourn, and Lenin was able to set up housekeeping, marry a fellow Communist, receive books, and write a scholarly book about Communism. This is in sharp contrast to the brutal treatment of prisoners under Stalin in Siberian concentration camps.

In 1903 Lenin, during meetings of social democrats in Brussels and London and with clever political maneuvers, was able to get a temporary majority to support his idea of a disciplined party to lead the revolution. Thereafter, he continued to use the name "Bolshevik," or majority, for his faction.

In January 1905 the seeds of the first major Russian revolutionary movement were planted after the massacre of perhaps as many as 500 people when soldiers fired on a mass demonstration of 200,000 people trying to petition the tsar. They were demanding an eight-hour work day and protesting the economic distress caused by the Russo-Japanese war. The following winter, when strikes and demonstrations escalated, Lenin returned to Russia, but he was not able successfully to escalate revolutionary activity and was forced again to flee the country. During this revolution, soviets, or committees elected at workplaces by the workers, were formed. Although these soviets were broken up by the police, they were revived in 1917 and played a key part in that revolution. The tsar did grant limited reforms as a result of the 1905 unrest, including the establishment of a parliament, or Duma. The Duma had limited power and was subject to being prorogued by the tsar, but it would play an important part in the 1917 revolution.

Lenin managed to keep a prominent position in the social democratic movement by publishing articles and books on ideology and revolution and meeting with Russian and foreign revolutionaries. Before World War I he worked for the Russian revolution from abroad, in Austria, Germany, Poland, Finland, England, and Paris. In the early 1900s he had edited a revolutionary paper, *The Spark*, which was smuggled into Russia, and before World War I he was an editor of several publications, including *Pravda*, a Bolshevik newspaper published in Russia. During World War I he settled in Switzerland, where he was relatively isolated from Russia. He remained there during most of World War I, frustrated but carrying on meetings with other leftists.

The revolution that overthrew the tsar began in February 1917. On February 27, Alexander Kerensky, a delegate of the Social Revolutionary Party to the Duma, made a violent speech attacking the tsarist government. The Duma's power at that time was severely limited in relation to the tsar and his officials. Kerensky claimed that Russia was exhausted from fighting in World War I and that it was time to liquidate the war. On March 3, workers in one of the big factories struck because others had been dismissed. The management locked them out, all 30,000 of them. Meanwhile, the housewives of St. Petersburg could no longer tolerate the war and the bread shortage, so they organized a demonstration. The police lost confidence in the government when the Cossack units refused to break up the demonstration. On March 11, however, soldiers killed 60 demonstrators, and the crowd ran amok. The tsar ordered the Duma to be disbanded.

On March 12 one of the regiments defected. A group of deputies then formed an Emergency Committee of Duma members, which began to act for the government of Russia for the next seven months. During this period the socialists revived the soviets of 1905 by electing committees in the factories, and formed an Executive Committee of their party, which became a center of political power rivaling that of the Duma.

The Emergency Committee and the Executive Committee, through two Duma deputies who met with the tsar, demanded the tsar's abdication along with elections, freedom of the press, and equal rights for minorities. Tsar Nicholas, who could not name his son as successor to the throne because of the boy's hemophilia then agreed that the crown should go to the Grand Duke Nicholas, his brother. Kerensky was in a rage against efforts to preserve the monarchy. The Grand Duke agreed, however, to take the crown only if it were offered by a constituent assembly. This satisfied Kerensky, who said "you are the noblest of men." This was the "revolution" that deposed the Romanov dynasty and took over the Russian empire.

Lenin, who was living in Switzerland, had established a loyal following among socialists as a result of his prewar political activities. He was also recognized as a leader among the other radical Russian expatriates. The German government in a desperate move after the United States entered World War I arranged for Lenin, who opposed the war, to be sent across Germany to Finland in a sealed railway carriage, as though he had a disease. As the German general staff had planned, as soon as Lenin entered Russia from Finland in April 1917 he began preaching revolution, using the powerful slogan "peace, bread, and land." Another slogan was "All power to the soviets," which were being organized in the workplaces of major cities and even in military units. The Central Executive Committee, which represented the soviets, played a key role in the revolution.

U.S. President Wilson pressed Russia to stay in the war and offered a loan of $325 million. Minister of War Kerensky agreed to support a new offensive against Germany despite Russia's weakened position. On July 20, 1917, he became prime minister. His government issued an order for Lenin's arrest, which prompted Lenin to flee across the border to Finland.

The new offensive caused Russia's economic and political situation to deteriorate even more rapidly, with soldiers deserting and peasants taking over land that they tilled. In September General Kornilov tried to take advantage of the situation with a coup. He was defeated with the help of railway workers who would not haul the troops. By this time in October the Bolsheviks dominated the All-Russian Congress of Soviets and its Executive Committee. Lenin returned secretly from Finland and persuaded the Bolshevik Central Committee to start the revolution. On November 7 the Bolsheviks, with the aid of the soviets and defecting soldiers and sailors who were tired of the war, took over the government in the name of the soviets. It was a near bloodless revolution, or coup, with Kerensky fleeing and not being able to muster troops to come to the defense of his government.

Lenin established the Council of People's Commissars, which issued a string of decrees ending private ownership of land and nationalizing enterprises, annulling state debts, replacing criminal courts with revolutionary tribunals, declaring men and women equal under law, and replacing church weddings with civil ceremonies. The Council's major action was to order the Russian military not to resist the Germans and to negotiate an end to the war, even though initially this involved giving up extensive areas of western Russia to the Germans and agreeing to pay a large indemnity. After the war, Ukraine was returned to the Soviet Union by the Treaty of Versailles, but the Soviets lost Finland, Estonia, Latvia, Lithuania, Poland, and Moldavia.

The situation was chaotic for the next few years, which were known as the period of War Communism. At first unions took over control of factories and groups of workers requisitioned food from the countryside. The Communists also tried hiring bourgeoise specialists and using one-man management of factories.

In November the elections that had been scheduled by the Kerensky government for a constituent assembly were held. Out of 42 million votes, only 24 percent were for the Bolsheviks plus their allies including 5 percent for the Left Socialist Revolutionaries. The Bolshevik opponents, the Socialist Revolutionaries, received most of the votes with 38 percent. Nevertheless, Lenin consolidated his power by breaking up the assembly, and he dissolved it again with soldiers when it tried to meet in January.

This chain of events shows that the Communists did not come to power through an uprising of the masses as a result of economic exploitation but through a revolution or coup supported by soldiers who were weary of war. Lenin did not win in a fair election, and he had an utter contempt for constitutional democracy (which he called bourgeois democracy). He won because he had a disciplined party with military support and a program for a hungry, war-weary nation.

THE CONSOLIDATION OF COMMUNISM

Lenin helped maintain political control by establishing the Cheka, or security police, which brutally suppressed opposition. The Cheka's eventual successor, the KGB, was larger with more pervasive controls. It continued to be a powerful force in the Soviet Union.

By 1921 the Communists were in firm control but the economy was in shambles. The tremendous damage caused by the German invasion was made worse by the civil war waged with the opposition forces, particularly those assisted by military units of the British and French in the Caucausus. Moreover, the string of government decrees abolishing the market system and incentives for Russian farmers and businessmen brought about economic stagnation and starvation.

The situation was brought to a head on March 21, 1921, when the sailors of the Kronstadt military base revolted in protest. They demanded elections by secret ballot, freedom of speech and the press, and a free market for peasants, demands that were consistent with the Kerensky program before he was overthrown. The Communist government crushed the Kronstadt revolt, killing several thousand.

The crisis led Lenin to introduce a New Economic Policy (NEP), which largely restored free markets. Decrees were issued nationalizing banks, the railroads, and the press, but the production of food and other items during these first years was left to private owners of farms and factories. In the early 1920s a severe famine was relieved with extensive food aid provided by the League of Nations and Quakers, under Herbert Hoover, who later became president of the United States. Gradually the Soviet economy began to recover from the tremendous destruction of World War I and the ensuing civil war and intervention.

Lenin named Stalin as general secretary of the Communist Party. Born Josif Vissarionovich Dzhugashvili, Stalin had joined the Social Democratic Party in 1906 at the age of 17 and had become a follower of Lenin and the Bolsheviks. He was a son of peasants, and he was educated in a seminary. His power base arose out of his position as secretary of the party, which put him in charge of recruiting 700,000 new members and in control of important appointments to government and party positions. Stalin consolidated his personal control, and the party soon dominated the government and economic and social aspects of Soviet life.

Lenin's death in 1924 provoked a political struggle over his successor. Stalin took control and dominated the Soviet Union for the next 30 years. His idea was to build socialism in one country before promoting the world revolution, whereas Trotsky, his chief rival, emphasized promoting world revolution. Stalin won the support of the party, and Trotsky fled to Mexico where, years later, he was assassinated by a Soviet government agent.

Stalin instituted a series of five-year plans in 1929 with the aim of building the Soviets' heavy industry as a basis for further development. This was a natural extension of Marx's and Lenin's theories of abolishing private ownership and substituting socialist control of the means of production. In the early 1930s with the second and third five-year plans, Stalin used the heavy industry for an armament industry to strengthen the Soviet Union against the threat of Germany.

By this time it was evident that the state was not withering away as predicted by Marx and his followers, but that a huge bureaucracy was being built up. Stalin felt constrained to explain that a powerful state was necessary to protect the Soviet Union from capitalist encirclement and to guide it into the higher phase of communism.

The building up of heavy industry required food for the new work force. Stalin met this problem by forcing Russian farmers to give up their land to collective farms, which controlled production, and turn over the products to the state. Many resisted collectivization and refused to cooperate in producing more food than they needed for their own consumption. Estimates of the loss of life as a result of the disruption caused by the collectivization policy range up to many millions. The Communist Party and government were able to prevail in the forced industrialization policy, however, and by World War II the Soviets had a substantial armament industry.

By the mid-1930s Stalin's main concern was meeting the threat from Hitler's Germany. The Soviet Union's huge resources of labor plus its heavy industrial base gave it the basis for creating a formidable defensive force of more than 100 divisions, fairly well equipped with tanks, trucks, guns, and aircraft, all of which required the steel and machinery of heavy industry. The Russian consumer suffered, but by 1940 Stalin had built the basis of a powerful military machine that was finally able to stop Hitler at the gates of Moscow, and eventually with the help of the Allied equipment and forces bring about his complete defeat (van Tuyll 1989).

THE STALINIST MODEL

By the time the 1936 constitution was approved, Stalin had established the framework of a repressive bureaucratic system that lasted into the Gorbachev era (see Figure 2-1). The key element of that bureaucratic state was the Communist Party, although its importance was not recognized in the 1936 constitution. The general secretary of the party, the Politburo, the Secretariat, and the party secretaries were in fact the most powerful policy making elements of the government. These party bodies were completely different than the political parties of the United States. U.S. parties are mostly voluntary organizations that focus on getting a candidate elected and they have no real governmental policymaking function.

Lenin's original constitution of 1918 had provided for the soviets to replace the state, which was believed to be a bourgeois invention. Stalin's 1936 constitution, however, stressed the importance of the state apparatus and affirmed the state's sovereign powers. The constitution provided for a bicameral legislature and detailed political and economic rights (Hunt 1963, 228–229). The legislature and civil rights provisions were a facade for the domination by the Communist Party bureaucracy, which parallelled and directed the government. The

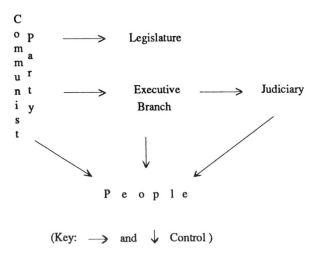

Figure 2-1   Government of the Soviet Union: Stalinist model.

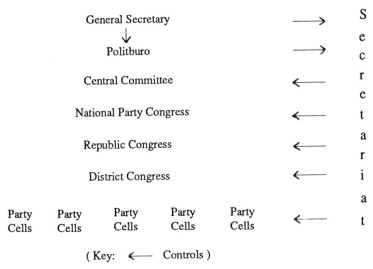

(Key: ⟵ Controls)

Figure 2-2 Communist Party: Stalinist model.

extensive bureaucracy of the Communist system was a natural result of the Communist Party's pervasive controls over economic and political life.

Another basic characteristic of the Stalinist model was what Khrushchev labeled the "cult of the personality," the deification of Stalin. Soon after Stalin established control over the party, his 50th birthday in 1929 was marked with pomp. He put his name on major construction projects, statues, a city, and the 1936 constitution, plus an increasing volume of propaganda publications as the years progressed. He was not an impressive public person and increasingly withdrew from public appearances. The party, then, increasingly became an instrument of his control.

The Communist Party

The major task of the Communist Party was to direct the activities of government officials. The party apparatus permitted an elite, and also a dictator like Stalin, to exercise totalitarian controls over the society. The Communist Party had two main elements—the organization of party members and the permanent secretariat of paid officials. The power and authority of the party flowed from the top down: from the Politburo of 12 or more members to the Central Committee, of about 300 members and 150 alternates, to the National Party Congress, which had about 4000 to 5000 members. The size of these bodies was greatly expanded after their founding (see Figure 2-2).

The Party Congress acted as a sounding board to hear speeches of the Politburo and Central Committee members and to ratify their programs. The Politburo was the most powerful organ in the government, and formerly the Central

Committee ratified decisions by it with little debate. Under Stalin the Party Congresses met more and more infrequently. In 1952, the year before his death, the Party Congress met for the first time since 1939. Stalin had so much power that he even tended to ignore the Politburo.

Party rules provided that lower bodies elect delegates to higher bodies starting at the lowest level of the primary party organs, or cells, and going up through the city, town, or district party conferences to the provincial conference, and finally up to the National Party Congress, which was held about every five years. The primary party organs were based on work units rather than geographic areas. The lower party conferences rarely lasted more than two or three days, whereas the national party conference lasted about a week or more. The print media were saturated with speeches that could last for hours.

The Secretariat serviced the party structure down to the local levels. The central secretariat was headed by the general secretary and 10 or more secretaries who supervised the heads of the department of the secretariat. These departments were responsible for defense, security, heavy industry, energy, and appointments and discipline of the party cadres. Below the central secretariat were perhaps 100,000 to 200,000 full-time party officials. The key official at any level was the party secretary, and the general secretary at the top was the most powerful official in the system. The party secretaries were like prefects, responsible for the economic success and political peace in their territories. They attended countless meetings, delivered countless speeches, and, depending on their personality, interfered in important government decisions including management of industrial enterprises. They dominated the party apparatus, purveying the party line and making sure that the right type of person was elected in party organs.

The power and structure of the Communist Party, which was the most important element of the Soviet government, are not described in the constitution. The 1977 constitution recognized the Communist Party's leading role in Article 6:

> The leading and guiding force of Soviet society and the nucleus of its political system, of all state organizations and public organizations, is the Communist Party of the Soviet Union. The CPSU exists for the people and serves the people.
>
> The Communist Party, armed with Marxism-Leninism, determines the general perspectives of the development of society and the course of the home and foreign policy of the USSR, directs the great constructive work of the Soviet people, and imparts a planned, systematic, and theoretically substantiated character to their struggle for the victory of communism.
>
> All party organizations shall function within the framework of the constitution of the USSR.

The Komsomol, or Communist Youth League, prepared young people for membership in the Communist Party. The age limit was 26 according to the 1936 rules. There were 9 million members of the Komsomol in 1939, more than twice the number in the party, which had been racked with purges (McNeal 1963, 115).

The Executive Branch

In line with the glorification of Stalin, he took over more of the leading state offices including chairman of the Council of People's Commissars (ministers), chairman of the State Committee of Defense (war cabinet), people's commissar of defense, and generalissimo of the Soviet Union. In practice he was also people's commissar of foreign affairs during World War II (McNeal 1963, 109).

The executive branch of the Soviet Union (Figure 2-3) differed from those of non-Communist governments in that it had ministries and other bodies to manage factories, farms, and other parts of the economy. Before the Gorbachev reforms there were more than 100 ministers and state committees in the council of ministers. These ranged from the conventional ministries, such as the foreign ministry, to ministries for the meat and dairy industry and the state committee for cinematography. The chairmen of the Council of Ministers of the Union Republics were also members ex officio of the Council of Ministers. The Council of Ministers directed both the work of its ministries and that of the Union Republics.

The Council of Ministers issued decrees and orders, and under the Stalinist model none were overruled by the Supreme Soviet or its presidium. Normally the career officials of the executive branch were not members of the highest

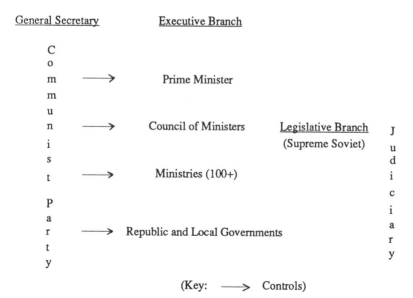

Figure 2-3   The four branches of government: Stalinist model.

party bodies. During the Brezhnev era Foreign Minister Gromyko and Marshal Grechko, the defense minister, were the first career professionals to sit on the Politburo (Macridis 1987, 354).

The major instruments of control in the Stalinist system were the security police, called the KGB since 1954, and the army. The security police were instruments of terror during the Great Purge in the latter part of the 1930s. By the mid-1930s Stalin had dictatorial control over the Soviet Union, and he used it to initiate purges that involved the death and imprisonment of millions of citizens. In Stalin's suspicious mind, hints of opposition were traitorous signs.

The purges began in December 1934 when Sergy Kirov, the Leningrad party secretary and a close associate of Stalin, was murdered. The record is clouded by pro-Communist and anti-Communist propaganda, so that it is useful to quote Khrushchev's famous speech before the Twentieth Party Congress in 1956 about the purge. In this speech he implied that the top functionaries of the NKVD (late the KGB) were guilty of Kirov's murder. Khrushchev was the Moscow party secretary sent to bring back Kirov's body for a funeral. Following are quotes from Khrushchev's speech, which shocked the delegates:

> Having at its disposal numerous data showing brutal willfulness toward Party cadres, the Central Committee has created a party Commission under the control of the Central Committee Presidium.
>
> The Commission has become acquainted with a large quantity of materials in the NKVD archives and with other documents and has established many facts pertaining to the fabrication of cases against Communists, to false accusations, to glaring abuses of socialist legality—which resulted in the death of innocent people. It became apparent that many Party, Soviet, and economic activists who were branded in 1937–1938 as "enemies" were actually never enemies, spies, wreckers, etc., but were always honest Communists; they were only so stigmatized, and often, no longer able to bear barbaric tortures, they charged themselves (at the order of the investigative judges—falsifiers) with all kinds of grave and unlikely crimes. . . .
>
> It was determined that of the 139 members and candidates of the Party's Central Committee who were elected at the XVIIth Congress, 98 persons, i.e., 70 percent, were arrested and shot (mostly in 1937–1938). [Indignation in the hall.]
>
> The same fate met not only the Central Committee members but also the majority of the delegates to the XVIIth Party Congress. Of 1,966 delegates with either voting or advisory rights, 1,108 persons were arrested on charges of anti-revolutionary crimes, i.e., decidedly more than a majority. This very fact shows how absurd, wild and contrary to common sense were the charges of counter-revolutionary crimes made out, as we now see, against a majority of participants in the XVIIth Party Congress. [Indignation in the hall.]. . . .
>
> The vicious practice was condoned of having the NKVD prepare lists of persons whose cases were under the jurisdiction of the Military Collegium and whose sentences were presented in advance. Yezhov would send these lists to Stalin personally for his approval of the proposed punishment. In 1937–1938, 383 such

lists containing the names of many thousands of Party, Soviet, Komsomol, Army and economic workers were sent to Stalin. He approved these lists.

A large part of these cases are being reviewed now and a great part of them are being voided because they were baseless and falsified. Suffice it to say that from 1954 to the present time the Military Collegium of the Supreme Court has rehabilitated 7,679 persons, many of who were rehabilitated posthumously.

The purges were drastic with trials that condemned millions to death or concentration camps, including most of the top Communist leaders. The purges fed on themselves, with the security police arresting and torturing prisoners to get false confessions incriminating the innocent. The purges can best be explained, as by Khrushchev, as a reflection of Stalin's paranoid fear of opposition.

Investigations of the abuses of power of the Stalin era continue today. The Soviet press agency Tass reported on January 5, 1989, that the Central Committee had asked the government to annul the verdicts of special three-person tribunals, known as troikas, that condemned Russian citizens to their deaths, labor camps, or exile during the 1930s, 1940s, and 1950s. "All citizens who were repressed by the decisions of the aforementioned bodies are to be considered rehabilitated" the party resolution said. This resolution was in response to a flood of letters to the press to create memorials to the victims of repression. The party resolution, which indicated that victims would be financially compensated (*NYT* 1/6/89, 1), specifically limits the rehabilitations to the period of Stalin's rule.

The Red Army was another major instrument of control, but one of last resort. Initially Lenin wanted to abolish standing armies, but he found it a necessary instrument to preserve the regime from attacks by opposition within the Soviet Union and from abroad. To prevent loss of control of the army, the system of political commissars was established to check on the commander and to indoctrinate the troops. This system created friction with professional army officers. During World War II the commissars were called *zampolit*, or deputy commanders for propaganda and morale, whereas the military commander was responsible for military decisions. After the war loyalty of the military was reinforced by its privileged position of a high military budget and first choice of quality products for military equipment. Khrushchev's maneuvering for power depended on military support. However, he allowed only one military officer to be a member of the Politburo, Marshal Zhukov, and that was only temporary.

In the economic area the excessive bureaucracy included the pervasive party apparatus, which, combined with the rigid state plans, hindered the economy. Stalin's harsh policies were based on developing heavy industry first to build up military strength and provide a consumer goods industry. The five-year plans, however, tended to put the economy in a straitjacket, and with the threat of Hitler, World War II, and later the cold war, the consumer goods industries were neglected.

After World War II the Soviet Union maintained extensive economic planning and bureaucracy, so that there were more than 100 cabinet-level positions, which mostly directed economic sectors. The five-year plans continued, and the demands of the cold war, described in the next chapter, kept the armaments industry busy. Consumers suffered both from this emphasis on the military and from economic inertia in the system that made it difficult to change plans to meet consumer demands. There was little incentive to produce new or better products, because rewards were based on meeting quantitative targets of the plan rather than on producing quality goods, meeting the demands of consumers, or using resources efficiently. Moreover, military production got first choice of products and resources. The Soviet Union was a superpower in terms of military strength, but its standard of living lagged far behind that of its chief rival, the United States, and well below that of Western Europe.

The Supreme Soviet

The 1936 constitution described the Supreme Soviet as the highest body of state authority for the USSR. It was elected for four years and had two chambers of 750 members each. One chamber was elected from equally populated districts; the other was from federal units of unequal population. Since the Supreme Soviet only met for about a week each year, it had no real legislative function. Its presidium of about 40 members acted for the Supreme Soviet when it was not in session. The laws and decrees it issued were proposed and approved by the Politburo.

Theoretically, the Presidium was the supreme body of the Soviet Union. Its head acted as the ceremonial head of state, but governments with serious business treated the general secretary of the party as the most powerful person in the Soviet Union. General Secretary Brezhnev took over both positions during his tenure. The Supreme Soviet formally received resignations and designations of new members of the Politburo and chairmen of the Council of Ministers. There would be no debate over such decisions made inside the party.

The soviets were elected, and until recently there was only one candidate for each position. The nominating process for these candidates was controlled by the party. Elections were a festive occasion that provided a facade of legitimacy for the system. A great effort was made to get over 99 percent participation.

Judicial Structure

The Marxist view of the law is that it is a weapon of the class struggle designed to promote control by the ruling class. Lenin initially abolished the courts, but the Communists soon found that they needed a detailed system of law and the courts in order to enforce actions of the state. By the 1930s socialist law was declared to express the will of the entire people, and it was used to strengthen the state and its struggle against capitalism. Punishments were particularly severe for crimes such as theft and espionage and other challenges to the state's authority.

There was a four-tiered judicial structure consisting of local people's courts directly elected, regional and territorial courts appointed by the corresponding soviets, the supreme courts of the union republics appointed by the soviets, and the supreme court appointed by the Supreme Soviet. The procurator general was also appointed by the Supreme Soviet, and he appointed and administered the procurators of the union republics and their national subgroups, and he confirmed the nomination of their procurators. These officials were closely supervised by the party. There was no independence of the judiciary under Stalin, and the court system was an instrument of the government and the Communist Party.

Social Groups

In addition to the control by the Communist Party and the government over the educational system, the news media, and religion, the rulers formed mass organizations to control the other groups. Stalin called these organizations transmission belts. Youth up to the third grade were indoctrinated in the Little Octobrists and after that in the Young Pioneers. They competed with one another in scholastics, athletics, and personal conduct, and they were encouraged to help in socially useful campaigns. The Komsomol, or Communist Youth Organization, for older youth ages 15 to 28, was an elite organization that provided a training ground for the Communist Party. The Komsomol was not technically a party body, but it was controlled by it.

The government organized trade unions to include almost all workers and salaried employees. Their organization was patterned after that of the party, and party members were careful also to control these organizations. They administered social insurance programs and sponsored a wide variety of athletic and recreational facilities, but under Stalin they were not allowed to agitate for higher wages or to strike.

The Soviet Empire

In 1917 the Communists inherited the Romanov empire, which, during its 300 years, had incorporated more than 50 ethnic and language groups. In the early years of the revolution Stalin, a Georgian, was the Communist Party's ranking expert on the nationality issue along with his other duties. About half of the people of the Soviet Union were non-Russian. Stalin's strategy was to give the republics nominal independence and to allow the various ethnic groups to use their own language and retain much of their culture, and at the same time to establish strict Communist Party controls over their political and economic life. There were copies of the USSR organs of the party, executive branch, and Supreme Soviet in the 15 union republics, all controlled by the Communist

Party. The strategy of control succeeded to such an extent that before World War II outside observers rarely referred to the Soviet Union as an empire.

The original 15 federal units of the Soviet Union were based on nationality, and these republics also included "autonomous" ethnic groups. The Great Russians made up about half of the population of the Soviet Union. This included 80 percent of the population of the Russian Soviet Federated Socialist Republic as well as sizeable percentages of the other republics. The non-Russian ethnic groups resented domination by the Communist Party, which was largely controlled by the Great Russians in Moscow. Very few of the non-Slavic people claimed Russian as their first language, and a sizeable minority could not communicate in Russian. Only one in five marriages was between individuals of different national origins. (Eklof 1989, 147–170).

The Communist Party used the same party organs and government structures used in the central government to control at the republic and local levels. At the lower levels prominent local personalities were often installed as head of the party organs without the formality of elections. The republic governments had a facade of independence including their own constitutions, flags, and even foreign offices. This facade was used to help assert their independence against the central government after 1989.

The pressures of World War II threatened to break up the empire, but moves toward independence were ruthlessly suppressed. Stalin deported entire populations to Siberia and Central Asia and confiscated their lands when he suspected them of sympathizing with Hitler. In *The Punished Peoples* Alexander Nekrich gives a detailed history of these deportations.

The Slavic leaders of Ukraine and Byelorussia shared in the Communist Party control but not in proportion to their population. In 1945 the Soviet Union had succeeded in getting Ukraine and Byelorussia recognized in the United Nations as separate governments with separate votes. However, Ukraine and Byelorussia did not take important initiatives in foreign policy. Until 1990 power was firmly in the hands of the central government for important matters such as allocation of funds.

The next chapter explains how the Soviet empire expanded to take in nations of Eastern Europe at the end of World War II. At first these nations were tightly controlled from Moscow, but beginning in 1989 they began to break away. Their success encouraged the nationalities of the Soviet Union to assert their independence.

The attitudes of nationalism stimulated by the "Great Patriotic War" (World War II) seemed to have consolidated the Soviet Union as a nation, while its military strength prevented serious challenges to Moscow's control over Eastern Europe until the time from 1989 to 1991. However, when it became clear that the KGB and military no longer were controlled by the hardliners of the Communist Party, the people's resentment of Communist controls exploded and broke up the Soviet empire. President Reagan's famous epithet for the Soviet Union as an "evil empire" was criticized by many as exaggerated. However, as the Soviet Union began breaking apart after the 1989 revolutions, the Soviet Union itself, as well as its system of control over former Eastern European satellites, was commonly referred to as an empire. As the national groups destroyed statues and symbols of Leninism and Stalinism, the adjective *evil* was recognized as appropriate for the Stalinist system.

To sum up, the network of the party, government, and mass organizations controlled society and suppressed opposition. Ethnic groups were able to use their own language and enjoy their culture, except for religious practices, but their economic and political life was strictly controlled by the Communist Party and its governmental structure. The structure concentrated power in the hands of a small elite, or in the era of Stalin, a dictator. The Communist elite was able to shop in special stores and buy foreign luxuries, get access to the best apartments, use special schools and hospitals, and vacation in exclusive recreation areas. Milovan Djilas, a former Yugoslav Communist official, published an indictment of these privileges in his classic book *The New Class* published in the early 1950s. The glasnost of Gorbachev threw light on these privileges and corrupt elements of the system. The Communist system held the internal empire together for 70 years and until 1989 seemed to be an effective instrument of control of the empire of satellites in Eastern Europe.

GORBACHEV'S REFORMS

After Stalin's death controls were relaxed and reforms were begun that culminated with Gorbachev's reforms and the demise of the empire. The main aim was to improve the Communist system by eliminating excessive bureaucracy, promoting incentives, and eliminating abuses. The reforms eventually got out of control and shattered the evil empire.

Stalin had created a bureau of nine men who would be the inner circle of the twenty-five member politburo, but Stalin gave the orders (Khrushchev 1970, 281–282). There was jockeying for power among the most powerful of these men including Khrushchev, first secretary for Moscow; Malenkov, head of the party personnel section; and Beria, head of the secret police. After Stalin died, Beria proposed Malenkov as chairman of the Council of Ministers, the head of the government, and this was accepted.

The top party members were in fear of Beria because of his position as head of the security police, and they suspected him of maneuvering for the top position in the party and the government. Khrushchev secretly arranged for his ouster, and at a meeting of top party officials had Beria arrested and imprisoned by the military, accusing him of many crimes including working with English intelligence and flagrant abuses of power in his position as head of the secret police. The charge about English intelligence appeared fabricated, but most of the others were not. Khrushchev in the next four years maneuvered first to head the party and then to replace Malenkov as head of the Council of Ministers. With both these positions Khrushchev was the leading figure in the government.

In contrast to Stalin, Khrushchev was a populist type of Communist leader who visited work places, made many speeches, and visited abroad. His sensational speech criticizing Stalin is described above. He followed this with action to release large numbers of prisoners from the labor camps. This contrasted with the millions imprisoned by Stalin. Khrushchev began holding Central Committee meetings and regular Party Congresses. His important foreign policy initiatives are described in the next chapter. He attempted agricultural and industrial reforms, but he did not fundamentally change the Stalinist economic and political structure. The failure of these reforms was at least in part responsible for his ouster.

Under Khrushchev the Politburo and the Central Committee increased in importance, so that they were able to determine who would lead the country. Khrushchev managed to stay in power with the help of a narrow majority of the Central Committee until 1964, when Brezhnev called a surprise committee meeting and ousted Khrushchev from power while he was vacationing in southern Russia. The Central Committee promoted Brezhnev, and he remained in a leadership position until his death in 1982. The Central Committee then elected Yuri Andropov, who died in February 1984, and Konstantin Chernenko, who died in 1985, as heads of the government. None of these latter three leaders made basic reforms in the system. In 1985 the Central Committee elected a younger, dynamic leader, Mikhail Gorbachev. Gorbachev as a student in Moscow during the Khrushchev era had been impressed by Khrushchev's denunciation of Stalin and was determined to carry out basic reforms.

Gorbachev's party and government reforms were approved in a stormy July 1988 Party Conference with a divided vote, and put into effect by the surprise Central Committee meeting in November (*NYT* 6/30/88, 1). The Conference endorsed seven resolutions, and the proposed changes were put into effect in September 1988 with only two days' notice. In this meeting Gorbachev consolidated his power by getting Andrei Gromyko, aged 79 and the most prestigious of the old Communist leaders, to retire from his position as president of the Supreme Soviet. Gorbachev then was elected as president pending election of a new Congress of People's Deputies established by the resolutions and described below. This gave Gorbachev even more power to pursue his perestroika policies.

Party Reforms

The Communist Party was used by Stalin to dominate the government and social organizations from the Communist Youth to churches and labor unions. Before the August 1991 coup attempt Gorbachev made major reforms in the Communist Party to reduce that domination. Previously the secretariat and top party officials chose the nominees for party positions, who were then elected without opposition. Gorbachev introduced the secret ballot and more than one candidate. As a result, many of the old hardliners were removed in the election,

Figure 2-4 Mikhail Gorbachev and his reforms (Courtesy: *The Economist*).

which of course helped Gorbachev continue reforms. Party leaders were limited to two five-year terms. About one-half to one-third of the Party Secretariat was removed. Party departments that oversaw branches of industry were replaced by commissions of Central Committee members rather than junior bureaucrats. Their mandate was for general policy direction of party affairs (such as membership and promotions of leading government officials), social and economic policy, and international affairs, rather than for specific sectors of the economy (*NYT* 9/21/88, 1).

In 1991 Gorbachev faced a challenge for leadership from Boris Yeltsin, the new president of Russia. Gorbachev responded by accelerating reforms. Gorbachev mounted an attack on Communist Party hardliners blaming them for the loss of 4.2 million party members. In July he gained acceptance of a new charter for the Communist Party accepting such ideas as a market economy and private property and a pluralism of views. This improved the atmosphere for President Bush's visit in early August, which was shortly before the August coup described below. After the coup the Communist Party was banned at Yeltsin's urging. This was challenged in court, which in November 1992, approved the banning of leadership structures but permitted grassroot cells.

Legislative Reforms

Gorbachev also plunged ahead with legislative reforms. The Communist Party in 1988 approved a new Congress of People's Deputies of 2,250 delegates, which was elected in the spring of 1989. Two-thirds was elected on the basis of geography, and between two and twelve candidates competed for each of these seats (Figure 2-5). Voters participated enthusiastically in the elections.

The most surprising results came in the elections for the one-third of the 750 seats that were presumably safe because they were unopposed as nominees of the Communist Party and other organizations such as the unions, which are also

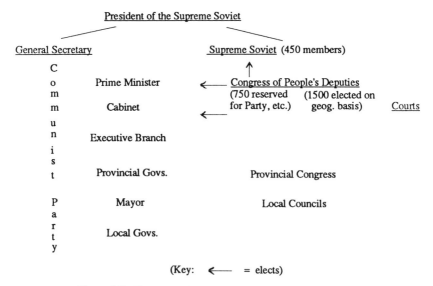

Figure 2-5 The communist government: Gorbachev model, 1989.

dominated by the party. In these elections a number of the unopposed prominent party leaders were defeated because more than a majority of voters crossed their names off the lists. Those that suffered such a humiliating defeat included the top five party leaders of Leningrad, the president and premier of Lithuania, and the commander of troops in East Germany (*NYT* 3/28/89, 1; 3/29/89, 12). The runoff elections for about 300 who did not get a majority in the March elections were held two weeks later. In July 1989 the top Leningrad party leader was dismissed from his party position because of his humiliating defeat.

Ironically the new Party Congress had 87 percent Communist Party members, a higher percentage than the 1984 body, which had 71 percent party members. The more open electoral process elected more intellectuals, who had party status, and fewer workers. Thus the future of reform after the first semi-democratic election depended on reformers within the party, and reformers from outside the party were able to achieve at best only a small minority under the new election system (*NYT* 5/15/89, A7).

The new Congress elected a new 450-person Supreme Soviet designed to act as a legislature. It planned to meet eight months of the year. The Congress did not elect to the Supreme Soviet a number of Moscow deputies who had called for faster economic and political change, including Boris Yeltsin, the popular former head of the Moscow party who had been particularly outspoken in his criticism of Gorbachev's policies. However, thousands of Muscovites rallied in Yeltsin's support, and many deputies reported that they received phone calls and telegrams from constituents protesting his defeat. As a result, Aleksei Kazannik, a university law lecturer from Omsk, announced that he would forfeit his seat in the Supreme Soviet if the Congress would give it to Yeltsin. This was approved, and the Congress in a special ballot reversed itself and elected Yeltsin to the Supreme Soviet with no one publicly opposing him, although 964 members had voted against him in the previous round of balloting (*NYT* 5/28/89, 2).

The Congress of People's Deputies also elected the president of the Supreme Soviet, and to no one's surprise at the beginning of 1989 it elected Gorbachev as the first president. The new president no longer occupied just a ceremonial position, but he actively managed foreign and domestic policy. Gorbachev retained his position as general secretary of the Party.

The Congress approved the cabinet, and in another of its first acts it blocked the nomination by Prime Minister Nikolai Ryzhkov of eight ministers out of the 71 Council of Ministers that led the executive branch. One of these was a protégé of President Gorbachev's, who he had proposed to oversee food production. The defeats were accepted without a fuss. No nominee of the government had been rejected by the rubber-stamp legislature of the past. The legislative committees also rejected three nominees to the Supreme Court and a deputy federal prosecutor accused of obstructing investigations into high-level corruption (*NYT* 6/26/89, 1).

During the first two weeks of debate in the Congress there was criticism of the one-party system. A poll of 686 of the deputies revealed that there was virtually an even split among supporters and opponents of the one-party system. In the fall session of the Supreme Soviet a group of deputies drew up a new law to allow automatic registration of public groups that could turn themselves into political parties. However, Gorbachev did not commit himself to that far-reaching reform.

The public followed the proceedings in the new Congress of People's Deputies and Supreme Soviet to an extent unknown in democratic countries. Until June 27 the proceedings of the Congress were broadcast live, with an estimated audience of 200 million viewers across 12 time zones. Members reserved speaking time days in advance. A dramatic speech by Yuri Vlasov, a deputy and former Olympic weightlifting champion, accused the KGB and Cheka of being involved in the murders of millions of people. The following day the chief of the KGB, Vladimir Kryuchkov, said that the new legislature should have authority over state security, including power to approve appointment of the KGB chairman. This proposal actually had been publicized a year before in the newspaper of the Communist Youth League. On June 26 the legislature decided to stop the live broadcasts for the Supreme Soviet, which convened for six weeks beginning at the end of June. The press agency TASS said that the leadership decided this after it learned that industrial production had fallen by 20 percent during the live broadcasts (*NYT* 6/9/89, 6; 5/30/89, 6; 5/31/89, 1; and 6/26/89, 1). However, highlights continued to be broadcast on the nightly news.

After 1989 the pace of the reforms was breathtaking as they seemed to feed on each other. Strikes and other demonstrations that had not been seen since the first years of the Soviet Union were permitted. There was frequent speculation in the foreign news media that unrest would lead to Gorbachev's removal. However, a major factor worked in his favor. He was the president elected by the Congress of People's Deputies, which meant he could not be removed by a quick meeting of the Politburo or Central Committee. Legally, removal would take a vote of the Congress of People's Deputies, which increasingly was asserting its authority and was not likely to commit suicide by supporting hardliners wanting to end the reforms. In the party hierarchy he periodically reinforced his position by appointments of supporters to top positions in the Politburo and Secretariat.

Why did Gorbachev make these drastic reforms? It is difficult or impossible to assess personal motives of reformers. They reject the easy noncontroversial ways of staying in power. Gorbachev challenged and changed what many thought was an impregnable system. As a law student in Moscow he was able to read writings of Western philosophers. During this period he had been impressed by Khrushchev's revelation of the repression under the Stalinist system, and he wanted to change that. He had worked in the Communist system and seen how it had been corrupted. Through his wife's research on farmers he knew that the agricultural system needed reforms. He visited abroad and saw the freer and more prosperous democratic systems.

He was bright and personable, and luck and hard work got him into a position to make changes.

In 1991 Boris Yeltsin emerged as the leader of the reforms using his presidency of the Russian republic as leverage. In 1990 Russia set up a Congress of People's Deputies and Supreme Soviet on the model of the Soviet Union. (This was confusing since sometimes in news reports it was not clear which Congress or Supreme Soviet was being referred to.) Yeltsin, who was elected to the Russian Congress with 90 percent support, was also elected as chairman of that Congress. In March 1991 he instigated a referendum calling for the popular election of a president in Russia and in June he won with a 60 percent vote. This was a key position since Russia had more than half the population of the Soviet Union.

In 1990 and 1991 he successfully opposed Gorbachev on key issues including Russia's ownership of coal mines and Gorbachev's attempt to keep the Baltic republics in the Soviet Union. In April 1991 in a meeting of 9 of the 15 republics Yeltsin convinced Gorbachev to recognize their sovereignty, which was a meaningful decision in contrast to the facade of independence they had under the Stalinist system. The prospect of the breakup of the empire triggered the August 1991 coup against Grobachev, and the failure of that coup sealed the fate of the Soviet internal empire.

THE FAILED COUP

Before the new constitutional process had a chance to consolidate, a group of hardliners attempted to depose Gorbachev. On Monday, August 19, 1991, a group of top Soviet officials led by Vice President Genady Yanaev, the heads of the three security services—KGB, Military, and Interior—plus the heads of the Soviet military-industrial complex attempted to take control of the Soviet Union in a coup. The coup was announced when Yanaev announced that Gorbachev, who was vacationing in the Crimea, was ill and that he, Yanaev, was taking over Gorbachev's duties. This was an obvious subterfuge to make the coup appear legal.

A few hours later Boris Yeltsin, the elected president of the Russian Federation, went to its parliament building in Moscow to denounce the coup and call for a general strike. In a dramatic gesture of defiance, he mounted one of the tanks under the command of the coup leaders that threatened the parliament and called on the soldiers for support. The tank commander did not stop him. Yeltsin called the coup a "rightist, reactionary, anti-constitutional coup," and appealed to the people of Russia to "rebuff the putschists" and "demand a return of the country to normal constitutional development" (*NYT* 8/20/92, 1). The coup leaders clearly did not anticipate this, probably expecting Yeltsin to flee to a hideaway.

On Monday afternoon and on Tuesday hundreds of thousands in various cities responded to Yeltsin's call for resistance. In Moscow they built barricades around the Russian parliament and prepared to defend it against attack. Yeltsin was successful in mobilizing national opposition to the coup and public disapproval from abroad. The next day the defense minister ordered troops to withdraw from Moscow, the coup leaders fled, and Gorbachev returned to Moscow to resume control of the government. Gorbachev was able temporarily to maintain his position as head of the Soviet state, which was no longer a Soviet union but a crumbling empire.

The question of why the coup failed is important for political scientists, many of whom found it hard to believe that a popular revolution could succeed in confronting an army and an entrenched Soviet bureaucracy.

The coup took place the day before Gorbachev was scheduled to return from vacation to sign a new union treaty that would have given many new powers to the republics at the expense of the central government. The new treaty appeared to be a desperate attempt to contain the nationalist pressures that threatened to tear the Soviet Union apart. The treaty probably triggered the coup by offending hardline Communists, including those in the military, who were unwilling to stand by while the Soviet Union disintegrated. Continued deterioration of the Russian economy and evidence that Gorbachev's government was unpopular with the majority of the Soviet people also encouraged the plotters.

What the coup plotters failed to anticipate was Boris Yeltsin's courageous opposition to the coup and the use of his great popularity, both of which led to his success. The turning point was his call for popular support for the Russian parliament and his mounting of one of the tanks of the coup forces to denounce the coup and call for a general strike. The message was broadcast by radio and by the Western news media. Hundreds of thousands of people heeded his broadcasted plea and came to the streets in major Soviet cities to demonstrate their opposition to the coup. Another key factor was a division among the top military commanders who refused to unite to support the coup and attack the people in the streets. Many of the republics refused to support the coup, and only Azerbaijan came out for it. The miners of the Donesk region threatened to close the mines.

Gorbachev, after he was released by the security forces, recouped some of his prestige by persuading the Soviet parliament on September 5 to approve a new government structure designed to hold the Soviet Union together in a loose arrangement, pending the drafting of a permanent constitution that would provide for an elected president. In broad outline the temporary government included (1) a State Council of the republics, headed by Gorbachev, to manage defense, foreign affairs, and security; (2) an elected Supreme Soviet of two houses—a Council of the Republics representing each republic equally and a Council of the Union representing each republic roughly according to its population; and (3) an Interrepublic Economic Committee to work out treaties governing economic relations among the republics (*NYT* 9/6/91, A10) (Figure 2-6).

The Soviet parliament formally pledged to honor existing agreements with other foreign nations, reassuring the United States about the far-reaching nu-

State Council	Supreme Soviet	
Executive panel headed by Gorbachev and made up of members of 12 republics. Responsible for foreign affairs, defense, and security.	Council of Republics	Council of the Union
	Each republic sends 20 delegates chosen from Congress of Soviet Deputies (Russia has 52 delegates). Each delegation has one vote.	Chosen by republic legislatures based on number of deputies each republic had in the Congress of People's Deputies.

Interrepublic Economic Committee
Coordinates economic policy and works out a treaty defining relations with the union. Chairman is named by the president with the approval of the council.

Figure 2-6 Structure of the Soviet government at the end of 1991.

clear arms reduction treaty that had been signed a few weeks earlier (*NYT* 8/1/91). It also suspended all activities of the Communist Party pending an investigation of its role in the coup. (The vote was 283 to 29 with 52 absentions, an index of the party's fall from grace. [*NYT* 8/30/91, 6]). Many of the republics, including the Russian Republic, had already closed Communist Party offices and seized its properties (*NYT* 8/30/91). Gorbachev, with Yeltsin's encouragement, used the crisis to sack top officials involved in the coup, including the cabinet, the head of the central bank, and the chairman of the Soviet parliament because they had not had the courage to oppose the coup.

On November 1 the Interrepublic Economic Committee decided to eliminate 70 ministeries and departments responsible for overseeing the centrally planned economy. The surviving ministeries included defense, energy, interior, railroads, nuclear energy, and industry. Initial budgetary cuts imposed by Yeltsin, President of the Russian Republic, caused the Soviet Union's Foreign Ministry to lose a large part of its staff and its large building in Moscow. Also, Yeltsin's aides announced that he planned to sign a decree that would, on November 10, abolish the Soviet government's monopoly on foreign exchange operations and allow the ruble to go to a market rate.

Meanwhile Yeltsin continued his basic reform strategy of removing Communist officials from power and asserting his enhanced influence. As the first elected president of the Russian Republic, he was in a strong position to do so. His government took over Soviet communications temporarily and got Gorbachev to put Yeltsin's candidates in key positions in the central government. This included naming Ivan Silaev as Soviet prime minister, in addition to his job as Russian prime minister. Yeltsin also persuaded Gorbachev to resign as head of the Communist Party, which had been discredited by its support of the coup.

Yeltsin's strategy was based on a belief that radical changes in the system would come from the republics, which would challenge the central control of the Communist Party. His strategy succeeded. The democratic elections in Russia and the republics released popular pressures and allowed them to break away from the Soviet Union, which ended the control of the party in Moscow. This meant that there was a link between demands for economic and for political reforms, both of which involved weakening the controls of the Communist Party. Political and market reforms have accompanied each other in the former Soviet republics (Morrison, 1991, 143).

THE END OF THE EMPIRE

The Baltic republics of Latvia, Lithuania, and Estonia had presented a particularly difficult problem for Gorbachev. Formerly part of the Russian empire before World War I, they gained their independence after that war. In 1939 the Soviet Union absorbed them as part of a pre–World War II deal with Hitler, when he took over western Poland and the Soviets took over the eastern part. Under glasnost the Baltic republics had reasserted their right to independence, believing they deserved again to link up with Scandinavia and Western Europe.

A dramatic demonstration for independence took place on August 23, 1989, when more than a million Estonians, Latvians, and Lithuanians linked hands across their three homelands and demanded independent statehood. A few weeks later Gorbachev rejected their demands and their claim that their independence had been usurped when they were taken into the Soviet Union in 1940. At the same time he moved up the time of the next Party Congress to consider their demands.

Gorbachev failed in 1990 to get the Baltic republics to compromise on his proposals for economic and political autonomy and eventual independence. During the August 1991 coup they asserted their formal independence. After the coup one of the first acts of the new State Council of 10 republics headed by Gorbachev was to recognize the formal independence of Latvia, Estonia, and Lithuania, which had declared independence during the August 1991 coup. This was the first peaceful loss of territory of the Soviet Union since it was formed. Surprisingly a public opinion poll carried out in Moscow indicated about half the people were also in favor of granting independence to the other republics. (*NYT* 8/29/91, A7). The previous Communist tactics of giving the republics a facade of independence had boomeranged because now the Russian people accepted their assertion of independence.

The defection of the Baltic republics set the stage for declarations of independence of other republics and the demise of the Soviet Union. The breakaway of Ukraine was the most dramatic. In December 1991 in a free election this nation of 60 million people voted 90 percent for independence. The defection of Ukraine, a Slavic nation, including Kiev, the birthplace of Russia, was a fatal blow to Gorbachev's Union.

At the beginning of December Yeltsin met with the newly elected president of Ukraine who agreed to call for Gorbachev's resignation and the formation of a new confederation of states. Two weeks later leaders of the 11 remaining republics of the Soviet Union (without Georgia) met in the capital of Kazakhstan and agreed to form a new Commonwealth of Independent States (CIS). Boris Yeltsin in announcing the new agreement on December 21, 1991, stated, "There is not one single state. There is a commonwealth of 11 independent states. . . . Now that we are no longer forcibly bound by the chains of the center, when the center has been destroyed and the totalitarian communist system has been destroyed, the field is open for forming a democratic commonwealth—the kind civilized countries should be in (*NYT* 12/12/91, 1)." The leaders of the 11 republics established a joint military command of Russia, Kazakhstan, Byelorussia, and Ukraine over the nuclear warheads of the former Soviet Union. They appointed former Soviet Defense Minister Yevegeny Shaposhnikov as head of the armed forces and agreed that Russia would inherit the Soviet Union's seat on the U.N. Security Council. They urged Gorbachev to resign with dignity and he complied. This was a historical first: a ruler permitting the breakup of an empire without a conflict. The next chapter describes the profound effect this had on international politics.

THE NEW REPUBLICS PICK UP THE PIECES

Russia dominated the new Commonwealth of Independent States with just over half of its population and about 60 percent of its output (Table 2-1). Although there was no civil war over the breakup of the internal empire, conflicts broke out among some of the ethnic groups of the former Soviet Union. The news media focused on these conflicts, particularly in Georgia and Azerbaijan. Yeltsin's drastic economic reforms for Russia, which took place at the beginning of 1992 as promised, received less attention, while major economic reforms in the other republics received virtually no news coverage.

The International Monetary Fund, the International Bank, and the European Community provided most of the technical assistance and financial support for the new reforms. In the first part of 1992 President Bush, urged on by former President Nixon, called on Congress to approve a $24 billion program for Russia, without mentioning that this was also part of an IMF proposal that would allocate a similar amount to the other new republics. On April 24, 1992, the $24 billion for Russia was endorsed by top officials of the Group of Seven (United States, United Kingdom, France, Germany, Italy, Japan, and Canada) (*IMF Survey*, 5/11/92).

A primary aim of economic reforms was to permit most prices to rise or fall to world market levels and by the beginning of 1992 this had been accomplished in the new republics (International Monetary Fund 1992, 38–39). In the first week of 1992 Yeltsin freed prices, except for bread and a few essentials, and at the end of February additional prices were freed, except for baby foods and medicines. In addition Russia and the new republics slashed military spending,

Table 2-1

Economic Measures of the Republics of the Former USSR Compared with Western Europe

Areas	Population (millions)[1]	Share of total GDP of former USSR (%)[2]	Income per capita compared to Russia (Russia = 100)[2]	Share of employment (%)[2] Industry	Share of employment (%)[2] Agriculture	Telephones per 1000 inhabitants[3]	Infant mortality rate (per 1000)[3]
Estonia	1.6	0.6	117	27.3	16.1	136.8	14.7
Latvia	2.7	1.1	113	27.5	18.6	175.0	11.1
Lithuania	3.7	1.4	105	27.5	19.1	147.4	10.7
Russian Federation	148.0	61.1	100	29.4	14.1	78.2	17.8
Belarus	10.3	4.2	88	29.3	22.3	108.2	11.8
Moldova	4.4	1.2	72	19.4	38.0	71.2	20.4
Ukraine	51.8	16.2	84	29.0	21.3	91.5	13.0
Armenia	3.3	0.9	70	28.3	18.8	138.2	20.4
Azerbaijan	7.1	1.7	58	16.2	31.1	68.3	26.2
Georgia	5.5	1.6	76	17.9	26.2	79.1	19.6
Kazakhstan	16.7	4.3	84	19.3	21.2	75.5	25.9
Kyrghyzstan	4.4	0.8	67	16.6	32.4	47.5	32.2
Tajikistan	5.2	0.8	56	11.9	40.2	31.2	43.2
Turkmenistan	3.6	0.8	71	9.0	40.1	46.4	54.7
Uzbekistan	20.3	3.3	61	13.8	38.2	49.5	37.7
Western Europe[4]	...	...	...	34.1	6.5	582.0	8.0

Sources: National authorities: International Monetary Fund, World Bank, Organization for Economic Cooperation and Development, and European Bank for Reconstruction and Development, *A Study of the Soviet Economy* (Washington: IMF, 1991); *Ekonomika i Zhizn* (Moscow: October 1990). p. 15; and Organization for Economic Cooperation and Development, *OECD Economic Surveys* (Paris: OECD, 1991); IMF, *World Economic Outlook, May 1992* (Washington, DC), p. 31.

[1] January 1, 1990.
[2] 1988.
[3] End of 1989.
[4] Arithmetic average for France, Germany, and Italy.

which had absorbed as much as 25 percent of the gross national product. On January 23, 1992, the Russian parliament approved a drastic budget, cutting military spending from around 25 percent of gross national product to about 4.5 percent and imposing a 28 percent value added tax. The Russian government also abolished the state trading organizations that had acted as a barrier to freeing consumer prices (*NYT* 1/25/92, 5).

As anticipated, these reforms had a severe economic impact. Many in the government and the military lost their jobs. The state-owned firms were accustomed to operating with heavy subsidies from the government budget and selling their products without competition. Ending government subsidies and protection left them stranded without markets for their products and without money to meet payrolls. Food prices skyrocketed as shelves emptied and customers rushed to stock up to meet anticipated shortages. The situation was worsened by attempts of the republics to protect their markets by holding back shipments of goods, particularly of food, to other republics. At the base of the food chain the officials of the collective farms were able to hold food off the market and take advantage of skyrocketing prices.

In the industrial sector a large part of the production of the former Soviet Union had been concentrated in single firms scattered among the republics. This led to a great volume of interrepublic trade. In 1987 this trade (one-half of exports and imports) amounted to 48 to 75 percent of total output of the new republics, not counting Russia with 31 percent (Table 2-2). The firms floundered as the controls and directions from Moscow were abolished. Consumer goods disappeared from the shelves. Citizens sold their belongings on street corners to get money for food. In the winter of 1991–1992 the shortages, even as admitted by Yeltsin, were comparable to the harshest days of World War II. Inflation soared 80 to 100 percent in the republics, spurred on by rises in the price of Russian oil, which had been sold formerly below world market prices.

The situation was most serious in areas devastated by ethnic wars. In 1991 output fell 25 percent in Georgia, 12 percent in Armenia, 12 percent in Moldova, and 10 percent in Kazakhstan (Table 2-3). As fighting continued in 1992 the economies remained in decline. The losses of production were much less in other republics as they struggled to adjust to a market system.

This situation encouraged bribery and corruption by those who could get control over food. Also, the government's privatization program invited corruption. Plant managers sold properties in deals that gave them control. In October 1992, Russia distributed free to the public ownership vouchers for state properties, but the rapid inflation encouraged Russians to sell them to speculators (*Economist* 10/10/92, 60).

In Russia, Yeltsin initially met the problems head on. In the middle of January 1992 he toured Russia, meeting with angry shoppers. He praised Russians for their patience and faith and warned them that the reforms could be reversed. Despite attacks from his vice president, members of the parliament, and the press, a poll showed that 40 percent supported Yeltsin against 34 percent who

Table 2-2

Republics of the Former USSR: Interrepublic Trade

(In percent, unless otherwise noted)

Republics	Total trade as percent of NMP[1]	Share of interrepublic trade in total trade[2]	Share of trade with Russia in interrepublic trade[2]	Balance of interrepublic energy trade (millions of rubles)[1]
Estonia	81.4	86.7	59.5	-144
Latvia	74.9	86.9	51.8	-545
Lithuania	75.6	88.2	59.4	-691
Russian Federation	30.9	59.0	. . .	6,087
Belarus	72.1	85.6	61.1	-814
Moldova	72.3	88.1	55.0	-652
Ukraine	47.2	78.5	70.1	-3,531
Armenia	74.5	89.3	54.4	-432
Azerbaijan	57.1	85.6	56.8	544
Georgia	60.8	86.3	56.9	-438
Kazakhstan	47.6	87.8	62.1	-441
Kyrghyzstan	63.4	78.0	43.4	-265
Tajikistan	58.5	88.3	45.9	-279
Turkmenistan	51.0	91.7	47.6	693
Uzbekistan	55.1	85.8	55.9	-383

Sources: Goskomstat, *Vestnik Statistiki*, No. 3 (Moscow: 1990); International Monetary Fund, World Bank, Organization for Economic Cooperation and Development, and European Bank for Reconstruction and Development, *A Study of the Soviet Economy*, Vol 1 (Washington: IMF, 1991). IMF, *World Economic Outlook, May 1992* (Washington, DC), p. 42. Trade is defined as the sum of merchandise exports and imports divided by 2.

[1]Based on domestic prices in 1988.

[2]1987.

Table 2-3
Eastern Europe and the Former USSR: Recent Economic Developments (Changes in percent, unless otherwise noted)

Areas	Real GDP		Consumer prices		Employment		Current account[1] (percent of GDP)	
	1990	1991	1990	1991	1990	1991	1990	1991
Eastern Europe[2] and former USSR	−2.9	−16.9	22.0	92.8	−0.8	−2.6	−1.1	−0.7
Eastern Europe[2]	−7.1	−16.6	149.1	134.7	−1.6	−5.8	−0.5	−2.2
Albania	−10.0	−21.1	—	40.0	0.2	...	−7.1	−18.1
Bulgaria	−10.6	−25.0	26.3	460.4	−6.5	−13.9	−5.3	−12.1
Czechoslovakia	−0.4	−16.4	10.8	58.7	−0.1	−6.6	−2.9	2.1
Hungary	−4.0	−7.5	33.4	33.0	−0.7	−1.1	1.2	1.4
Poland	−11.6	−8.0	585.8	70.3	−2.6	−2.4	4.0	−2.1
Romania	−7.4	−12.0	4.7	164.3	−1.0	−2.5	−8.7	−7.7
Yugoslavia[3]	−7.5	−29.3	584.0	270.0	−0.8	−10.0	2.2	−0.2
Former USSR[4]	−2.0	−17.0	5.6	86.0	−0.6	−2.0	−1.2	−0.2
Estonia	−3.6	−10.8[5]	17.2	211.8	−2.0	−1.0	−6.1	6.1
Latvia	−0.2	−7.9[5]	10.5	172.2	−6.0[6]	−4.7[6]	−5.3	4.4[7]
Lithuania	−5.0	−13.0[5]	8.4	244.7	−2.7	0.4	−3.8[7]	6.5[7]
Russian Federation	0.4	−9.0	5.0	90.4	−1.1	−1.1	−0.8	0.7
Belarus	−3.0	−3.1[5]	4.5	80.0	−0.9	−2.0	−2.0	3.4
Moldova	−1.5	−11.9[5]	4.2	98.0	−0.9	...	−3.0	...
Ukraine	−3.4	−9.6[5]	4.2	84.2	−3.0	−0.4	−4.9[6]	−6.4[7]

(Table continues on next page)

Table 2-3

Eastern Europe and the Former USSR: Recent Economic Developments (Changes in percent, unless otherwise noted) *(Continued)*

Areas	Real GDP		Consumer prices		Employment		Current account[1] (percent of GDP)	
	1990	1991	1990	1991	1990	1991	1990	1991
Armenia	−8.5	−11.8[5]	10.3[8]	100.3[8]	...	...	−11.8[7]	...
Azerbaijan	−11.7	−0.7[9]	7.8	87.3	...	...	4.6	5.3[7]
Georgia	−12.4	−25.0	4.8	81.1	...	...	−6.2[7]	−5.0[7]
Kazakhstan	−1.5	−10.0[5]	4.0	181.0	...	...	−4.2	−3.5
Kyrghyzstan	4.0	−2.0[5]	3.0	103.0	−0.4	−2.0	−6.2	12.2
Tajikistan	−0.6	−8.7[5]	4.0	90.0	3.0	0.4	13.5[7]	3.9[7]
Turkmenistan	1.5	−0.6[5]	4.6	90.0	3.4	2.6	−8.4	13.8
Uzbekistan	4.3	−0.9[5]	3.1	82.2	2.8	0.4	−15.0[7]	−1.1[7]

Source: IMF, *World Economic Outlook, May 1992* (Washington, DC), p. 31.

[1] Current account in convertible and nonconvertible currencies. The aggregates are the ratio of the combined current account to aggregate GDP/NMP.

[2] Excluding Albania.

[3] The territory of Yugoslavia as it existed in 1990.

[4] Reliable, comparable economic data for the republics of the former USSR are not generally available; the estimates presented above should be interpreted as indicative of broad orders of magnitude.

[5] Net material product.

[6] State sector.

[7] Trade balance as a percent of NMP/GDP. For Ukraine, balance of foreign and interrepublic trade.

[8] NMP deflator.

[9] Preliminary.

did not (*NYT* 1/17/92, A6). Similarly on January 18 he met with 5000 military officers who vented their frustration by attacking politicians for the major cuts in the military (*NYT* 1/18/92).

Robert Strauss, ambassador to Russia, testifying before the U.S. Senate Foreign Relations Committee on March 13 indicated that he had confidence in Yeltsin. Strauss said he had suggested that Yeltsin might fire a prime minister after six months to take some of the political heat off of Yeltsin caused by the economic hardships. Yeltsin refused this tactic saying that he had complete confidence in Deputy Prime Minister Yegor Guidar who was carrying out Yeltsin's economic policies.

The International Monetary Fund and the International Bank played a key role in advising Russia and the other new republics. In line with their advice most or all of the republics liberalized most prices, prepared for monetary reform in 1992, drafted laws for privatization, and levied value added taxes and other taxes that would allow them to institute government budgets along the lines of Western models (International Monetary Fund 1992, 38–39).

It is significant that these economic reforms accompanied the political reforms mentioned above. However, they lagged several years behind the economic reforms of Eastern Europe, some of which, as we will see, began before 1989.

Meanwhile there was political turmoil in the republics. At the beginning of 1992 a civil conflict raged in Georgia between supporters and opponents of President Gamsakhurdia, who was accused of becoming a dictatorial demagogue after being elected by an overwhelming majority in 1991. The conflict, which involved opposing military units, began when national guardsmen fired on an opposition demonstration.

Gamasakhurdia was forced to retreat to a neighboring region of Georgia where he set up a rump parliament. In April 1992 Eduard Shevardnadze, Gorbachev's former foreign minister, took office as head of Georgia's State Council of 60 members, many of them fierce opponents of the Communist government he once served. Parliamentary elections were scheduled for the fall to reinstitute democracy. In April Shevardnadze stated that he opposed Georgia's membership in the Commonwealth, which he predicted would not survive. Shevardnadze was a popular leader with his popularity increasing from 30 to 70 percent in a poll, but he himself indicated that could change in the face of soaring inflation and a sharp drop in industrial production (*NYT* 4/20/92, 8).

Yeltsin also failed to stop the conflict between the republics of Azerbaijan and Armenia. The conflict centered on Armenia's demand for the Nagorno-Karbakh autonomous region, which had been made part of Azerbaijan in 1921 even though a large majority was ethnically Armenian. The Armenians were Catholic while the Azerbaijanis were Moslem, which widened the split. At the beginning of 1992 as many as 2000 had been killed in the fighting. In March 1992 President Mutalibov, who had been popularly elected six months earlier, resigned in the midst of demonstrations demanding further action against the

Armenian separatists (*NYT* 3/7/92, 3). The Russian Vice President Rutksoi, in a revealing public statement showing the weakness of the CIS, said that the regular troops of the CIS should withdraw and that the sovereign nations of Georgia, Azerbaijan, and Armenia should work out their own problems. In May 1992 the presidents of Armenia and Azerbaijan met in Teheran to sign a cease-fire mediated by Iran (*NYT* 5/9/92, 1). However, sporadic fighting continued.

Despite ethnic conflicts and economic hardships, the new republics made democratic reforms, which included free elections for parliaments and presidents. In some republics the elections were not free and Communist Party members maintained control, but even in these cases public pressures brought about concessions to democracy. Both the hardliners and the reformers agreed they did not want Communist controls reimposed from Moscow.

Since the 1950s Freedom House, a nonprofit organization, has evaluated governments' actions to suppress or extend political freedoms. Its experts and consultants use published materials and on-site investigations to grade governments with uniform criteria. Its major criteria are whether a government permits free elections, including a free selection of candidates, and provides for political rights and freedoms. The 1991–1992 Freedom House assessment shows dramatic moves toward democracy by the former republics of the Soviet Union, as well as by Eastern Europe (Figure 2-7).

In addition to the reforms of the Soviet Union, the most progress in the past few years was made by the Baltic republics and Ukraine. The major problem of freedom and civil rights in the three Baltic republics centered on their residence and language measures to exclude Russians from citizenship, some of whom had lived there since the beginning of World War II. Each republic carried out generally free elections for parliaments that then addressed the important issues of reform. Even those that were graded least free carried out elections (Uzbekistan, Turkmenistan, and Georgia). Their major problems were civil conflicts and domination by Communists in the new governments that did not give an opposition a fair chance (Freedom House 1991–1992). Figure 2-7 gives a rough picture of the close relationship of political and economic reforms. This graph of economic progress is based on a rough estimate of the extent to which prices were freed.

The reason for this initial linkage of political and economic reforms is not some mysterious historical force but simply that leaders and people of the republics wanted to free prices and prepare a basis for moving toward the relative prosperity of Western Europe. Moreover, the IMF and World Bank experts advising them had the leverage of being able to grant sizeable loans for such an adjustment. Although the IMF and World Bank experts had no experience in helping Communist economies readjust, over past decades they had had relative success with other countries abolishing governmental controls and moving toward market economies.

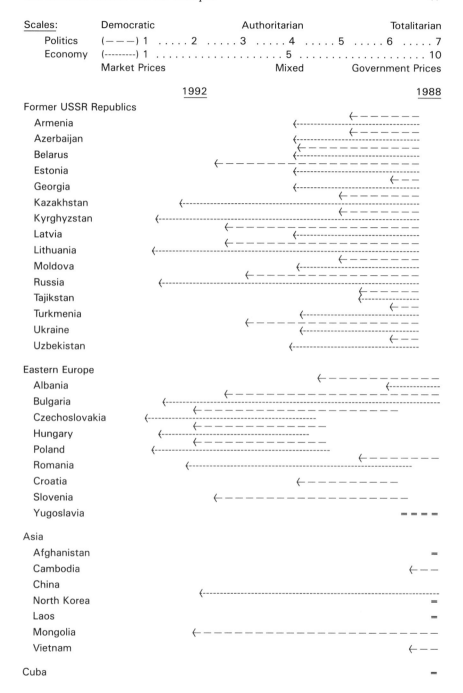

Figure 2-7 Trends toward freedom of Communist governments and toward free prices in former USSR republics and Eastern Europe 1988–1991. (Sources: See Table 2-4.)

Table 2-4

Trends toward Freedom of Communist Governments and Degree of Government Price Control in
Former USSR Republics and Eastern Europe, 1988 and 1991

Country	Type of government 1988	Type of government 1991	Degree of government price control (%) 1991
Former USSR Republics			
Armenia	6.5	5	50
Azerbaijan	6.5	5	50
Belarus	6.5	4	50
Estonia	6.5	2.5	50
Georgia	6.5	3	50
Kazakhstan	6.5	4.5	20
Kyrghyzstan	6.5	4.5	10
Latvia	6.5	2.5	50
Lithuania	6.5	2.5	10
Moldova	6.5	4.5	50
Russia	6.5	3	10
Tajikistan	6.5	5	50
Turkmania	6.5	5.5	50
Ukraine	6.5	3	50
Uzbekistan	6.5	5.5	50
Eastern Europe			
Albania	7	4	80
Bulgaria	7	2.5	10
Czechoslovakia	6.5	2	5
Hungary	4.5	2	10
Poland	5	2	7
Romania	7	5	20
Croatia	5.5	3.5	
Slovenia	5.5	2.5	
Yugoslavia	5.5	5.5	
Asia			
Afghanistan	7	7	
Cambodia	7	6	
China	6	6	20
North Korea	7	7	
Laos	7	7	
Mongolia	7	2.5	
Vietnam	6.5	6.5	
Cuba	7	7	

(Table footnotes appear on next page)

SUMMARY

Until 1989 the military and the police as instruments of the Communist Party had held the internal empire together. When it became clear that Gorbachev would not use force to preserve the Eastern European empire, it broke apart within a few months. After Yeltsin rallied democratic forces to defeat the attempted coup by the hardliners, the internal empire crumbled. The first to go were Latvia, Lithuania, and Estonia. They had resolutely insisted on independence, and most of the world soon officially recognized them. After the defection of Ukraine the game was over, and other republics declared their autonomy and independence through referendums and legislative action. The breakup was confirmed a few days later when Yeltsin met with the leaders of Ukraine and Byelorussia, renamed Belarus, to declare that the Soviet Union no longer existed.

Until 1989 the West had regarded the Soviet empire as a cold war opponent able to subvert and control weaker countries with the Communist doctrine and apparatus. It is important to evaluate the forces that tore the empire apart before looking at the foreign policy implications.

The basic weaknesses were the resentment by the various ethnic groups of the rigid system of totalitarian control from Moscow, along with the special privileges and corruption of the Communist elite. Gorbachev's glasnost removed the lid on this resentment. Under Stalin the security police had suppressed opposition and executed and imprisoned millions. Gorbachev and others who later reached positions of power remembered repression of their grandfathers, fathers, relatives, and friends, and refused to copy Stalin's methods.

People resented the special stores, apartments, vacations, and other privileges of party officials. Studies have shown marked differences in income and privileges of the party elite compared to the ordinary worker. Although some studies indicated the differences were not as great as in the Western capitalist societies (Rossi and Inkeles 1957; Connor 1979), perceptions are more important than reality. In the summer of 1989 strikes of Russian coal miners that threatened the entire economy had reflected their resentment of privileges of

---

Note: The approximations shown in the table are based on Freedom House's *Freedom in the World* 1987–1988 and 1991–1992 assessments of political freedom and the IMF's *World Economic Report May 1992* assessment of the freedom of prices. For governments a grade of 1 indicates a democracy and a 7 indicates a totalitarian government. A grade of 1 indicates market prices while a grade of 10 indicates government control of prices. The governments had about 100 percent control of prices in 1988. The degree of price liberalization exaggerates progress toward a market economy because at the beginning of 1992 little progress had been made toward privatization, and the government still exercised licensing and other controls on the economies. The estimate of China's price liberalization is from *The Economist*, 7/25/92, p. 34.

officials. The perceptions of special privileges helped bring about the humiliating defeats of the Communist Party in the free elections of 1990.

Closely related to resentment of special privileges was resentment of corruption. Gorbachev faced a dilemma with his glasnost policies. Relaxing controls on the news media and criticisms were used as tools to reveal fraud and eliminate abuses. However, publicizing such information eroded what little support the Communist Party had.

Gorbachev's glasnost was far-reaching but his perestroika did not accomplish the basic restructuring of allowing an opposition party, freeing prices, and permitting private ownership of important parts of the economy. He seemed to believe he could carry out a partial reform along these lines, or perhaps a gradual reform with a one-party Communist system. Many have criticized him for gradualism, but such critics often forget how they had assumed even his limited reforms were not possible against opposition by the Communist bureaucracy. Critics overlooked the difficulty of disposing of state-owned property, which in other countries has taken many years to turn over to private ownership. They also failed to acknowledge that Hungary and Czechoslovakia were able to carry out gradual reforms with limited success. (See Chapter 4.)

Before Gorbachev's reforms, elections were a fraud. The Communist Party controlled the nominations, and only one candidate was on the ballot. In rare cases where there was more than one candidate, the government did not permit an organized group to campaign. After Gorbachev's initial reforms, competition for nominations was allowed. This reform resulted in removal of hardline Communists from positions of authority, which helped strengthen his position to continue limited reforms. However, it was only a partial political reform because there was still no organized opposition. In the summer of 1988 a group trying to organize an opposition party called the Democratic Unity Party mounted demonstrations in Moscow, but they were easily broken up by the police and leaders were arrested. For more than five years Gorbachev performed a balancing act between the hardliners and the reformers as he moved forward haltingly with reforms.

Gorbachev broke with much of Leninist tradition, but he seemed to want to maintain Communist Party domination. Lenin's major contribution to Marxist theory had been an insistence on strict discipline in his Bolshevik faction. Lenin attacked the Mensheviks who supported democratic procedures, and he broke up the democratically elected constituent assembly of 1918 because his party had only a minority of the seats. Lenin established the Cheka, which grew into the repressive KGB. Gorbachev by pulling the teeth of the KGB and permitting criticisms of the regime, released pressures for reform that led to erosion of Communist one-party control and to the break-up of the empire.

Opposition to the Communist policies then became evident in elections to the Communist Party, in elections to the parliament, in public opinion polls and other indices of popular opinion. Yeltsin from the wings called for fundamental democratic and market reforms. His policies were popular enough to get him elected president of the Russian Republic. This gave him enough democratic legitimacy after the abortive coup in 1991 to take a leading role in the new confederation of the Russian republics, the Commonwealth of Independent States. In 1992 he made good on his promises of reform with decrees freeing prices and slashing the bureaucracy built up under the Communist system.

In 1992 it was not clear how long it would take for the market reforms to work. There were serious food shortages and stores were emptied of other goods as people used their accumulated savings to hoard food and convert almost worthless rubles to buy available goods.

As of the end of 1992, however, the pessimistic predictions of starvation, food riots, and chaos had not materialized. I visited Ukraine in December 1991 and was told that the people would somehow make it through the winter with the help of free market shops, bartering, and standing in lines. This is the way they survived. There was no opportunity in the first months of 1992 for a payoff for price incentives for agricultural production.

Success in the crop year of 1992 was problematic. Soviet farmers for many decades had worked as laborers on collective farms. Those few that took advantage of new laws permitting private ownership found it difficult to get good land from the collectives. In the first months of 1992 machinery and buildings were still in the name of the collective farms and seed and fertilizers were still controlled by the bureaucracy. Managers held back food from city markets to get exorbitant prices. However, privatization of farmland accelerated early in 1992.

Initial reports of the grain crop for 1992 indicated a good harvest and a reduced need for imports of grain. The problem in the coming months would be to promote distribution of food crops through market incentives. Outside of Russia about 20 to 40 percent of the people were employed in argiculture, and maintenance of food production and distribution in these republics would be crucial.

The industrial sector faced similar problems. Rubles had little value since huge amounts were held in savings, and prices had little relationship to market values. Obtaining raw materials and marketing goods still required approval of government bodies and deals with state firms. Gorbachev began by abolishing ministries and reducing the bureaucracy. He then proceeded with a monetary reform to soak up excess rubles, free prices, and make the ruble freely convertible into foreign exchange, steps that would create access to goods and price incentives to produce. Yeltsin at the beginning of 1992 had freed most prices and ended the monopoly of state stores.

Yeltsin's position, as president of Russia and the leading figure in the Commonwealth of Independent States, would continue to be tenuous until food came back to the shelves. The fundamental problem was political—to keep political support for removing old hardline officials from power and substituting market decisions. I will assess the probabilities of success after looking at the experience of other Communist systems and the success and lack of success in changing them.

Those who believe in the democratic system with its checks and balances and rule of law, which are designed to prevent officials from exploiting their power, were not surprised that tyranny had developed under Communism. They were surprised, however, at the revolutions against tyranny. How did the Communist system permit reformers such as Gorbachev and Yeltsin to assume leadership? In the first place its economic and political failures demanded reforms. The system was harder to maintain as knowledge spread of the success of the democratic, market-oriented European Community. The accident of Gorbachev's leadership triggered reforms. It was as simple as "A-B-C." After all, if Andropov, Brezhnev, or Chernenko had lived longer, Gorbachev might have missed a chance to rise to power. In 1985 there were no other dynamic reformers at the top. Gorbachev won on a close vote in the Politburo, and his supporters obviously did not know what was in store. Like Lenin, he dominated Russian history of his era. Both started processes with tremendous momentum. Once perestroika and glasnost started, the hardliners (dinosaurs) were not able to reverse them.

Russia and the 14 other former Soviet republics faced serious interrelated problems. After the removal of totalitarian controls, ethnic and religious wars broke out. Other conflicts occurred as Communist cadres tried to hold back the public pressures for reform. In a few cases there were authoritarian reactions by leaders and political groups. In the economic realm the normal shock of removing totalitarian controls was made worse by the blockage of trade between republics and inflation caused by excess rubles accumulated under the Communist system.

In the first two years it appeared that people had been better off under the Communist economic system. Their faith in a market system was stretched thin. It will take until the end of the century before the success of this experiment in political and economic reforms can be determined. However, the events after 1989 discredited Communism among intellectuals, so that it was no longer a serious ideology. In the 1930s and after World War II Communist ideals of equality and social justice had attracted many intellectuals, who then failed to acknowledge repression under Stalinism, Maoism, Castroism, and other forms of Communism. After 1989 Communism and its ideology seemed to be in the dustbin of history. We will now look at the equally dramatic foreign policy changes reflected in developments of this period of reform.

Chapter 3

The Dynamics of Soviet
and Russian Foreign Policies

The cold war started at the end of World War I, although it did not get that name until after World War II. In the 1930s the fear of Communism prevented alliances against Hitler's Germany. After Germany attacked France and Western Europe in 1940 and the Soviet Union in 1941, the United States and Britain formed the Grand Alliance with the Soviet Union, and relations were at a high point until the end of the war. After World War II and until 1989 world policies revolved around the cold war, moderated at times by agreements to limit nuclear arms. After 1989 the cold war ended, and foreign offices began sorting out policies for a world without a serious Communist threat.

ORIGINS OF THE COLD WAR

After World War I, Lenin, Stalin, and other Communist leaders were not prepared for the problems they faced. They hoped for a world revolution to help them consolidate control in the Soviet Union. Instead, they faced large-scale intervention by hostile capitalist powers.

From the beginning the Communist government called for workers in other countries, particularly in Germany, to overthrow their governments. The Soviet Union established the Comintern, or Third International, in March 1919 with the aim of promoting revolution throughout the world. In the Soviet city of Baku in September 1920, the Communists held a Congress of the Peoples of the East calling on Moslems to wage a holy war against British imperialism. They hoped the British would be thrown out of Turkey, Persia, Afghanistan, and India. The Soviet Communists also encouraged Communist revolutions in Europe, which resulted in temporary Communist regimes in Hungary and in Bavaria, Germany. On March 21, 1919, Bela Kun proclaimed a Hungarian proletarian government in Budapest. As the Allied armies smashed the German armies in September 1918, Lenin offered the support of Red soldiers to the German workers to help smash capitalism. There was a Communist uprising in Berlin, but the Social Democratic party managed to take control of the government with the support of what was left of the German army.

Allied intervention in Russia initially arose during World War I. After Lenin negotiated peace with Germany, American troops landed at Archangel and Murmansk, the northern ports supplying Russia, to protect munitions that were being sent to the previous Russian government. British and French forces also landed there ostensibly for the same reason. The British and French, however, supported factions fighting the Communists. U.S. President Wilson was anti-interventionist, and there were no serious clashes between American and Bolshevik forces. After World War I ended, Wilson withdrew U.S. forces the following summer when the ports were cleared of ice (Kennan 1960).

In southern Russia, British and French forces numbering about 110,000 supported the troops of Russian Admiral Kolchak, with the aim of helping to overthrow the new Communist government. Winston Churchill's book *The Aftermath* has a frank account of this British and French intervention. In the east the Japanese invaded Siberia with 73,500 troops with the aim of taking control of eastern Siberia. Czechoslovakian prisoners of war rebelled and for a while controlled large stretches of the Trans-Siberian railroad. In the west a Polish army under Pilsudsky pushed into Soviet territory. The Red Army counterattacked, but finally the Soviets were forced to settle on a boundary that gave up Soviet territory to the new state of Poland established by the Treaty of Versailles. As the Red Army fought back and gained control in other areas, the Allied armies of intervention were withdrawn.

The Allied intervention is remembered with bitterness in Soviet histories. In the West the Soviet support of revolutions created a fear of Communism. This was the origin of the mutual hostility that became known as the cold war about 25 years later after World War II.

European nations established correct but not friendly diplomatic relations with the Soviet Union in the 1920s. The major breakthrough was the Treaty of Rapallo in 1922, in which full diplomatic recognition was granted to the Soviet Union by Germany. This action by two outcasts of the Treaty of Versailles shocked other nations into restoring diplomatic contacts to forestall a closer relationship between these two potentially powerful adversaries. There was also a secret agreement in which the German military established a base in Russia to work with modern military equipment forbidden by the Treaty of Versailles. This gave both Germans and Soviets training that was useful in World War II.

In the 1930s Soviet diplomacy at first tried to get the Western nations to oppose Hitler. After that failed at Munich, when Britain and France approved of Hitler's taking over part of Czechoslovakia, an ally of the Soviet Union, Stalin joined in the notorious 1939 pact with Hitler. Stalin suspected the West of wanting Hitler to attack the Soviet Union. After the pact was signed, Hitler attacked Poland in the west while the Soviets took over eastern Poland and parts of Eastern Europe including the Baltic states of Latvia, Lithuania, and Estonia, as a protective buffer (map, page 1). Hitler's attack against Poland brought Britain and France into World War II.

Stalin's pact with Hitler in 1939 disillusioned many Communists in other countries, and the world Communist movement, already reeling from the purges of the 1930s, never recovered from this cynical pact. The Soviet Union then moved to attack Finland, which after offering surprisingly strong resistance, negotiated a favorable truce that preserved its independence. Hitler, with the Soviets neutralized, successfully conquered France, Belgium, Luxembourg, the Netherlands, Denmark, and Norway and tried to conquer Britain. But Britain maintained air superiority and discouraged an invasion, so Hitler tore up his pact with Stalin and attacked what had been his main target, the Soviet Union. Hitler targeted the Soviet Union as the leader of world Communism and owner of the largest area of "lebensraum," land and resources, that Hitler wanted for his Greater Germany.

Britain and the United States, finally realizing Hitler's ambitions to rule the world, supported the Soviet Union by shipping military equipment and food to the Soviet forces (van Tuyll 1989). The Soviet superiority in manpower was instrumental in stopping Hitler's attack at the gates of Moscow. At about the same time Japan attacked the United States and made the war worldwide in scope.

The Grand Alliance of Britain's Prime Minister Churchill, America's President Roosevelt, and Russia's Stalin during World War II was the high point of Soviet cooperation with the West and brought victory against the German-Italian-Japanese Axis. The cooperation was sufficient to form the United Nations, determine the boundaries of many countries involved in the war, and write the peace treaties. This established a framework for the postwar world that remained until 1989. At the same time, the Soviet occupation of the East European buffer and the controversy over policy toward Germany promoted the cold war, which, as described below, dominated international politics after World War II.

CONSOLIDATION OF THE EAST EUROPEAN EMPIRE

The creation of the East European bloc of buffer states after World War II was based on the Soviet leaders' overriding fear of Germany, which had devastated western Russia twice in the twentieth century, and also by the Soviets' suspicions developed during World War II. Russian fears were reinforced by fundamental tenets of Communist ideology that the capitalist system generates war and aggression. The ideology holds that the German fascist system of the 1930s was a historical result of the workings of the capitalist system. Moreover, during World War II Stalin kept asking the Allies for a second front to take the pressure off the Soviet Union, which was suffering millions of casualties. Unfortunately, President Roosevelt indicated to Stalin that the United States expected to form a second front in 1942, but it was not until two years later that such a front was actually established (Sherwood 1948, 577). The British opposed an early second front for sound military reasons: the U.S. forces were just beginning to be mobilized, and the British did not think their troops together were strong enough to land on the continent. This delay, however, helped reinforce the suspicion in Soviet minds that the Allied capitalist nations wanted Soviet forces chewed up by the Germans, particularly since the USSR was taking the bulk of the casualties from the German attack.

The cold war resumed between the Soviet Union and Britain over the Polish issue. Britain had entered World War II because of Hitler's invasion of Poland and, therefore, was concerned about its future. To the Russians, Poland geographically was an essential part of the buffer against a German threat. In the meetings before Yalta, Churchill insisted that the conservative Polish regime under Mikolajczyk with headquarters in London should have a 50/50 balance in a new Polish government against the group of Lublin Poles, who were dominated by the Soviets. No clear understanding was reached on this point, but in February 1945 at Yalta the three powers agreed to establish the provisional Polish boundaries that exist today (Churchill 1953, 227, 365–402). Under this arrangement Poland took over areas of eastern Germany and gave up part of eastern Poland to the Soviet Union.

The text of the Yalta agreement of March 24, 1945, stated that the three governments would assist the East European people to form "interim governmental authorities broadly representative of all democratic elements in the population." Under this wording, the Soviet Union consolidated its control with Communist leaders trained in the Soviet Union and used the Soviet armed forces as a lever to impose an empire dominated by Moscow. Within a few years the Soviets had firmly established a series of friendly Communist governments under Soviet domination all through Eastern Europe. Prime Minister Churchill on June 4, 1946, dramatized the situation by his now famous phrase, "the iron curtain," which had descended between Eastern Europe and the West.

Khrushchev's memoirs give an example of how the Soviets dominated East European governments after World War II. Stalin personally selected the leaders of Poland with the assistance of Khrushchev and other Soviet officials using as the main criteria whether the new leaders shared Soviet goals and would be "faithful" later on. The election was rigged for the Communist leaders trained in the Soviet Union to take over control of Poland (Khrushchev 1974, 173, 197–250).

The breakaway of Yugoslavia in 1947 from the Eastern Bloc was a shock to the Eastern European empire, but it increased the determination of the Soviets to consolidate their control of other East European countries. When the East German revolt occurred in 1953, it was put down with Soviet troops, and East Germany became one of the most subservient states of the entire Eastern Bloc (see Chapter 4).

Another shock to the Soviet–East European system came with Khrushchev's denunciation of Stalin in February 1956 at a Party Congress attended by foreign delegates. Khrushchev's slashing attack shattered the myth of Stalin's infallibility. Many Communists interpreted the speech as heralding a relaxation of Soviet domination of Eastern European governments. This helped encourage the Polish workers of Poznan to protest about low wages, and failing to get satisfaction from Warsaw, they rioted. The Polish government put down the revolt with its armed forces in June 1956, but it later made concessions to the workers. Unrest spread a few months later to Hungary, and in late October 1956 a revolution broke out led by students and workers. Imre Nagy, the leader, proclaimed Hungary's neutrality and demanded that Soviet troops be withdrawn. Within a few weeks Khrushchev ordered Soviet troops to intervene to arrest the leaders. Despite protests of U.N. bodies, where the Soviets were outvoted, the Soviets arrested Nagy and executed him (see Chapter 4).

The East European empire was stable for 12 years after the Hungarian revolution, but in August 1968 nationalist pressures erupted again when Czechoslovakian officials demanded liberalization. The Czechoslovakian government, under the leadership of Dubcek, set goals of developing toward a socialist type of democracy; however, Chairman Brezhnev moved Soviet and Eastern European troops into Czechoslovakia announcing that the USSR was determined to defend the interests of the "Socialist Commonwealth," and that Soviet and East European troops would give mutual assistance to countries where the existence of "socialism" was threatened. This became known as the Brezhnev Doctrine. Under Soviet occupation Dubcek was forced out and replaced with a government that agreed to the stationing of Soviet troops.

Although at the end of 1978 Romania openly challenged Soviet demands to increase the Warsaw Pact budget, other East European countries closer to the historic invasion route of northern Europe did not challenge Soviet dominance. The Warsaw Pact and the economic arrangements of the Council for Mutual Economic Assistance provided the treaty framework for continued Soviet control of its East European empire.

RIVAL MILITARY AND ECONOMIC ALLIANCES

In retrospect, the rebirth of the cold war and the formation of rival alliances appear to have been inevitable. The Soviets were determined to create a buffer of friendly states, which, to the Western leaders who had just fought Hitler, appeared to be a form of aggression. At the same time the Soviets wanted to keep West Germany weak. On the other hand, the United States and Britain did not want a "basket case" on their hands. So they began supporting Germany. They scrapped the plan to put strict limits on its industry, and began lifting the controls on industrial production. At the same time they moved toward granting it self government and sovereignty.

After World War II the Soviets tried without success to obtain four-power control of the Ruhr valley and also control Germany's major warmaking potential. They hoped to use their Communist view of the dominance of economic factors in politics as leverage to prevent Germany from ever again becoming a threat. The United States and Britain, faced by the pressures and responsibilities of keeping the Germans alive and wishing to restore the health of Western

Europe, unified their two occupation zones and took steps to let Germans manage their economic and political affairs without the threat of a Soviet veto on their decisions. When Britain and the United States allowed West Germany to issue its own currency, the Soviets saw it as a plot to rebuild a powerful, capitalist Germany that might again threaten the Soviet Union. Stalin, in a power move, responded by blockading access to Berlin to back his demands that the Western powers give the Soviets a veto on German recovery. President Truman, assisted by Great Britain, countered with the 1948 airlift to Berlin over the Russian zone of occupation.

Meanwhile, Western Europe felt threatened by the Berlin blockade and the Communist coup in Czechoslovakia. It organized the Brussels Pact, which later became a core of the North Atlantic Treaty (NATO), joined by the United States. The Soviets belatedly realized that the Berlin blockade was stimulating the alliance process, and they lifted the blockade in the spring of 1949. This was too late to stop the momentum for NATO, and on July 21, 1949, the Senate ratified the North Atlantic Treaty. In the fall a provisional West German government was established.

The final step of arming West Germany did not take place until more than five years later. Again the Soviets sped the process along by supporting the Korean War in 1950. At the same time they were secretly forming a paramilitary force in East Germany, which later was converted to military units for the Warsaw Pact. There was a reluctance, particularly in France, to rearm Western Germany, but when the Soviets gave the signal in the Korean War that Communism would commit aggression where there was weakness, this alarmed leaders of the West. They accelerated the rearming of Germany.

At the end of 1954 British Foreign Secretary Anthony Eden proposed to expand the Brussels Treaty (France, Britain, Belgium, the Netherlands, and Luxembourg) to take in West Germany and Italy. To calm French fears, Britain agreed to maintain four British divisions in Germany along with a tactical air force. The United States also committed forces in Germany. As part of this deal the German chancellor signed the "ABC" agreement, which committed Germany, along with the Benelux countries, not to make atomic, bacteriological, or chemical weapons.

Germany regained sovereignty and joined NATO in 1955. A few days later the Soviets concluded the Warsaw Pact of 1955 with their East European satellites as a balance-of-power response. The preamble of the Warsaw Pact makes clear that the entry of West Germany into NATO was the rationale for the Pact. All the East European countries were members of the pact except Yugoslavia and Albania. It was a mutual defense treaty, reinforced by bilateral treaties between members.

The treaty followed the NATO pact in a number of key provisions, and it, like NATO, was loosely tied to the United Nations. Article 11 had an interesting balance-of-power provision that provided for dissolving the Warsaw Pact when an all-European collective security treaty was signed. This implied that if U.S.

forces were withdrawn from Europe, a treaty could be negotiated in Europe terminating the Warsaw Pact. In fact on July 1, 1991, after the cold war ended, the Soviet Union and five Eastern European countries terminated the pact. It had been more of an instrument for Soviet domination of Eastern Europe than a treaty for mutual defense. The Soviets had stationed their forces in Czechoslovakia, Poland, East Germany, and Hungary and had provided military advisers under the treaty. They had used it as a cover for their invasion of Czechoslovakia in 1968, and ironically the meeting terminating the pact took place in Czechoslovakia. President Havel noted at the time that the invasion of Czechoslovakia in 1968 had been the only military action taken by the pact.

The Warsaw Pact and NATO provided a framework for military confrontation in Europe. A minor step toward easing such confrontation was taken by the provisions of the Conference on Security and Cooperation in Europe (CSCE) of 1975, which permitted observers from each of the pacts to observe military maneuvers involving more than 25,000 troops. This lessened chances to misinterpret practice maneuvers. Before Gorbachev became general secretary, desultory discussions also took place between the two pacts for Mutual Balanced Force Reductions (MBFR) in Europe.

The major challenge to the two pacts arose from the dramatic developments in 1989, described in the next chapter, as the Brezhnev policy of intervention was discarded. In its place Gorbachev's government press spokesman, Gerasinov, announced the "Sinatra policy" of letting the Eastern European countries do things their way (*NYT* 11/12/89, 1, 12).

The unilateral withdrawals of Soviet forces in 1989 were accompanied by announcements of major reductions in East European forces. The East European governments demanded withdrawal of Soviet forces and by the end of the year Hungary and East Germany had begun negotiations to accomplish this with the Soviets. As indicated in the following chapters, Communist Party controls were discarded. Military observers for years had noted that the East European troops would not be reliable in an offensive operation, and with these developments they completely discounted their value in an offensive war (*Economist* 1/27/90).

President Bush used the above arguments in the middle of November 1989 when he announced that he had asked the secretary of defense to start planning for a cut of $180 billion in projected spending for the U.S. defense budget over five years. Since spending was projected to increase, this meant about a $90 billion cut from the 1989 levels of spending (*NYT* 11/18/89). More drastic cuts followed in subsequent years.

In the economic realm the Communist challenge in Western Europe after World War II stimulated support for aid for Europe. When General Marshall took over as secretary of state in January 1947, Greece was faced with a deteriorating economic situation and a Communist insurgency supported from Albania, Yugoslavia, and Bulgaria. Undersecretary of State Acheson pictured the threat as if the Communist infection of Greece could easily spread to the Middle

Figure 3-1 President Boris Yeltsin and President Bush signing the Strategic Arms Reduction Treaty (START) on June 17, 1992. (Courtesy: Susan Biddle, The White House).

East and Africa and to Western Europe, where domestic Communist movements were already active. The Truman administration got Congress to approve the Marshall Plan for all of Western Europe. Although helping economic recovery was emphasized as the Plan's purpose, Acheson in his testimony to Congress stressed the political threat of Communism sweeping through an impoverished Western Europe.

This started Europe on the road toward the European Community,* which perhaps as much as NATO strengthened Western Europe in relation to Eastern Europe. The major motive of Jean Monnet, the French founder of the European Community, was to establish an integrated economic community in Western Europe that would make war between France and Germany inconceivable. The master plan succeeded, and it also succeeded in making the European Community the most dynamic economic area in the world. It has far outpaced Eastern Europe and exerted what turned out to be an irresistible lure for the Eastern

---

*The European Community started out as the Schuman Plan or Monnet Plan. Western Europe established the European Coal and Steel Community, which was later expanded into the European Economic Community, aimed at abolishing trade restrictions on all products, not just coal and steel. The European Economic Community was expanded into the European Community, which includes the European parliament and other European institutions. The European Community had twelve members in 1989.

European nations to make political and economic reforms and loosen their ties to the bureaucratic Communist economies.

In 1949 the Soviets had set up the Council for Mutual Economic Assistance (CMEA or COMECON) as a counter to the Western initiatives of the Marshall Plan, and later the European Community. CMEA was not actually activated until five years later, after Stalin's death. The countries that belonged to the Warsaw Pact were members, with other Communist nations as observers. The CMEA embraced 300 million people including 250 million Soviets. All members of the CMEA theoretically were equal and all decisions were unanimous, and it did not develop the type of supranationality that the European Community did. Despite the broad aims of CMEA, its main accomplishments were trade agreements among the members and provisions to strengthen the ruble as an instrument for clearing trade balances between the various countries. One of its aims was to coordinate economic plans of the Eastern European countries, but this was resisted by the Eastern Europeans. To the extent it succeeded with the bilateral trade agreements, it held back economic progress that comes naturally with multilateral trade. Even Gorbachev criticized the CMEA as a device for countries to dump unwanted goods on each other.

The East European countries looked longingly at the success of the European Community, which had supported Western Europe's remarkable record of economic growth. Gorbachev's call for a ''Europe House'' for all of Europe encouraged Eastern European countries to apply to join the European Community. East Germany already had access to the Community through tariff-free trade with West Germany. In a summit meeting in the summer of 1989 the Western powers agreed that the European Community would coordinate aid to Eastern European countries to help in any programs of market reforms. Eastern Europe would need assistance as its governments undertook the painful adjustments to a competitive system free of the subsidies and controls that had held back economic progress.

DÉTENTE AND NUCLEAR ARMS CONTROL

Détente is a French word that means a relaxation of tension and not a comprehensive settlement of issues. Coexistence is a similar term in the Communist dictionary. In essence these words described pragmatic policies of the Soviets and the United States to coexist to survive in a nuclear world.

There is no agreed chronicle of détente or its opposite, the cold war. Most Americans regard détente as a development of the 1970s, but moves toward détente began after Stalin's death in 1953 and Khrushchev's taking control of Soviet foreign policy. In the years after Stalin's death, Soviet and Western policymakers concluded a series of agreements including the Korean War Truce in 1953, the Geneva Agreement to end the war in Indochina in 1954, and Austrian Treaty, which had been under negotiation since the end of World War II. Khrushchev not only withdrew troops from Austria, which was under joint occupation with the Western Allies, and allowed it to regain its sovereignty, but he did the same for Finnish territory and reduced Soviet troops in Eastern Europe. His motives seemed to be pragmatic—to reduce causes of friction with East European allies and to reduce the expense of maintaining these forces (Khrushchev 1974, 250–262, 279–298). His later nuclear détente with the United States after the Cuban missile crisis seemed based on a genuine fear of the potential of these terrible weapons.

Khrushchev's gestures toward détente received a setback with the revulsion in the United States and Europe to the 1956 repression by Khrushchev's troops of the Hungarians' revolt for freedom from Soviet control. Tension increased in 1958 when he supported China's offensives against the offshore islands held by Taiwan with a statement threatening Soviet use of nuclear weapons if the United States used them. This was a high point of tensions, but soon after that Mao's reckless statements about nuclear weapons helped create the split between Peking and Moscow (see Chapter 7). This split more than a decade later permitted the détente between the United States and the People's Republic of China. Khrushchev restored better relations during his 1959 visit with Eisenhower at Camp David, but this was shattered in 1960 by the reaction to the Soviets' shooting down of an American U-2 spy plane over the Soviet Union.

The cold war intensified in 1962 with Soviet pressures on Berlin and installations of nuclear missiles in Cuba. Probably the major motive of the Soviets was to try to catch up with Americans in long-range strategic missiles. Placing Soviet intermediate-range missiles in Cuba would have brought American cities within range of a larger number of Soviet missiles and in one dramatic move narrowed the missile gap with the United States (Allison 1971). This was a high point of the cold war.

Khrushchev was shocked by President Kennedy's demand to remove the missiles. For a while the world seemed to teeter on the brink of nuclear war. U.S. policymakers mobilized support for Latin American nations in the Organization of American States and the backing of other allies. With carefully escalated power politics, including partial mobilization, a threat to attack Cuba, and a "quarantine" of Cuba designed to cut off shipments of nuclear weapons, and with the informal assurances to the Soviets (Kennedy 1959) that the United States would remove its missiles from Turkey, President Kennedy managed to get the Soviets to withdraw their missiles. This was considered by most observers a triumph of American diplomacy. However, the Soviets intensified their development of long-range missiles and within 10 years had redressed the balance of power with larger and more terrible weapons of destruction.

In 1963 there was a brief revival of détente with Ambassador Averell Harriman's conclusion of a partial nuclear test-ban treaty. Most laypeople regarded the treaty as designed to keep nuclear fallout out of the atmosphere, but it had perhaps the even more important side effect of preventing the testing of large new weapons. There was also the hot line agreement during this period that established emergency communications between the Kremlin and the White

House, but détente soon was submerged by the escalation of the Vietnam War under President Johnson in 1965. The Soviets were a major supplier of arms to the North Vietnamese, and the cold war intensified while the hot war in Southeast Asia escalated (see Chapter 8).

Détente was revived and became a household word in the early 1970s as Kissinger pursued the SALT negotiations and negotiated an end to the Vietnam War. President Nixon and Chairman Brezhnev signed the first SALT agreement in Moscow on May 26, 1972, at a summit meeting. There were two major parts—"interim" agreements limiting the number of long-range missiles, not including those in bombers, and an Antiballistic Missile (ABM) Treaty. The interim SALT I Agreement was approved overwhelmingly in a joint Senate-House resolution and the ABM Treaty was approved by a vote of the Senate, with only two in opposition. The Supreme Soviet of the USSR ratified for the Soviets.

The ceilings and subceilings were not complicated. Under SALT I the United States was limited to a total of 1710 intercontinental ballistic missiles (ICBMs) and sea-launched ballistic missiles (SLBMs) with an option to substitute new submarine missiles for old land missiles. The Soviets had a higher ceiling of 2358 ICBMs and SLBMs with an option for a similar substitution. Opponents of the agreements attacked them on the basis that they allowed the Soviet Union a higher ceiling with more and bigger missiles. Defenders pointed out that the United States had more warheads on bombers and on multiple independently targeted reentry vehicles (MIRVs) with a higher destructive power. Bombers and MIRVs were not covered by SALT I. Moreover, the U.S. submarines were quieter and harder to detect, and its submarine missiles had a longer range.

A technological breakthrough that permitted conclusion of the agreements involved satellite photography that captured details of missile silo construction, the missiles themselves, and submarine construction. This is called monitoring by "national means," and the agreements specified that the Soviet Union and the United States should not attempt to interfere with this process. This finessed the difficult problem of on-site inspection. The Soviet military authorities historically had opposed letting foreigners inspect military installations.

The accompanying antiballistic missile (ABM) agreement limited each country's defensive system to two ABM sites. The purpose was to deter a nuclear attack by leaving both sides vulnerable to mutual assured destruction (MAD) in case of a nuclear war. Neither side was able to develop an effective ABM defense against enemy missiles, and both sides, therefore, would be devastated in a nuclear war.

In November 1974, President Ford met with General Secretary Brezhnev in Vladivostok, Russia, and they agreed on a framework for a further SALT agreement that would also include bombers and missiles with multiple warheads (MIRVs). President Jimmy Carter later negotiated the SALT II agreement using the Vladivostok ceilings as a guide. SALT II set equal ceilings for both sides of 2250 on strategic nuclear missiles by 1981, which would involve only minor reductions in missiles already on hand. The agreement covered bombers and MIRVs as well as intercontinental and submarine-launched missiles covered in SALT I. SALT II was observed for many years, although it was never ratified.

Other nuclear arms agreements negotiated by the Soviet Union and the United States during the Nixon and Ford administrations included:

1. The hot line agreement of 1971, a follow-up to the 1963 agreement that established a quick communications link between Washington and Moscow.
2. A Nixon administration protocol to the original ABM Treaty that limited ABM systems to one rather than two sites.
3. A 1973 executive agreement between the United States and USSR to consult in case of a nuclear confrontation.
4. A Ford administration treaty that would limit nuclear tests underground to 150 kilotons or less. This was honored, although the Senate did not act on it, and the issues of inspection were not settled until 1989.
5. A 1976 agreement, not approved by the Senate, for controls on peaceful nuclear explosions. However, it also was honored.

Meanwhile, in 1975 détente continued in other fields with the signing of the Final Act of the Conference on Security and Cooperation (CSCE) concluded at Helsinki, Finland, by 32 Eastern and Western European countries plus the United States and Canada. The act included prior notification of military maneuvers, exchanging observers, increasing cooperation in the cultural and scientific fields, and promoting respect for human rights and fundamental freedoms. Both Western and Eastern European countries strongly supported the CSCE agreement.

Germany's Ostpolitik (politics toward the East) occurred at about the same time as the first SALT agreements and was as important to détente in Europe as the nuclear arms agreements were to the United States. Willy Brandt, mayor of Berlin during the Berlin blockade, was the author, and his blockade role gave him anti-Communist credentials. He became chancellor of Germany as head of a Social Democratic coalition in the early 1970s, and he concluded treaties with the Soviet Union and with Eastern European countries that recognized the boundaries imposed on Germany after World War II, including the division of Germany and the loss of territory to Poland. His treaty with East Germany recognized that there was still the idea of one German nation, but it provided for formal diplomatic recognition of the two Germanys. Both Germanys were subsequently admitted to the United Nations. The Soviets were delighted at the official recognition of their postwar transfer of territory to Poland, which could have provided the basis for German revanchism.

The Federal Republic of Germany gained permission for more economic and cultural contacts between the two Germanys, which in reality is the substance of German unity. In the years after the treaties were signed, as many as 8 million

East Germans visited West Germany annually, representing a 300 percent increase in four years. The Soviet Union also permitted 10,000 Germans to emigrate and reunify with their families in the Federal Republic of Germany (*Economist* 8/28/76, 43).

President Carter's strong advocacy of human rights complicated his policy of détente with the Soviet Union. The principles of human rights were at odds with the controls of Soviet society. Whereas the Soviets could resist the pressures for human rights within their own country, the issue caused them considerable uneasiness in Eastern Europe. The nationalists of Eastern Europe resented Soviet dominance over their societies, and the human rights issue provided them with internationally recognized slogans to attack such controls. The human rights issue also affected the Western European Communist parties, which after 1976 began demanding a fundamental change in the Soviet position on this issue.

President Carter's human rights campaign began in 1977. During that summer, the CSCE, set up during the Ostpolitik era, met in a preliminary session at Belgrade. The Soviets made a sharp attack on the Carter statements on human rights, saying that they undermined détente, and accused the West itself of human rights violations. They also stepped up arrests and action against Soviet dissidents who were demanding that the Soviets live up to obligations under the CSCE Final Act. The Soviet leaders obviously saw the human rights campaign as a challenge to their own totalitarian system and a threat to their East European buffer by encouraging Eastern European leaders and people who wanted to achieve independence from Soviet domination.

In preparation for the 1976 Berlin meeting, the French and Italian Communist parties had issued a "Eurocommunism" manifesto calling for independent roads to Communism and listing liberal democratic rights. They even criticized Soviet treatment of dissidents and abuse of prisoners in labor camps. In March 1977 leaders of the Spanish, French, and Italian Communist parties agreed on the Declaration of Madrid, again calling for respect of universal suffrage, political plurality, and individual freedoms. The host, Spanish Communist Party leader Santiago Carrillo, publicly said that the meeting was not meant to be a challenge to anybody, but a prominent Czechoslovak party member labeled the Eurocommunists as traitors (*Washington Post* 7/1/76, A1). Moscow waited until after the Spanish elections to attack Carrillo, knowing full well that other Communists would get the message. The Soviet *New Times'* official line attacked Carrillo's proposal for an independent Europe and his vague call for a European defense arrangement as supporting the imperialist policy of arming Western Europe against world socialism (Haseler 1978; Tokes 1978; Leonard 1978; Tannahill 1978).

In the closing days of 1979 and into early 1980, prospects for détente and ratification of the SALT suffered another severe setback when about 100,000 Soviet troops entered Afghanistan to put down a rebellion against the Communist leader, who showed signs of independence, and replace him with a reliable leader whom they could trust. Although the United States had not reacted two years earlier when there was a Communist coup since there was no evidence of direct Soviet intervention, the new move was outright aggression (Garthoff 1987). The United States, its Western allies, neighboring countries, and other governments objected strenuously. Although technically a case could be made under international law that a sovereign government can invite Soviet assistance, reports of Soviet intervention in the coup itself and the massive and rapid entry of its forces into Afghanistan indicated that the call for help by the Afghanistan government was a fraud. The Soviet invasion was imperialism that was in a different category than its previous indirect support to "national liberation" and revolutionary movements in the Near East and Africa.

President Carter took the lead in mobilizing condemnation of the Soviet aggression. His major psychological move was a U.S. boycott of the Moscow Olympics in the summer of 1980. Germany, Japan, Arab countries, and more than 60 other countries joined the boycott. Although other European and Olympic committees decided to participate, the athletes of 16 of these nations refused to fly their nations' flags at the ceremonies. Other moves joined in varying degrees by other governments included sharply curtailing grain exports and Soviet fishing privileges, suspending scientific and cultural exchanges, and restricting exports of high technology and other strategic items. Carter also withdrew the request for Senate approval of the SALT II agreements, which was doubtful in any event. The president, however, still made clear that the United States would continue to observe the SALT II limits unless the Soviets moved first to exceed them. Meanwhile news reports indicated that the Afghanistan people were mounting massive resistance to the Soviets including demonstrations and guerrilla action even though they were outgunned by modern Soviet weapons (*Economist* 9/4/76, 82–87). This was another high point of tensions in the roller coaster of the cold war and détente.

By the 1980s the Soviets and Americans had slipped back into cold war rhetoric and postures. The Western European nations, also demanding a withdrawal of Soviet troops from Afghanistan, continued diplomatic approaches to persuade the Soviets to withdraw. As usual the Western Europeans held back and let the United States take the lead in coercive policies. However, they gave support to U.S. pressures against the Soviets, and they agreed to take more of the burden of NATO defense to ease the burden of the U.S. build up in the Persian Gulf area.

In a speech in May 1982 President Reagan proposed that each side drastically reduce its strategic missiles. Few observers took him seriously, because he had appointed hardline opponents of the SALT treaties in key negotiating positions, he had openly criticized the Soviet Union as an "evil empire," and he had begun a massive military buildup. In 1983 he complicated the nuclear weapons negotiations in a speech calling for designing and building a system of space weapons, dubbed Star Wars, with the aim of destroying offensive missiles before they could reach U.S. soil. Although Reagan would not admit it, this would violate the ABM Treaty. Seemingly fruitless negotiations were carried out in Geneva on reducing strategic and medium-range missiles. At the end of 1986 Reagan formally ended the SALT II ceilings, but both sides stayed close to them.

A marked change in atmosphere and a basis for a breakthrough occurred in a brief October 1986 Iceland summit, when President Reagan and General Secretary Gorbachev agreed on principles for removing and destroying intermediate nuclear warheads in Europe from a Soviet total of more than 1400 to only 100, and for reducing strategic missiles by 50 percent. However, final agreement was not reached because the Soviets insisted that the United States not implement the Star Wars plan, while Reagan insisted on forging ahead with it.

The breakthrough came in 1987 in a Washington summit when the two leaders signed an INF (Intermediate Nuclear Force) agreement for eliminating throughout the world all medium-range nuclear and "shorter-range" missiles with ranges of 300 to 3400 miles. Provisions were made to monitor the destruction of the missiles and to make detailed on-site inspections in more than 100 sites in the Soviet Union and 30 sites in Europe and the United States to determine that the missiles were destroyed. Moreover, they pledged to press forward to negotiate an agreement to eliminate 50 percent of their strategic missiles and to reduce conventional forces in Europe. The Star Wars issue was left unresolved with both sides agreeing to conduct research, development, and testing as permitted by the ABM Treaty, without addressing the Reagan administration's assertion that this allowed extensive testing of Star Wars systems in space. Both the Soviets and later the U.S. Congress said the Reagan interpretation of the ABM Treaty was not justified.

The implications of the INF Treaty were breathtaking. For the first time entire classes of missiles totaling about 2000 were destroyed. To confirm the agreements, extensive inspections of military facilities were permitted in the Soviet Union. Moreover, this took place in extensive media coverage of Gorbachev and the Russian delegates. It was obvious to the world that Gorbachev had taken control in the Soviet Union and that he was determined to end the nuclear arms race. The opening of Russian military bases for inspections was a dramatic extension of his glasnost policy.

Both leaders appeared determined to press forward to eliminate 50 percent of their strategic missiles. This was not an idle promise as evidenced by the fact that they settled important issues for a future treaty including establishing a framework for counting weapons and starting an inspection system. This was a dramatic reversal in the cold war atmosphere that had prevailed. Observers reasoned that if President Reagan, who was known as a hardline anti-Communist, approved, this would ensure future U.S. government support of this type of agreement, promising a historic end to cold war tensions (U.S. Department of State 1987).

The détente based on nuclear arms control negotiations and centered in Europe was accompanied by conclusion of negotiations sponsored by the United

Figure 3-2   Vice President Bush, President Reagan, and General Secretary Gorbachev, December 1988 (Courtesy: David Valdez, The White House).

Nations for the Soviet Union to withdraw from Afghanistan. The invasion in 1980 had been a high point of cold war tensions; the withdrawal relieved those tensions and promoted détente. This, plus similar moves of Vietnam, the Soviet ally, to withdraw from Cambodia laid the groundwork for the normalization of diplomatic relations between the Soviet Union and China that took place in May 1989.

A NEW ERA OF COLLABORATION

After 1989 with the break up of the Soviets' East European and internal empires, détente blossomed into collaboration that included aid from the West. Drastic arms reduction treaties were superceded by unilateral reductions of nuclear and conventional arms that even optimists had not hoped for. Gorbachev opened the bidding in December 1988 before the United Nations when he announced reduction of Soviet armed forces in Europe, including 500,000 soldiers, 10,000 tanks, 8500 artillery systems, and 800 combat aircraft (*NYT* 12/8/88, 6).

Formal negotiations on conventional arms began in May 1989 in Vienna between NATO and Warsaw Pact members. This so-called Negotiation on Conventional Armed Forces in Europe was a successor to the Mutual and Balanced Force Reductions (MBFR) negotiations that were abandoned in February 1989 after 15 inconclusive years. Andrey Kokoshin of the USSR Academy of Science in testifying before the U.S. Congress stated that the decision by the USSR to make unilateral reductions of weapons in part had been caused by discouragement over the failure of the MBFR talks to make progress. He suggested unilateral reductions by both sides since they had huge margins beyond what was needed, particularly in strategic weapons (U.S. Department of State, 1987, 15–16).

President Bush countered with a proposal that the United States and the Soviet Union each cut their troops in Europe to 275,000, a modest cut for the United States, but a major cut for the Soviet Union. This was accepted. Talks continued on conventional weapons until the end of 1990 when the Iraq attack against Kuwait set the stage politically and militarily for subsequent, more drastic cuts of strategic weapons. Secretary of State Baker consulted closely with Gorbachev and Foreign Minister Bessmertnykh about acting against Iraq. The Soviets had been the principal arms supplier and ally of Iraq, so they appeared to be in a good position to pressure President Saddam Hussein. The Soviets approved the U.N. resolutions for sanctions against Iraq, including the one authorizing the United States and other nations to use force to carry out U.N. resolutions. Iraq refused to withdraw and the United States led the attack. After a month of heavy bombing, the U.N. anti-Iraq coalition defeated Iraq in a seven-day attack. The Iraqi forces armed with Soviet equipment were decimated, which indirectly degraded Soviet military prestige.

The U.S.–Soviet cooperation in the Gulf War set the stage for the signing of the START treaty in July 1991 after about ten years of negotiation. It would drastically reduce the number of nuclear warheads, for the first time. (Table 3-1). The Senate approved the treaty in October 1992. It required legislative action by Kazakstan, Belarus, and the Ukraine to get rid of the weapons and sign the Nuclear Non-Proliferation Treaty. (*NYT* 9/30/92, 4). The START treaty allows seven years for the complicated job of disposing of the nuclear weapons.

As Gorbachev struggled to hold the Soviet Union together in the fall of 1991, President Bush announced the United States would unilaterally withdraw, and destroy, all its nuclear weapons in Europe, except for tactical weapons on aircraft, and cut back further on strategic weapons. This dramatic move included removing tactical nuclear weapons as well as dropping plans for the strategic mobile MX and Midgetman missiles. Chancellor Kohl gave his "heartfelt thanks" on behalf of all Germans for the Bush offer, while British Prime Minister Major announced he would scrap Britain's similar systems while keeping nuclear submarines. The United States retained strategic weapons along with tactical nuclear bombs that the U.S. air force could deliver. Bush's motives, as revealed in press reports, were to act while Gorbachev was still in power, and to give Gorbachev indirect political support in maintaining a policy of cooperation with the United States.

The United States implemented its offer by removing about 1300 artillery shells and 850 short-range ballistic missile warheads from Europe and about 500 nuclear weapons from ships and submarines. (See Table 3-1.) There were no provisions for stringent verifications or inspections. Defense Department officials stated that changes in the Soviet Union made such measures unnecessary. Changes in the Soviet political and social culture, with a freer press and outspoken leaders made it easier to track military developments in the Soviet Union. Inspections of strategic weapons would continue, and the United States wanted to reopen talks on the ABM Treaty.

On February 17, 1992, Russian President Yeltsin and Secretary of State Baker announced agreements on assistance in dismantling Russia's nuclear arsenal. These included the United States supplying 25 specially fitted boxcars and 250 special containers to transport nuclear warheads to storage sites. When these were dismantled, the highly enriched uranium and plutonium would be entombed in underground bunkers to be monitored by the International Atomic Energy Agency or converted to use in nuclear reactors or for research. On June 16, 1992, Bush and Yeltsin initialled an agreement for more drastic cuts of up to

Table 3-1

Agreements on Nuclear Weapons Ceilings (number of warheads)

Agreement	Strategic (more than 3400 miles)		Intermediate (300–3400 miles)	Tactical (0–300 miles)
	ICBMs, SLBMs	Bombers		
SALT I (1972)	1710–2358 (12,000)	Unlimited	Unlimited	Unlimited
SALT II (1978)	——— 2250 ——— (12,000)		Unlimited	Unlimited
INF (1988)	—		0 (2000 destroyed)	Unlimited
START (1991)	——— 1600 ——— (6900–8600)		0	Unlimited
Missiles left under Bush's unilateral proposal (September 1991)	——— 1600 ——— (6900–8600)		0	Most tactical weapons removed from Europe and destroyed.
Bush-Yeltsin Agreement (June 1992)	——— (3000–3500) ———		0	

66 percent in remaining strategic nuclear weapons, and negotiators began to put the agreement in treaty form.

After the Soviet republics declared their independence with no signs of a serious challenge from Moscow, Western Europe and the United States seized the opportunity to recognize them and confirm the demise of the Soviet empire. The major concern of President Bush was that the United States might be faced with four nuclear powers (Belarus, Kazakstan, Russia, and Ukraine) rather than one. The United States offered technical assistance to the republics in dismantling the strategic nuclear weapons.

At the beginning of February 1992 Secretary of State Baker made a swing through most of the republics that had broken away from the Soviet Union. He met with the new heads of state of Moldova, Armenia, Azerbaijan, Turkmenistan, Tajikistan, and Uzbekistan. Press reports indicated an emphasis on their observation of human rights as a condition for official recognition by the United States. It was evident, however, that Baker was also interested in promoting their status as states independent of Moscow. Also he probably encouraged them to send back any tactical nuclear weapons to Moscow's control and permit others to be under central control from Moscow so that disarmament commitments could be verified. Background reports indicated that he was concerned that a rebel group or other unreliable group might get control of nuclear weapons.

Western offers of aid also were used to help get the four republics with nuclear weapons (Kazakhstan, Belarus, Russia, and Ukraine) to ship all their tactical nuclear weapons to Russia for destruction. They also placed their strategic nuclear missiles under joint control with Russia. In addition, they agreed to accept the restraints of the nonproliferation treaty and arrangements to control export of missile technology (*NYT* 3/31/92; *NYT* 4/29/92). On May 23, 1992, in Lisbon the four nuclear republics of the former Soviet Union signed a protocol agreeing to implement the START missile-reduction treaty, which then would be presented to the U.S. Senate and the Russian parliament for final ratification.

In June 1992, in a red-carpet visit to the United States, President Yeltsin and President Bush signed a treaty for drastic cuts in the remaining strategic nuclear weapons. Each side would reduce the long-range weapons from the START ceilings of 6200–8600 to 3000–3500. The job of destroying those weapons is so time consuming that it was estimated it would take until the year 2000 or 2003 to complete the task. The U.S. spokesman pointed out the new agreement provided for destroying the huge land-based weapons that are the most threatening for a first strike. Despite the drastic cuts in weapons, the United States still maintained a tremendous nuclear retaliatory capacity against Russia and the republics.

The above figures were dramatic, but the most important elements of the agreements were that the psychological elements of the cold war were dismantled. Technical assistance for nuclear arms reductions was worked out in NATO with meetings between East and West defense chiefs (*NYT* 3/31/92). The relaxation of tension was demonstrated in a poll taken in Russia, Ukraine, and Uzbekistan that showed that only 6 to 8 percent of the people saw a threat to their country from a foreign country (*NYT* 4/23/92, 3).

Yeltsin, with his arms control concessions, his drastic economic reforms, and his restraint in letting the Soviet empire break up earned the confidence of Western leaders. This was demonstrated in the large aid and stabilization program proposed by President Bush and Chancellor Kohl. The amount ($24 billion) was significant, but it was also important to note that much of the aid was conditional on Russia and others meeting the conservative, market-oriented guidelines laid down by the IMF (*NYT* 4/27/92, 6). Although Yeltsin asserted he would not be dictated to by the West, he supported membership in the IMF and World Bank, which hinged on meeting market-oriented conditions (*NYT* 4/30/92; 4/26/92). The prospect for this aid was used in parliamentary debates in Russia to support the conservative goals that were approved by the IMF.

What Bush did not mention was that the IMF estimated the other 14 republics would have an additional need of about $24 billion in 1992. These were staggering amounts, but IMF director Michel Camdessus noted they could be financed by 7 percent of the defense budgets of the industrial countries (*IMF Survey* 4/27/92).

SUMMARY

The cold war was over, and pundits attempted to assess the potential of a new era of collaboration. The fear of Communism had dominated Western foreign policy since the end of World War I, when Lenin seized power from a struggling new democracy. Not only was the cold war over, but Communism was discredited among intellectuals and the common people. This was dramatically demonstrated by mass demonstrations against the symbols of Communism and by the free elections in which hardline Communists were able to get only a small percentage of the vote. In former satellites reformed Communists even discarded the word *socialist* because of its association with the former Communist regimes.

The Soviet Union and its external empire appeared to be a broken egg with its fragments impossible to put together again. Nationalism based on ethnic, religious, and cultural differences had broken up the Eastern European empire, with the historic nations of Eastern Europe asserting their independence soon after it became clear Gorbachev would not send troops. The most dramatic event was the rush through the Berlin Wall, when the East German President Egon Krenz ended restrictions on visiting West Germany. This surprising development, more than any other event, symbolized the end of the cold war, because if the Soviet military would allow this, it meant they realized NATO forces were not a threat to the Soviet Union. Soviet leaders finally realized Germany had been defanged by its pledge not to make weapons of mass destruction, and tamed by its profitable association with the European Community. Implicitly, the Soviet leaders recognized that the Marxist-Leninist doctrine was wrong in asserting the capitalist world would initiate wars to prosper.

Not surprisingly the breakup of the East European empire led to the crumbling of the Soviets' domestic empire. The first to go were the Baltic states, which had been taken over by Stalin in the notorious deal with Hitler at the beginning of World War II. Again, the signal that predicted their splitting away was the reluctance of President Gorbachev to use force against them, and his attempts to get them to negotiate their independence while retaining close ties to the Soviet Union. Perhaps historical research will reveal how the decisions to use limited force against Lithuania and Estonia were made, but Gorbachev publicly did not take responsibility. He blamed it on overzealous military commanders. This encouraged not only the Baltic republics, but also other republics to continue to press for independence.

The domestic Soviet empire then unraveled. The coup de gra was the defection of Ukraine after a referendum at the end of 1991 gave overwhelming support to independence. Even the minority Russian community in Ukraine gave a strong vote for independence. Ukraine's moves toward independence were accepted by many Russians, in part because since World War II it had a facade of independence, including membership in the United Nations.

Western leaders observed the events in Eastern Europe and the former Soviet Union with amazement but with restraint. They had been born and raised in the cold war, and they found it hard to believe their good fortune that the Soviet Union was breaking up and was no longer a threat. A few hardliners proposed that the West react by actions to "drive a stake through the heart" of Communism. More moderate councils prevailed. President Bush's actions were restrained, reflecting a view that bragging and belligerence might cause a nationalistic reaction against the West. The United States and Western Europe offered billions of dollars of aid to the floundering Soviet economy.

After the Soviet Union officially broke apart into 15 republics, the Commonwealth of Independent States, the Western powers quickly gave them official recognition to bolster their position. Secretary of State Baker visited many of them to reinforce their new status, to encourage a Western orientation, and also to help make arrangements for the safe disposal of nuclear weapons.

The International Monetary Fund, a specialized agency of the United Nations, played a key role in the market reforms of the former Communist empire. It arranged to provide assistance linked with technical advice to the new republics as well as to most of the East European states. It was estimated that about $4 billion in loans would arrive in 1992. (*NYT* 3/3/92). By September 1992 fourteen of the fifteen former Soviet republics were admitted to the IMF. The aid to them was conditioned on economic reforms including actions to balance the budget, bring an end to inflation, reduce trade barriers, and make the currency convertible. Although Russia accepted the conditions, at the end of 1992 it had not implemented all of them.

Gorbachev had initiated the movement that became an avalanche to destroy Communism. He was a political genius who balanced between the Communist hardliners and the younger reform Communists. Pundits soon found ways to criticize his actions, but they were surprised he lasted as long as he did. He had an attractive, dynamic personality that initially appealed to Politburo leaders after their experience with three short-lived party leaders. After the pundits' initial amazement at reforms, they proposed that the demise of Communism was inevitable because of its economic failures. No explanation was given as to why they had been so surprised if the development really had been inevitable.

Some Western leaders were initially reserved in their reaction to Boris Yeltsin, who was elected president of the Russian Republic and replaced Gorbachev as a spokesman for the CIS. He was not as smooth or as personable as Gorbachev; however, he was popular with the Russian people. He had capitalized on his political strength by forcing Gorbachev's resignation and taking over the foreign policy position of the former Soviet Union. After he led the opposition to the August 1991 coup, Western leaders embraced him. Moreover, he delivered on promises, supporting moves toward independence of the republics and instituting radical market and economic reforms. His popularity in Russia waned as the economic crisis deepened in the winter of 1992, but he courageously met with irrate shoppers and angry military leaders to hear out their complaints.

Yeltsin carried out an even more radical disarmament policy than Gorbachev did by cutting back the Russian defense budget to a reported 4.5 percent of GNP. He met Bush's unilateral cuts in nuclear and conventional arms with even more drastic cuts and more radical proposals. He accepted the U.S. proposals for assistance in disarming nuclear weapons and for employing nuclear and weapons scientists in peaceful research.

During the breakup of the Soviet empire the CIS leaders began close collaboration with the West on settling long-standing international disputes. Formerly the disputes had been subordinated to the cold war with the superpowers supporting the side most likely to embarrass the other. Much of the new collaboration was through the United Nations. For example the Soviet Union supported action against the aggression of Iraq, a former ally, to force it out of Kuwait and to destroy its strategic weapons. (However, the Soviets did not provide arms, and the Supreme Soviet forced Foreign Minister Shevardnadze to get its prior approval before providing such arms.) The Soviets helped sponsor a Mideast conference that for the first time brought Israel and Arab states together to negotiate. It put pressure on North Korea to work for peace with South Korea. The Soviets were instrumental in pressuring Cuba to agree to withdraw troops from Angola to bring about a truce in the long-standing civil war. It gave political support to ending the civil war in Nicaragua, cutting back on aid to Cuba, which had been a major arms supplier to the Nicaraguan government. It helped bring about a truce in Cambodia and supported sending U.N. peacekeeping troops to that area. It agreed with the United States to stop supplying arms to opposing sides in Afghanistan. Russia continued these policies after the formation of the Commonwealth of Independent States.

Pundits suggested that the United Nations could finally act as its founders hoped. For the first time the U.N. Security Council could act in major crises without a veto by the Soviets or the Western powers. Both sides could now work for peaceful solutions instead of an advantage in the cold war. Also, with the end of Communist ideological tirades against capitalism, the International Monetary Fund began to play an important role in promoting market-oriented reforms in former Communist countries and making them a condition for aid.

As the twentieth century drew to a close, nations cut back on military budgets and began to give more attention to the remaining conflicts and other problems of a troubled world. I now will examine the effects of the breakdown of Communism on Eastern Europe.

Chapter 4

The End of Communism
in the Northern Satellites

Ironically, the most successful moves against Communism occurred first in the northern tier of Eastern European states—Poland, Hungary, East Germany, and Czechoslovakia. These countries included the areas most strategically important to the Soviet Union, since they had been used by Germany as an invasion route in World War I, and by Hitler in World War II to attack the Soviet Union. They were areas where the Soviets placed most of their occupation troops and exercised the most direct control. This chapter traces the struggle of the northern tier of satellites, particularly after 1989, to free themselves from the controls of the Communist cadres, who were installed by the Soviet Union's occupation forces after World War II.

After World War II turned in the Allies favor, Prime Minister Churchill visited Moscow in October 1944 and informally agreed with Stalin on the division of postwar influence in Eastern Europe. Trying to obtain the best deal for British influence, Churchill won Stalin's agreement for dominant British influence in Greece by a ratio of 90 to 10 and 50 to 50 in Hungary and Yugoslavia. They agreed in the Soviet's favor 75 to 25 in Bulgaria and 90 to 10 in Romania (Churchill 1953, 227). No agreement was reached on Poland. The United States was not a party to this arrangement and declared that this was only an interim arrangement valid for a few months.

Despite the Soviet pledge in the Yalta Agreement early in 1945 to allow Western allies to share in the occupation of East European countries and to assist the East European people to establish "democratic" governments there representing the will of the people, the Soviets began placing Communists in key positions, particularly in the military and police, and purging non-Communist leaders. (Churchill 1953, chap. 15, 578–584; Hull 1948, chap. 106, 1451–1471; Byrnes 1947, 52–57; Khrushchev 1974, 173, 197–250). This so-called salami policy by the Communists continued by purging the army and controlling it, infiltrating and controlling the secret police, forcibly merging the socialist parties, undermining the peasant and other opposition parties, and finally taking over complete control. Top leaders personally chosen by Stalin included Walter Ulbricht (East Germany), Matyas Rakosi (Hungary), and Bolesaw Beirut (Poland).

The East European states, except for Yugoslavia and Albania, became part of the Soviet empire. In the early years after the war the Soviets extracted heavy reparations, perhaps as much as $20 billion, mostly from East Germany. Not only did Eastern Europeans resent foreign control and their lack of freedom, but they also resented privileges of the Communist elites, who were backed by Russian troops and the threat of Russian intervention.

The major motive of the Soviet policy was to establish a buffer against the revival of Germany, which had invaded Russia twice in the lifetime of its leaders. Also, many Communists believed in the Leninist doctrine of promoting revolution to establish a worldwide commonwealth of Communist nations and that this was historically inevitable and would bring an end to wars. Leaders of the United States and other democracies held the opposite view—that a predominance of democracies brought peace and security. The cold war was based on these opposing ideologies and reinforced by the Soviet takeover in Eastern Europe. The world did not challenge Soviet hegemony in Eastern Europe after World War II, since it appeared that the USSR would have responded to such a challenge with World War III.

Action against Communist and Soviet domination began in Czechoslovakia after World War II, but the democratic government was overthrown in a Communist coup in 1948. Yugoslavia successfully broke from the Soviet bloc in 1948, but General Tito continued with his own brand of Communism. Before Gorbachev came to power, the high-water marks of the surges of anti-Communism were in the northern tier—the 1953 East German demonstrations, the 1956 Hungarian revolt, the 1968 Czechoslovakian revolt, and the Polish Solidarity movement toward democracy in the early 1980s. These were suppressed. The successful moves to dissolve the Soviet East European Empire and end Communist rule took place after Gorbachev was elected as general secretary of the Communist Party in 1985. After examining the patterns of success in the northern tier of former satellites, I will examine reasons for the different patterns of political development in the southern tier of Eastern European states.

HUNGARY'S ANTI-COMMUNISM

In 1919 in the aftermath of World War I, Hungarians, following the lead of the Russian revolution, established a Communist government in Hungary that lasted only 133 days. It was replaced by a dictatorship under Admiral Horthy. During World War II there were divisions in the Horthy government about supporting Hitler and strong opposition by left-wing groups. Horthy's government was persuaded to support Hitler with his offer of the lure of northern Transylvania and part of Yugoslavia, areas that had formerly been part of the Austro-Hungarian empire. Hungary provided troops and materiel support to Germany, and allowed German troops transit to attack Romania and Yugoslavia. Toward the end of the war a new fascist government liquidated political opponents and ruthlessly sent Jews to German extermination camps (Seton-Watson 1961, 98–105).

In the closing months of World War II Hungary was "liberated" by the Soviet troops with the aid of Hungarian units that defected under General Miklos. In the last months of the war Admiral Horthy tried without success to conclude a peace treaty with the Soviet Union. In December 1944 the Hungarian Communist Party, together with the Smallholders' (peasants') Party, the National Peasants Party, and the Social Democratic Party, set up a provisional assembly and government. It passed a number of acts eliminating the large land holdings, and the government took over the banks, power stations, and oil wells.

Using salami tactics the Communists took over control of the government slice by slice during the next few years. Under the ambiguous wording of the Yalta declaration the Soviets would claim that the government was broadly representative of the democratic elements of the population. In the parliamentary elections of November 1945 the Communists had polled only 17 percent of the vote, whereas the Smallholders won the majority of the seats (57 percent). However, in the spring of 1947 the police, which were controlled by the Communists, arrested Bela Kovacs, the Smallholder secretary general. He was a member of a group that was opposed to Communism and hoped to gain independence from the Soviet Union. In June 1948 the Social Democrats were forced to merge with Communists in the Hungarian Workers' Party, and other political parties were dissolved.

The climax of the salami policies included establishing a national front coalition, putting Communists at the head of key ministries including police and defense, creating front organizations where Communists would take key positions, and trumping up charges against opponents. In 1949 Hungary was proclaimed a people's republic.

The following reasons have been suggested for why the Red Army and the Hungarian Communists waited three years before taking over complete control: (1) an immediate takeover would have ended chances for Allied cooperation with the Soviet Union in their joint occupation of Germany; (2) the Communists did not want to alienate left-wing parties in Western Europe (economic conditions were grim there, and Communist parties were gaining strength); and (3) the Communists were a minority and needed time to erode the opposition.

Under the constitution the Hungarian Socialist Workers Party, or Communist Party, was the "leading force of society." The party followed the Communist model with a Party Congress, which met every five years, a Central Committee, and the Politburo and Secretariat in control. The premier was a member of the Politburo.

The mass organizations of youth, women, labor, etc. belonged to the Patriotic People's Front (PPF) along with the Communist Party, which controlled the organization. This front organization was a common device that the Communists used to control other parties in Eastern Europe. It nominated the candidates for the unicameral parliament of about 350 members. After 1956 there were multiple candidacies for parliament, all approved by the PPF. The parliament met four times a year for about two days. Between sessions the Presidential Council or Presidium acted as a parliament. This was a standard device in Eastern Europe that permitted a small body of leading Communists to control legislation. The cabinet was formally elected by the parliament, but in fact it was selected by the party. There was a limited amount of self-government by local government bodies.

Imre Nagy, who later became leader of the revolution, was prime minister from 1953–1955. He was not successful in reversing the emphasis on heavy industry in order to produce more consumer goods. By 1955 Rakosi, with Soviet support, took control of the party. He was not an intellectual, but a Stalin type with a worker's background. He framed Rajk, a popular, rival Communist leader, and had him executed. His stress on promoting heavy industry did not work, and as economic conditions deteriorated, the intellectual opposition grew.

Khrushchev's anti-Stalin speech in 1956 made a big impression in Hungary, and the government allowed some movement toward relaxation. Rakosi acknowledged his part in the frameup of Rajk, and he began to rehabilitate those who had been jailed unjustly. This was too late, however, to prevent a political crisis. Nagy was released from prison and became a leader of the opposition to Rakosi. He took part in a huge procession honoring Rajk in October 1956.

The Petoefi Circle, which stimulated opposition to the Communist order, first came to public attention in March 1956. It was a Communist-type debating society, attracting many of the Communist intellectuals and others who had been purged and who supported Nagy. It organized debates on Marxist topics, but rigged them so that the Communists trying to defend Rakosi's policies were defeated. In the heat of the debates, demands were made that Rakosi resign and end governmental and police interference with the press.

After a visit to Budapest by Mikoyan, the deputy prime minister of Russia, the Hungarian government announced Rakosi's resignation in July 1956. The Petoefi Circle members were encouraged by this, and on October 14, 1956, Nagy was readmitted to the party. On October 17 university students were demanding a reduction of courses on Marxism-Leninism, more athletics, room and board improvements, and abolition of required study of foreign languages (Russian). On October 20 the Writers Association was asking for a new Communist Party Congress with a democratically elected party leadership. By this time news reached Hungary of a successful workers' strike and demonstrations in Poland and Gomulka's successful defiance of Khrushchev, described below. Hungarian students upped the ante to demand withdrawal of Soviet troops. They also came up with the idea for a public demonstration on October 23 to affirm the friendship between Poland and Hungary. Major demands circulated at that time included free elections, freedom to form political parties, freedom of press and speech, and the right to strike, all under Nagy. At that time two Soviet divisions were stationed in Hungary.

On October 23, 1956, the demonstrations got out of hand. The streets were full of people singing songs and waving flags. Imre Nagy spoke briefly asking the crowds to go home peacefully, but Gero, the party chairman, spoke harshly indicating that he would not speak with the students. This made the crowds angry. One group attacked a large statue of Stalin and demolished it. Another group was fired on by the security police. Workers joined the demonstration, but on October 24 Soviet troops appeared in Budapest. On that day the Central Committee claimed to have elected Imre Nagy prime minister and to have called for Soviet troops. Actually, Soviet troops were already on the move before the meeting (Mackintosh 1963, 169–170). People resisted the Soviet troops with stones, barricades, and home-made bombs. Mikoyan returned to Budapest to try to find a solution. Soviet tank commanders fired on the crowd.

On October 26 Nagy announced that Soviet troops would withdraw, and by October 28 there was an official cease-fire. By this time the Hungarian army and police were destroyed as a pro-Soviet force. Unofficially elected bodies were set up that demanded political freedoms throughout Hungary. Nagy was the obvious leader and seemed to be associating with the more radical elements. On October 30 his government abolished the one-party system, and former political groups such as the Smallholders Party and the Social Democratic Party were reestablished.

On October 31 the Soviets announced they would negotiate the withdrawal of troops from Hungary, but instead began moving troops back into Budapest. That night Nagy delivered a protest to the Soviets and then announced that Hungary had withdrawn from the Warsaw Pact. He formally declared its neutrality and formally appealed to the U.N. that all troops be withdrawn. This puzzling statement of defying the Soviets by withdrawing from the Warsaw Pact has been explained by the fact that Soviet troops were already moving across the border before Nagy declared neutrality. Also, Nagy was asking for a neutral status similar to that granted by the Soviets to Austria two years before. Janos Kadar, a top Hungarian party official who had claimed to be a supporter of Nagy, went to the headquarters of the Soviet commander in chief and apparently made a deal. On November 4 Soviet troops suddenly attacked Budapest and took key positions in the city. By this time 200,000 Soviet troops had entered Hungary.

Meanwhile a new pro-Soviet government appeared led by Janos Kadar. On that day Soviet officers kidnapped Nagy as he was returning from the Yugoslav Embassy, breaking a promise to the Yugoslavs not to molest him. The Hungarian authorities executed him. It is estimated that 20,000 Hungarians were killed and at least 200,000 out of a population of 10 million fled to Austria and Yugoslavia (Schmid 1985, 26–29). During the revolt many military men headed by General Pal Maleter joined the uprising. The Soviets describing this intervention used the familiar charge that Soviet troops had crushed a counter-revolutionary revolt led by international imperialistic reaction.

The U.N. Security Council was blocked by a Soviet veto, but an emergency special session of the General Assembly called on the Soviets to withdraw and instructed the secretary-general to investigate. The major concern of the United Nations at that time, however, was the Israeli-British-French attack against the Suez Canal. In succeeding months the General Assembly condemned Russia's intervention in Hungary and its violation of the U.N. charter and denounced Hungary's execution of Imre Nagy. The Soviets ignored the condemnation. They asserted that they were suppressing the "counterrevolutionary terror" in Hungary.

Kadar had 2000 people executed and 20,000 put in prison. On the other hand, in subsequent years he removed leading Stalinists and concentrated on relaxing controls to promote economic development.

The Hungarian demonstrators in 1956 showed great courage in the face of overwhelming Soviet military strength. President Eisenhower quickly ruled out any attempt at military intervention. After 1956 the Hungarian government under Kadar did not openly challenge Soviet rule.

In the 1960s Hungary began to relax the strict controls of the Communist system. In the 1960s and 1970s Hungary experimented with relaxing economic controls and developed one of the highest living standards in Eastern Europe. It also relaxed political controls, even to the extent that its newspapers were banned in other Eastern European countries. There were two taboos—criticism of the leadership and criticism of the Soviet Union. This allowed, for example, discussion of economic and even political reforms, as long as the reforms were in the distant future. The Communist Party leaders hoped to continue in power by a "negative consensus," that is by avoiding open opposition even though the public was dissatisfied with the economic malaise and the lack of political freedom (Szoboszlai 1991, 195–212).

The Hungarian economy was regarded as more dynamic than its East European neighbors. Its cooperative farms did not produce according to a master plan. Although the government controlled prices of grain and major products, much of the meat and produce was produced on private plots and sold at free prices. There was experimentation with market prices for other consumer items, although basic energy and industrial prices were controlled. Small private enterprises in the food and service sectors were allowed, and moonlighting was common.

In 1985 the Hungarian Socialist Workers Party (the Communist Party) allowed competition for elections for its offices, three years before Gorbachev's party reforms along these lines. After 1985 the growth of a class of small entrepreneurs and the aging and retirement of the old, hardline Communists changed the balance of the Communist Party in favor of activist reformers. Their call for democratic reforms was not challenged by party leaders, as long as the reforms were advocated for sometime in the future (Tokes 1991, 226–

286). The political moves toward ending Soviet domination and Communist Party rule gathered speed and momentum after Gorbachev took power in 1985. Only in retrospect did success seem likely. At the time the reformers and revolutionaries in Eastern Europe feared Soviet suppression, like that of 1956, or an invasion like in Afghanistan in 1979, or a putsch like that in Poland in 1981. Pundits were amazed at how quickly the Soviet empire collapsed.

At the Polish Communist Party Congress in 1986 Gorbachev had said he would make sure no one undermined the socialist community. However, in March 1988 in a visit to Yugoslavia he pledged no interference under any pretext in the internal affairs of another state. Later that year, before the U.N. General Assembly, he repeated that pledge saying freedom of choice is a universal principle. At the same time he was withdrawing troops from Afghanistan. At this point the rapid collapse of the Soviet empire was not foreseen. Even those who believed he had good intentions doubted that the Soviet Communist elite, the secret police, and military bureaucracies would permit a breakup of the empire.

In Hungary the lead was taken by Communist Party reformers, in particular Imre Pozsgay, Reszo Nyers, and Miklos Nemeth. Although they did not cooperate closely, they were moving in the same direction, while keeping an eye on Soviet reactions.

At the end of 1987 the aging leader Janos Kadar was kicked upstairs to the largely ceremonial position of president. A conservative, Karoly Grosz, took over as party leader. The conservatives hoped he could restrain the reformers, but he did not have enough popular support or support within the party to do that.

By the end of 1988 Pozsgay was promoted to the Politburo. He soon announced that the Politburo had agreed to free the press, and he claimed they were moving very fast toward further reforms (*CSM* 11/28/88, 11).

Reforms went into fast forward in 1989. In February 1989 Pozsgay took the lead in pushing through the Communist Central Committee a schedule for parliamentary elections for 1990 and 1995 that would establish a multiparty system. The party set up an extensive system of roundtable talks with various political groups, which became the nuclei of future political parties. The party leaders planned to rewrite the constitution and hold a referendum on it early in 1990. Meanwhile the Communists would control the foreign policy, the police, and army, and would retain a guaranteed number of seats in the new parliament. The new constitution would specify that the economy be dominated by public ownership (including cooperatives) and the "system of alliances would be taken into consideration" (Warsaw Pact). The Communist censorship and monopoly of the press was ended, and more than 100 new publications appeared, ranging from political tracts to girlie magazines (*CSM* 6/29/89, 3). Under Khrushchev and Brezhnev, these developments would have triggered a hardline and even military response. There was no immediate reaction from Moscow, and only a belated criticism in one of the party publications two weeks after the February meeting.

Figure 4-1 The Hungarian parliament, 1989 (Courtesy: Embassy of Hungary).

Grosz did not have enough political support to delay the reform movement. Reportedly he was impelled, not by democratic sentiments, but by a fear that if he did not compromise, there might be another 1956 revolt with Soviet tanks called in to suppress it (*Economist* 2/18/89).

In May 1989 the party expelled the old and ailing Kadar from his position in the midst of public criticism of his role in the 1956 invasion. Leaders of the Communist Party, however, stated that they would continue to honor the Warsaw Pact (*NYT* 6/25/89). This made the July 1989 visit of President Bush more palatable. During the visit the government presented him with a plaque of barbed wire from the border fences that Hungary had dismantled between it and Austria. Hungary, citing its commitments under the U.N. treaty on refugees, rejected East German and other East European demands that it prevent their nationals from fleeing through the Iron Curtain. This started the flood of East Germans through Hungary to West Germany that led to the end of the Berlin Wall.

At the beginning of 1989 Imre Pozsgay had also pushed through the Central Committee a resolution to reevaluate the 1956 revolution, called a counterrevolution by the Communists. The party's relabelling of it as an "uprising" implied that a popular movement had taken place against the Soviets and against their Hungarian Communist allies. This point was dramatized in June 1989 by the reburial of Imre Nagy, the leader of the 1956 uprising. Top Communist Party leaders attended this celebration, which in effect buried the Hungarian Communist Party. In October, the Hungarian Socialist Workers Party confirmed this by taking the name of the Hungarian Socialist Party.

In October 1989 the parliament purged the constitution to establish a Western-style democracy. This was symbolized by dropping "People's" from the country's name so that it became the Republic of Hungary. It provided for privatization of state property. The parliament also excluded Communist Party cells with their privileges from the workplace.

The new Hungarian Socialist Party of old Communists officially supported freedom and democracy and claimed it would pattern itself after the socialist parties of Western Europe. By this time, however, socialism was a dirty word in Hungary because of its association with the one-party dictatorship of the Communists. The new Hungarian Socialist Party suffered a stunning defeat in the March 1990 elections, winning only 13 percent of the seats.

Even the new Social Democratic Party, which patterned itself after the Western European socialist parties got only 3.6 percent of the vote. Ironically it, too, suffered from the stigma of the word *socialism*, even though a large proportion of Hungarians favored socialist programs such as social insurance and public health and education programs of states like those of northern Europe.

In the parliamentary elections in the spring of 1990 the Democratic Forum won 43 percent of the vote and 165 seats, and the Free Democrats (prodemocracy and private enterprise) won 24 percent and 92 seats. The Democratic

Forum formed a coalition government under Josef Antall as prime minister with the Smallholders (11 percent and 43 seats) and the Christian Democrats (5 percent and 21 seats).

The strategy of the reformers had succeeded. Imre Pozsgay had led the movement by pressing for reform within the Communist Party framework, with one eye on the reaction of Gorbachev's government. The breakthrough was in January and February 1989 when he got Central Committee approval for roundtable discussions on reform with opposition groups, and when he succeeded in getting a reevaluation of the 1956 revolution, which was labeled a "popular uprising," implying criticism of the government and the hardliners who suppressed it. Subsequently the reburial in May of Imre Nagy, the hero of the popular uprising, signified the burial of the Hungarian Communist Party. The end of the Soviet Communist empire occurred in July 1991 when the last of the Soviet troops withdrew. Ironically, Pozsgay, the reforming Communist, was prevented from the likelihood of being elected president in national elections by opposition parties who distrusted him because of his Communist connections. They managed to defeat a proposal for a popularly elected president, and substituted a parliamentary election instead where they managed to defeat Pozsgay's candidacy.

In 1968 the Hungarian government had begun limited economic reforms called the New Market Mechanism (NEM) (Pollock 1987). There was slow progress on reforms and the economy continued to be dominated by the state sector. Economic reform accelerated after the 1989 revolutions. Major effects of the reforms by 1991 were to promote trade with the West and tourism, to liberalize prices, and to allow managers of state enterprises to make their own business decisions on prices and investment and production strategies. Exports to the competitive markets of the West increased to 70 percent of the total in 1991 from 40 percent in the mid-1980s. Hungary, with a population of 10.3 million, hosted 38 million tourists in 1990, an increase of 50 percent over 1989. It earned Hungary an estimated $2.6 billion, which compares with exports of goods of $9 billion.

By 1991 about 90 percent of prices were liberalized and Hungary was close to having a convertible currency (*IMF Survey* 3/3/92; U.S. Embassy Budapest, 1992). At the beginning of 1992 the Hungarian economy appeared to be dynamic with stores crowded with customers. Most prices were free, and imports were liberalized. It was making slow progress toward privatization. The government announced in November that it was reducing its foreign debt from $22 billion to $19.9 billion, and that its hard currency reserves had increased to $2.4 billion. Hungary still had by far the highest per capita foreign debt in Eastern Europe, but with IMF support and encouragement it was retiring it. In 1992 GNP was expected to fall, and unemployment increase as it continued difficult adjustments to a freer economy. International Monetary Fund officials concluded in their evaluation that Hungary had the best chance in Eastern Europe of succeeding with its reforms.

POLAND'S SOLIDARITY STRIKES FIRST

Poland is located along the historic invasion route used by Germany in World War I and World War II to invade the Soviet Union, so Stalin was determined to keep Poland as a buffer under tight control. However, Poland was the most homogenous ethnic and religious area (Polish-Catholic) in Eastern Europe, which made Soviet domination difficult. During World War II the Soviets established a camp in Lublin in the Soviet Union to indoctrinate a special group of Poles, who then took over the Polish government after the war.

Churchill in an October 1944 meeting in Moscow with Stalin agreed on the relative shares of influence in Eastern Europe except for Poland. The Soviets were determined to place their Lublin Committee of Communist Poles in control of the government, whereas the British and Americans supported the Polish government in exile in London. Britain had a major interest in the Polish issue demonstrated by its going to war over Poland in 1939.

Polish boundaries were another issue. The Soviets insisted on taking over eastern Poland and compensating for that with an industrial area of eastern Germany. Poland lost 70,000 square miles of its former territory to Russia, which gave it 40,000 square miles of former German territory including the valuable industrial area of Silesia. After the Holocaust and after the Germans fled west after World War II, the Poles ended up 98 percent ethnic Polish and 90 percent Roman Catholic.

Despite their best efforts, Roosevelt and Churchill could not get Stalin to permit democratic elections and relax the strict Communist Party control of Poland. The United States had little leverage because it rapidly demobilized and withdrew most of its troops from Europe after the end of the war.

The Soviet occupation troops and domination were bitterly resented by the Poles. The Soviets had three counts against them. The first was the Nazi-Soviet accord of August 1939, which had prepared the way for Germany's attack on Poland. In line with this agreement the Soviets had joined with Germany in attacking Poland and had taken over the eastern part. The German attack had brought Britain into the war and officially opened World War II. The second count against the USSR was the massacre of about 15,000 officers when the Soviets occupied eastern Poland. The Soviets accused the Nazis, but the Poles believed the Soviets were responsible. This was confirmed in October 1992 when the Russian government released documents showing that Stalin personally ordered this massacre (*NYT* 10/13/92, 1).

The third count against the USSR was when Soviet tanks approached Warsaw in 1944. There was an uprising against the German occupation by the Jews of the Warsaw ghetto and by other Poles. The Soviet army delayed in pushing on to the city. It was alleged that Soviet troops delayed entering Warsaw so that the Germans would eliminate the potential center of power opposing the Lublin Committee of Communist Poles. These events reinforced the natural resentment of the people against an occupation army that forced a government on them.

The Soviet occupation, as in other satellites, was ensured through manipulated elections in which Polish leaders friendly to them were installed in controlling positions. In December 1948 the Polish Socialist Party was purged of anti-Communist elements and merged into the Polish United Workers Party. One year later all major parties were controlled in the National Unity Front dominated by the Polish United Workers Party, hereafter referred to as the Communist Party. The party had the standard Politburo, Central Committee, and Party Congress that met infrequently, with a permanent secretariat to control the party apparatus. For many years until the confrontation with Khrushchev in 1956, Marshal Rokoskovsky, a famous Russian general, was in charge of the Polish armed forces.

There was major unrest in Poland after the Khrushchev anti-Stalin speech in 1956. Polish workers were dissatisfied with wages and working conditions. They struck, and Polish security forces put down the strike with 22 killed. The government was shaken up by the strike, and the workers who were arrested were released except a few who were tried for murder or theft. Gomulka, a respected party leader who had been arrested and imprisoned from 1951 to 1954, was released, readmitted to the party, and then made first secretary. Reportedly the Soviets, alarmed at the workers' demonstrations, threatened to come in with troops. Gomulka told the Soviet leaders that if their troops came in, the Poles would fight them. Khrushchev backed down before the united party and country. He then relieved the Soviet head of the Polish armed forces along with other Soviet advisers. As noted previously, news of the Polish strikes and success in facing up to the Soviets in 1956 encouraged the Hungarians to rebel against the USSR.

Another major challenge to the Polish Communist government, and by implication to the Soviet Union, occurred in 1980. At that time strikes broke out in many cities of Poland with workers objecting to increases in meat prices. In August representatives of 21 enterprises met in Gdansk to set up a strike committee to coordinate demands and actions. The name Solidarity was adopted for the movement, and Lech Walesa, a former electrician who had been fired, was elected as chairman.

Solidarity organized translation services for foreign visitors and published a bulletin on strike news. The government reluctantly negotiated with the strikers and agreed to many of Solidarity's demands, including recognizing self-governing trade unions as "authentic representatives of the working class." These pressures resulted in major changes in the government including replacement of Gierek as chairman of the party. Solidarity increased its demands including democratic changes in the government. This meant increasing the power of the Sejm (parliament), and during this crisis the Communist Party did come to the Sejm for authority for its actions. Lech Walesa meanwhile attained the prestige of being awarded a Nobel Peace Prize.

Solidarity's demands in 1981 became so far-reaching that the Communist Party promoted General Jaruzelski from minister of defense to a position where he could crush Solidarity. In February he was promoted to prime minister and then later in the year he took over as party leader. In December, he disbanded Solidarity and Poland was placed under a strict Communist military dictatorship. Moscow, which had threatened to invade Poland, commented favorably on suppression of this resistance to the Communist regime.

The workers engaged in periodic, minor demonstrations, until 1988 when a series of strikes broke out as a result of rises in prices of consumer goods, amounting to as much as 200 percent. Lech Walesa stepped forward as the spokesman for the strikers, supporting workers' demands for recognition of Solidarity. The unrest continued into August when the government agreed to negotiate with representatives of the workers, including Lech Walesa, without recognizing Solidarity. Lech Walesa finally agreed, and negotiations continued sporadically for about a year.

The Sejm before 1989 had already achieved more power than other Communist parliaments of Eastern Europe. The nominees for its 450 seats were selected by the Communist Party. It had two sessions that lasted two to three months each. It ratified the decisions of the supreme organs of the Communist Party including the laws and the budget. Committees examined the work of the government. As in other Communist countries the Council of State acted for the Sejm when it was not in session. The Council of State also supervised the local governments, ruled by elected councils.

In the second wave of strikes in the summer of 1988 protesting against wage

Figure 4-2   The Polish parliament (Sejm) (Courtesy: Embassy of Poland).

cuts, Jaruzelski asked the Central Committee to approve broad-based talks to resolve the country's economic ills. In his closing address to the Central Committee, the general admitted to shortcomings in government policies, but he said there would be no search for scapegoats. In a televised address he said that a decision about the future of the government would be made by the Sejm the following week when it would meet in a special session. At that session the Sejm surprised observers by electing Mieczyslaw Rakowski as prime minister. Rakowski was deputy prime minister in 1981 when he defended martial law and attacked the Solidarity trade union.

In 1988 Rakowski was faced with an inflation rate of 60 percent, and a foreign debt of $39 billion, as well as the problem of getting the cooperation of the workers through making peace with Solidarity (*NYT* 8/29/88; *NYT* 8/30/88; *Economist* 10/1/88, 52).

Rakowski began a vigorous campaign to revive the economy, but ran up against disputes and lack of cooperation among the workers. In January in a spirited debate in the party's Central Committee, Jaruzelski said that "an atmosphere of militant disputes and unrestrained claims must give way to attitudes of co-government, co-management, and co-responsibility for the development of Poland's prospects." He threatened to resign unless Solidarity was legalized (*NYT* 1/19/89, 1, 4). Rakowski agreed to legalize Solidarity and accept elections to the Sejm on the condition that Solidarity abide by Poland's Communist system and reject radical groups calling for the abandonment of Communism. In subsequent negotiations the government agreed with Solidarity on elections for the lower house and a new upper house of the Sejm, allowing Solidarity to campaign for seats.

In June 1989 elections Solidarity achieved a stunning victory, winning 99 of the 100 seats in the upper house and all 161 seats it was allowed to contest in the lower house. Moreover, in the Communist-only runoffs the candidates endorsed by Solidarity won. More embarrassing was the defeat of 33 of 35 high-ranking officials, including 8 Politburo members. Solidarity initially refused an invitation to join a coalition government with the Communists, because its sweep of the election gave it veto power over legislation. Moves to make the economy more efficient and pay off foreign debts would work hardships on the workers and the consumers over the short run, and, therefore, would be politically hard to implement.

On June 30, 1989, Jaruzelski announced that he would not seek election by the new parliament to be president. He said he would support Comrade General Czeslaw Kiszczak for this position. This action not only recognized the strong opposition of hardliners to Jaruzelski, blaming him for the electoral humiliation, but it also recognized the power of the Polish army in the situation. General Kiszczak had purged the interior ministry of pro-Soviet officers and hardliners. He had also negotiated terms for elections in which Solidarity had won the seats (*NYT* 7/1/89, 1–2).

The elections set the stage for President Bush's visit to Poland in July 1989.

He received a correct welcome from General Jaruzelski and a warm welcome from the Polish people and from Solidarity members. At the subsequent summit of Western leaders in Paris they announced programs of aid and trade concessions to Poland.

Subsequently Lech Walesa indicated that he would support General Jaruzelski or any other candidate put forward by the Communist Party (*NYT* 7/15/89, 1). A few weeks later General Jaruzelski changed his mind and ran for president. He won the election in the Sejm by only one vote, with the aid of Solidarity votes and abstentions. Communist hardliner, Miecyslaw Rakowski, took over as head of the party.

Solidarity then successfully wooed the Peasant Party and the Democratic Party out of their alliance with the Communist Party. They had been forced to support the Communists since 1948. This gave their alliance the strength in the Sejm to name as prime minister a Solidarity activist, Tadeusz Mazowiecki. For the first time in history a Communist country named a non-Communist as prime minister. Reportedly Gorbachev agreed (Roskin 1991, 136). Prime Minister Mazowiecki was still under a Communist president, however, and he still had to deal with Communist officials in key positions throughout the government. But it was a historic breakthrough toward a democratic system.

Several factors worked in Solidarity's favor in 1989. About 98 percent of the population is Polish, and the Poles are strongly nationalistic. Their past history indicates their willingness to fight against foreign domination. Catholicism is strong and Solidarity was allied with the Catholic church. Solidarity members attended worship services at the plants while they were on strike, and Catholic prelates, including Pope John Paul II, gave them cautious support. Prime Minister Mazowiecki is a Catholic lay leader who had strong backing from the Catholic church. Meanwhile, General Jaruzelski asserted he was committed to democracy and he claimed that he continued to have backing of the military.

In September 1989 Prime Minister Mazowiecki began formulating a plan to transform the state-run Polish economy into a market system. In December the government got approval of extensive legislation cutting the list of subsidized goods by two-thirds and freeing most prices. Factories formerly getting subsidized interest rates would get loans only on a commercial basis. The Polish currency (zloty) was devalued and made fully convertible.

The budget was balanced with the aim of bringing the *monthly* inflation rate down from 50 percent to 5 percent. The government expected unemployment to rise, but a safety net of unemployment insurance was provided to ease adjustments (*NYT* 12/24/89, 9). This reform program was used to negotiate a major agreement with the International Monetary Fund for as much as $4 billion in Western aid from all sources. Twenty-four Western nations, including the United States, pooled their resources to back the negotiations with the IMF (*NYT* 12/14/89, A10).

The Communist Party was humiliated on January 29, 1990, when it voted to

(a)   (b)

(c)

Figure 4-3 (a) Prime Minister Tadeusz Mazowiecki (Courtesy: Embassy of Poland). (b) President Wojciech Jaruzelski (Courtesy: Embassy of Poland). (c) Lech Walesa visits President Bush at the White House, November 1989 (Courtesy: David Valdez, The White House).

dissolve. Its own resolution stating that the Communist Party bore responsibility for violating democracy and damaging the nation's economy passed 1228 for and 32 against. The great majority of the delegates formed a new party, the Social Democratic Party. Its program attacked evils of unbridled capitalism and called for a mix of private and government ownership. A group of about 100 dissidents broke off to form a competing party also along social democratic lines (*NYT* 1/29/90, A7). Another report indicated that the enormous party apparatus was being dismantled, cutting from 20,000 down to 2000 party workers. Part of its headquarters was being rented out to businesses. Also its monopoly on virtually all newspapers, magazines, and books was broken up. Most of the 270 newspapers had run at a deficit despite huge tax breaks (*CSM* 1/26/90, 4).

In December 1990 Walesa was elected president of Poland, capping a year of dramatic political activity. In April 1990 the first Solidarity national party congress confirmed his position by electing him as its leader. In May, before the local and regional elections, he lashed out at the government for its lack of concern for the workers who were faced with huge increases in prices of food and other essentials after price controls had been lifted. In the May elections candidates picked by Solidarity won a plurality of 40 percent of the votes. About 38 percent of the votes was won by independent candidates. However, there was voter apathy with only 42 percent of the voters participating.

Solidarity then split when both Mazowiecki and Walesa announced they would run for president. General Jaruzelski withdrew even though his term would not have ended until 1993. In the November 1990 elections Walesa ended up with 75 percent of the vote. Walesa, as the new president, continued to try to stay above the political fray and lend support to the austerity program, which continued to cause hardship on workers, particularly those forced out of jobs in the inefficient state enterprises.

The next democratic elections in October 1991 were inconclusive and Poland was faced with a period of weak governments unable to command a stable majority. None of the 29 parties won as much as 13 percent of the vote. This left more power in the hands of President Walesa, who finally selected Jan Olszewski from the muddle of parties as prime minister. He could command only one-fifth of the votes in parliament. He had to contend with a greatly increased budget deficit of 18 trillion zlotys or about $1.5 billion.

As in other East European countries the IMF was playing a key role in the economy. It would hold off continued lending to Poland unless it met stabilization targets. Moreover, the creditor governments of the Paris Club would not complete writing off half of Poland's $35 billion debt unless it met conditions of the IMF (*Economist* 2/22/92, 41–42).

In May 1992 the Polish Sejm challenged the prime minister and the IMF by exceeding the IMF limits in the budget when it increased pay for public sector employees and retirees. The Polish finance minister resigned and IMF negotiators met with the Polish officials on the issue.

In the resulting governmental crisis, President Walesa appointed a new prime minister, Hanna Suchoka, Poland's first woman prime minister. She bridged the gap between traditional Catholic voters and those who wanted to press forward with market reforms. At the beginning of September 1992, she won a victory by forcing striking workers in two important industries to scale back wage demands. Observers saw this as a decisive step to reinforce the big bang market reforms threatened by weak governments based on the fragmented political system (*NYT* 9/3/92, 4).

The news media also featured the pollution problems that had developed under the Communist system, where people had no vote to pass environmental laws. The problem arose from the Stalinist emphasis on heavy industry and the failure to modernize equipment. News reports exaggerated the problem by not reporting steps to correct the situation. For example, in Nova Huta in Krakow, formerly one of the worst polluters in Europe, the management instituted new waste management and new equipment to clean up emissions. Also, the plant closed down a major steel furnace and about half of the coke batteries and blast furnaces (*Interview* by author on 12/17/91; *NYT* 5/13/92, 1).

In 1992 Poland continued to face difficult problems of adjusting to a market economy. With its shops stocked with goods, it appeared to be much better off than the former Soviet Union, although Polish workers were faced with severe hardships. Poland's private sector was growing at a rapid rate but private industry still produced less than one-fourth of total industrial production (*NYT* 3/8/92, C8). However, agriculture was 90 percent privately owned and prices were free. Over 80 percent of industrial prices were free and 800 small firms and 20 large firms had been privatized. Moreover, imports were liberalized (*IMF* May 1992).

Poland's problems were essentially political and it was trying to face them with governmental rules held over from Communist days. It needed a constitution approved by a democratic process that would provide a government with a stabilized majority (Zbigniew Brzezinski, C-Span, 3/8/92). Agreement with the IMF would be essential for economic stabilization, but the IMF needed to recognize it was dealing with a democracy needing support of workers faced with severe hardships.

CZECHOSLOVAKIA—THE THIRD TIME IS THE CHARM

Czechoslovakia was established by the Treaty of Versailles after World War I from the former Austro-Hungarian Empire. Before World War II Czechoslovakia was the only democracy in Eastern Europe. It had alliances with France and the Soviet Union, but the latter appeared to be its only real friend when Czechoslovakia was threatened by Hitler in 1938. The Soviets offered to support Czechoslovakia against Hitler and maintain Soviet alliance commitments if France also kept its alliance commitment with Czechoslovakia. France refused because it was afraid of war with Germany. Two years later Germany conquered France in about six weeks. This offer of Soviet support created a reservoir of goodwill for the Soviets, even though the offer had little chance of helping. The other Eastern European countries were not willing to let the USSR help Czechoslovakia, since they were more afraid of Soviet troops moving through their territories than they were of Hitler. Their leaders said they would fight the USSR if Soviet troops entered their land. Most of these countries were dictatorships and some were fascist in contrast to Czechoslovakia, which was a flourishing democracy.

After World War II the liberating Soviet armies, mostly of fellow Slavs, had high prestige in Czechoslovakia, whereas the Czechs held lingering resentment against the Western allies for selling out in 1938. In the first free election of 1945, the Communists won a plurality of 38 percent of the vote, winning the premiership as well as the key positions of interior and defense ministers. For a time Czechoslovakia enjoyed a free press and free parliament.

By 1948 it was evident to the Communist leaders that they would suffer severe losses in the upcoming elections. Voters were alienated by reports of Communist brutality and corruption in the provinces and of attempts to intervene in education. The Communists started to make their move to consolidate control when the Communist police chief dismissed certain non-Communist police officers. This was opposed by the cabinet, which resigned, expecting President Benes to call new elections. However, the Communist Party chief, Gottwald, intimidated Benes with street demonstrations and a threat of revolution, and Benes, who was ill, allowed a Communist-dominated cabinet to take control. Soviet Deputy Foreign Minister Zorin flew to Prague to manage this coup with Soviet troops prepared to intervene if necessary. The pro-West foreign minister, Jan Masaryk, committed suicide or was killed, and the non-Communist president Benes resigned.

This Communist coup was followed by years of Stalinist purges and strict economic controls with an emphasis on promoting heavy industry. The Communist Party, which dominated the government, had two elements—Czech and Slovak parties. The party had the standard structure, headed by a Presidium or Politburo, serviced by a secretariat, both of which controlled the system. Under the Politburo were the Central Committee and the Party Congress. There was a similar structure for the Slovak Communist Party, but it was under the main party structure and had the status of a regional organization. There were two Czech and two Slovak non-Communist parties—they had virtually no political influence. They were controlled by the National Front, which was controlled by the Communist Party as in other East European satellites. There were also standard mass organizations also controlled by the National Front.

A bicameral legislature, the Federal Assembly, served as a facade—the House of the People with 200 deputies and the House of Nations with 150 deputies, half Czech and half Slovak. Each of the two houses approved legislation by a majority vote. Before the 1989 reforms it met only a few days a year. The candidates were nominated by the National Front, as in the other East

European satellites, and there was no significant competition for seats. The legislation was guided and controlled by Communist Party bodies.

The president was elected by the Federal Assembly on the proposal of the party. The president was head of state and commander in chief of the armed forces, but in the past, as in the 1968 crisis, his actions were controlled by the Politburo.

By 1967 the party permitted some liberalization. Press and broadcast censorship was relaxed. By December 1967 issues were being debated in the Central Committee in a democratic fashion with Alexander Dubcek, the secretary of the Slovak Communist Party, leading the attack against the head of the Communist Party.

A political movement for reform developed in 1968. Growing dissatisfaction with the hard line of the Communist government resulted in Alexander Dubcek, the reformist leader of the Slovak Communist Party, being elected as head of the Czechoslovakian Communist Party. Under him the parliament abolished censorship and prepared for democratic elections. Eight out of eleven in the Politburo were replaced as well as top echelons of the party secretariat. Dubcek pledged to maintain a firm link to the Warsaw Pact, but the Soviets saw his democratic reform movement as a threat to Communist rule in Eastern Europe. In July 1968 the Soviets, backed by officials of Hungary, Poland, East Germany, and Bulgaria, sent a letter to Prague warning it about hostile forces threatening its socialist system. Dubcek responded stressing the need for cooperation with the Soviet Union but also respect for national sovereignty.

On August 21, 1968, Soviet troops, along with those of four other Communist states of the Warsaw Treaty Organization, took control of Czechoslovakia. The president, General Svoboda, denounced the Soviet invasion. Also, the Czechoslovakian U.N. delegate denounced the invasion as a violation of its sovereignty, but he was quickly replaced. The Czech government ordered the military not to resist, so resistance and casualties were minimal.

The next day the U.N. Security Council voted on a draft resolution declaring that the action by the USSR and others was a violation of the U.N. Charter and that the people of Czechoslovakia had the right to exercise self-determination. It called on states to exercise their diplomatic influence to bring about implementation of the Council's resolution. Only the USSR and its East European satellite voted against, whereas 10 members of the Security Council voted for the resolution; it failed because of the USSR veto.

Chairman Brezhnev's troops had intervened under what became known as the Brezhnev doctrine of protecting the "socialist" order. In a speech of October 29, 1968, to visiting Czech officials Brezhnev quoted an August 3, 1968 meeting of Eastern bloc nations saying that supporting, strengthening, and defending the aims of socialism "are the common international duty of all the socialist countries." Brezhnev also cited a treaty of friendship and mutual assistance committing Czechoslovakia and the Soviet Union to assist each other if attacked. In April 1969 the Communist Party forced Dubcek out and replaced him with Gustav Husak, who purged the party and finished reversing the reforms.

In October 1968 a new agreement was signed allowing Soviet troops to be stationed in Czechoslovakia. Dubcek was sent as ambassador to Turkey, and while he was there, he was expelled from the party.

After the 1968 rebellion the conservative elements of the Communist Party successfully prevented reform. As a result of the purges, more than 150,000 people went into exile. Opponents of the regime were punished by preventing them from getting jobs in their fields.

Challenges to the government and its subservience to the Soviet Union continued with demonstrations keeping the memories of the 1968 revolt alive. On August 21, 1988, a crowd of 10,000, celebrating the twentieth anniversary of the revolt, marched through the streets of Prague shouting "freedom" and "Russians go home." The police allowed the demonstration to continue, but detained a few people (*NYT* 8/22/88, 3). On August 22, 1989, about 370 people were arrested in Prague in a similar demonstration. A spokeswoman for the Czechoslovak human rights organization Charter 77 said that participation of Hungarians and Poles in the demonstration had tempered police violence (*NYT* 8/23/89).

In the late 1970s the Charter 77 organization was formed in line with the Conference on Security and Cooperation in Europe (CSCE), which as already noted was set up to negotiate major issues between Eastern and Western Europe. The Chartists, as they were called, numbered about 1000 and made reports on human rights conditions in Czechoslovakia despite their repression by the regime.

In December 1987 there was an unusual transfer of power in Eastern Europe—peacefully and without a crisis—when Gustav Husak gave up the party leadership and kept the dignity of the presidency. His successor, Milos Jakes, appeared to promise hardline pro-Soviet Communism. Jakes had supervised the purge of the party in the years after the 1968 uprising against Communist rule (the Prague Spring). On October 10, 1988, Jakes removed Czechoslovakia's best-known reformer, Lubomir Strougal. At the same time he replaced the foreign minister, the interior minister, and others with hardliners. The man who imposed Brezhnevism appeared unlikely to bring the reforms of Gorbachev to Czechoslovakia (*Economist* 12/26/87, 10–11; 10/15/88, 60–61).

Meanwhile the economic situation continued to deteriorate, and people looked with envy at the relative prosperity of their West European neighbors. Reportedly air pollution was the highest in Europe. Worker morale was low and Czechoslovakian products, once known for their quality, had trouble finding markets, even in Eastern Europe (*Washington Post* 8/29/88; 9/4/88, 6–7).

The memories of democracy were still alive and brought forth annual demonstrations of thousands in Prague to commemorate the 1968 and 1948 reform movements. The Charter 77 organization and Catholic church were centers of opposition. The access to outside news media opened doors to the winds of reform sweeping through Eastern Europe. In November 1989 reformers were encouraged with an official message from the Kremlin warning that further delays in reforms would cause serious trouble (*NYT* 11/22/89, 14).

On November 20, 1989, after the Berlin Wall came down, 200,000 Czechs hit the streets demanding free elections and democracy. A broadly based group, Civic Forum, took command of demonstrations of more than 500,000. Workers cooperated with a two-hour general strike (*NYT* 11/16/89, 1). The police quickly gave up attempts to suppress the movement. On November 25 the Politburo in an emergency meeting replaced 13 members. A new Communist Party head was elected who promised a new constitution and cooperation with the opposition (*NYT* 11/26/89, 1, 8).

On December 10 the Communists proposed a new cabinet with 16 of 21 ministers as Communists. Civic Forum threatened a general strike, and the Communists yielded and took only 10 cabinet seats with 11 for non-Communists. The Communist Party then elected a new leadership by secret ballot and expelled 32 top leaders, including Gustav Husak, who had led the party since the 1968 Soviet-led invasion (*NYT* 12/21/89, 14). On December 29 parliament elected Vaclav Havel as president of Czechoslovakia. A popular author, he was a founder of Charter 77 and the opposition to the Communist Party. His inaugural speech criticizing Communism in Czechoslovakia will be long remembered (Appendix 2). Alexander Dubcek, leader of the aborted 1968 revolution, was elected chairman of the parliament. The Gorbachev policy of nonintervention had permitted another domino to fall.

In the 1990 elections on June 8 and 9 turnout was 96 percent. The Forum and its Slovak twin, the Public Against Violence, won most of the seats. In Czech lands of Bohemia and Moravia the Forum won 53 percent of the vote and Christian Democrats came in a poor second. Calfa of Slovakia formed the government in alliance with the Christian Democrats, who did well in Slovakia. The Communists won only 14 percent.

The new government then negotiated the withdrawal of Russian troops over a two-year period. The troops withdrew almost a year ahead of schedule, with the last troops leaving in June 1991. By this time Czechoslovakia had become a full-fledged democracy. Political parties were free to organize, and the news media were not subject to government control. However, ethnic and political tensions between Czechs and Slovaks continued that were only partially allevi-ated in 1990 when the legislature changed the name of the country to the Czech and Slovak Federative Republic.

In 1992 Czechoslovakia faced serious political issues, including how to di-vide powers in a new constitution between the Czech and Slovak republics, how to divide the budget, how to treat former Communists, and how to form a government to address these problems for a bevy of small parties. President Havel had proposed a referendum to settle the constitutional issue of federalism or separatism, but this was opposed by Slovak parliamentary delegates who feared they would lose. They used the threat of Slovak separatism to get budget and other concessions for Slovakia, the poorer half of the country. Public opinion polls indicated that the people would vote for a federal solution, but they also indicated that separatist candidates had a strong following (British Embassy 11/27/91; *NYT* 6/4/92, 5). In October 1991 authorities began screening civil servants to determine if they should be dismissed because of collaboration with the former Communist regime.

The June 1992 elections did not decide issues. In Czechoslovakia the conservative, promarket reform coalition headed by the Civic Democratic Party won about one-third of the vote for the parliaments of the Slovak Federation and Czech republic. The Slovak Nationalist Party for Slovak Sovereignty won about the same amount in the Slovak parliament and the federal parliament. Former Communists won about 14 percent. The two major parties were polarized on the issues of national unity and reform, while polls indicated that the people did not want to split the country (*NYT* 6/8/92, 7).

President Havel favored slower movement toward market reform than his finance minister. The Czechoslovakian economy, which sent 30 percent of its exports to the Soviet Union, had been more closely tied to the Soviet economy than other Eastern European countries, a fact that caused problems in finding new markets. At the beginning of 1992 it had attracted only $800 million in foreign investment, which was only about one-third of Hungary's total. With the shock of adjustment to a market economy output fell 16 percent in 1991 (Table 2-3, p. 43).

Czechoslovakia was prudently managed. Inflation was only 10 to 15 percent at the end of 1991, despite the comprehensive price liberalization earlier in the year. Almost all imports had been liberalized (*IMF May 1992*, 32–33). There was active tourism, and shops were well stocked as a result of market reforms, although prices for ordinary people were high. Czechoslovakia also was pushing forward with its privatization plan of distributing shares through low cost coupons to its citizens. Although this permitted more abuses than a slower program, observers expected success over the long run (*NYT* 3/5/92, 1).

Prospects for the economy darkened in 1992 after June elections in which the parties for partition strengthened their position. At the end of August, the new parliament finally came to a decision to split the country into the Czech and Slovak republics. Parliamentarians set a target for the beginning of 1993, and the split became official on January 1, 1993. Although its leaders talked of a borderless customs union like Benelux, a unified military command like NATO, and a fixed exchange rate, this appeared to be too optimistic. There would be basic problems of adjusting economic policies. The Czech economy was stronger with more advanced development and a strict budget policy, while the Slovak government had a weaker economy inclined to deficits and economic intervention. Splitting the country promised to add to the troubles of ending controls of the Communist command economy and carrying out market-oriented reforms. One of the few bright spots was that the split was being carried out peacefully, and at least the politicians had ideas for alleviating the adjustments (*Economist* 2/22/92, 13).

FOCUS ON EAST GERMANY

East Germany was the most strategic and the most sensitive area of Soviet control in Eastern Europe. After World War II the Soviets stationed 400,000 troops there, the largest Soviet contingent in Eastern Europe. The Soviets, of course, feared a revival of German fascism and militarism. It is ironic that Germany, where Marx and Lenin thought the world Communist revolution would begin because of its high industrialization and the size of its proletariat, had given birth to the opposing ideology of German fascism that in World War II had devastated the USSR, the cradle of Communism. Following is a sketch of that history, with an account of how Communism was established and then opposed in East Germany.

There had been a strong Communist movement in Germany after World War I at the time of the Russian Revolution. For a while it was touch-and-go whether the Communist forces under Rosa Luxembourg and Karl Liebknecht would seize control of the government after the kaiser abdicated, or whether the Social Democratic forces would take over. The Social Democrats won by obtaining the support of the German military to oppose the Communists and establishing a government that could meet the Allied armistice demands, which included reparations and a war-guilt clause. About 15 years later that government's acceptance of Allied demands was the Achilles' heel that Hitler attacked in his propaganda to get political support to seize control of Germany. After a rough period of adjustment in the early 1920s, the Social Democrats and the Center parties provided stable governments until the Great Depression of the 1930s.

In the early 1920s the Communist Party tried again to seize power. This helped stimulate the growth of the Nazis, who were aided by fear of Communism, particularly by the German middle class and some of the big industrialists. In the 1930s Hitler's Nazis, aided by anti-Communist hysteria, won a plurality of votes by promising to revive German strength and lead it out of the depression. A senile president appointed Hitler as chancellor. He quickly eliminated political opposition, rearmed Germany, and led it into World War II.

During the war the Soviets prepared for the occupation of East Germany by setting up the Free Germany Committee in Moscow to recruit German Communists and prisoners of war for political training. In defeating the German armies the Soviets made major territorial gains that allowed them to establish a buffer in Eastern Europe. They annexed a major part of eastern Poland, and at the same time gave the Poles the German areas of East Prussia and the Silesian coal and industrial area. About 13 million refugees were forced off this land by the Soviets or fled from other parts of Eastern Europe into Western Germany. These Soviet territorial grabs of territory were not recognized by the Allies until about 25 years later when West Germany completed its Ostpolitik policies of recognizing the division of Germany and the new boundaries established by the USSR after the war.

At first the Soviets ravaged their zone of occupation in East Germany by taking plant and machinery as reparations. The Nazis had destroyed much of western Soviet Union and there were stories of Soviet troops taking revenge as they entered Germany. Millions of Germans fled in terror to the West. The Soviets installed a government led by Germans from the Free Germany Committee.

The Soviets realized that the Communist Party could not win an election, so they merged parties by force under the Sozialistische Einheitspartie Deutschlands (Socialist Unity Party of Germany—SED) dominated, of course, by the Communist leaders trained in the Soviet Union. Then when the Soviets saw that the Western powers were determined to allow West Germany's economic and political recovery, which the Soviets saw as a threat to their own security, Stalin imposed the Berlin Blockade to try to stop the process, closing the highways through East Germany to Berlin. Khrushchev described Stalin's action with the Leninist phrase—prodding the capitalist world with the tip of a bayonet. (Kim Il Sung used this same phrase in describing his attack on South Korea in 1950.) President Truman instituted an airlift to Berlin, which could have been challenged only by direct military actions against Allied aircraft. After a year in which the United States and the British proved they could supply the former capital, the Soviets ended the blockade. As Khrushchev described it, the capitalists proved to be too strong for Stalin, and he was forced to capitulate in Berlin (Khrushchev 1974, 219–220).

In 1949 when the West established the West German government, the Soviets countered with the East German Communist government installing the faithful Communist Walter Ulbricht at its head. Soviet policy was embodied in article 6 of the East German constitution—calling for a "perpetual and irrevocable alliance" with the USSR. The other part of the foundation was the Stalinist political and economic model established through the salami slice-by-slice policy. Political parties were merged and purged so that the Socialist Unity Party of Germany (SED) would be dominated by the Communists. Industry was nationalized, and large-scale farms were expropriated.

West Germany's prosperity contrasted with the harsh economic conditions in Eastern Germany. This led to resentment and unrest.* On May 28, 1953, the East German government, in an attempt to get more production without raising wages, raised the wage norms. This led to demonstrations. Communist officials were attacked and the Communist flag was torn from public buildings. On June

---

*I was on the Department of State's German desk watching developments during this period, and it was clear from intelligence reports that before the rebellion their was a great deal of internal opposition to Soviet control and to East German government policies, even in the East German military.

17 Russian tanks moved into Berlin in sight of Western reporters. There are dramatic pictures of demonstrators throwing rocks at the tanks, illustrating the courage of the demonstrators, and the restraint of individual Soviet soldiers with their cannons and machine guns. They took control, but the East German government granted many of the strikers' demands.

The Communist Party was able to maintain control after these demonstrations, but between 1945 and 1961 the German Democratic Republic lost several million refugees to the West. By 1961 Khrushchev and the East Germans considered the flight of East German workers as a hemorrhage and a "disastrous" situation. The workers would go to West Berlin and then be flown out, so they would not be picked up at East German checkpoints. In his memoirs Khrushchev admitted that "Unfortunately the GDR—and not only the GDR—has yet to reach a level of moral and material development where competition with the West is possible." He added that under the dictatorship of the working class there can be no such thing as freedom (Khrushchev 1974, 456).

The issue came to a head during the Kennedy administration when he met with Khrushchev in Vienna. Khrushchev declared there that the problems with East Germany stemmed from the lack of a peace treaty, which the Soviet Union intended to sign. Kennedy asked if such a treaty would block access to Berlin. Khrushchev replied that it would and that any continued Western presence inside East Germany after a peace treaty would be illegal and a violation of East Germany's borders, and those borders would be defended (Sorenson 1966, 662). Kennedy, after returning to the United States, responded by asking for a major increase in the military budget, stepped-up draft calls, and issued a warning about defending West Berlin. On August 13, 1961, Khrushchev backed down and ordered the building of the Berlin Wall in lieu of challenging the West by cutting off Berlin. Soon Berlin, as well as all of Germany, was divided by barbed wire patrolled by soldiers who would shoot to kill East Germans trying to escape. It was a humiliating solution for Khrushchev, who claimed lamely that the wall would protect East Germany from CIA and hostile influences. After the wall was set up, only about 2000 people a year managed to escape from East Germany.

In the early 1970s the tensions were reduced when Willy Brandt, the foreign minister and then chancellor, carried out the Ostpolitik of reconciliation with East Germany and other East European countries. As mayor of Berlin during the Berlin Blockade, he had good credentials in the West for achieving détente. The key was recognizing two Germanies and nailing down access to Berlin and its international status through a treaty. The treaty, however, included the phrase "one German nation," which implied the aim of eventual German unity. Moreover, West Germany's constitution (Basic Law) in the preamble called on the entire German people "to achieve by free self-determination the unity and freedom of Germany." At the same time Brandt reassured the East European countries of West Germany's peaceful aims by concluding treaties of friendship, cooperation, and mutual assistance with them that reestablished diplomatic relations and recognized boundaries imposed by the Soviet Union after World War II.

The Soviets were pleased because Ostpolitik recognized their territorial gains, the new boundaries in Europe, and the buffer they had created against possible future German aggression. The West Germans were pleased because the Ostpolitik agreements created the framework that initially permitted 10,000 Germans to emigrate with their families and allowed millions of visits annually back and forth between the two Germanies. It was a remarkable concession by the West German government to the facts of life in Central Europe. In the process the East German party secretary, Walter Ulbricht, who was dragging his feet on Ostpolitik because he thought it threatened the SED, was replaced by Erich Honecker, former leader of the New German Youth.

East Germany had the Stalinist political system with the Politburo dominating the government. Under it was the Secretariat, the Central Committee, and the Party Congress, which met infrequently. In 1989 the General Secretary Erich Honecker was also chairman of the Council of State, which promulgated the laws, and of the National Defense Council. The chairman of the Council of Ministers, Willi Stoph, and the ministers of defense and of state security were also members of the Politburo. In addition to the SED there were four other political parties: the Christian Democratic Union, the Liberal Democratic Party, the Democratic Peasants' Party, and the National Democratic Party. They were represented in the legislative body, which was called the People's Chamber, but they were elected from a single list of candidates selected by the Communist Party through the National Front. The People's Chamber had 500 members. Its function as a facade in 1989 was indicated by the fact that it met only in plenary session and only four times a year for one day (Furtak 1986, 124), during which meeting it elected the Council of State.

The Council of Ministers and its chairman were elected by the People's Chamber. In 1989 they were nominated by the SED. The Council of Ministers had 40 members, with a controlling body called the presidium of relatively few members. There were also the standard mass organizations, which, as in the other East European satellites, were embraced in the National Front of the GDR. The National Front appointed candidates to the representative bodies and managed elections.

The East German leaders were worried about Gorbachev's political reforms. Gorbachev visited East Germany in 1987 and greeted the comrades with a barrage of criticism. The East Germans were not accustomed to such frankness. After the visit Gorbachev's speeches were censored in the press or largely ignored (Michielsen 1988).

The East German economy, without accompanying political reforms, did well in comparison with the other satellites. Its per capita GNP for 1988 was estimated at $11,680, the highest in Eastern Europe but still well below that of West Germany. About half of East Germany's foreign trade in 1989 was with West Germany, and the East German economy suffered in comparison from obsolete industrial equipment and poor quality production (Childs 1988; *NYT* 8/15/89).

In the summer of 1989 the East German government witnessed a humiliating flight of its people to West Germany. Initially the departures took place through Hungary, after it announced that it was removing the barriers between it and Austria. East Germans with visitor's visas for Hungary kept going across the border into Austria and then to West Germany, which welcomed them as full-fledged German citizens. Hungary refused East Germany's demand that it stop the flow, asserting it would stand by other commitments not to stop refugees. About 37,000 East Germans had fled by September 1989.

East Germans also crammed into the West German Embassy in Czechoslovakia, and after a few weeks of press attention and embarrassment, the East German government at the beginning of October agreed to allow them to leave in trains across East Germany into West Germany. The world's news media featured their travel and joy at being able to leave East Germany. Smaller numbers of refugees managed to flee through Poland and even through the American Embassy in East Berlin.

These dramatic developments took place before Gorbachev's scheduled visit to help East Germany celebrate its 40th anniversary in October. Prior to his visit East Germans demonstrated for Gorbachev to support their demands for reform of the hardline Communist system. However, Erich Honecker, the 77-year old ailing Communist Party leader, defiantly claimed that the Communist state had brought happiness to the East Germans and that it would maintain its political system (*NYT* 10/1/89, 1).

Gorbachev played it cool during his visit. He had enough trouble at home without being accused of promoting unrest in the strategic area of East Germany. He presented the image of support for Honecker and said he was not there to tell the East Germans what to do, although at another point he said that danger awaits those who do not react to events (MacNeil/Lehrer 10/7/89). The Western news media noted that Gorbachev in the past had encouraged the East Germans to reform, and that he was probably repeating these warnings in private. After he left, tens of thousands demonstrated in Leipzig calling for freedom and democracy with signs reading "Gorby." Some signs said "we want you to stay."

After Gorbachev left, Honecker reportedly gave written orders to the Leipzig police to break up a scheduled demonstration by imposing a "Chinese solution" along the lines of the Tiananmen Square repression (Chapter 7). Police were given live ammunition and told to shoot if necessary. On October 9 Egon Krenz, who was the Politburo member in charge of security, flew to Leipzig and cancelled the order, thereby allowing the mass demonstration to occur without serious incidents.

Within 10 days the Politburo after debating the issues forced President Honecker to step down and elected Krenz as party leader, head of state, and chairman of the defense council. On November 1 Krenz flew to Moscow to consult with Gorbachev. After returning he announced that East Germans who wanted to settle in West Germany could travel freely through Czechoslovakia. Meanwhile, 44 top cabinet officials resigned along with 5 of the Politburo's hardliners. Modrow, the Communist Party leader from Dresden who had led demonstrations in previous weeks, was selected by the Politburo as prime minister.

On November 9 in a press conference carried on TV the government spokesman announced that the Central Committee had approved a new law allowing East Germans to go freely into the West. That evening in effect the Berlin Wall came down. New entrances were opened, and in the first weekend 3 million East Germans flooded across the border into West Germany (*NYT* 11/19/89, 1, 15). The world's news media featured the celebration as Berliners danced on the wall.

Government spokesmen pledged to keep the barriers down and to proceed with political reforms, while pleading with the East Berliners to stay. It was a gigantic gamble in the most sensitive area of the Eastern bloc, and the strategy succeeded, at least initially. In the first week only about 10,000 sought to remain in the West, one-third of 1 percent who had gone sightseeing in the West.

Prime Minister Modrow obtained unanimous approval by the 500-member parliament for his streamlined 28-member cabinet in which the Communist Party kept control of defense, foreign affairs, and interior. Eleven posts were given to the smaller parties. He promised a new election law, and deputies elaborated by saying that it should provide for multiparty elections and a secret ballot (*NYT* 11/18/89, 4).

Soon the media reported on the luxurious homes of the Communist elite and their large foreign bank accounts. The resentment forced Krenz to resign. A non-Communist, Manfred Gerlach, replaced him as head of state, and Gregor Gysi was elected Communist Party chairman in December 1989. A new constitution was approved and elections were scheduled for May 1990.

In January 1990 reports indicated that Gorbachev had accepted German unity as inevitable. Chancellor Kohl of West Germany pressed forward with plans for unification. In March East Germany held free elections. Chancellor Kohl as well as other party leaders campaigned in the East, and his Christian Democratic Party won along with other conservative parties. On July 1, 1990, Kohl promised monetary union with East Germany, which proved to be a major psychological step toward unification. In June Poland was reassured about its border areas, which it had taken over after the war, when the German parliament renounced any territorial claims against Poland. The possibility of Germany someday claiming these areas had been a major concern of European countries and the United States since the end of World War II.

The four powers with residual occupation rights, particularly in Berlin, negotiated arrangements for withdrawal of their troops. Secretary of State Baker insisted on Germany remaining in NATO. The Soviets reluctantly agreed in return for reductions of German troops to 370,000. The final treaty reaffirmed Germany's commitments not to make atomic, bacteriological, or chemical weapons. It also reaffirmed the eastern borders with Poland. Soviet troops agreed to withdraw over a period of four years, and Germany agreed to pay billions of dollars to help resettle them in the Soviet Union.

After weeks of debate the East German parliament on August 4 voted to accept West Germany's invitation for unification. On October 3 Germans again danced on the Berlin Wall as German unity was finally achieved. All German elections took place on December 2 with the Christian Democrats winning throughout Germany. Kohl, the architect of German unity, stayed on as chancellor.

For more than 100 years the dangers inherent in German revanchism had been a major concern of European politics. The concern was intensified after World War II when Poland took over the rich Silesian industrial area and other East German areas. This fear, of course, motivated the Soviets to establish hegemony over Eastern Europe, which restarted the cold war. Western Germany was enlisted through NATO to help protect Western Europe from the Soviet Union, but also to forestall the development of a powerful, reunified, revanchist Germany that could threaten the European balance of power.

After 1989 the moves toward unification took place so rapidly that Western and Soviet diplomats did not have time to put up roadblocks to prevent the recreation of a German nation that could dominate Europe militarily. They recognized publicly that there was so much pressure in Germany for reunification there was no way of stopping it. They rolled with the punch, but they did succeed in keeping the German army integrated into NATO and in reaffirming the German commitment against obtaining weapons of mass destruction.

There were two somewhat contradictory economic concerns about reunification. One was that the costs would undermine the German economy, which would cause political reactions in Germany and also harm the European economy. The other concern was that a unified Germany would dominate the European economy and perhaps leave the European Community. Both fears proved to be exaggerated.

The West German economy was strong enough to bring about slight increases in GNP for the unified German economy in 1991 and 1992. After a fall of 26 percent in the first year the East German economy increased by 7 percent from that level in 1992. This required a subsidy of about 4 percent of West Germany's GNP. Germans grumbled but Chancellor Kohl managed to keep support of his party (*Economist* 10/31/92, 47–8).

However, there were repercussions throughout Europe from drastic changes taking place in Europe's most powerful economy. In order to help finance the huge investment in the East and control inflation, German financial authorities raised interest rates. This attracted funds from other European countries that weakened their currencies. By September 1992 the other European currencies could not stand the pressure, so they ended arrangements for tying their exchange rates to the German mark. Some moved to protect their currencies by huge increases in interest rates, while Britain lowered its rate to stimulate its economy. In the fall of 1992, the outcome was not clear, but politically the financial turmoil weakened the drive for the European Community's Maastricht Treaty, which would have created a common European currency by the end of the century.

Concern about the new Germany's strength had been heightened after 1989 by the huge amount of investment of German firms and the German government in Eastern Europe including the Soviet Union. By the beginning of 1992, this amounted to $60 billion (*Economist* 2/29/92, 51), which revived memories of Germany's prewar economic push toward the East (*drang nach osten*). Germany, before World War II, developed a flourishing trade with Eastern Europe, exchanging manufactured items for agricultural goods and raw materials. As a result of German influence, German, not Russian or English, still tends to be the lingua franca of Eastern Europe.

Despite the forces working for German economic influence in Central and Eastern Europe, Germany continued to be one of the strongest advocates for strengthening integration of the European Community. Germany helped lead the way at the 1991 Maastricht summit for creation of a common European currency. Also, the European Community continued to negotiate associate memberships with the northern tier of East European states and explore such arrangements with other East European countries.

SUMMARY

In 1992 a peaceful, economically strong Germany, and not a revanchist Germany, was causing economic waves. Germany was still leading the moves for further European integration, which had made inconceivable another war with Germany at the center. Despite the financial flurry caused by the strains of German unification, the European economy was basically sound. Moreover, German trade and investment in Eastern Europe would help its adjustments to democracy and a private enterprise system.

After 1989 the countries of Eastern Europe, which had been close physically and historically to Western Europe, were coming closer to the European Community. East European revolutions had been motivated by an attraction to the freedom and prosperity of Western Europe, as well as by strong Hungarian, Polish, Czech, and Slovak nationalism that had resented Communist controls and Soviet hegemony.

With the problem of German revanchism solved and Soviet troops withdrawn, the northern tier countries could concentrate on domestic problems. The most serious economic problem was adjusting to a market economy. Poland, Hungary, and Czechoslovakia liberalized most of their prices and liberalized foreign trade. Their foreign exchange rates were close to a free market rate. They were assisted in these adjustments by advisors and financial support from the IMF and World Bank. Their serious political problem was to maintain support for the drastic economic adjustments that were necessary, and this was compounded by weak coalition governments. With the new democracies there were many small parties representing special interests.

As of the end of 1992 the northern tier of former satellites was not cursed with the type of ethnic conflicts that had fractured its neighbors. The horrible example of the Yugoslavian conflicts was a deterrent. However, there is a threatening potential. The Romanian government has continued repression of the Hungarian minority in Transylvania. Hungarians regard Transylvania as having been taken from them unjustly after World War I because it contained large areas where Hungarians were a majority. There is also a large Hungarian minority in the Vojdovina in northern Yugoslavia, who are threatened by the virulent Serbian nationalism that has torn that country apart. Moreover, there is a large Hungarian minority in Slovakia. That government is damming up the Danube, a border river, despite strong Hungarian government objections that the Slovak action violates international law (*Economist* 10/31/92, p. 50–51; *Zoltan* 11/10/92). In Czechoslovakia the coming division of that country was causing political tensions. There is hope that they can separate peacefully, but this could cause a setback there to the encouraging economic progress with their market reforms.

We will now examine the slower progress of the southern tier countries toward democracy and market economies.

Chapter 5

The End of Communism
in the Southern Tier

Yugoslavia was the first East European country to establish its independence from the Soviet empire. It had never been integrated into the Soviet bloc, and its rejection of Moscow's guidance was the first obvious crack in what was regarded as monolithic Communism. However, Yugoslavia did not reject Communism. General Tito established his own brand of Communism, following much of the Stalinist model. Tito's strong leadership and his legacy were able to hold the country together until the shocks of 1989.

Albania asserted its independence from Moscow and from Yugoslavia about the same time, but its Communist system was even more rigid than that of the Soviet Union. Romania initially was controlled from Moscow, but it, too, asserted independence, and also established a rigid Communist dictatorship that was probably the most corrupt in the satellites. Bulgaria on the border of the Soviet Union remained as one of the most hardline Communist regimes, and was among the last to cast off Communist controls. This chapter focuses on the postwar politics of these satellites, how they broke away from the Soviet empire, and why their pattern of development differed from that of the northern tier.

YUGOSLAVIA LEAVES THE SOVIET BLOC

Yugoslavia was created in the wake of World War I. A gang of Serbian terrorists had triggered World War I by assassinating the heir-apparent to the Austro-Hungarian empire. Their aim was to incorporate into Serbia the Serbs of the empire. The empire retaliated, and its attack triggered mobilizations that escalated into World War I. Yugoslavia was created by a coalition between Serbia and competing national groups of southern Slavs of the Austro-Hungarian empire. Yugoslavia was composed of Serbia and Montenegro, and the areas of Slovenia, Croatia, Dalmatia, Vojvodina, and Bosnia-Herzegovina, which were formerly part of the Austro-Hungarian empire. The Serbs, with a strong army and government apparatus, dominated the new state, which was confirmed by the Treaty of Versailles.

Yugoslavia (the land of southern Slavs) was a federation of Slavic nations. The strong ethnic divisions were reinforced by different religions (Eastern Orthodox, Catholic, and Moslem), and two different alphabets, Latin and Cyrillic. The major ethnic groups in Yugoslavia were: Serbs, 8 million; Croats, 4.4 million; Slovenes, 1.8 million; Albanians, 1.7 million; and Moslems, 1 million.

Josip Broz, who took the name of Tito, was a Croat who was a prisoner of war in Russia in World War I. He took part in the Russian Revolution and became a professional revolutionary after he returned home to Yugoslavia. In 1937 he was the secretary of the Communist Party in Yugoslavia.

Tito's partisans with materiel help from the British dominated Yugoslavia's resistance against the German occupation and tied down many Axis divisions during World War II. Tito had the prestige of being on the winning side against the Germans. He controlled the dominant military force, and his Communist organization took control of the country under the National Liberation Front, later named the People's Front. Elections under Communist control were held after the war, and the monarchy was eliminated. On November 29, 1946, Tito proclaimed the Federal People's Republic of Yugoslavia, based on the principle of equality of the country's principal national groups. The constitution made him president for life.

At the end of World War II Tito had a force of about 800,000 loyal men. When the cards were down, their fighting potential permitted Yugoslavia to assert its independence from the Soviet threat. Geography also played a major role. The Soviets were much less concerned with Yugoslavia, with its mountains and relatively nonstrategic position in relation to the Soviet Union, than they were with Germany and Poland, which lay on the historic route of attack against Russia. The German armies had not fought major battles in Yugoslavia, but initially drove through Poland into the Soviet Union.

The war had cost the lives of about one-ninth of the Yugoslavs, and Yugoslavia then had a tremendous job of economic and political reconstruction. Tito's Communists controlled the police and set up a government on the Communist model. It punished those who had collaborated with the Germans. Businesses of collaborators were nationalized. Those who had actively or passively collaborated with the enemy lost the vote. Opposition newspapers were suppressed, and the opposition was prevented from organizing meetings. In frustration the leaders of the main opposition party appealed for a boycott of the polls in November 1945. As a result, 96 percent of those voting supported the government. The government proclaimed a new constitution based on that of the Soviet Union. Tito appeared for a while to be an enthusiastic pro-Stalin leader.

Nevertheless, there were underlying differences between Tito and Stalin. During World War II when Stalin urged Tito to collaborate with his Yugoslav enemies, the royalist forces, against the Germans, Stalin created a basis for Tito's suspicion and resentment. After the war Stalin's weak backing of Tito's claims to Trieste and the poor behavior of Soviet troops in Yugoslavia added to the friction. Also, Tito accused the Soviets of creating a network of secret agents for undermining the Yugoslav government (Rubenstein 1985, 38). Moreover, Stalin opposed Tito's proposal for a Balkan federation, although Stalin originally had supported the idea. Stalin obviously was beginning to worry about Tito's independent attitude and did not want to see a Balkan bloc dominated by him.

By 1948 the frictions had developed to the point where Stalin withdrew Soviet advisers and expelled Yugoslavia from the Communist Information Bureau (Cominform), which had replaced the Comintern. Stalin then persuaded the Council for Mutual Economic Assistance to boycott Yugoslavia. The great mass of the Communist Party members in Yugoslavia were loyal to Tito, and he became more popular than before. Only two major Yugoslav leaders followed the Soviet lead in criticizing him.

In 1951 the Yugoslav Ministry of Foreign Affairs published a White Book listing the pressures that the Soviets had exerted against Yugoslavia including espionage and terrorist actions. At Yugoslavia's Party Congress in 1949 Tito accused Stalin of many crimes and called the Soviet Union imperialistic, bureaucratic, and antisocialist. The London Royal Institute of International Affairs published letters showing that the Soviets were angry because Tito had accused their army officers of behaving "worse than the British" and that he had Soviet subjects watched by Yugoslav's state security. By 1953 Yugoslavia was supporting China as the example of authentic revolution and contrasting it with the imperialistic Soviet Union. Years later when the Sino-Soviet split occurred, the Soviets' propaganda attack on Yugoslavia was a code word for an attack on China's policies.

After the break with the Soviet Union, the Yugoslav Communist Party searched for an ideological alternative to Soviet-style Communism. The Sixth Congress of the Yugoslav Communist Party in 1952 asserted that the leading role of the Communist Party was to be confined to political education. The party name was changed to the League of Communists of Yugoslavia to emphasize its new decentralized structure. Nevertheless, no other parties were permitted to challenge the Communist Party's political supremacy.

The new system emphasized workers' democracy—that factories belonged to the workers. Workers' councils were authorized to approve production and price decisions and "workers' self management" received a lot of attention. Unions theoretically had the right to regulate the type of product, the scope of production, the distribution of income, and conditions of work. The workers also had the right to decide certain basic policies with a referendum and in meetings. In reality, however, the discussions and decisions were dominated by management, which had superior access to information. Meetings and referenda were seldom used.

In agriculture the officials were wise enough to abandon forced collectivization in 1953. By 1980 farmers owned 85 percent of the agricultural land. The rest was under cooperatives and collectives. A free market for food was introduced, and the private sale and purchase of land were allowed. As a result there were substantial increases in agricultural production. Although the regime discriminated against the private farms, the farmers resisted joining collective farms (Staar 1982, 234).

Stalin died in March 1953, and it became evident that many of the problems had been caused by his personal animosity toward Tito. By June the Soviets under Malenkov were proposing resumption of normal diplomatic contacts. By the fall of 1954 the Soviets closed down their anti-Yugoslav radio. This trend continued under Khrushchev, and in April 1956 a triumphant Tito toured the Soviet Union. He made a speech about moving "shoulder to shoulder" with the Soviets. He also improved his relations with the Chinese. Even the Soviet invasion of Hungary did not cool the relationship. In November 1956 Tito excused the Soviet intervention in Hungary, although he attacked the Stalinists of various Communist parties.

For many years Tito, like Stalin, dominated Yugoslavia's Communist Party. After Tito's death in 1980 there was some concern that the Soviets might intervene, but there was never a serious threat of invasion. Tito's successors attempted to keep good relations with the United States, which they saw as a counter to the Soviet Union. The United States encouraged Yugoslavia's independence for power-politics reasons as well as for psychological reasons.

In 1984 Yugoslav President Mika Spiljak, and in 1985 the Yugoslav prime minister, met with President Reagan. By maintaining good relations with the Soviet Union and the United States, the Yugoslavs preserved the image of nonalignment that they promoted in the Third World. Moreover, they severely criticized Cuba's membership in the "nonaligned" movement because of its close alliance with the Soviet Union.

The main concern of rulers of Yugoslavia, including Yugoslavia's first Communist president, Marshal Tito, was the ethnic rivalries that threatened to split the country. The Croats and the Slovenes in the north were the most economically developed and predominantly Catholic. In the center of the country were the Serbs, who were the first to emancipate themselves from Turkish rule. They nominally are of the Eastern Orthodox faith. The smaller ethnic groups were in the south. Yugoslavia was a federation of six socialist republics of six ethnic groups. By the 1960s and 1970s there was a resurgence of hostility among some of the groups, in part due to the different levels of economic development. In the south the Bosnians, Macedonians, Montenegrins, and Albanians were poor and they suspected the Serbs of using the central power of the government to maintain their relatively favorable economic position.

The government was set up to allow fair ethnic representation throughout and to try to contain ethnic rivalries. There was a high degree of federalism with the republics considered to be self-managing. They had jurisdiction over education, health, and social welfare. They even maintained contacts with organizations in other countries.

Also, the Communist Party (League of Communists of Yugoslavia-LCY) had a federative character with decentralized authority. Leaders of the republic-level party agencies dominated the central organ of the party in Belgrade. The Socialist Alliance of the Working People of Yugoslavia (SAWPY) was the front organization controlled by the Communists that incorporated the mass organizations. The Federation of Trade Unions cooperated with the SAWPY in nominating candidates for organs of government.

Ethnic representation was insured for the collective chief executive which had a membership of nine persons with different ethnic backgrounds. The chairmanship rotated every year. The Federal Executive Council, or cabinet, also had equitable representation of the different ethnic groups.

The national legislature was called the Federal Assembly, which participated actively in drafting legislation and debating programs. It had two chambers, one elected by each of the eight federal units. The other was selected by members of the labor organizations. Voters elected local assemblies, which elected communal assemblies, which then elected the Federal Assembly. The republic and provincial assemblies had a good measure of autonomy in economic policy and local matters (Banks 1985; Bertsch 1985, 116–117; Furtak 1986).

Demonstrations for stronger Serbian influence in the government, generated by the dynamic leader Slobodan Milosevik in the fall of 1988, stimulated comments that Yugoslavia and other East European Communist systems were losing control. At that time, Milovan Djilas, former Communist official and author of the classic, *The New Class*, in a MacNeil/Lehrer television interview, suggested that the Yugoslavian demonstrations could be a good sign of protest and pressure to change a "calcified" system. On the other hand, he was not optimistic that Milosevik would change his authoritarian ways if the party gave him further powers. Djilas' reservations were confirmed early in 1989 when Milosevik maneuvered to establish Serbian control over Kosovo province, which was 90 percent Albanian. These moves generated protests by the Albanians and by non-Serbian ethnic groups in Yugoslavia.

The policy concerns for rights of ethnic groups led to a lack of economic discipline. The central bank could not control the money supply and the central government controlled less than one-third of public spending. In the late 1980s there was less trade among Yugoslavia's republics than there was in the 1970s. Few firms had branches outside their home republic or made investments across local borders (*Economist* 8/12/89). The lack of discipline coupled with a relative free price system led to monumental inflation by 1989.

The revolutions of 1989 that swept away the monopoly of power of the Communist parties of Eastern Europe also swept through Yugoslavia. The anti-Ceausescu revolution in neighboring Romania was serialized on Yugoslav television and intimidated the Communist Party's Congress of January 1990 in Yugoslavia. In a stormy session the Congress voted to allow multiparty elections, but it then was suspended as it debated whether it should be reconstituted as a confederation of independent republic organizations.

At the end of 1989 a new prime minister, Ante Markovic, ignored the Congress and its ethnic debates and went forward with an economic reform agenda. During 1990 he showed good success in controlling inflation, which had reached 1000 percent in the year before he took over. In a program worked out with the International Monetary Fund he started implementing a program of a balanced budget and a convertible currency. Initially the economic program showed success. However, after the various republics held elections and began asserting their independence, in 1991 civil war broke out in the north that ultimately spread and destroyed the economy and even Yugoslavia's political system.

In 1990 multiparty elections were held in the provinces. Except in Serbia the parties of former Communists fared badly and the nationalist parties won. In Serbia the former Communist Party, renamed the Socialist Party, was headed by a nationalist, Slobodan Milosevic, whose party won 194 seats out of the 250-member parliament. Milosevic was popular with the Serbs because as prime minister of Serbia he had suppressed Albanians in the autonomous provinces of Kosovo and Vojvodina, located within Serbia but home of 70 percent of the country's Albanians.

The Christian Democrats won in Croatia with the Communists gaining only 20 percent of the seats. The Democrats won in Slovenia with Communists getting 17 percent of the seats. In the free elections in Bosnia-Herzegovina parties were split along ethnic lines. The radical nationalist party won most of the seats in Macedonia. These governments in 1991 declared their independence from Yugoslavia (Freedom House 1991, 394–398).

Serious fighting broke out in the summer of 1991 as the northern republics of Slovenia and Croatia declared their independence and the Federal Army fought to keep Serbian communities in Slovenia and Croatia independent of their control. The European Community in a series of meetings with the opposing sides attempted to mediate a cease-fire that would hold. It had only limited success in preventing a full-scale war, and deaths were in the hundreds while the fighting continued sporadically. After 13 truces had been declared and broken in the fighting, the issue was turned over to the U.N. Security Council. Cyrus Vance, former U.S. secretary of state under President Carter, was named as the U.N. mediator. After a series of meetings he negotiated a cease-fire that was accepted and the U.N. Security Council began putting in place peacekeeping units 14,000 strong. Their job was to police the three Serb enclaves in Croatia, disarm the militia, and stop the attacks by the federal army. The problem of making peace was complicated by Serbs having moved into Croatian homes during the fighting and vice versa. The cost to the U.N. was estimated initially at $400 million per year. The war had taken 5000 lives with more than 500,000 forced out of their homes (*Economist* 2/22/92, 13). Germany led the way in recognizing the independence and sovereignty of Croatia and Slovenia. The European Community and the United States followed suit.

Bosnia-Herzegovina also claimed independence. It had three major communities—Moslem (40 percent), Serbs (33 percent), and Croat (18 percent). In a referendum boycotted by Serbs, an overwhelming majority voted for independence. Serbian military units attacked with the aim of absorbing Serbian communities and a large part of Bosnia-Herzegovina. At least, initially, they were supported by the rump Yugoslavian government, although it disclaimed responsibility. The Serbian units targetted Serbian communities of Bosnia-Herzegovina to force evacuation of Moslems. The term "ethnic cleansing" was used to describe Serbian policy, and horror stories of mass killings of the Moslem minorities had overtones of Hitler's racism.

The world was shocked as Serbian units attacked civilian targets and laid siege to Sarajevo, the capital of Bosnia-Herzegovina. It fought back and called on the United Nations for assistance. In May 1992 the Security Council imposed strict economic sanctions, including stopping oil shipments to Serbia, with demands that the fighting stop. However, the Serbian military units controlling areas around Sarajevo prevented planes from bringing relief supplies to Sarajevo, and attacked U.N. and Red Cross convoys of food for the civilian population. The new Secretary General Boutros-Ghali on Friday, June 26, reported that the Serbs were breaking a cease-fire by tank and artillery attacks against civilians. That weekend French President Mitterand broke the siege by personally flying to Sarajevo with relief supplies. The United States and the European countries sent air and naval units to the area but held back on a decision to send infantry against a guerilla army.

The United Nations began sending convoys of relief supplies to other parts of Bosnia-Herzegovina, but fighting continued. The United Nations was faced with the dilemma of fighting that was being carried out by local units that the Serbian government said it did not control. The Security Council demanded inspection of prison camps because of atrocity stories, and a number of camps were opened to inspection. On August 10, it authorized using any means necessary to deliver relief supplies. On October 7, 1992, the U.N. Security Council approved setting up a war crimes commission, modelled after the 1943 commission on Nazi war crimes, to collect evidence for trials.

The U.N. High Commissioner for Refugees called an international conference in Geneva on July 29, 1992, for what was described as the largest flow of refugees in Europe since World War II. Germany had absorbed most of the refugees and Britain and France hardly any.

In August, at a conference in London, the Serbs agreed to permit U.N. monitoring of the heavy artillery around Sarajevo. Working groups were set up in Geneva to arrange a peace. There was hope that peace could be achieved. The moderate Serbian Prime Minister Panic, an American citizen, seemed to be gaining political strength in comparison with the militant president, Milosevic. The unfinished tragedy that the Geneva working groups would try to resolve was that the Serbs were gaining their goal of expelling Moslems from their homes in order to create a greater Serbia. In September, as the fighting continued, the United Nations authorized further U.N. units to go to the area along with NATO units and to use force, if necessary, to protect the convoys of relief supplies. By a vote of 127 to 6, the U.N. General Assembly suspended U.N. membership of Yugoslavia, which was now a truncated state with a divided government.

Summary

Tito's Communist system had held Yugoslavia together for more than 40 years. The democratic revolutions in Eastern Europe triggered pent-up ethnic and cultural pressures that split Yugoslavia apart in a bitter civil war. Communism proved also to be a divisive factor, since the northern provinces of Croatia and Slovenia, with their European heritage, resented the Communist controls of the Serbian-dominated central government. The European Community had to call on U.N. peacekeeping forces to try achieve a truce in Croatia and Slovenia. They were recognized as independent states, and in 1992 the EC and U.N. continued to work together to establish a peace.

The Serbs' attacks in Bosnia-Herzegovina continued in the winter of 1992. The deaths and destruction, particularly the attacks against civilians, were featured in the news media and horrified the world. The U.N. and NATO increased pressure against the Serbs by tightening the blockade. Croatian units were involved in the fighting in Bosnia-Herzegovina. It was a tragic situation because Yugoslavia had made good political and economic progress before the conflicts broke out.

ROMANIA REVOLTS

Romania is 90 percent ethnically Romanian with Hungarian and German minorities. The Greek Orthodox Church is the largest religion. In World War II Romania participated with Germany in the invasion of the Soviet Union, in part to get back Bucovina and Bessarabia, which the Soviets had taken in 1940. In August 1944 young King Michael, in league with the armed forces and political elements, overthrew a military dictatorship and declared war on Germany. This did not save his position, however, and in March 1945, after the liberation by the Soviet army, the USSR imposed a coalition government dominated by Communists, and the king was forced to abdicate. In the peace treaties Romania gained Transylvania back from Hungary but lost Bessarabia and Bucovina to the Soviet Union.

The Soviets imposed Communist control of a coalition government. At the end of 1947 Romania was proclaimed a people's republic. In April 1948 a new constitution was adopted similar to that of the Soviet Union, followed by nationalization of important sectors of the economy and collectivization of agriculture. By the end of 1948 the coalition had ended and the Communists had taken over completely. The Romanian alphabet was Slavicized, proper names were changed to show a connection with Russia, and the study of Russian was made compulsory in the schools. Five-year economic plans were adopted, and the peasants were lured and forced off farms into the cities.

After talks with Romanian leaders, Khrushchev was persuaded to withdraw troops in 1958. Following this withdrawal Romania asserted that it would forcibly resist a Soviet invasion and developed a military strategy to reinforce this statement. The Soviet's developing split with China and Romanian neutrality in the dispute helped discourage any Soviet reaction to the assertion of independence. By 1961 Romania was refusing to accede to further economic integration in COMECON. By 1962 and 1963 it was erasing many of the signs of Russification, such as street names, and was closing Russian cultural institutions. Even the Slavicization of the Romanian language was reversed. Romania declined to permit Warsaw Pact maneuvers on its soil and restricted military integration with Soviet forces. In 1968 it refused to join in the invasion of Czechoslovakia.

Nicolae Ceausescu succeeded to power in 1965 overcoming the challenge of the head of the secret police. Ceausescu was a populist type of Communist leader, who attended endless meetings and made many speeches. He used the party's totalitarian controls to establish a personality cult that rivaled those of Stalin, Kim Il Sung of Korea, and Castro of Cuba. In the late 1970s and early 1980s he expanded the cult to include his wife and son, who headed government bodies. His son was named secretary of the Union of Communist Youth, and his wife and three dozen other members of his family held high posts. Ceausescu was the head of state, head of the party, commander of the armed forces, and head of other state institutions. Subordinates in the government were rotated to prevent them from building a power base. He used the Communist system to create a personal dictatorship (Wesson 1978, 161).

After 1960 Romania reduced trade with the Soviet bloc and reasserted its ties with the West. After its foreign debt rose to $10 billion, Ceausescu imposed a strict austerity program to eliminate it. He kept strict Stalinist controls on the economy while supporting prestige building projects and wasteful farm commune construction. The economic situation was the worst in Europe outside Albania (*Economist* 8/12/89, 15).

As one Communist regime after another fell in Eastern Europe, observers waited for trouble in Romania. Ceausescu defiantly staged several public rallies in which his supporters cheered him on.

The revolution began December 17, 1989, with a demonstration in Timisoare to support an ethnic Hungarian priest who had defied the regime. The security police mowed down demonstrators and buried them in mass graves.

On December 22 Ceausescu called a mass rally. (The following version is based on an account of a young Romanian who was an eyewitness.) The Romanians were required to go to the rally, and with security police with guns looking down on them from buildings around the square, the Romanians were forced to applaud. However, someone exploded a noise bomb—perhaps it was a firecracker. The crowd dispersed and gathered in a small square nearby with anti-Ceausescu slogans and speeches. The next day there was a huge anti-Ceausescu rally in the square. In alarm Ceausescu fled in a helicopter. The pilot kept the military informed of his location, and when he landed, the military arrested Ceausescu. He and his wife were given a quick trial and then executed.

Meanwhile the elite security police were trying to defend what was left of the government. The revolutionaries, with the support of army units, took control of the radio and television station. The army took control and established a provisional government. Former Communists in the government, who claimed they had opposed Ceausescu, scheduled elections for May the following year.

On May 20, 1990, elections were held for a two-year parliament with 396 lower house seats and 190 upper house seats. In the elections the National Salvation Front led by ex-Communists won 66 percent of the vote. Ion Iliescu, a former Communist, was elected president on May 20 with 85 percent of the vote. The prime minister was also a member of the National Salvation Front.

A week later riots broke out against the new government. Demonstrators rallied in the middle of town next to the Intercontinental Hotel where they could be viewed by foreign reporters. At the end of May the police moved in to break up the demonstration and clear the square. This infuriated the demonstrators who then attacked a police station and seized some guns and made Molotov cocktails. They then attacked the television station but were repelled with about six killed. These events reminded citizens of the former repression, and there was widespread criticism of the government in the news media, and official protests including one by the United States.

The new prime minister, Petr Roman, aged 43, appointed 22 ministers with an average age of 48. In introducing them to parliament he emphasized their studies at Western universities and memberships in Western professional organizations (*Economist* 7/7/90). Roman freed 80 to 90 percent of the prices and liberalized almost all imports. A privatization law was passed that would take effect in 1992. The exchange rate was unified. However the reforms did not control inflation, which was 164 percent in 1991. Roman's liberal market reforms split the National Salvation Front. Former Communists represented by President Iliescu were not willing to implement all the reforms and give up their positions and influence to the market. Output dropped 12 percent in 1991 (Table 2-3 p. 43).

During miners' riots supporting Iliescu in Bucharest in November he used the crisis to sack Roman, who remained head of the National Salvation Front. The new prime minister, Theodor Stolojan, had no more success in reviving the economy, as it struggled to break away from the Stalinist controls. Meanwhile the opposition coalesced around the idea of getting rid of the old Communists.

In elections of September and October, 1992 Iliescu retained his position as president, and his party kept enough of a plurality to stay in control of the government. The question was whether the government would be able to keep on the difficult economic course set by the IMF.

In 1989, the winds of reform blew away the corrupt Stalinist system dominated by Ceausescu. Democratic demonstrations escalated into a successful revolution marred with violence and death. After the May 1990 elections, the new government headed by reform Communists instituted economic reforms, perhaps more extensive than Poland's big bang. The Romanian reforms included privatization of industry and agriculture, freeing most prices, reforming the banking system, and freeing the exchange rate. In 1991 and 1992, the economy was faced with inflation and falling GNP, but the government was able to hold to its course (*IMF Survey* 6/22/92, 204–208). There seemed to be no chance that the democracy would return to a corrupt Communist dictatorship like the one the people had overthrown. However, the regime was not popular, and there was no certainty that the democracy could stand up to a military or populist authoritarian coup, which would exploit its economic troubles.

EVEN BULGARIA REFORMS

At the end of 1989 reverberations from events in Eastern Europe led to the overthrow of Communist control of Bulgaria. This had been one of the most solidly entrenched Communist governments.

In 1919 the Bulgarian Communist Party was the first Eastern European Communist Party. Georgi Dimitrov, a Bulgarian, headed the Comintern from 1924 to 1944. However, the Communist Party made little progress in Bulgaria before World War II. During the war the country allied with the Axis. At the end of the war Moscow declared war on Bulgaria, and Soviet troops invaded and occupied the country in September 1944.

The Fatherland Front, a coalition of various antifascist forces including the Communists, the agrarian party, and the social democrats, took control of the government during the Soviet occupation. Bulgarian Communists trained in the Soviet Union took over the key positions of the ministry of interior (police) and the ministry of justice. The bureaucracy was purged of "fascist-bourgeoise" elements. On the basis of a referendum the monarchy was abolished in September 1946, and Bulgaria was proclaimed a people's republic. At the manipulated elections the Fatherland Front received 78 percent of the votes and Georgi Dimitrov became prime minister. Bulgaria adopted a constitution similar to that of the Soviet Union in 1947. The salami tactics of getting rid of opposition slice by slice continued. After the June 1947 peace treaty with Bulgaria was ratified, the principal agrarian leader Petkov, leader of an opposition group, was arrested, tried, and executed.

Bulgaria had a standard Communist Party organization, with the party including almost 10 percent of the population. Candidates for the National Assembly were nominated by the Fatherland Front. The Council of State, the permanent organ of the National Assembly, exercised power on behalf of the Assembly. The first secretary of the Communist Party, Todor Zhivkov, who was put in power with Khrushchev's help, was chairman of the Council of State.

Until the end of 1989 Bulgaria had a repressive, Stalinist type of government. Its economy had stagnated with serious shortages, which were alleviated somewhat in 1985 by a Politburo decision to devote more funds, including imports, to consumer goods. Agriculture was collectivized, but farmers were allowed private plots, which amounted to about 15 percent of the cultivated land. The weakness of the collective farm system was demonstrated by the fact that these small plots produced about half of total agricultural output. Like other satellites Bulgaria was integrated into the CMEA which took about two-thirds of Bulgaria's trade. The dissolution of that organization and the ending of subsidized oil imports provided a major shock to the economy in 1990 and 1991.

Bulgaria joined the IMF in September 1990 and instituted a major economic reform program in February 1991. The reforms included eliminating restrictions on most prices, sharply reducing government subsidies and general government expenditures, and liberalizing foreign trade. In return the IMF provided a credit of about $80 million to meet increased petroleum costs and standby credits of over $300 million (*IMF Survey* 3/18/91). The initial effects of the program were severe with GDP dropping to 68 percent of its 1988 level (*IMF Survey* 4/14/92).

In the late 1980s Bulgaria had serious problems with Turkey because of Bulgaria's policy of forced assimilation of Turks, who made up 10 percent of Bulgaria's population. In 1989 the Communist authorities launched a reign of terror against the Turkish minority forcing more than 300,000 to flee to Turkey.

The news of the crumbling of the Berlin Wall in November 1989 reverberated throughout Bulgaria, and in the following week Zhivkov was replaced as party leader by a reformist, Petar Mladenov, former foreign minister. He announced he was committed to parliamentary democracy and free elections. He also ended the persecution of the Turks and invited them to return to Bulgaria. The parliament on the same day repealed a repressive law against free speech, and took up restructuring the economy as first priority (*NYT* 11/19/89, 14).

The following day 50,000 Bulgarians filled the cathedral square in the center of the capital to celebrate in the first free demonstration since World War II, with an end to the "totalitarian regime" and free elections as pervading themes. Zhivkov was caricaturized in banners as Hitler and denounced as a despot.

The Bulgarian parliament in April 1990 adopted legislation providing for Bulgaria's free multiparty elections. The Communist Party began to reform, its cells were disbanded in the workplace, and mass organizations were dissolved (Bell 1990, 417–420). Both the former Communist Party and its major opposition ran against the previous Communist regime, and both parties supported democracy and the market system. In the June 1990 elections the Bulgarian Communist Party, renamed the Bulgarian Socialist Party, won a decisive majority after the runoff elections, with 211 seats of the 400-seat parliament. The main opposition party, the Union of Democratic Forces (UDF), won 144 seats, the Turkish minority party 23, and other small parties 22 seats. Bulgaria thus became the only country in Eastern Europe where the reform Communists were able to form a new government. Mladenov headed the new government, but in July he was forced to resign after students protested the fact that in December 1989 he had called for tanks to smash an antigovernment protest.

To mollify the protesters a UDF chairman, Zhelev, was elected as a new president, although the leader of the Bulgarian Socialist Party, Lukanov, was retained as prime minister. Lukanov attempted to institute market reforms without the cooperation of the opposition UDF party. He managed to free 80 to 90 percent of the prices and liberalize imports subject to tariffs. He also freed the exchange rate and freed interest rates. He was not able to control inflation, however, which was fueled by the currency overhang left over from the Communist system. Prices rose 460 percent in 1991 (*IMF May 1992*, 31–33). A cutback in oil supplies from the Soviet Union and Iraq compounded the country's difficulties. Then four of the six Chernobyl-type nuclear plants were closed for safety reasons. Demonstrations against the government continued and on November 29 Prime Minister Lukanov resigned. A nonparty man, Dimitur Popov, was named as an interim prime minister until the October elections.

In October 1991 new elections were held to try to resolve the crisis of confidence in the government. The elections were determined fair by international observers. In the elections the right of center Union of Democratic Forces edged out the Bulgarian Socialist Party of the reformed Communists by a margin of 34.5 to 33.1 percent. The Movement for Rights and Freedom of the Turkish minority got 17.3 percent of the vote and the rest less than 4 percent. It was ironic that the Turkish party, which had been persecuted under the old Communist government, held the balance of power. Dimitrov of the UDF formed the new government, but a year later he was forced to resign because he did not get the support of the Turkish party.

During the political turmoil the government was able to maintain the 1990 market reforms. However inflation of 460 percent was a serious problem in 1991 originating largely in the overhang of currency from the previous Communist regime and the inability to meet competition in the world markets (*IMF May 1992*, 31–33). Inflation could undermine support for Bulgaria's new democracy. Also, former Communist officials could attempt to maintain their positions and influence and discourage democratic reforms.

ALBANIA, THE LAST HOLDOUT

Albania under King Zog was invaded by Italy in 1939. In 1941 Enver Hoxha, a school teacher, helped found the Communist Party and became its first secretary. By 1944 the Communist-led National Liberation Front under Hoxha, by then a general, was able to proclaim Albania's liberation from the Axis and assume control of the country.

The Albanian Communist Party was the only authorized political organization, and it prided itself on its ideological purity. The constitution prohibited granting of concessions or even accepting loans from bourgeois countries. In 1967 it declared itself to be an atheist state, although most of its citizens were Moslems and Christians (Furtak 1986, 33–34). The government then proceeded to destroy churches and symbols of religion.

Yugoslavia dominated Albania after World War II much as the Soviets dominated Eastern Europe. By 1948 Albania even feared annexation, so in July Hoxha broke off diplomatic relations with Yugoslavia. Yugoslavia was weakened at that point by its expulsion from the Cominform. Albania maintained a close alliance with the Soviet Union but normalized its relations with Yugoslavia after the death of Stalin. After Khrushchev's denunciation of Stalin in 1956, which offended Hoxha, he openly broke with Khrushchev. In 1961 Albania broke relations with the Soviet Union and aligned itself with China. In mid-1977 after China's détente with the United States, Albania severely criticized China as an imperialist-revisionist regime.

In April 1985 Hoxha died after a prolonged illness. Ramiz Alia, the head of state and a close associate of Hoxha's succeeded him as first secretary of the party. Albania's relations with East European nations were so poor it sent back their messages of condolences except those of Romania. Its major thrust in international fora was to protest the suppression of the Albanian minority in Yugoslavia.

Albania, which claimed to be the only truly Marxist-Leninist regime in the world, was the most isolated and backward country in Europe. Visiting there was like going back in time with ox carts, donkeys, and rattling Czech trucks in the countryside and decrepit buses in the cities. Statues of Hoxha and Stalin abounded (*NYT* 11/13/89, A9). It was far from the industrialized, capitalistic society that Marx said was necessary for the revolution, but in 1989 it was the last European holdout for Stalinism.

The winds of reform eventually affected Albania. In January 1990 President Alia, at a meeting of the party's Central Committee, supported a number of reforms including democratization of the economic and political system. He spoke of competitive elections, decentralization of planning, and opening up the economy to tourism and to foreign technology.

On March 31, 1991, Albania had its first multiparty elections. They had been postponed for six weeks in response to striking coal miners who demanded time for opposition parties to organize. The former Communist Party (Party of Labor) won 169 of 250 seats, and the opposition Democrats won 75 seats. The elections were not entirely free, and foreign observers were not permitted to monitor them. President Alia lost his seat to an unknown, but the Party of Labor reelected him president.

The opposition party leader was killed in a demonstration after the elections, but the Democratic party forced the government to arrest and indict officials for trial. Demonstrations and unrest continued and the president dissolved the new government and named a coalition government pending new elections in 1992. The new cabinet renounced party affiliations (Freedom House 1991–1992).

In the March 1992 elections the Socialist Party of former Communists won only 38 of 140 seats. During the campaign the Democrats pledged to oust Alia. On the eve of the meeting of the new parliament Alia resigned as president, leaving the selection to the new parliament (*NYT* 4/2/92, 5).

Economic conditions worsened in 1991 and 1992. Albania lagged far behind other East European countries in price and foreign trade reforms. Output dropped about 20 percent in 1991, which did not reflect the shock of market reforms, but social unrest and a sick economy (*IMF May 1992*, 30–33). There was some hope in the countryside where peasants were beginning to work their newly privatized fields. However, in the cities food was short. There were a few food riots, but Italian army relief operations helped stave off starvation. An influx of refugees from Kosovo, the Albanian province of Yugoslavia, brought some capital and skills, but this did not materially help the immediate crisis.

PATTERNS OF STALINIST CONTROLS
AND THE DEMOCRATIC REVOLUTIONS

Figure 2-7 (p. 47) shows more than 23 countries in the space of four years making gigantic steps from totalitarian Communism toward democracy and market systems. As of the spring of 1992 they had not turned away from these reforms. These events are some of the most significant of the century. Following is an analysis of underlying reasons for their occurrence.

After World War II Soviet occupation forces imposed Communist systems on friend and foe alike. They manipulated elections and politics so that by 1948 Communist parties were able to control the "people's democracies" as they were called. Following are patterns of consolidation of the Stalinist model before it collapsed beginning in 1989.

1. The Soviet occupation put local Communists in control, many of whom had been trained in the Soviet Union. Under the shadow of Soviet armies the Communists took over in the so-called salami policy. Social democrats, farmers' parties, and other political groups were forced into coalitions controlled by Communist activists. Opposition leaders were purged or arrested on some pretext such as former collaboration with the Germans.

2. The Communist Party structures allowed strong leaders such as Husak, Hoxha, Zhivkov, and Ceausescu to take control as general secretaries of the Communist parties. Following Stalin's example they controlled levers of power through the secretariat, Politburo, central committee, down to the party cells. The secretariats with the nomenklatura system placed reliable Communists in key positions.

3. The governments under control of the Communist parties established Stalinist, totalitarian controls over the economy and mass organizations. Key instruments of control were the security police and the armed forces,

which had Communist officers attached to units for indoctrination and control. The economy was controlled by rigid economic plans emphasizing heavy industry, giving little attention to consumer goods.

4. Eastern Europe was regarded as a sphere of Soviet influence dominated by its military power. The East European armies were controlled under the Warsaw Pact. Economic plans were tied to the Soviet economy through the Council of Mutual Economic Assistance.

5. Through the years Communist elites consolidated control under the above system backed by their security police, the military, and the threat of Soviet troops.

There was an underlying resistance to the Soviet empire that was suppressed until the Eastern European revolutions of 1989. Following are the patterns of those historic events:

1. The basic element in international relations almost by definition is nationalism. Marx and Lenin called for an end to nationalism, for workers of the world to unite across national boundaries, but this did not work. Workers in Eastern Europe along with the general population remained loyal to national ideologies and symbols. That nationalism exploded in resentment against the domination of the Soviet Union.

2. People resented the perks of the Communist elite including better housing, limousines, special stores where they could purchase foreign delicacies, vacation homes, and travel abroad. People also resented the hypocrisy of their privileges when they were supposed to represent the proletariat and common man.

3. Ironically, the revolutions were the opposite of Marx's prediction that the workers would overthrow capitalism. Instead, the people, including workers, overthrew the Communist elites and called for democratic and free-market reforms. The proletariat helped the revolutions with supportive strikes.

4. The people wanted freedom and democracy as demonstrated by the slogans of the demonstrators and freedom from Communism associated with Soviet domination. Polls taken in Western Europe by Radio Free Europe of tourists and other visitors from the Soviet bloc showed that the Communist parties would have received only 5 to 15 percent of the vote in a free election (Radio Free Europe 1981; Hart 1984). The polls were confirmed in elections after 1989. The placards and party programs of demonstrations against governments mostly called for freedoms and not for economic benefits. The people wanted freedom to travel, to change jobs, to speak out against injustice without fear of arrest or reprisal, and other democratic freedoms that are taken for granted in the West.

5. The demonstrations were remarkably peaceful considering the history of repression. The potential for violence was there, however, as demonstrated when the Romanian security police tried to crush the demonstrations.
6. The security police were a special target of resentment in Poland, Romania, Czechoslovakia, the Soviet Union, and elsewhere because of their brutality in supporting the old regime. The military on the other hand played a key role in supporting reforms late in the game in Poland, Romania, the Soviet Union, and Czechoslovakia. As of the first part of 1992 the military had not moved to overthrow the reform movements in Eastern Europe. This reflected in part the nationalistic orientation of the soldiers and the attitude that Communism was imposed as a foreign ideology.
7. The controls and extensive bureaucracy of the Stalinist model had held back economic expansion. Eastern Europeans, who had access to the West, looked with envy on the Western economies. There was experimentation, particularly in Hungary, Poland, and Czechoslovakia, as well as in Russia to freeing trade from extensive controls. Moreover, the sectors of relatively free markets in the former Communist countries that were the most productive included the small farm plots in the Soviet Union and the retail and small industry sectors in Hungary and Czechoslovakia. This created self-reinforcing support for reform.
8. Leadership was a crucial factor in the revolutions. The people, including their Communist leaders, deeply resented Soviet domination. When it became clear Gorbachev would not order Soviet troops to suppress reform and independence in Eastern Europe, events escalated. Local leaders, such as Communist leaders Imre Pozsgay and Egon Krenz, as well as non-Communist leaders Lech Walesa and Vaclav Havel, triggered the revolutions. Backed by mass demonstrations of support, leaders of the former satellites demanded and obtained agreement from Gorbachev to withdraw Soviet troops. This ended the Soviet external empire.
9. Why did these leaders want reform? Many had traveled in the West and had contacts with it. This indicates that the increase in travel and communications across national borders was a basic cause of the growing pressures for reform. The economic stagnation in Eastern Europe contrasted with the economic prosperity and democratic freedoms of Western Europe. There was considerable travel to the West by the 1970s and 1980s, and there was even access to Western television along the borders of Eastern and Western Europe and to Western radio throughout Europe.
10. The East European Communist countries had a built-in Achilles' heel of a democratic framework with a parliament and even opposition parties, which were in existence, although they had no real power. The leaders

of these parties asserted themselves through these institutions when they got the chance.

11. Reforms aimed at ending the Communists' bureaucratic restrictions on management and farmers. This meant cutting back on the Communist Party's domination, suggesting that economic reforms were linked to the political reforms of working toward a pluralistic, democratic system.

12. The access to the West also led to the problem of heavy debt burdens. Heavy debts caused heavy demands on the workers to produce and repay the debts incurred from the West. The countries most heavily in debt were Poland, Hungary, and East Germany. However, they were much better off economically than Romania, which suffered while paying debts under Ceausescu, and Albania, which did not incur many debts. Those countries that did meet debt obligations, such as Hungary, created confidence that began attracting foreign investors with sizeable resources, including management and technical skills.

13. The lack of violence was surprising since conventional wisdom was that the Communist elites would not give up their power and privileges without a fight. Communist parties participated reluctantly in the reform. The ideals and examples of Western democracies apparently undermined the loyalty of party members, particularly the younger ones. As the older cadres who had taken over control at the end of World War II retired, the movement for change gained strength. Also, about 90 percent of the people opposed the Communists, and at critical periods they demonstrated this opposition.

More specific country-by-country causes of the revolutions were:

1. Yugoslavia's leaders asserted independence early because Tito's powerful army liberated it, and Soviet troops never controlled the country. The Soviets did not challenge Tito because Yugoslavia is on the periphery of the Communist bloc outside the historic invasion route to the Soviet Union.

2. East Germany was close to the highly successful West German economy. In 1989 the Communists, encouraged by reforms in the Soviet Union and other satellites, let the wall come down.

3. Czechoslovakia had a tradition of democracy before World War II and its people resented the loss of freedom under Communism.

4. Hungary also was off the main invasion route. Hungary's unsuccessful revolt in 1956 was encouraged by the Soviet withdrawal from Austria, Khrushchev's denunciation of Stalin, and Poland's successful defiance of the Soviets. It cautiously began reforms in the 1960s and it was ready for revolution when Gorbachev gave the green light.

5. Poland is one of the most intensely nationalistic countries of Eastern Europe. The Marxist theory worked in reverse with Polish workers strik-

ing for higher wages, a free trade union, and democracy. There was such widespread support for these demands and opposition to Communism that General Jaruzelski gave up resisting the workers.

6. Ceausescu achieved a measure of independence from Soviet domination. His hardline, corrupt dictatorship was blown away by the winds of reform throughout Eastern Europe.

7. Bulgaria's revolt also spontaneously combusted, ignited by news of neighbors' revolts.

8. Albania has a similar geographic position and it was able to achieve independence from the Soviets and Yugoslavia by playing one major power against the other.

The new democracies faced a difficult period of economic adjustment. With varying degrees of speed they dismantled Stalinist economic controls. East Germany was quickly integrated into the West German economy. The other East European countries, with the exception of Albania, freed 80 to 90 percent of their prices. This was particularly hard on city elites who were used to low prices for apartments, bread, transportation, and other essentials. Rural areas without access to these subsidies had a lower standard of living, but at least they had better access to food.

The East European countries, except for Albania, also liberalized 90 to 100 percent of their imports and unified the exchange rates so that their rates were close to market rates. They also took major steps to reform taxes and the government budget. They established a safety net of unemployment benefits, but the benefits were limited because of budgetary constraints (*IMF May 1992*, 32–33).

The northern tier of former satellites—Hungary, Czechoslovakia, Poland, and East Germany—were markedly better off in 1992 than the southern tier. Their drop in output in 1991 was about half of that of Albania, Bulgaria, and Yugoslavia (Table 3-3). In 1992 they were bottoming out in their adjustment toward a market economy.

The southern tier lagged behind the northern tier. Yugoslavia was in deep trouble because of civil wars. Eastern Europe's output dropped 17 percent in 1991 and 10 percent in 1992, but it was expected to rise in 1993. The northern tier was expected to start recovery in 1992 (*IMF Survey* 5/25/92, 162–163; *IMF World Economic Outlook* 10/92, 7).

There were no widespread food riots in the first years of freedom. People were dissatisfied that reforms were not paying off, but they were not revolting. Some political leaders were forced to leave office because they could not achieve the impossible—an early rise in the standard of living. There was speculation that economic troubles would bring populist dictators who would exploit the political disillusionment.

A key to the future lay in whether political stability could be maintained until the new crops were harvested in 1992. Agricultural production and improvement in food distribution within the framework of market reforms would be important to success. People could postpone purchases of manufactured goods, but not food.

Why did the northern tier of former satellites lead the others in revolution and reform? Geographically, historically, and culturally they had closer connections with the West and its example of freedom and relative prosperity. The people of the northern tier of states had a higher standard of living and were better educated than their southern neighbors and thus were more receptive to the lure of Western Europe. Also, as the reforms began, they tended to reinforce reforms in neighboring states. For example, when Hungary let East Germans flee to the West, the Berlin Wall began to crumble. The northern tier was more important strategically, and Soviet controls and presence were more obvious, and thus more resented by the people. Interestingly, the above conclusions about the northern tier of satellites also apply in part to the two northern provinces of Yugoslavia, Croatia and Slovenia, which were the first to break away from the Yugoslavian Communist system.

The new East European democracies were anxious to make contacts with the West. They gave high priority to agreements with the European Community and the International Monetary Fund, which made that aid conditional on market reforms.

In 1991 the IMF committed over $5 billion to five East European countries and helped mobilize over $20 billion in total flows from all sources. (*IMF Survey* 2/3/92, 35). The Eastern European countries, particularly the northern tier, pressed forward with reform. They also began holding meetings to arrange for regional trade and economic agreements, encouraged by the European Community and the IMF. Hungarian, Polish, and Czechoslovakian representatives met early in 1991 to discuss issues of common concern. Austria, Czechoslovakia, Poland, Hungary, Yugoslavia, and Italy formed a Hexagonal Group, formerly a Pentagonal Group, in which prime ministers discussed matters of regional concern such as investment projects, environmental matters, and ethnic minority problems (Dienstbier 1991; Klosowski 1991, 1).

These developments acted to encourage private investment in the new democracies. Germany was the most active, but other Western entrepreneurs also began investing. Such investments normally take a long time to germinate. The northern tier, and particularly Hungary, which had begun market reforms in the 1960s, was the most successful in attracting new investments.

Both the CIS and East European countries also held meetings with NATO authorities. The most successful contacts involving security were with the U.N. mediator Cyrus Vance, who in 1991 negotiated a cease-fire in Croatia and Slovenia, and in the spring of 1992 began to explore mediation in the dispute between Armenia and Azerbaijan. Just as the European Community succeeded in diverting historic Franco-German frictions, the political moves toward regional arrangements could help sublimate the many ethnic and boundary rivalries in Eastern Europe.

The importance of the leadership factor stands out in the patterns of successful breakaways from Communist Party controls and Soviet domination. Gorbachev came to power only after the deaths of the hardliners Brezhnev, Andropov, and Chernyenko. General Tito successfully fought against challenges to his leadership during World War II and then was the unchallenged president of Yugoslavia until his death in 1980. He had been the first to break away from Soviet domination of Eastern Europe. Stalin knew that Yugoslav nationalism and geography would help make Tito's forces formidable opponents if he tried to force Yugoslavia back in the fold.

Lech Walesa was the first to lead the charge in the 1980s against the entrenched East European Communist regimes. He was silenced in 1981 when millions of union backers pressed too far toward democratic reforms. In 1988 Poland's economic crisis and strikes forced General Jaruzelski to deal with Walesa. Meanwhile Gorbachev gave his blessing to Polish and East European reforms. By this time General Jaruzelski formed an alliance with Walesa and Solidarity to bring Poland out of its economic slump. Negotiations were often close to a breakdown, but Walesa and Jaruzelski steered them to at least initial success.

Egon Krenz amazed the world with his bold initiative to tear down the Berlin Wall. His meteoric career ended as East Germans were told of scandals in the Communist Party, but his decision was so popular that rebuilding the wall seemed out of the question.

In Czechoslovakia the popular writer Vaclav Havel, who had spent five years in jail for his opposition to Communism, was released by Communist reformers. He organized a center of political opposition, Civic Forum, that took up the torch from the Poles and Germans. With strong popular backing the legislature chose him as the new president of Czechoslovakia.

The revolts in Bulgaria and Romania were more like spontaneous combustion fanned by winds of reform from the Soviet Union, Poland, Czechoslovakia, and Berlin. They had heroic leaders, too, but they were not as prominent as the masses who demonstrated there for democracy and freedom. This points to another dominant part of the pattern—the mass support for reform. Millions of Solidarity members backed Walesa, and millions of East Germans swept through the Berlin Wall soon after Krenz announced it would come down. Security police readily gave up half-hearted attempts to suppress these huge demonstrations.

Another major force behind the revolutions was nationalism. Communism was associated with Russian domination. The revolutions were based on resentment against this domination and the system it imposed rather than class conflict and economic oppression, as predicted by Marx. The revolution of alienated workers against the Communist elites was a mirror image of Marx's predictions, but 150 years later. Marx would have been confounded to see the new governments instituting capitalist reforms.

Next, developments in the other Communist systems are examined before assessing the political significance of the democratic and free market revolutions.

Chapter 6

Communism Chinese Style

The Chinese revolution after World War I is reflected in Mao Zedong's life even more than the revolution in Russia was focused on Lenin. It is questionable whether the Chinese revolution would have succeeded without Mao, just as there is doubt that the Russian Revolution would have succeeded without Lenin. A related question is whether the Communist system naturally led to the cult of the personality and a repressive regime like that under Mao. Examining these issues also helps throw light on the main question of whether a change toward democracy and more market reforms are likely in China. This depends on their leaders and we will examine how the history of the Chinese Communist system affected the thinking of the different generations of Chinese leaders and the people they attempt to control. The way they think, of course, will determine China's future.

The Chinese Communist system is unique in part because the Chinese Communist leaders resisted the Soviet Union's attempts to dominate them. This resistance finally developed into a split with the Soviets. Gorbachev's reconciliation did not entirely succeed because Chinese leaders were alarmed at the results of his reforms.

This chapter examines the Chinese Communist revolution and its government with special attention to changes after Mao's death. The next chapter analyzes Chinese foreign policy, particularly as it related to the United States and the Soviet Union.

ORIGINS OF THE REVOLUTION

Mao Zedong (for old spellings, see Table 6-1) dominated the Chinese Revolution and the establishment of its Communist system, and his life mirrors these developments. Mao was born in 1893 when China was being humiliated by imperialist powers. In a series of battles the British had forced China to give it long-term leases on Hong Kong. Japan conquered Formosa (Taiwan) in 1893 and detached Korea from China at the beginning of the twentieth century. During Mao's youth, foreigners controlled important areas of port cities of China, where their laws prevailed, and they even collected taxes to make sure that their loans were repaid. In certain major cities Chinese were treated like inferiors by

Table 6-1
Names of Major Chinese Officials: New (and Old) Romanization

Sun Yatsen (Sun Yat-sen), former president of China
Mao Zedong (Mao Tse-tung), former chairman of the Communist Party
Zhou Enlai (Chou En-lai), former premier
Deng Xiaoping (Teng Hsiao-p'ing), formerly most powerful Politburo member
Hua Guofeng (Hua Kuo-feng), former party chairman
Liu Shaoqi (Liu Chao-ch'i), former president
Peng Dehuai (P'eng Te-huai), former defense minister
Lin Biao (Lin Piao), former defense minister
Zhao Ziyang (Chao Tzu-yang), former party chairman
Hu Yaobang (Hu Yaopang), former party chairman
Jiang Qing (Chiang Ch'ing), Mao's wife

---

foreigners. The government was run by a corrupt group of mandarins around the empress, and it was too weak to prevent humiliations by foreigners. Mao called China a semicolony at this time.

The son of a middle-income peasant, Mao moved to the city for middle school, where he was much poorer than other students. During his youth Sun Yatsen assumed leadership of the Chinese revolution, and Mao supported him. In 1918 Mao moved to Beijing where he held a minor post in the university library. His superior was a Marxist who organized a study group. At this point Mao read the *Communist Manifesto* and other Marxist literature that called for a social revolution in China, and he helped organize Communist cells. He participated in the revolutionary movements, including the May Fourth demonstration in 1919 against Japan's demands for special rights in Shantung and the rest of China.

The Russian Revolution was admired by Mao and other Chinese students, particularly when the new Russian regime renounced the special rights and interests of the tsarist regime in China. In 1920 three representatives of the Comintern went to China to help Sun Yatsen organize the government. At this time the Soviets helped Sun Yatsen to build a military academy, with Chiang Kaishek as its first head. For a while Sun Yatsen's and Chiang's party, the Kuomintang (KMT), and future Communist leaders including Mao and Zhou Enlai, worked together in the academy. In 1921 Mao participated in the Communist Party's first national congress.

After Sun Yatsen died, Chiang assumed leadership of the government. He unified China by defeating the warlords, and in the process he turned on the Communists and attacked them. By 1926 Chiang controlled most of China. Mao, meanwhile, was working for the Communist Party, organizing revolts among the peasants. This not only was a challenge to Chiang, but it brought Mao into conflict with the Soviet advisers, who believed that the organizing efforts should be with the urban proletariat and not the peasants. Mao lost his position as an alternate on the party's Politburo during this period.

Mao went into the countryside where he organized a small army of peasants that later became a part of the Red Army. Chiang Kaishek tried to suppress these groups. During this period and the early 1930s Mao developed his skills as a commander of guerilla warfare. In October 1934 his forces broke out of Chiang's encirclement and began the Long March, which is celebrated as an epic military feat, although, in fact, Mao lost about nine out of ten of the 85,000 soldiers who started it. The remnants of the Long March and the many replacements that joined it retreated 5000 to 6000 miles to Shensi in west-central China, where they organized local soviets and built up their troops to fight Chiang's forces and later the Japanese.

In 1936 Chiang flew to Xian to get the cooperation of the local warlord, Zhang Xuiliang, in suppressing the Communists. Zhang, who actually was cooperating with the Communists, arrested Chiang and let the Communist forces decide his fate. There was a major argument in the leadership with Mao advocating his execution, but Moscow sent the Chinese Communist leaders a stiff telegram threatening to denounce them if they did not cooperate with Chiang in fighting the Japanese. The Soviets were obviously thinking of their own interest in keeping the Japanese occupied in China so they would not take over Siberia with the support of Hitler. Mao lost the argument and Chiang was released, but Mao's resentment against Soviet interference was reinforced.

Japan renewed its attacks against China in 1937. There was limited Communist cooperation with Chiang's forces until Pearl Harbor in 1941 with Mao's forces waging guerilla warfare against the Japanese. The cooperation lessened after 1941, and Mao's units were able to build up their strength and organize their areas politically, whereas Chiang's forces took the brunt of casualties waging conventional war against the Japanese. The Japanese took over most of China, with Chiang forced to establish his capital in Chongqing in the south. At the end of the war the Chinese Communists had built up their army to almost 1 million, and they controlled areas with a population of 70 to 90 million. By this time Mao had emerged as their leader.

Chiang's KMT forces were exhausted after fighting the Japanese. The Chinese had been virtually cut off from the rest of the world. Chiang's forces had suffered an estimated 2 million deaths, far more than the Communists. The Chinese economy was a disaster with runaway inflation and with destruction of bridges and railroads and other extensive war damage. Corruption was rampant.

The next chapter describes the failure of U.S. General George Marshall to get Chiang's and Mao's forces to cooperate. By 1947 they were fighting a full-scale civil war. In the next two years the Communist forces won in a genuine revolution, in contrast to the Russian Revolution, which was more like a coup. The Chinese revolution was backed by military forces manned by the peasants, and not the proletariat, led by the Communist Party. The party at that time was virtually equivalent to the People's Liberation Army.

The Chinese Communists had the following advantages over Chiang's forces: (1) the KMT troops had suffered heavy casualties in World War II, whereas the Communist forces conserved their strength; (2) the KMT army was poorly paid with the commanders living off their troops' allowances; (3) the Communists were well disciplined, used guerilla tactics, and took over control of the countryside with relatively low casualties; (4) they were well supplied with Japanese arms, which the Soviets allowed them to take after the Japanese surrendered at the end of the war; (5) Chiang's forces overextended themselves in trying to control Manchuria; and (6) the economy was disrupted and could not support the war.

The United States withdrew its advisers and military units from China after January 1947, when General Marshall gave up and cut back on U.S. aid programs, reasoning that Chiang's forces already had adequate supplies from those turned over to it after World War II.

In 1949 Chiang was forced to flee to Taiwan in defeat with his government's remaining 1 million troops and civilian officials. There he reestablished his government, which claimed to represent all of China. The Soviet Union immediately recognized the new Communist government on the mainland, and Soviet recognition was followed by the other satellites. Within a few years Britain and a few other countries had also recognized it. The United States continued to recognize Chiang's government as China's government until the Carter administration.

Mao and his Communist cadres performed a remarkable feat in pulling the country together after 1949. In the cities the Communists instituted self-criticism and indoctrination campaigns to weed out potential opposition to their program.

The following factors contributed to Mao's success in winning and consolidating the revolution: (1) he had a simplistic but powerful Communist ideology blaming foreign imperialist forces for Chinese troubles and calling for attacking Chiang as an agent of imperialism appealed to the Chinese; (2) the Communists had obtained valuable administrative experience during the war in controlling western China; (3) their army was well organized and they ruthlessly crushed resistance; (4) they had high morale and team spirit from fighting together for decades; (5) they instituted a monetary reform to abolish the excess currency and end the inflation; law and order and reliable currency will do wonders for an economy—Germany and Japan after World War II are examples; (6) the Soviets provided assistance and an effective model for organization, indoctrination, and control; and (7) the mass executions of the Communists' land reform and mass trials intimidated the Chinese people.

China's relations with the Soviet Union were close until 1958, and the Soviets provided assistance as well as a political and economic model for Chinese development. China's Communist Party was the center of power with the standard Politburo, Central Committee, and Party Congress supported by the secretariat and by Communist Party cells in various enterprises throughout the country. The National People's Congress theoretically was the highest organ of state power, and it approved the constitution in 1954. The second and third constitutions of 1972 and 1978, however, recognized the reality of the Chinese Communist Party (CCP) as the "core of leadership" of the Chinese people. As in other Communist governments, the executive branch, headed by the State Council, controlled the society under the direction of the Communist Party.

THE GREAT LEAP FORWARD AND ECONOMIC DISASTER

There was much ruthless maneuvering within China's political framework that disrupted its political and economic life until the late 1970s, when Deng Xiaoping emerged as a powerful leader to institute reforms that gave the Chinese a respite from economic hardships. The Chinese political process is difficult to understand. Mao did not control the Communist Party and the Chinese government during most of the postwar period, as some imagined, but Chinese politics involved the party leaders taking away his authority and leaving him with only honorific titles. This was done subtly, and the maneuvers, of course, were not reported by the government news media. Mao's reaction was unique. He used his influence with the people to generate mass movements against his opponents, which were tactics outside the scope of normal politics in Communist societies.

In the agricultural sector squads of poor peasants were organized for "land reform" in the early 1950s; they were given free rein to take land from the richer peasants. It has been reported that between 750,000 and 2 million peasants were killed during this period (Chou Ching-wen 1960; Clubb 1964, 317–318; Hinton 1982, 29; Rice 1974, 127). Subsequently, peasants were organized into cooperatives with the aim of sharing implements and labor and increasing production. With about 90 percent of the Chinese people living in rural areas, their organization into cooperatives also permitted the Communist Party and its government to extend controls over the society.

Challenges to Mao's control began after the brutal land reform program that he initiated soon after the Communist victory in 1949. His excesses in this program helped encourage an unsuccessful attempt to limit his power in 1954. He countered by purging his critics. However, Khrushchev's 1956 speech attacking the abuses of Stalin reverberated throughout Chinese leadership as well as the rest of the Communist world. The Communist leaders reacted by revising the Communist Party constitution in 1956 to limit Mao's powers. They eliminated references to the thought of Mao Zedong as a guiding principle for all members to study and added an insert stating that no one is free from mistakes. The Communist Party Congress also gave Mao a semi-inactive position as the party chairman and elected Deng Xiaoping into the key position of General Secretary of the party.

With the help of Soviet experts and equipment and with favorable weather conditions, the Chinese economy during the first five-year plan ending in 1957 expanded annually about 5 to 8 percent. This was from a very low base as a result of the destruction and stagnation in the previous decades of conflicts.

The modest increases in production during the first five-year plan were not enough for Mao; Soviet credits were running out and had to be paid for. In 1958 just as the second five-year plan was scheduled to begin, Mao persuaded party leaders to embark on a radical Great Leap Forward program to increase production. One of the main elements was to amalgamate farms into communes about the size of an average U.S. rural county, where Communist cadres would direct production of agriculture and small-scale industrial production. Also, under the slogan of the General Line, millions of people were mobilized to work on dams and irrigation projects. This was not a new experience for Chinese peasants, who for more than a thousand years had been mobilized for this type of work. Mao set targets, one more ambitious than the other, for increased agricultural and industrial production, hoping that the Communists could inspire peasants and workers to meet the targets.

For a while there was optimism in China and in foreign countries that the Chinese could succeed. Statisticians caught the spirit of the Great Leap Forward, and at one point claimed that the Chinese had trebled grain production. They then retracted, claiming doubled grain production, and finally admitted that the increase was one-third. Even this was grossly overestimated, and the real figures were close to what they were before the plan (Yoder 1961).

There was a prodigious waste of effort in the Great Leap Forward with its emphasis on self-sufficiency. For example, the Chinese people were mobilized to build backyard blast furnaces that produced useless crude iron, and to build local irrigation projects that were ill-planned and counterproductive. The efforts took farmers away from their normal intensive cultivation of crops. The new factories constructed with the help of the Soviets were run day and night without proper maintenance.

The first major signs of dissatisfaction with Mao's policies appeared at the December 1958 Central Committee meeting, which announced Mao's decision to retire from chairmanship of the government. This reduced his authority, although it did not diminish his stature with the common people. In 1959 agricultural production fell as a result of the Great Leap Forward and bad weather.

In the spring of 1960, Khrushchev, dismayed at the waste of Soviet industrial equipment through overuse and lack of maintenance, ordered all Soviet technicians to return home. As indicated in the next chapter the controversy over nuclear weapons policy also played a major part in this decision. Trade with the Soviet Union, including the supply of spare parts, fell drastically, and with further poor harvests the Chinese economy slid into a severe depression.

In July and August the prestigious defense minister Peng Dehuai severely criticized the failures of the Great Leap and, by implication, the chairman. Mao was furious and still had enough political support to get Peng dismissed from office. Communist Party organs reasserted the correctness of the commune and Great Leap Forward policies, but by January 1961 the Central Committee was admitting errors, and retrenchment began with dismantling the communes to the levels that existed before the Great Leap. By this time Mao's political support among the top cadres was undermined. He was out of the center of the action, and, as he put it, he became a "Buddha on the shelf."

THE CULTURAL REVOLUTION

Mao fought back to promote support for his failing policies and to restore his waning influence. When he had Peng Dehuai dismissed as head of the Chinese armed forces, Lin Biao replaced him and backed Mao enthusiastically. Lin had secret ambitions to take over the government. He arranged for the printing of millions of copies of Mao's Red Book of wise sayings for the armed forces and others, and the General Political Department of the People's Liberation Army promoted the study of Mao's thought.

With the military's backing, Mao in 1966 began the Great Proletarian Cultural Revolution. The eventual reaction to this plus the chairman's growing senility resulted in his loss of power and the development of the reform movement under Deng Xiaoping.

A major theme of Mao's organized attack on government and party officials, known as the Cultural Revolution, was to gain support against a reactionary gang of "capitalist-roaders." Although Mao had been removed from positions of authority in the party and in government, he was still the chairman, and "great helmsman," and he used his mass following to fight back against Communist Party leaders and to reform the political system.

In August 1966 the Central Committee convened a special meeting packed with revolutionary students, teachers, and officers who approved the guidelines for the Cultural Revolution. The youth of the country were mobilized, starting at Beijing University and other college campuses, to attack reactionary, Western-oriented professors. Within a few months Mao, who was supported by a radical party faction, had called forth millions of Red Guard units of youth to march around the country, to attack officials and Western-oriented intellectuals, and to assemble for a mass rally in Beijing. At the rally Defense Minister Lin Biao gave a eulogy of Mao. Liu Shaoqi, the president, was not present, and it was evident that he was the principal capitalist-roader under attack.

By the spring of 1967 the leaders of the Cultural Revolution were establishing new power centers in the government called Provincial Revolutionary Committees. These consisted of representatives of the army, party, and mass organizations. Lin Biao ordered the People's Liberation Army (PLA) to give active support to these organizations.

The Chinese are still suffering from the chaos of this period. At times there were civil conflicts in the cities with political factions, including those backed by the military, fighting each other for control. Estimates of the numbers killed range from the official tally of 34,000 to as much as 400,000. The number of persecuted reached the millions (Butterfield 1982, 348–349; Wang 1989, 25).

Even top military leaders and government officials were purged for being capitalist-roaders and anti-Communist. Red Guards roamed from city to city attacking local party and government officials. Officials were publicly humiliated to the point that many committed suicide. Universities were closed and professors forced to go into the countryside to perform menial tasks. In most cases they were not welcomed. The peasants were struggling to grow enough food without the burden of supporting city officials and professors who knew little about agriculture and who could not work efficiently in the fields.

During this period the influence of the military grew. Mao finally ordered an end to the chaos by instructing Lin Biao in January 1967 to use the armed forces to restore order. The military took over leadership positions at all administrative levels and assumed major police responsibilities. The 1969 Party Congress consisted of about 40 percent military officers. The new constitution in 1969 even named Lin Biao as successor to Mao. At this point the party cadres began to coalesce to reduce the power of the military and to remove Lin.

There is no agreed version of what happened next. Lin Biao was a radical favoring revolution throughout Asia, suggesting that the countryside encircle the cities, and that the Third World encircle the developed countries. He was also against détente with the United States even though China at that time was being threatened by a nuclear attack from the Soviet Union (see Chapter 7). Mao's lack of support for Lin at a major party meeting in March 1970 alarmed Lin. As he sensed that the party was against him, he secretly planned a coup. During this period Mao was becoming senile and increasingly under the influence of a radical political faction headed by his wife, Jiang Qing.

In August and September 1971 Lin Biao and his son apparently plotted to overthrow Mao and assume control of the government. Mao and others learned of the plan and plotted his assassination. Either Lin was killed by an army unit after a dinner with Mao, or, according to the official version, he crashed in Mongolia in a plane fleeing to the Soviet Union (Ming-le 1983; Wang 1986, 25–28; Meisner 1989, 365–370). Whichever version is correct, Lin was removed as the successor to Mao, Communist Party supremacy was confirmed, and the move toward détente with the United States continued without interruption. Moreover, after Lin Biao's death, the military representation in the government organs of China was sharply reduced through purges of the top officers from the Central Committee and other party organs. President Nixon's visit with Mao went forward as planned in February 1972.

POLITICAL AND ECONOMICAL REFORMS
UNDER DENG XIAOPING

When Lin Biao disappeared, Premier Zhou Enlai moved into the second-rank position in the party. His success in reducing the influence of the military was shown by reduction of the army officers in the Central Committee to 30 percent. He also strengthened the party by bringing back Deng Xiaoping, who had been attacked by the radicals.

Moderates were put into decision-making positions, but the radicals controlled propaganda and education, so the struggle for political control of the party continued. Zhou left his sickbed in February 1975 to preside over the Fourth National People's Congress. He signaled a change in policy by calling for "four modernizations"—agriculture, industry, national defense, and science and technology. This implied an emphasis on consumer goods and incentives at the expense of heavy industry and central planning. In August 1975 the radicals attacked Zhou and Deng as revisionists and capitalist-roaders—indirectly through attacking the hero of a Chinese classical novel, *The Water Margin.*

Zhou Enlai died on January 8, 1976. Deng gave the eulogy, but after that he was purged from power for the third time. Apparently Mao, getting more senile and coming more under the influence of radicals, refused to back Deng. In a compromise, Hua Guofeng, the fifth-ranking member of the Politburo and head of the security police, was made the acting prime minister and tagged as Mao's successor. Hua Guofeng's claim to fame was that he had Mao's confidence after building a special hall in Mao's honor in the village where he was born.

On March 25, 1976, a Shanghai newspaper offended many Zhou supporters by calling him a capitalist-roader. Then on April 4, a traditional day when Chinese honor the dead, tens of thousands of people loyal to the memory of Zhou Enlai visited Tiananmen Square in the center of Beijing to lay wreaths at the monument there. Some of the wreaths had slogans attacking the radicals. Some slogans made it clear that they were also attacking Mao. On April 4 all the wreaths were removed. This stimulated a counterdemonstration, and on April 5 a crowd of more than 100,000 gathered there chanting slogans and demonstrating for Zhou (and indirectly for his protégé, Deng). The crowd was finally dispersed, but there were similar demonstrations throughout China. In the weeks that followed the demonstrations were blamed on Deng. Reportedly the police punished 40,000 who participated.

In late July 1976 the Tangshan earthquake struck northern China killing 200,000. Many Chinese believed that this was a portent of the death of an important leader. In fact, on September 6, 1976, Mao died apparently from natural causes. Hua presided at the funeral. Reportedly a gunman shot into a procession in which Hua was riding, and confessed when caught that he was acting on behalf of Jiang Qing, Mao's wife. The military on the orders of Hua in October arrested Jiang Qing and the rest of what was called the Gang of Four, who were subsequently tried and convicted. Meanwhile troops arrested more radicals. Hua Guofeng was then named party chairman. He had double-crossed radicals who had helped get him elected as prime minister.

The propaganda machine tried to build support for Hua Guofeng, but he did not have the authority, prestige, experience, and party support to be convincing as Mao's successor. Moreover, a wall poster campaign started calling for the return of Deng. The posters also criticized those who had arrested the demonstrators for Zhou.

In October 1976 Deng wrote a letter to Hua praising him as a wise leader and offering to be of assistance. Hua invited Deng back into the government. Deng had a reservoir of support among the top leaders, and in July 1977 the Politburo restored him to his former posts making him the most powerful figure after Hua, who nominally was still chairman of the party and of the Military Affairs Commission, which controlled the armed forces.

Divisions continued in the elite, reflected in criticisms and the trial of the Gang of Four as ultra-rightist, whereas other critics connected the gang with Lin Biao, who had been discredited. Temporarily Deng began pressing for the "Great Four Freedoms," which included speech, airing views, debates, and writing big character wall posters. This was the period of "Democracy Wall" in the center of Beijing where people gathered to read posters put up by individuals and political factions. By April 1980, however, when Deng had achieved power, he had the four freedoms removed from the constitution. Placing such posters on Democracy Wall and other places was prohibited.

During this period, when Deng was consolidating his position at the expense of Hua Guofeng, Chinese relations worsened with the Soviets and its close ally Vietnam. In the spring of 1978 Hanoi closed down private businesses, most of which were run by ethnic Chinese, and thousands fled, including the "boat people" who often perished at sea. On November 3 Moscow concluded a mutual defense treaty with Hanoi.

At the same time Deng started improving relations with the United States. On December 15, 1978, a normalization of relations treaty with China was announced by the Carter administration. Deng visited the United States. He received a warm welcome and much good publicity. He kissed children at the Kennedy Center and visited the space center in Texas, where he piloted a mock space capsule.

In China Mao's pictures were removed from some public places, and in November the Gang of Four was tried and convicted on 48 counts. In September 1980 Zhao Zhiyang, a protégé of Deng, was appointed prime minister replacing Hua, who later resigned as party chairman and was removed from the Politburo. Zhao's appointment signaled the beginning of economic reforms and a record expansion of the Chinese economy.

Zhao was 59 years old at the time, the son of a wealthy landlord. In 1967 he had been denounced by the Red Guards and forced to wear a dunce cap. He spent four years doing manual labor. Later, his five-year tenure as first secretary of Sichuan brought him to Deng's attention. Zhao had boldly introduced policies in Sichuan that gave material incentives to farmers and manufacturers. Private plots were expanded through lease agreements giving the farmers incentives to produce more. In three years agricultural production there rose 25 percent and industrial production rose 81 percent.

Zhao instituted this reform, called the responsibility system, throughout

China. The key concept was that farm households contract with a collective farm for plots of land to deliver a specified quota of crops. Any production above the quota could be sold at higher prices or in the free market. Letting farmers cultivate a definite plot of land and earn extra income on the free market had a dramatic effect on production, and Chinese farmers doubled agricultural incomes in about seven years. This was demonstrated in free markets throughout Chinese cities and new brick cottages in the countryside.

Zhao also instituted the responsibility system for some sectors of industry, allowing more freedom for marketing consumer products, but this proved difficult to manage. Overall production in the economy averaged about a 10 percent increase in the early 1980s. There were phenomenal increases in durable consumer goods such as washing machines, TVs, and electric fans. Village industries grew at a rate of 18 percent per year.

Ironically, the free market reforms of Deng and Zhao accomplished a great leap forward in Chinese agriculture that Mao failed to bring about by his government controls through the commune system. The agricultural reforms and free markets stimulated the entire economy and indirectly helped support the market reforms in the industrial economy.

Before 1974, when a strict policy of family planning was introduced, the population had increased as much as 3 percent or more a year. After the one-child-per-family policy was initiated, the population increase fell to about 1.1 percent by 1984 and then increased to 1.4 percent in 1987. Local neighborhood committees supported measures to reduce the population. The strict limits on population growth contrasted with the European-American model where economic development reduced population growth.

The Chinese believed that China could not afford to wait with its population already over the 1 billion level. The population control program was implemented by laws raising the age of marriage, and penalties in wages for couples having more than one child. The measures had wide support in the cities but ran into difficulties in rural areas. There was a major increase in population in the countryside in the 1980s after the responsibility system was implemented and peasants left the production teams. This made it harder to control the peasants because they could no longer be penalized at workplaces for more than one child. Despite these problems, the Chinese government has so far succeeded in implementing one of the strictest family planning programs in history (*People's Republic of China Yearbook* 1988–1989, 505–510).

Zhao Ziyang, who was promoted to general secretary, and Li Peng, the prime minister, in 1988 reinstituted some economic controls to try to restrain inflationary pressures, but they still asserted the aim of ultimately moving toward a freer economy.

As the economy surged ahead with economic reforms, Deng began limited political reforms. These were reflected in the 1982 constitution that dropped a specific reference to the Chinese Communist Party and emphasized the role of the executive branch over the party and even the military (Nethercut 1983, 30–

46). Meetings of the National People's Congress became more regular after 1978, and its Standing Committee drafted important legislation. The president was elected by the National People's Congress (NPC) under the 1982 constitution, but he generally performed only ceremonial functions. There was somewhat less party interference in government business, which was managed by a premier and cabinet ministers, also elected by the NPC. Also, many of the old cadres were retired. Nevertheless, the leaders discouraged moves toward a pluralistic system, and they continued to give obeisance to Marxist-Leninist theories.

At the end of 1986 student demonstrations throughout China called for reforms. After a period of uncertainty, Deng gave the signal that demonstrations were to be suppressed even if some students were hurt. Some, indeed, were hurt and were arrested, and the demonstrations stopped. Hu Yaobang, the party secretary, was blamed for the student unrest, and he was replaced by Zhao Ziyang, the premier and another protégé of Deng.

At the end of 1987 there were sweeping changes in the Central Committee and other top positions in line with Deng's program for reform. Virtually all the old party leaders retired, and Deng himself stepped down from all positions except what later proved to be the key position—chairman of the Military Affairs Commission. However, news reports at the time indicated that he would play a major role in party and state decisions (*CSM* 11/2/87, 2; *NYT* 11/2/87, 1). About 43 percent of the Central Committee and three of the five members of the standing committee of the Politburo were removed. Li Peng was installed as premier in 1988. Nevertheless, a few of the old cadre still exerted influence from behind the scenes.

Official statements continued to support the four basic principles—socialism, the dictatorship of the proletariat, the leadership of the Communist Party, and Marxism-Leninism and Mao Zedong thought. At the same time, Deng and Zhao made it clear that economic reforms would continue to include giving plant managers more authority by lessening the influence of party cadres and decentralizing decision making. Deng retired older cadres from high positions and reduced the military by 1 million men.

REACTION TO TIANANMEN

Until the summer of 1989 Deng's strategy seemed to be successful in pressing forward with economic reforms and limiting political reforms—limiting in the sense of not allowing any opposition to the Communist Party to organize. Chinese could even get away with criticisms of the government and the party as long as they did not break the law, such as committing violence or giving military information to a foreigner. Deng's strategy, however, had the seeds of tragedy. The "openness" or new open door policy also opened windows to the outside world. Millions of tourists visited China every year, many of them Chinese. Publications, personal contacts, television shows, and Western news

Figure 6-1   Deng Xiaoping, 1989 (Courtesy: *Beijing Review*).

media influenced the society. Students and teachers, in particular, had access to the outside world as tens of thousands went abroad and began to return. Students in China learned about the West and competed to get scholarships and permission to study abroad.

Democracy in the West appeared to them to promise the good life of more personal freedoms and more consumer goods. A similar process, as we have seen, was working in the Soviet Union and Eastern Europe. China opened its door first, and the process had been working about 10 years before it exploded in the spring of 1989. The student demonstrations for democracy in 1987 had been suppressed without much pain. There were no reports of students being killed, or even jailed for more than a short time. An anti-bourgeoise liberalization campaign was developed, but it had a minor effect on the open door policy.*

In the spring of 1989 students seized an opportunity to express their dis-

---

*I was teaching in Beijing at this time. The foreign teachers were called together for a special admonition. The theme was that Chinese society is different from the West and that the West has problems, too, such as excessive sex and violence, and AIDS. Privately I was assured that the bourgeoise liberation campaign was aimed at the party and it should not affect my teaching. I continued teaching courses in government and foreign policy much as I taught them in the United States, and there was no criticism. Some of my American colleagues in other universities noticed a cooling-off of relations with Chinese, but my wife and I after the demonstrations did not notice any difference in attitudes toward us.

satisfaction with the slowness of reform, the privileges of the Communist elite, and the suppression of political dissent. In April 1989 Hu Yao Bang died; he was the leader who had been dismissed because he had permitted students to demonstrate in 1986. Demonstrations to honor his death started with between 500 and 1000 people marching to Tiananmen Square at the center of government in Beijing. The parallel with demonstrations 12 years before at Chou Enlai's funeral was obvious. Those demonstrations had given political support to his protégé, Deng Xiaoping and had become part of a chain of events that allowed Deng to take power and start the original open door reform program.

The government during the first weeks did not suppress the demonstrations even though by the beginning of May they included as many as 150,000. Some of the demonstrations pointedly criticized Deng by including a broken bottle in the wreaths—Deng's name in Chinese sounds like small bottle. On May 15 when Gorbachev visited Beijing to normalize relations in what was to be a crowning achievement for Deng, hundreds of thousands of students demonstrated in the center of Beijing against the government and called for democracy and reforms. Some signs asked for reforms like those by Gorbachev. All this occurred in front of the world's news media.

By this time there was a split between Zhao Ziyang, who wanted to meet with the students and discuss the problems in a calm and reasonable way, and Deng, who was furious and wanted to suppress the demonstrations with the military. Deng reportedly asserted that Zhao was behind the demonstrations. Premier Li Peng supported Deng. On June 3 more than 2000 unarmed troops headed toward Tiananmen Square to restore order but were blocked by hundreds of thousands of students and Beijing residents who surged into the streets. Tens of thousands remained in the square, some on a hunger strike. It was apparent from news accounts that the youth, who were too young to remember the violence of the Cultural Revolution, were leading the demonstrations. It was also clear that many youths were prepared to sacrifice their lives for the democratic ideal.

Early on June 4 armed troop units began moving in on Tiananmen Square. The first troop units were attacked by crowds and some soldiers were killed. In the confusion of the early morning hours, troops attacked in force firing indiscriminately on citizens, killing what the *New York Times* later estimated to be between 400 and 800 people, and wounding many more (*NYT* 6/21/89, 8). Strikes broke out in other major cities of China with buildings being burned and citizens killed. Foreigners were evacuated after a few days of disorder.

Within a few days, however, Deng's troops had cleaned up the square and restored a police-state type of order. In the first few weeks 27 of those accused of violence were executed and many arrested. It was obvious to the Chinese city people and to foreigners that the Communist Party was opposed by huge numbers of demonstrators and could maintain control only with military force. The news media and leaders of many countries criticized the excessive violence by the troops, with the United States and European countries applying minor sanctions of stopping sales of certain military equipment and of cancelling high level visits to China. Deng sacked Zhao and replaced him with Jiang Zemin, a hardliner from Shanghai. Li Peng, who had opposed Zhao, stayed on as prime minister.

After Tiananmen the government reversed moves toward political reform. At the end of 1990 it claimed that it had completed the trials of 715 cases related to the demonstrations, but Western sources estimated that 215 still awaited trial. The government renewed jamming of Voice of America and the BBC, and it harassed and arrested some Catholic priests. It maintained a draconic birth control policy except among ethnic minorities. Thus, any moves toward political reform were deterred or suppressed (Freedom House 1991–92, 151–156).

The above repression had a marked economic impact. In the first year after Tiananmen economic expansion ended. Before the massacre China earned about $2.2 billion a year from tourism. In the following 12 months this fell off by more than $1 billion. Foreign investments were cut back with the World Bank suspending new loans of $700 million. The Japanese government postponed a seven-year $5.8 billion loan to China. However, by the second half of 1991 lenders resumed activities, which helped the economy to resume its expansion. After a period of retrenchment the government shifted to expansionary credit policies and consumers increased their spending. The government meanwhile restricted imports and began an export promotion drive, which by 1990 generated a $9 billion trade surplus. The momentum of agricultural production continued with a record harvest in 1990 (Naughton 1991, 259–263). In 1991 there was rapid growth of industrial output and exports (*NYT* 7/28/92).

Meanwhile, the undercover struggle over economic policy continued within the Communist Party. Deng Xiaoping at age 87 intervened in the spring of 1992 by visiting the southern China special economic zones (SEZs) in Guandong Province, where investors could establish factories with the benefit of no tariffs and access to cheap Chinese labor. Guandong Province became one of the dynamic development areas of Asia, somewhat like the "four dragons" of Asia (Hong Kong, Singapore, Taiwan, and Korea). Most of Guandong's industrial production came from private firms. Deng praised their achievements and called for reforming of the stock market and liberalizing laws on enterprises. In mid-October 1992 the Communist Party Congress, which is held every five years, confirmed the new direction of economic policy. Jiang Zemin, the general secretary of the party, in his speech setting the party line, called for the building of a "socialist market economy" and placing a priority on economic growth. He called for modernizing China by liberating economic forces. At the same time, he called for strengthening the "people's democratic dictatorship." The new trend was confirmed by promotion of free market reformers to the powerful seven-member standing committee of the Politburo. Deng appeared briefly to approve the new line (*NYT* 10/13/92, 3; 10/19/92, 5; 10/20/92, 1, 6).

(a)

(b)

Figure 6-2 (a) Jiang Zemin, chairman of the Chinese Communist Party addresses a conference on propaganda in Beijing, 1989 (Courtesy: Liu Jianguo, *Beijing Review*). (b) Prime Minister Li Peng and Mikhail Gorbachev in Beijing, 1989 (Courtesy: Xue Chao, *Beijing Review*).

THE LEGACIES OF MAO AND DENG

Marxism-Leninism was a powerful revolutionary weapon in the hands of Mao. He mobilized the peasants and others with slogans attacking imperialism, capitalism, and the rich farmers for the ills of China. After he succeeded in overthrowing the government, weakened by 15 years of fighting the Japanese, Communism gave him a model of organization for the revolutionaries to control society. In the early years of the People's Republic of China, the Soviets helped with technical assistance and aid, but Mao's party was able to resist Soviet domination.

Some of the special characteristics of Chinese-Maoist Communism are that Mao realized that the revolution did not have to depend on a proletariat but on the people, who happened to be mostly peasants. The Communist Party and Chinese military were inseparable in the revolution, and Mao's guerilla techniques of revolution were used successfully by others, including the Vietnamese, against more powerful forces. The military continued to play a key role in Chinese politics supporting the Great Leap Forward, the Cultural Revolution, and the coup against the Gang of Four. It backed Deng Xiaoping and suppressed the people's demonstrations in the summer of 1989. Mao's saying that political power comes out of the barrel of a gun helps explain the political developments of this century in China.

Mao initially used popular front techniques to win power and then consolidated it behind a facade of opposition parties. After peasants killed the well-to-do peasants, Mao's Communists instituted a massive political reeducation campaign for the urban classes and opponents, rather than liquidating them (Lowenthal 1964). China developed self-criticism and brainwashing meetings to a fine art.

The leaders maintained control of the party and the government by drastic political maneuvers. Although Mao was revered by the people as the chairman and great helmsman, and is still revered by many, he did not control the government after the Great Leap Forward. He instituted the Cultural Revolution to try to purge the bureaucracy and regain control of policy. This was followed by political struggles for domination—between the military and the civilian cadres, between the Gang of Four and Hua Guofeng, between Deng and Hua, and between Deng and Zhao Ziyang. During the initial contests for power, Zhou Enlai until his death in 1976 "minded the store" as premier in charge of the government, which was the number three position or finally number two in the hierarchy, whereas the number twos (Liu Shaoqi and later Lin Biao) were removed during their political struggles for control.

Mao developed a mass following, or personality cult, that allowed him to take control of mass movements over the opposition of the party elites. The two major mass movements, the Great Leap Forward and the Cultural Revolution, had disastrous effects, and the party leaders finally put Mao on a shelf after the Cultural Revolution failed.

Deng Xiaoping chipped away at the worst economic and political aspects of Maoism, afraid to try to shatter it because Mao was still revered by many. He made progress in lessening interference of party cadres in economic enterprises, and in reducing the role of the military. This created enemies. There was increased emphasis on the rule of law and on legislation on reform issues. Political prisoners were released, and many were reinstated and their charges were erased. Many of the older cadres resigned or were forced out.

The most dramatic results of reform were in the economic area where the economy surged ahead at about 10 percent a year during the 1980s. At the end of the 1980s there were problems of inflation that caused the government to reinstitute price and allocation controls.

Deng's legacy, however, was also the tragedy of Tiananmen. The good feeling engendered abroad by his reforms was wiped out in a single night as the news media featured troops killing demonstrators and restoring order in the center of Beijing. A year after the Tiananmen tragedy the economy resumed its rapid growth, but the political reaction continued.

At the end of 1989 Deng resigned from his last Communist Party position as head of the Communist Party's Central Military Affairs Commission. He resigned from the parallel position of the government's military affairs committee in the spring of 1990. Deng's health was frail, but he and a small group of old-timers still had powerful behind-the-scenes positions. After the Tiananmen tragedy the government leaders were nervous enough about their positions to black out the news of the Berlin demonstrations (*NYT* 11/12/89, E3). At the beginning of 1992 he took an initiative to reinforce support for his economic reforms by his well-publicized visit to the special economic zones.

In 1992 it appeared only a matter of time before the old hardliners would be replaced by younger reformers who would want to press forward with economic and political reforms. There is a tendency among observers to stress economics and overlook the importance of political factors. However, the Tiananmen demonstrations were not caused by economic hardships; they occurred after 10 years of unprecedented economic expansion. They occurred in cities where people were subsidized by low prices for housing, transportation, education, and basic foods. The leaders of those mass demonstrations were emphasizing demands for political reforms and freedoms. The symbol of the uprising was a statue of liberty. Gorbachev with his record of glasnost was a hero of demonstrators. The open door economic policy has continued, but the population is still sullenly resentful of the Communist Party domination.

Other factors worked toward eventual political reforms. There is no clear line between political and economic policy. China's open door economic policies included sending students abroad and exposing Chinese society to the outside world through education, tourism, business investment, and modern communications. These reforms educated students who had helped organize the demonstrations. Moreover, students in large numbers continued to go abroad and return to China, and these students someday would take over from older leaders. The students were not yet the reformers, and most of the Tiananmen demonstrators were not students. Many signs of continuing popular resentment against the Communist system were evident to reporters in the years after the tragedy.

Such openness under the heading of economics or politics is likely to have an unsettling effect on a totalitarian society. This is the dilemma Communists face as they try to control a society at the same time they try to keep up with the outside world and give incentives to produce. We discuss this issue further in the concluding chapter.

China was in a somewhat different position than East European satellites, which were swept by waves of reform. Those reforms had been bottled up by the threat of Soviet intervention, and when this was removed, there was a political explosion. Chinese leaders were relatively insulated from these movements. Moreover, as the Soviet Union fell apart, the hardliners got support for their repressive policies by pointing to the chaotic conditions in the Soviet Union. However, only the oldest leaders had been schooled in the ruthless experience of revolution, and younger Chinese leaders of the future would probably be less willing to use force to keep a privileged position. Even the older leaders who had suffered under Maoism would not return to the chaos and repression of that era.

In 1992 China's rulers were pulling in two directions. They were supporting an open door economic policy on the one hand and reaction to political reform on the other. However, the hardline Communists' days were numbered. As the old and respected leaders left the scene, the way was prepared for a Chinese Gorbachev to rejuvenate the party and proceed with the reforms that were interrupted by Tiananmen. At that time hundreds of thousands demonstrated in the cities for reform. In 1992 many expected a political crisis to occur after the death of Deng Xiaoping, then 89.

China's home-grown Communism proved to be more lasting than the East European transplanted kind. However, the combination of economic reforms and new ideas of the younger generation as it takes over leadership positions would open the door further to pressures that swept away the European Communist regimes.

In the interim period of uncertainty it was harder for the Chinese government to maintain discipline on complicated issues affecting the United States and other countries. These issues, in addition to human rights issues, included China's control of the sales of sensitive nuclear and missile technology, controlling narcotics from the Golden Triangle, and monitoring unfair trade practices. The challenge to the United States was to exercise patience and persistence on problems rather than to close the door with ineffective, unilateral trade sanctions (Oksenberg 1991).

Chapter 7

China's Relations with the West and the Communist World

China with its 1 billion people has come to play a major role in international politics. At the beginning of this century it was still a sleeping giant, but the traders of the world forced it to awaken. The United States with its open door policy supported its independence at the beginning of the century. Continued U.S. support of China triggered the Japanese attack at Pearl Harbor that brought the United States into World War II. After the war China turned toward Communism and the Soviet Union, but that alliance was broken in the early 1960s. After the Vietnam War, China turned toward the West, and as a result Asia has enjoyed a relatively peaceful equilibrium. China's suppression of the Tiananmen Square demonstrations and the West's reaction ended their growing détente, but relations were restored in the following years. There was still ill will generated by periodic attacks in the United States on China's human rights record. This chapter examines the politics of China's foreign policies relating them to the internal political maneuvers described in the previous chapter.

RELATIONS WITH THE UNITED STATES BEFORE WORLD WAR II

At the end of the last century China was the focal point of imperialist ambitions. By 1900 it had already lost Hong Kong, Taiwan, and Korea. Also, Russia secured boundary adjustments in its favor in northwest China and along the Amur River in the east. This is a sensitive point in the relations between the two countries. In recent years China has demanded discussion of the boundary issues and at least recognition of the injustice of the changes, but until recently the Soviets resisted such discussions.

Western ideas and some Western technology were introduced by the Western powers attracted by trading possibilities and the possibility of carving out spheres of influence. As new ideas took root in China, the activists blamed the Manchu rulers, who were not Chinese, for their weakness in the face of Western challenges to its sovereignty. Just before World War I rebels inspired by Sun Yatsen overthrew the Manchu dynasty, and revolutionaries installed a parliamentary government.

The conventional explanation of the U.S. open door policy at the beginning of the twentieth century stresses the trade motive. However, there was also a strong element of wanting to protect Chinese sovereignty against colonial ambitions. In 1900 two diplomats, William Rockhill of the United States, who was an old China hand, and Alfred Hippisley of Great Britain, who was part of the international customs administration of China, met informally and agreed that it was important to preserve China's integrity. They respected China's people and culture, and they wanted to avoid imperial wars over China.

Hippisley encouraged Rockhill in 1900 to ask Secretary of State John Hay to circulate a diplomatic note emphasizing the importance of maintaining equality of commercial opportunity (the open door) and China's integrity. They drafted the original open door note, adding other reasons they could think of to get support for the policy, including the advantage of opening up the Chinese market to all on an equal basis. Historians reading the documents have assumed that commercial reasons were the only important ones, but more careful study of the lives and motives of these men indicated that they had in mind China's interests, the interest of avoiding war, and, probably thirdly, commercial interests.

From 1898 to 1900 the Boxer Rebellion occurred, an antiforeign, religious rebellion that was put down only by intervention of British, German, and American forces to rescue the foreign community in China. Although China was forced to pay an indemnity, the U.S. government used the funds for scholarships for Chinese students. American missionaries had been very active in China establishing schools and colleges, and helping to bring Western agriculture and medicine to China. These missionary activities and those of charitable foundations in China continued until World War II broke off normal contacts.

The United States in later international agreements and treaties reinforced the principle of recognizing the territorial integrity of China. The open door notes and these treaties were much more than pieces of paper. They came to reflect a fundamental U.S. interest in supporting China against the imperialistic drive of Japan, as well as keeping China available for trade opportunities.

In 1931 Secretary of State Stimson mobilized the world community to object to Japan's attack on Manchuria and its establishment of a puppet state called Manchukuo. This was the principal industrial area of China. With the encouragement of Senator Borah, chairman of the Foreign Relations Committee, Stimson circulated a note refusing to recognize the so-called State of Manchukuo because it was established contrary to international commitments against war.

The League of Nations committee investigating the situation criticized Japan, and in face of this pressure Japan withdrew from the League, while maintaining its occupation of Manchuria. The League action was more than a slap on the wrist, because Japan had been an active member. Secretary of State Stimson, who later was secretary of war under President Roosevelt, said in his memoirs that this Stimson Doctrine was the accomplishment he was most proud of. It did have a practical effect, because after Japan was defeated in World War II, there was no hesitation in returning Manchuria to China.

The momentum of this pro-China, anti-imperialistic policy carried the United States into a confrontation with Japan that triggered Pearl Harbor. U.S. government officials, and particularly Secretary of State Hull, objected to Japan's renewing aggression against China at the end of the 1930s. Hull and Stimson supported economic sanctions against Japan, including stopping shipments of strategic materials such as aviation gasoline, scrap iron, and metals. Finally in the summer of 1941 the United States imposed financial controls that cut off shipments of petroleum to Japan. Although Japan had over 1-1/2 years of civilian supply on hand, it needed more petroleum supplies to support its military attacks against China. The Dutch East Indies (Indonesia) was an attractive source.

Japanese military leaders believed that in order to take over the oil areas of the Dutch East Indies, Japan would have to eliminate the ability of the U.S. navy to block such an action. They, therefore, began the plan to attack the United States at Pearl Harbor and the Philippines. There were detailed negotiations of the China issue with Secretary of State Hull before the attack, but Hull insisted on the Japanese withdrawing from China as a condition of resuming normal trade and commercial relations. Japan refused. Its leaders had ambitions for a Greater East-Asia Coprosperity Sphere led by Japan that would eliminate Western imperialism from Asia. The Japanese then launched the surprise attack at Pearl Harbor in December 1941, which brought the United States into World War II.

Why did Hull support the embargo against China? Many historians emphasize trade, but trade with China never amounted to more than 1 or 2 percent of the U.S. total. If the United States was interested just in trade, it would have increased trade with Japan, a major trading partner, and let Japan exploit China. Hull's two major aims and accomplishments help us to understand his position. He received the Nobel Peace Prize for his part in promoting the United Nations. His other major accomplishment was legislation for the reciprocal trade agreements with nondiscriminatory principles, which have been accepted and have greatly expanded United States and world trade. He also believed in collective security as the way to promote peace. Japan's aggression was a direct challenge to these principles.

On January 13, 1941, Hull explained to Congress the rationale for opposing Japanese aggression:

> . . . the proposed new order in the Pacific area means, politically, domination by one country. It means, economically, employment of the resources of the area concerned for the benefit of that country and to the ultimate impoverishment of other parts of the area and exclusion of the interests of other countries.
>
> It means, socially, the destruction of personal liberties and the reduction of the conquered people to the role of inferiors (Hull 1948).

Before Pearl Harbor the United States encouraged the voluntary military aviation unit called the Flying Tigers to be formed in China, and Americans from the U.S. armed forces volunteered for service. During the war the United States was a close ally of China, supplying arms at considerable U.S. cost.

Although most U.S. forces were sent first to defeat Hitler, a major segment of the U.S. navy fought the Japanese, and the United States made great efforts to supply the Chiang Kaishek government.

Although there are numerous examples of U.S. support for China in the era before World War II, and the United States was even drawn into the war because of this, there has been little or no reservoir of goodwill in China from this history. The history of good U.S. intentions was eroded by decades of anti-West propaganda. Even Chinese friends of the United States would see the U.S. support of China before World War II as a reflection of our perceived interests in opposing Japan, or in promoting trade and investment, rather than as any evidence of idealistic support for Chinese territorial integrity in the interest of world peace. What goodwill does exist in China results more from many personal contacts and educational and religious activities, rather than from the foreign policy record.

ORIGINS OF THE SINO-SOVIET SPLIT

The Communist leaders of the Soviet Union also wooed China, but their attempts to control its policies eventually backfired. In the years after the revolution in Russia, Lenin established relations with world revolutionary movements. The Soviets declared that although China was not advanced enough industrially with a proletariat for a Communist revolution, they were prepared to help the new nation. Dr. Sun Yatsen soon asked for assistance. The Comintern sent Michael Borodin in 1920 to help with the reorganization of the Kuomintang (KMT) nationalist party, and the Soviets invited Chiang Kaishek, the recognized leader after Sun Yatsen, to the Soviet Union for three months before he became the head of the Whampoa Military Academy. Soviet military advisers were assigned to the military academy, and as a result the Communists and leaders of the KMT became well acquainted. Zhou Enlai, later the premier of Communist China, was the chief political commissar under Chiang.

When Sun died in 1925, the Russians persuaded the Chinese Communists to cooperate with the KMT. In 1926 Chiang attacked the leftist elements of the KMT as well as the warlords who stood in the way of a united China. Stalin, who was in a contest with Trotsky for the leadership of the Soviet and world Communist movements, called for the Chinese Communists to cooperate with Chiang, but at the same time asked them to prepare secretly to overthrow him. The instructions were publicized, and Chiang attacked the Communists again, shattering the leftist forces in Wuhan (Pye 1984, 138–139). Chiang then took over control of China's government. The United States was the first to recognize his new government in 1928. This was in line with its traditional policy of supporting the sovereignty of China and discouraging colonialist powers from moving in.

During the 1920s Mao Zedong, who became the revered leader of the Communists, was a minor figure who disagreed strongly with the Soviet policy of cooperating with Chiang Kaishek. Moreover, Mao differed from the Soviet advisers since he believed that the Chinese revolution should be based on the peasants rather than the urban proletariat. Mao then spent the 1920s organizing peasant resistance to Chiang's government. When Communist forces were surrounded by Chiang's government forces in the early 1930s, Mao led them in the Long March to western China, where they established a base of operations that later allowed them to launch their final attack on Chiang's government.

RED CHINA CONFRONTS THE UNITED STATES

After Pearl Harbor the United States focused on the European war, but it continued to support the Chinese Nationalist government in the war against Japan. As China kept Japanese troops occupied, the United States made strenuous efforts to supply China over the Burma Road and by flights "over the hump" from India into China. The Chinese Communist forces under Mao fought a guerila-type war against the Japanese in northwest China, but the major fighting was a conventional war between Chiang's forces and the Japanese. It is estimated this cost more than 2 million deaths. The Chinese Communist casualties were far fewer since their strategy was based on guerila warfare. Chiang's strategy was defensive, waiting for American and other forces to attack the Japanese. He also wanted to strengthen his armies to prepare for a struggle with the Communists.

After World War II China was racked by a vicious civil war between Chiang's forces, which were exhausted by the war, and the Communist forces which were relatively fresh and well organized. In 1946 and 1947 the United States, through General George Marshall, attempted to mediate a cease-fire. He finally gave up trying to find a basis for trust and compromise between President Chiang Kaishek and Chairman Mao that would permit the building of a coalition government. During this period the United States continued to provide economic and military aid to Chiang Kaishek's forces. The U.S. aid was drastically reduced after Marshall left China, but it did continue, and after the victory of the Chinese Communists in 1949, the United States was their foremost enemy.

The Chinese Nationalist government fled to Taiwan; the United States withdrew its military mission from there and was not providing military aid to Chiang's government at the outbreak of the Korean War. Although in 1949 and 1950, 14 non-Communist governments wanted to establish diplomatic relations with the new government called the People's Republic of China, it established formal relations immediately with only 6. The initial Chinese Communist attitude toward Western missions was one of contempt. The new regime seized American property belonging to the American consulate in Peking and mistreated and arrested an American consul, Angus Ward. President Truman, on the other hand, refused to negotiate with the new government. As a result, the United States withdrew official personnel from China.

The Korean War (1950–1953) was an avalanche consolidating the hostile confrontation between China and the United States that was not changed for 20 years. The war came from a North Korean initiative, secretly approved by Stalin, while China acquiesced. There was evidence that the Chinese Communists were assembling boats to invade Taiwan, so President Truman "neutralized" the Taiwan Strait with the U.S. Seventh Fleet to protect Taiwan immediately after the outbreak of the Korea War. The Chinese Communists reacted with angry propaganda against the United States, and, in a cable to the United Nations, accused the United States of armed aggression against the territory of China (Taiwan).

The Chinese Communists, and particularly Mao, feared the effect of having North Korea, which bordered China's major industrial area, occupied by U.S. troops. Zhou Enlai, the foreign minister, warned in a public statement on September 30 that China would not tolerate seeing its neighbor, North Korea, invaded by imperialists. China later relayed a direct warning through the Indian ambassador in Peking of China's intention to intervene if American forces crossed the 38th parallel into North Korea. After the U.N. troops, mostly Americans under General Douglas MacArthur, drove into North Korea, Chinese Communist troops appeared as "volunteers." In November 1960 hundreds of thousands of Chinese volunteers helped drive the U.N. forces back beyond the 38th parallel into South Korea. After severe fighting the front was finally stabilized near this line close to where the fighting began (Figure 7- 1).

Meanwhile, the United States took the lead in the U.N. in organizing a strict trade embargo. After the cease-fire was established in 1953, the United States led the fight in the U.N. year after year to keep Communist China out. Moreover, the United States provided large amounts of military and economic aid to Taiwan, its U-2 spy planes flew over mainland China, and its Seventh Fleet patroled the Taiwan Strait, although the neutralization of the strait by the Seventh Fleet was officially terminated after the Korean War.

As the war in Vietnam heated up, U.S. relations with China continued to be hostile with many American leaders and most of the American public seeing North Vietnam as a satellite of the Russians and/or the Chinese. More perceptive observers and most of the State Department policymakers whom I knew, as the war escalated in Vietnam, realized that North Vietnam was obtaining aid from both China and the Soviet Union, and playing them off against each other. Meanwhile, the U.S. policy of isolating China as well as Chinese propaganda attacks against the United States continued, and there appeared to be little chance under President Nixon to improve relations.

THE SINO-SOVIET SPLIT

Chinese nationalism, along with its nuclear weapons policy, had a major impact on China's relationship with the Soviet Union. The Chinese Communist leaders resented how Soviet Communist advisors had tried to dominate them during the 1920s. At that time there had been factional conflicts between the Chinese

Communists, and particularly between a group led by Mao and one by Moscow. Mao had built his appeal on Chinese nationalism, and his ideas had come into conflict frequently with policies of Soviet Communist advisors, whose goal had been to strengthen Moscow as the center of world Communism and support those Chinese who looked to Moscow for advice.

President Chiang Kaishek exercised de facto control of the government of China by the mid-1920s after fighting with Communists and purging them from his party while battling the Chinese warlords. Chiang's running battle with Communist forces under Mao forced them into the Long March of the 1930s.

In 1936 Chiang was kidnapped by Communist sympathizers in Sian in western China, but after a strong message from Moscow, the Chinese Communist leaders, over Mao's objection, released Chiang and agreed to cooperate with him in fighting the Japanese. Stalin's nationalist motive was to build an anti-Japanese coalition in China that would keep the Japanese armies occupied and reduce the Japanese threat to Siberia. Stalin at that time was worried about the growing power of Hitler and did not want to divert troops to defend Siberia from Japan, which was allied with Germany.

Since World War II there have been periods of close cooperation between the Soviet Union and the Chinese Communists, but most of the time since the

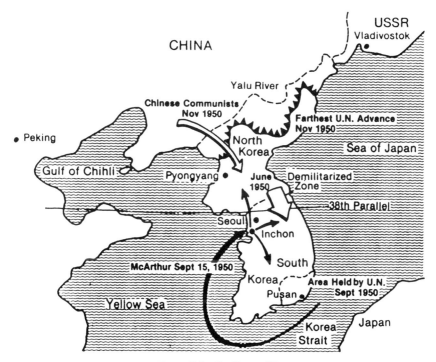

Figure 7-1 The Korean War.

formation of the Peoples' Republic of China in 1949 has been characterized by strife. At the close of World War II the Soviets were preoccupied in getting better access to the Pacific through control of railroads in Manchuria and concessions in Port Arthur. For this reason and with U.S. encouragement, they completed a treaty of friendship with Chiang Kaishek's Nationalist government. However, after the Soviet Union accepted the surrender of the Japanese troops in 1945 in Manchuria, the Russians secretly handed over surrendered arms to Chinese Communist forces under Mao. Thus the Soviets were getting concessions from the official Chinese government and taking out insurance by supporting the Communist rebels.

The period after 1949 following the victory of the Chinese Communist forces was the high point of Sino-Soviet cooperation. The Soviets were the first to recognize the new Chinese Communist government that was set up in 1949 after Chiang Kaishek and his remaining forces fled to Taiwan. The Soviets even refused to participate in U.N. Security Council meetings in 1950 until after the outbreak of the Korean War, because the Chinese Nationalist government still represented China in the Security Council. This was a tactical error since it permitted the Western powers led by the United States to mobilize the Security Council quickly to oppose the aggression of North Korea against South Korea. Since North Korea had been occupied by the Soviet Union after World War II, had numerous Soviet advisors, and had been heavily supplied with Soviet arms and equipment, it was clear that Soviet leaders had approved the invasion. The Soviets, however, carefully avoided involving their troops in the Korean War.

From December 1949 to February 1950 Mao Zedong visited Moscow. During this visit he agreed to Kim Il Sung's plan to attack South Korea (Khrushchev 1970, 271–272). The Sino-Soviet Treaty of Friendship and Assistance was revised so that if either state was attacked by Japan "or any State allied with it," the other partner would immediately render military and other assistance "by all means at its disposal." This extended defensive coverage of the treaty against an attack by the United States, which was allied with Japan. When China felt itself threatened as the U.N. forces led by General MacArthur approached the Yalu River boundary between Korea and China, hundreds of thousands of Chinese came across the Yalu to drive back the U.S. and U.N. troops. China saw its action as protecting its borders, but it was pulling Russian chestnuts out of the fire by preventing a defeat of Russia's North Korea protégé. China was covered in the new treaty by the Russian guarantee of assistance if the United States had attacked China. Truman prevented the danger of extending the war by strict orders not to attack Manchuria, which was being used by the Chinese as a base for their attack. The controversy over this decision led to his firing of General MacArthur.

The North Korean attack on South Korea in June 1950 had a far-reaching effect on the power politics of the Far East. President Truman interpreted the open aggression of North Korea as a move by the Communist powers to expand their influence by aggression, and he mobilized U.N. support around the concept of collective security. Many nations responded and the aggression was repelled after a bitter and costly war. The Korean War and its implied threat to weak nations also helped consolidate the NATO alliance by encouraging the rearming of Germany.

President Eisenhower and Secretary of State John Foster Dulles created a series of formal alliances around the periphery of the two Communist giants to deter future aggression of this type. The treaty system against China included the alliance with Japan (1951), Korea (1958), the Republic of China on Taiwan (1954), and the SEATO, or Southeast Asian Collective Defense Treaty (1954), which included the United States, Australia, Britain, France, New Zealand, Pakistan, the Philippines, and Thailand. The treaty texts were similar to the NATO pact, but the Asian treaties have not come close to NATO in the strength of commitments (see Figure 8-1, p. 172).

In the early 1950s the Soviet Union provided hundreds of millions of dollars of aid through loans, grants, and technical assistance to Communist China. The Soviet steel and machinery plants were the basis of industrialization in the first five-year plan for China, which permitted the Chinese to rebuild their industry after the terrible destruction of the civil war. Early in 1955 the Soviet Union began assisting the People's Republic of China in nuclear energy through providing an experimental reactor and training scientists at Dubna in the Soviet Union. China, in fact, helped finance this major nuclear research center. By October 1957 China had made an agreement with the Soviet Union to eventually provide China with a sample atomic bomb and technical data for its manufacture (*Peking Review* 1963, 14; Halperin 1965, 79–80; Rice 1974; Khrushchev 1974, 306).

Also in 1957 the Soviet Union tested its first intercontinental missile, and on October 4 it put Sputnik I into orbit. The Americans were dismayed and the Chinese were delighted. Mao journeyed to the Soviet Union in November 1957 to celebrate the 40th anniversary of the revolution. In his speech at the Moscow airport he praised Soviet achievements in space, thanked them for their generous assistance, and stated that "there is no force on earth which can separate us" (Schram 1969, 436). Soon thereafter, in a meeting with a group of Chinese students studying in Russia, Mao stated that the launching of the Russian satellite marked a turning point in the struggle between the socialist and communist camps and that now the "East wind prevails over the west wind" (*Peking Review* 9/6/63, 7–16; Griffith 1964, 371–387).

In this speech Mao said that the Communist countries would not be the first to unleash a nuclear war, but if one were started by the imperialists and "worse came to worst and half of mankind died, the other half would remain while imperialism would be razed to the ground and the whole world would become socialist. Then the victorious people would very swiftly create on the ruins of imperialism a civilization thousands of times higher than the capitalist system and a truly beautiful future for themselves." He put this position more crudely during the conference in terms of the Chinese producing more babies. Implications of these statements were profoundly disturbing to Soviet leaders and foreign observers (Khrushchev 1970, 290–291).

At this time the Chinese were secretly asking for a sample of a nuclear bomb, but the Soviets stalled. This was a reasonable position on their part; even the United States does not turn over nuclear weapons to its allies without retaining ultimate control over their use.

In 1957 most experts and observers perceived the Sino-Soviet alliance as solid, cemented not only by the leaders' Communist ideology, which saw Communist countries threatened by a hostile capitalist world led by the United States, but also cemented by economic interests, in which the strong Soviet heavy machinery capacity could help Communist China build a base for industries paid for by Chinese shipments of raw materials. Even without this ideological and economic cement, they could have allied on strictly balance of power terms against the United States. However, within two years this unity was to be shattered, and experts are still not agreed on the principal reasons for the split. The cracks started to show during the 1958 offshore islands crisis after Mao's "East wind–West wind" speech.

In August 1958 Communist China started a heavy bombardment of the offshore islands located a few miles from the mainland of China but still held by Taiwan. During this period the American press carried stories of the U.S. military build-up in the Taiwan area including nuclear capabilities. American naval ships helped convoy supply ships up to the last three miles of territorial waters of the offshore islands with Chinese Nationalist forces under fire taking the supplies the rest of the way.

On September 6, 1958, Premier Chou Enlai announced that Communist China had no desire for war with the United States and proposed a resumption of the Sino-American ambassadorial talks in Warsaw. The following day Khrushchev for the first time intervened with a statement that an attack on the People's Republic of China would be regarded as an attack on the Soviet Union. On September 19, in an even stronger stand in a formal note to the United States, the Soviets stated that "our side" also has nuclear weapons—a reply to reports in the U.S. press that nuclear weapons might be used to defend the offshore islands (*NYT* 9/20/58, 1). Years later when the Chinese Communists and Soviets were trading abuse and referring to the offshore island crisis, the Chinese asserted that the Khrushchev statements were too late to do any good; nevertheless, the Chinese did not suspend bombardment of the offshore islands until October 1958, a month after the Soviet statements of support were made.

Many analysts take the Chinese assertions about Khrushchev's statements at face value, but in view of the propagandistic nature of the later exchanges that occurred in the 1960s, it is reasonable to assume that the Chinese were attempting to minimize the Soviet statements of support in 1958. This is supported by the fact that on January 28, 1959, Premier Zhou Enlai referred to the "unbreakable unity" of the Communists, the "correct leadership" of Comrade

Khrushchev, and the "fraternal assistance" of the Soviet Union (*Peking Review* 2/3/59, 6). In February 1959 the two countries signed a long-term trade agreement including technical assistance, which was their largest economic agreement to that date (*Peking Review* 2/10/59. 12). In retrospect the Soviet support during the offshore island crisis of 1958 risking a nuclear confrontation with the United States was impressive despite China's later belittling of that support.

In any event, the Chinese Communists did not attempt to cash in on the offer of Soviet nuclear support of September 1958, and on October 5, 1958, they announced a one-week cease-fire, which was later changed to shelling the islands on odd-numbered days. The islands in 1978 were still subjected to bombardment with propaganda shells, but in 1979 this ended after the United States recognized China.

By the middle of 1959 Sino-Soviet relations were fractured when in June the Soviet Union secretly tore up the agreement on "new technology" for national defense and refused to provide China with a sample of a nuclear bomb and technical data concerning its manufacture (Griffith 1964, 351; *Peking Review* 8/16/63, 12). In October Khrushchev attacked economic policies of the Great Leap Forward and "arrogant" leaders in the Chinese Communist camp. These Soviet actions occurred at the time Mao was purging the top military leader, Peng Teh-huai, who was friendly with Moscow.

By July 1960 tensions and pressures had developed to such a point that Khrushchev abruptly terminated the Soviet economic aid agreement, and he recalled all 1390 Soviet scientists and technicians from China within a few weeks. Trade was cut back. The effect on the Chinese economy was disastrous because ambitious plans of the Chinese had depended on imports of Russian capital, equipment, and technical advice. This, joined with abortive economic policies of the Great Leap Forward and a poor harvest, led to a Chinese depression.

The next crisis in Sino-Soviet relations occurred after 1963 following the negotiation of the partial nuclear test ban treaty, and when the dust had settled, Khrushchev had been deposed. At the end of 1962 the Soviets informed the Chinese of their intention to negotiate a nuclear test ban treaty with the United States. The Chinese were furious since one of the articles of the treaty, which was ratified in 1963, foreclosed Soviet nuclear weapons assistance to other nations such as the Chinese.

The Chinese pressed forward with the development of their own nuclear arsenal and on October 16, 1964, exploded their first atomic device. Significantly, a few days before this Khrushchev had been deposed, and one of the accusations against him by the Central Committee was "hare-brained scheming." In the Communist dictionary this could have covered plans for a preemptive strike against China (Rice 1974, 474).

Chinese nuclear weapons progress accelerated after the first test. On October 27, 1966, the Chinese Communists fired a medium-range missile with a nuclear warhead, and on June 17, 1967, they exploded their first hydrogen bomb. The

Soviets countered with moving strategic missile units into Mongolia, within range of the area where the Chinese carried out their tests (Rice 1974, 475).

The dispute in 1969 entered a critical phase that later led directly to the Chinese move for détente with the United States. During this period reports circulated in the press and among the Communist parties of Europe that the Soviet Union was seriously considering a strike against China to forestall its developing fusion weapons that could threaten European Russia. It is even reported that the Soviet Union approached the United States in 1969 to explore what its attitude would be if the Soviet Union carried out such a strike, but that the United States discouraged it (Hinton 1975, 108; Kissinger 1979, 183–186). This was soon after the Soviets led an invasion to put down a liberalization tendency in Czechoslovakia and announced the Brezhnev Doctrine, proclaiming the right of the Soviet Union and its allies to intervene when "socialism was in danger." In the latter part of 1969 the Chinese carried out more tests of thermonuclear weapons culminating in the successful test in December 1969.

On August 28, 1969, a *Pravda* editorial stated, "The military arsenals of the Maoists are filling up with all the latest weapons, and a war, should it break out in present day conditions, what with existing weapons and lethal armaments and modern means of delivery, would not spare a single continent."

A Soviet weekly at the same time was claiming the Chinese were building fortifications in Manchuria for war with the Soviet Union. It accused the Chinese of a reckless, adventurous policy and warned that "any attempts to speak with the Soviet Union in the language of arms to encroach on the interest of the Soviet people, which is building Communism, will meet with a firm rebuff." It added that the "Chinese people are being alerted for possible nuclear war and border clashes are part of a chain of hostile actions by the Peking leadership which does not cease its absurd territorial claims on the Soviet Union" (*NYT* 8/29/59, 1, 4).

The Chinese retort in October accused the Soviet Union of intending to launch a nuclear war against China. They stated that they would never be intimidated by threats and that there would be war should a "handful of maniacs dare to raid China's strategic sites in defiance of world opinion." It is clear that Chinese leaders saw Soviet statements as threats of a preemptive strike, and that the dispute over nuclear weapons was at the heart of the split. A few months later on December 18, 1979, Mao indicated to Edgar Snow, a reporter, the desire to have conversations with President Nixon. This was an important statement that cleared the way for détente (Snow 1971, 47).

Historians and political scientists continue to debate the many other issues underlying the Soviet split with China. Many observers stress competition for leadership of the world Communist movement. The Soviet Union, after the Great October Revolution of 1919, saw itself as the leader of the socialist camp. Mao Zedong and the Chinese Communists, however, also aspired to lead the world Communist movement. Both sides have competed for influence in Vietnam, Laos, Cambodia, and many of the Communist parties of the world. Moreover, there have been numerous border disputes and clashes along the 5000-mile border between the Soviet Union and China. Major Soviet and Chinese military forces faced each other along this border (Ginsberg 1978). There was also friction between two proud and powerful leaders, particularly after Mao's "East wind–West wind" overtures to Khrushchev in Moscow were rejected. However, the failure of the Soviet Union to carry through on the commitment to help China develop nuclear weapons was at the center of the break.

THE OPEN DOOR TO THE UNITED STATES AND THE WEST

The events described prepared the way for the historic reconciliation of China and the United States. An incredulous world received the announcement on July 15, 1971, that President Nixon had sent Henry Kissinger to Peking to meet with Premier Chou Enlai on July 9–11. The amazement continued when President Nixon visited Peking February 21–28, 1972, with full coverage by the news media. As already noted, it appears that the Chinese invitation was motivated by their fear of the Soviet threat to their northern border and of a Soviet nuclear strike.

The February 1972 communiqué established the basic framework for "normalization" of relations between the United States and the People's Republic of China. The dilemma of reconciling basically different ideologies and views toward Taiwan and toward Far Eastern policies in general was finessed in the Shanghai Communiqué, by setting forth in diplomatic language each side's view of these issues, and then indicating agreement on some general principles and disagreement on others. The areas of agreement included a desire to work toward "normalization" of relations, to reduce the danger of war, and not to seek "hegemony" in Asia. The Chinese side stated the Communist line that the nations want liberation and the people want revolution as an irresistible trend of history and that the Chinese firmly support the oppressed—including the people of Vietnam, Laos, and Cambodia. The United States in the communiqué made it clear that it wanted a negotiated solution to the Vietnam problem and that it would maintain its close ties and support for the Republic of Korea, its friendly relations with Japan, and that it wanted a peaceful settlement of the Taiwan question by the Chinese themselves.

On July 1, 1977, President Carter reaffirmed the Shanghai Communiqué and stated that he hoped the United States could work out an agreement with China for "full diplomatic relations" and still make sure of maintaining the "peaceful lives of the Taiwanese" (*Washington Post* 7/1/77, A12). Intensive and secret negotiations with the Chinese were carried out in 1978, and at the end of the year Carter announced that the United States would establish full diplomatic relations with the People's Republic of China on January 1, 1979, while breaking off diplomatic relations with Taiwan. He also announced U.S. intentions of abrogating the mutual defense treaty with Taiwan in one year, in accordance with the termination clause of the treaty. The Chinese request to terminate it immediately had been the sticking point in the secret talks, and the new Chinese government, apparently controlled by Deng Xiaoping, had finally yielded to permit a one-year notice of termination. Carter persuaded Congress to approve the new relationship, which created a nondiplomatic office in Taiwan. The Taiwan issue was the most sensitive in the new arrangements for China. After a difficult negotiation, President Reagan approved a compromise on the arms-to-Taiwan issue by agreeing to a communiqué by which the United States expected a gradual reduction of arms sales to Taiwan, with the ultimate objective of ending them.

Later, President Reagan, the most hardline anti-Communist president in the post–World War II era, confirmed the new diplomatic relations with China in a visit to Beijing. Even the U.S. congressional members who were the strongest supporters of the Nationalist regime on Taiwan realized that their fight against the new U.S. China policy was over.

China strengthened its new open door policy by welcoming tourists, inviting U.S. and other foreign experts to teach and to train Chinese workers, and encouraging businesses to establish joint enterprises in China. By 1989 there were 40,000 Chinese students studying in the United States, and the United States relaxed controls on exports even of "defensive" military items.

China reinforced the new moderate open door policy in a treaty with Great Britain providing for the return of Hong Kong in 1997 at the expiration of the lease of that territory. The arrangement guaranteed the continuation of Hong Kong's social system, defined as capitalism, for 50 more years. China made it clear that this was an inducement for Taiwan to reunite with the mainland under similar conditions, and it offered to allow Taiwan to reunite with the mainland while keeping a military force but giving up control of foreign policy. The Taiwan regime refused because it had not given up on its ultimate goal to represent all of China.

As the permanent member of the Security Council, the new China played a constructive role in the United Nations. It condemned Soviet aggression in Afghanistan and called for the withdrawal of Vietnamese troops from Kampuchea. China continued its normalization of relations with the Soviet Union on resolving these issues. It also condemned U.S. support for CIA attacks against Nicaragua and the U.S. invasion of Grenada. Although China supported Security Council Resolution 598 calling for an end of the Iran-Iraq War, the Chinese military continued to sell missiles and military equipment to Iran and Iraq presumably to get hard currency for strengthening the Chinese military. Until the suppression of the Tiananmen demonstrations in 1989, its prestige was high and most countries of the world periodically beat a path to Beijing to reinforce diplomatic relations with a future superpower.

China's open door policy of increasing ties to the West created a new balance of power in Asia and in the world. The new balance of power strengthened China's position in Asia and attracted Western technology. For the United States

(a)

(b)

Figure 7-2   (*a*) Deng Xiaoping and Vice President Bush in Beijing, 1983 (Courtesy: *Beijing Review*). (*b*) Mikhail Gorbachev, Deng Xiaoping, and Raisa Gorbachev in Beijing, 1989 (Courtesy: *Beijing Review*).

the new relationship ended a threat of a resumption of a hostile Chinese-Soviet alliance.

AFTERMATH OF THE TIANANMEN TRAGEDY

By the summer of 1989 there was major progress toward solving the three blocks to normalization of relations with Russia—withdrawal of Soviet troops from Afghanistan, withdrawal of North Vietnamese troops from Kampuchea, and negotiation of border issues—and Deng and Gorbachev met formally toward this end. The student demonstrations at that time distracted the world's attention from this reconciliation and to some extent lessened its impact.

In June 1989 China's brutal suppression of student demonstrations at Tiananmen Square seriously threatened U.S.–China détente. The U.S. news media and Congress reacted indignantly, calling for harsh sanctions against the government. President Bush, however, a former ambassador to China, settled for relatively minor moves, including the suspension of military sales and high-level military visits. Bush indicated geopolitical considerations were important as well as those of human rights. The Soviet Union's reaction was a mild expression of disapproval.

The Chinese actions against the demonstrations threw cold water on the developing affair between China and the United States and forced it and other countries to take a more realistic view of the Chinese government. In terms of geopolitics there seemed to be little chance of a renewal of the hostile alliance of the Soviet Union and China like that of the early 1950s. Meanwhile, Gorbachev continued the détente with China and the West, and his popularity abroad soared, although at home it was threatened by strikes and ethnic unrest.

In December 1989 President Bush sent senior U.S. officials to Beijing to lift the ban on high-level visits. This triggered widespread criticism in the United States for "selling out" to the Chinese hardliners and undermining U.S. support for democratic reforms in Eastern Europe. China's subsequent gesture of lifting martial law did not appease many critics.

In May 1991 Jiang Zemin visited Moscow, the first visit by the head of the Chinese Communist Party since 1957. The visit produced an agreement on the eastern sector of the border, including demilitarization of the frontier, and China also extended a credit of $730 million. Also in 1991 in the wake of an agreement on Cambodia, Beijing and Hanoi renewed their ties. This was a concluding action to end what had been a perceived threat from the Soviet encirclement around Chinese borders arising from the China–Soviet border dispute, the war in Afghanistan, the war in Cambodia, and the Soviet–Vietnam alliance.

In the United Nations, the Chinese took actions consistent with international law in condemning Iraq's invasion of Kuwait, but called for further negotiations. China abstained on the U.N. resolution to use force against Iraq. The abstention was attained after strong pressure from the United States not to veto the resolution. China also cooperated to limit the power of the Khmer Rouge in the U.N.-brokered agreements on Cambodia and in other U.N. actions.

The most sensitive issue in U.S. relations with China continued to be the U.S. attitude toward Taiwan. Normalization of relations had been bought with President Carter's renunciation of the U.S. mutual defense treaty with Taiwan. Taiwan is regarded by Chinese leaders as a rebel regime, and continued arms sales to Taiwan had threatened the new relationship under the Reagan administration. Secretary of State Haig, with considerable effort, had managed a compromise communiqué with China stating that it was the ultimate intention of the United States to end those arms sales, and meanwhile the United States would gradually reduce them.

This compromise held for 10 years until the U.S. political campaign in 1992, when President Bush announced approval of a $6 billion sale to Taiwan of fighter jets, which are manufactured in Texas, one of the swing states in the 1992 presidential election. This would be a massive increase over past sales of military equipment. The presidential approval came during a trade dispute in which Congress was trying to end most-favored national treatment of China, and both sides were threatening to raise tariffs. Members of Congress, under fire from the news media, found it easy to criticize China for human rights abuses arising from Tiananmen and to threaten to end most-favored-nation (MFN) trade treatment.

The Democrats were leading the denunciations of China and criticizing Bush for being too lenient, so the new Clinton administration was expected to continue pressure. Friendship with China was no longer a strong card for the United States to play against the Soviet Union in the cold war, which had ended. China did have a veto in the United Nations, however, and the dispute threatened to end China's cooperation in the Security Council, which had allowed the U.N. Security Council to function effectively in the years after Gorbachev came to power. The dispute could also close the door that had opened for tens of thousands of Chinese students in the United States and could discourage the many commercial contacts that had developed. Bush's move was highly political, disregarding what the Chinese and others regarded as an international agreement about Taiwan.

The final chapter examines the relationship of the open door policies and glasnost to the democratic revolutions in the Communist world. The following chapters look at developments in other Communist states that were strongly influenced by China and the Soviet Union.

Chapter 8

Asian Communist States and Their Wars

There have been four major international wars in Asia started by the Communist nations since World War II. These were not anticolonial wars or internal revolutions, as pictured by Communist propaganda, but aggression as defined under international law. There is a difference of opinion about the Vietnam War, which is discussed below, but that, too, in the last phase was an international war. Following is an account of these wars, of the nature of the Communist societies that supported them, and of the ideological and power factors that determined their outcome. After the wars ended and the Eastern European empire had collapsed, Mongolia also emerged from under the shadow of Soviet domination.

KIM IL SUNG'S NORTH KOREA

At the beginning of the century Russia and Japan were competing to take control of all of Korea. In the 1904–1905 war Japan won and later made Korea a colony. Japan suppressed the nationalist movement, but in the 1930s the Korean nationalists formed an anti-Japanese movement led by Syngman Rhee. An ardent Korean nationalist, Rhee had received an M.A. at Harvard and a Ph.D. at Princeton.

During World War II the United States was anxious to get the Soviet Union into the war against Japan. Russia had maintained neutrality with Japan not wanting to fight a war on two fronts. So at Potsdam in 1945, as part of the agreement for the Soviet Union to fight Japanese troops in Manchuria and Korea, the United States agreed that the USSR would occupy North Korea after the war and the United States would occupy South Korea—south of the 38th parallel.

At the end of World War II, Kim Il Sung and his followers arrived in North Korea along with Soviet troops. Kim was born in 1912 in Korea near Pyongyang. He had joined the Russian army during the war as a guerilla fighter in Manchuria, and had risen to the rank of major. He spent a month looking over the situation, and then on October 10 he organized the North Korean Central Bureau of the Korean Communist Party. The leader of the local Communist

Party was conveniently assassinated after he met with Soviet and Communist leaders. The assassin was never apprehended.

In 1946 a single Democratic National Front was formed of organizations cooperating with the Soviets. The Front, of course, was dominated by the Communists. Kim purged the Communist Party of non-Communist elements by arresting or assassinating the opposition. During this period about 2 million refugees fled to South Korea from the north. This is similar to the pattern of mass flights, after the Communists took over in Eastern Europe, from Cuba, from China to Hong Kong, and from North to South Vietnam.

The United States and the Soviet Union could not reach agreement on a unified occupation and government for Korea, so in 1947 the United States turned the problem over to the U.N. General Assembly. The General Assembly adopted a resolution stating that elections should be held in Korea to form a government. A U.N. commission made up of states that were not superpowers was formed to supervise the election that was set for 1948. North Korea refused to admit U.N. representatives, so they supervised the election in the south. Syngman Rhee and his party won, and the General Assembly declared South Korea as the only lawful government in Korea. This did not imply that it had authority over the north.

The Soviet Union withdrew its forces in 1948 and the United States withdrew its forces in June 1949 leaving only 500 officers in a Military Assistance and Advisory Group (MAAG). Kim Il Sung became premier of the new Democratic People's Republic that was established in the north when the Soviet forces left. At the beginning of 1990 he was still in control.

The Korean War that broke out in 1950 had a major impact on U.S. foreign policy for a generation. It not only brought about a war and confrontation between the United States and China, but it stimulated a system of alliances designed to prevent Communist expansion in Asia and prepared the way for the United States to take part in the Vietnam War.

North Korea's open aggression challenged the principles of collective security of the U.N. Charter. An unusually frank and apparently genuine account of the planning for the war is given in Khrushchev's memoirs. He states that he was transferred from the Ukraine to Moscow at the end of 1949, and Kim Il Sung arrived to consult with Stalin. Kim said that "the North Koreans wanted to prod South Korea with the point of a bayonet" (a Leninist metaphor). He anticipated that the first poke would touch off an internal explosion in South Korea and that the "power of the people" would prevail. Khrushchev continued that, naturally, Stalin could not oppose the idea because it appealed to his conviction that this would be an internal matter that the Koreans would settle among themselves. The idea also appealed to Khrushchev because the North Koreans wanted to give a helping hand to their brethren who were under the heel of Syngman Rhee. Stalin told Kim to go home and come up with a more concrete plan. Kim later returned to Moscow and assured Stalin of the plan's success. Khrushchev explains that Stalin believed if the war were fought swiftly, U.S. intervention could be avoided. Khrushchev adds that no real Communist would have tried to dissuade Kim Il Sung from his compelling desire to liberate South Korea from reactionary U.S. influence. To have done so, Khrushchev said, would have "contradicted the Communist view of the world."

Mao Zedong was also in Moscow during Kim's initial trip and supported Kim's plan. Mao, according to Khrushchev, also was of the opinion that the United States would not intervene since the war was an internal matter. At a dinner with these leaders, Khrushchev reported that Kim said that Korea with this move would get agricultural products in the South such as fish, rice, and other food to combine with the raw materials for the Korean industry from the north.

Khrushchev then related how the plans did not go as hoped. First, the internal uprisings did not materialize. Then the MacArthur landing in Inchon near Seoul cut off the North Korean forces, which at that time had reached the tip of South Korea. MacArthur's surprise counterattack completely changed the character of the war (see Figure 7-1, p. 157). At this point, Khrushchev says, after the Americans began to move north, Zhou Enlai appeared in Moscow to discuss what to do. At first, the opinion was that it was fruitless to intervene, but then it was agreed in Moscow that China should give support to North Korea in order to save the situation from disaster.

Note the following points: (1) Kim Il Sung initiated the attack, (2) Stalin and Mao supported the attack "as good Communists," (3) by Khrushchev's admission there was not substantial support in the south, and (4) the USSR and China agreed on the Chinese intervention but Stalin was strongly against direct Soviet participation.

With U.N. observers as well as the world press to report on the North Korean attack, there was no doubt that North Korea had started the war. The United States took it to the Security Council. The USSR was absent because it objected to having the Republic of China (Taiwan) there instead of the People's Republic of China, which it had pledged to support. The Soviet Union's absence made it easier for the United States to mobilize support from members of the United Nations.

Later that year, after MacArthur's counterattack, the Chinese "volunteers" attacked suddenly and drove the U.N. forces back to a bloody stalemate along the 38th parallel. The Chinese soldiers were not volunteers—that title was used to avoid China formally waging war against the United States.* The bloody fighting lasted along the 38th parallel until the armistice in 1953.

The main issue of negotiating a truce concerned the prisoners of war. In the

---

*As one of a group of foreign experts in the fall of 1986, I was invited to stay overnight at a crack infantry division's headquarters, about 60 miles south of Beijing. We were shown around the camp and I was able to observe maps displayed of their campaigns, which included fighting in the Korean War.

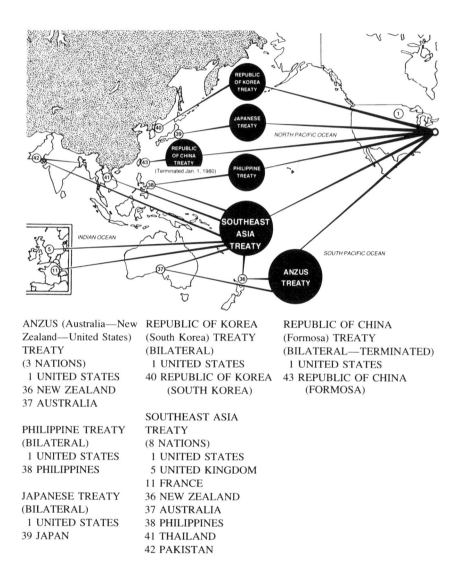

ANZUS (Australia—New Zealand—United States) TREATY
(3 NATIONS)
  1 UNITED STATES
 36 NEW ZEALAND
 37 AUSTRALIA

PHILIPPINE TREATY
(BILATERAL)
  1 UNITED STATES
 38 PHILIPPINES

JAPANESE TREATY
(BILATERAL)
  1 UNITED STATES
 39 JAPAN

REPUBLIC OF KOREA
(South Korea) TREATY
(BILATERAL)
  1 UNITED STATES
 40 REPUBLIC OF KOREA
    (SOUTH KOREA)

SOUTHEAST ASIA
TREATY
(8 NATIONS)
  1 UNITED STATES
  5 UNITED KINGDOM
 11 FRANCE
 36 NEW ZEALAND
 37 AUSTRALIA
 38 PHILIPPINES
 41 THAILAND
 42 PAKISTAN

REPUBLIC OF CHINA
(Formosa) TREATY
(BILATERAL—TERMINATED)
  1 UNITED STATES
 43 REPUBLIC OF CHINA
    (FORMOSA)

Figure 8-1   United States collective defense arrangements in Asia.

course of the fighting, the U.N. forces captured 25,000 Chinese and North Koreans. President Truman did not want to force them to go back to Communism and insisted on their being allowed to make a choice. The North Korean and Chinese commands insisted on their unconditional return. After long negotiations in the United Nations, it was finally agreed that a neutral commission would interview them. Just after this decision was reached, Syngman Rhee ordered the prisoners released, and they faded into the South Korean countryside. This solution strangely enough was probably more acceptable to the Communists than the interviews, since they would have lost face with prisoners refusing to return. Eventually more than 20,000 of these prisoners, of which two-thirds were Chinese, were settled in countries of their choice (United Nations 1968, 32). The free choice of many of the prisoners to settle outside their country raises serious questions about the commitment of peasant soldiers to war and to the Communist ideology. The truce was signed July 27, 1953, but there has been no peace treaty between the two Koreas since then.

The effect of the war was disastrous. Almost 3 million North and South Koreans were killed, including 1 million civilians (Sivard 1991, 31). There was a tremendous job of reconstruction in the capital of South Korea, which was fought over four times since it is close to the border. North Korea was devastated by bombing. It received considerable aid from China and the Soviet Union in rebuilding its economy, including over $600 million in gifts. There have been no major clashes since the end of the war, but there have been serious incidents along the truce lines and terrorist incidents instigated by the North Koreans.

An important result of the war was to convince many doubters that Communism was a world movement led by the Soviet Union that would take advantage of weakness and that arms and alliances were the only effective way to contain Communist aggression. The reaction to the war gave strong political support to NATO and to U.S. alliances with Asian Communist countries. A few years after the war started the United States concluded alliances with Japan (1951), the Philippines (1952), Australia and New Zealand (1952), Korea (1953), and the Republic of China (1954). In 1954 the United States negotiated the SEATO Treaty, which included Britain, France, Australia, New Zealand, the Philippines, Pakistan, and Thailand and also a commitment to protect Vietnam, Laos, and Cambodia if they were the object of Communist aggression (see Figure 8-1). This consolidation of the cold war delayed the U.S. détente with China about two decades.

The failure to establish peace between North and South Korea and the North Korean probes against the south heightened tension in the area. In the 1970s the U.S. forces still stationed on the 38th parallel discovered elaborate tunnels dug under the border. The obvious purpose was to infiltrate raiders and terrorists to the south. There have been periodic incidents involving the capture and killing of U.S. soldiers who closely patrol the border and Panmunjon, where representatives of the two forces meet periodically to snarl at each other. In October 1983 North Korean terrorists infiltrated Burma and killed 17 including four South Korean cabinet officers on a friendship tour of the country. Two of the North Korean terrorists were apprehended by Burmese authorities and sentenced to death after their confessions. In November 1987 two South Korean terrorists, later captured by the Japanese, planted a bomb that destroyed a South Korean passenger plane in the Indian Ocean. One confessed to North Korea's instigation of the attack.

Tensions rose again as South Korea hosted the Olympic Games in the summer of 1988. North Korea refused to accept the consolation of hosting only four events, and there was fear that it would try to disrupt the Games by further terrorist incidents. In this atmosphere, talks about negotiating peace and eventual reunification made little headway.

Kim Il Sung had personal responsibility for these events. He used the Communist Party structure to consolidate a personal dictatorship of himself and family members. He was secretary-general of the Communist Party (Workers' Party of Korea), president of the supreme body of state power, the Central People's Committee, which directs the work of the executive branch, commander in chief of the armed forces, and chairman of the National Defense Commission. There were pictures and statues of Kim Il Sung all over Korea, which reminded outside observers of the personality cults of Stalin and Mao. Although Kim Il Sung exercised close to absolute power, there was evidence of below-the-surface opposition to his family's privileges that threatened his aim to have his son, Kim Chong-Il, accepted as his successor.

The constitution of the Democratic People's Republic of Korea asserts that the government was formed on the basis of the worker-peasant alliance led by the working class. It claims, therefore, to represent the whole Korean people and not just the working class. The guiding principle is *chuch'e*, which means self-reliance in politics, economics, and national defense. This philosophy is reflected in the relative isolation of North Korea from the rest of the world, reflected by a low volume of foreign trade.

The Communist Party of North Korea emphasizes propaganda and indoctrination. Its membership of 3 million or about 16 percent of the population is a greater proportion than in any other Communist nation. However, the party had little power. The supreme organ, the Party Congress, was convened only three times between 1961 and 1980.

At the end of 1990 North Korea, by implementing its policy of *chuch'e*, had become one of the most isolated and reactionary of the Communist regimes. Economically it had fallen far behind with a standard of living variously estimated at only one-half to one-fifth that of South Korea. North Korea started out with a focus on heavy industry using obsolete Soviet equipment, and that had not been modernized. It suffered from severe electricity shortages and brownout. In 1990 and 1991 the shortage was particularly harsh since coal production had fallen because of flooded mines. What little foreign trade it had was oriented toward the Soviet Union. It was delinquent on the few foreign loans it did obtain.

It was as reactionary politically as it was economically. Kim Il Sung had used the Communist system to build a family dictatorship that was grooming his son to be his successor. The news media were strictly controlled, and children and young adults were forced to attend indoctrination camps. Christians and Buddhists were persecuted. In 1990 it is estimated that there were more than 100,000 political prisoners. Apparently fearing the effects of exposure to pro-democracy ideas of the revolutions in Eastern Europe, North Korea recalled about 2000 North Korean ambassadors and officials from there in 1990 and scattered students and officials to remote provincial areas (Freedom House 1990–1991).

In 1991 North Korea, reacting to pressure from the Soviet Union and China, started to break out of its Communist cocoon. For years North Korea had opposed the idea of two Koreas, and the Soviet Union and China had cooperated by blocking South Korea's admission to the United Nations. In 1991 both governments increased their commercial dealings with South Korea and informed North Korea that they would no longer veto the admission of South Korea into the United Nations. North Korea, not wanting to give the South that advantage, also agreed to join. Both were admitted on July 8. Over North Korean objections the Soviet Union announced on October 1 that it would resume formal diplomatic relations with South Korea.

In 1988 North Korea had agreed to a series of interparliamentary and official tasks with the south, but they made little progress until 1991. In October the two sides finally agreed to end hostilities, respect each other's political and economic systems, and conduct trade and economic exchanges.

In 1992 North Korea's drive to make nuclear weapons remained a serious obstacle to normalization of relations with the outside world. Although its standard of living was low, North Korea, like other Communist regimes, devoted the best of its scarce resources to the military. With only half the population of South Korea, North Korea had more men in the armed forces. North Korea used its scarce engineering resources to build nuclear fuel plants, reportedly capable of producing weapons-grade plutonium. In 1986 it had signed the nuclear nonproliferation treaty, but it refused to allow inspection of its plants until U.S. nuclear weapons were removed from South Korea. In September 1991 the United States complied in connection with its withdrawal of tactical nuclear weapons from Europe. The United States also cancelled the annual military exercise along the border of the two states.

Japan, the United States, and other nations refused to resume normal economic and political relations with North Korea until it met its commitment for inspection of its nuclear facilities by the International Atomic Energy Agency (IAEA). On April 15, 1992, Kim Il Sung's birthday, North Korean television showed the three plants and announced that they would be opened for inspection from the outside. Kim Il Sung made a similar statement in an interview with the *Washington Times* (*AP* 4/16/92). In May it handed over to the IAEA an inventory of its nuclear processing facilities, but American intelligence sources suspected North Korea of holding back information on secret sites (*Economist* 5/6/92, 42).

Superficial reports indicated that Kim's program of indoctrination had convinced many of his own people of his greatness. He had made a showcase of the capital for foreigners, including evacuating disabled and mentally retarded people (*NYT* 7/19/89, A6).

What brought about resumption of contacts with the outside world by a country that had remained rigidly isolationist for more than 40 years? Political factors played an important part in instigating the 1991 changes. It was obvious that pressure from the Soviet Union and China had pushed North Korea into the United Nations. The 1988 Summer Olympics in Seoul, which allowed South Korea to show its dynamic economy, also forced a response from the North.

Many observers pointed to the need for trade, credits, and outside technology in explaining the changes in North Korea. Its economy continued to decline in 1991, which contrasted with the south's record as one of the fastest developing economies in the world, averaging growth of about 9 percent annually. North Korea had a poor harvest and its mines were flooded, causing a severe drop in electricity production. Production fell in 1990 and 1991 as a result of problems with coal production, a poor harvest, and a cutback in trade and credits from the Soviet Union, which was experiencing its own economic and political problems.

There was little chance to evaluate the effect of economics on internal Korean politics because the society had been insulated from reporters and outside observers. However modern communications and Kim's policy of trying to make North Korea a showcase for foreigners caused cracks in the insulation, as did its proximity to South Korea and Japan, which had prospered under democratic and market systems, and to China, which had prospered under open door economic policies. North Korean efforts to show off its capital attracted many thousands of visitors from the outside who came in contact with the people. For example, its 1989 World Youth Festival attracted 25,000 delegates, including 20 U.S. reporters. Internally, significant political opposition must have existed since North Korea reportedly had more than 100,000 political prisoners. Moreover, its worldwide reputation was badly tarnished by its terrorist attacks against the south and by its general backwardness compared with the south's relative progressiveness.

North Korea's own propaganda for reunification may have convinced its people of the need for change. The propaganda even convinced many South Korean students of North Korea's desire for reunification. These students demonstrated against the South Korean government and against U.S. troops still stationed there, and the South Korean government forcefully prevented the demonstrators from attending the World Youth Festival in North Korea (*CSM* 7/ 3/89, 3).

The openings to the outside world are likely to increase pressures for reform. Moreover, Kim Il Sung, who has been president for almost 50 years, is expected to step down and attempt to place his son in his stead. The young Kim has been associated with the terrorist attacks by the north, and is not expected to be a reformer. However, reports indicate the change might generate opposition within the ruling clique.

There appears to be little chance for reunification as long as the Communist cadres control North Korean society. In any reunified democratic system the democratic south, with twice the population of the north, would dominate. The north has held out for equal north-south parliamentary representation or a confederal system, which would preserve the Communist system in the north (Zweig 1989). However, the Berlin Wall fell in one day, and a dramatic reunification cannot be ruled out.

HO CHI MINH'S VIETNAM

The Korean War prepared the way for the Vietnam War in two ways. First, the attack of Korea backed by the Soviet Union and China convinced U.S. leaders that world Communism was probing for weak spots and that the answer to this challenge must be strength and alliances. The United States created most of the Asian alliance system, including the South East Asian Treaty Organization (SEATO), after the Korean War. South Vietnam was specifically included although it did not sign the treaty. The United States specified that its commitment to act against aggression under the treaty applied to Communist aggression. Second, after the Korean War China was able to provide military equipment and a sanctuary for Ho Chi Minh for his attacks against French colonial troops. This assistance was important in Ho Chi Minh's victory at Dien Bien Phu in 1954, which forced the French to surrender North Vietnam to his control.

War of Independence

North Vietnam's creation was the result of a long anticolonial struggle, and the momentum of that struggle carried Ho and his successors to victory against the United States, the strongest military power in the world, when it tried to protect South Vietnam. Ho Chi Minh dominated the history of Vietnam, which was formed from the French colony of Indochina. He led the prolonged war against the French and then against the United States. Here Ho Chi Minh's life is examined, including how he succeeded in using the Communist ideology to help defeat the United States. Then the government of Vietnam and how successfully it addressed its political and economic problems after the war is evaluated.

Ho Chi Minh was to the Vietnamese what Lenin and Stalin were to the Soviet Union. He was born about 1890 to a rich peasant who had been well educated and who had passed the tough mandarin exams that allowed him to become an official in the imperial administration in Hue. Ho had several names, including the Vietnamese equivalent to "the patriot" and "he who will be victorious." He finally settled on Ho Chi Minh, "he who enlightens." Ho's father was dismissed from government service when he refused to work for the French colonial regime after it took control. He and Ho were involved in a nationalist opposition movement against the French.

Ho attended Indochina's best high school, which was the only such school to use the Vietnamese language in instruction. Ngo Dinh Diem, Ho's future opponent in South Vietnam, as well as other future Communist officials such as Pham Van Dong and General Giap, also attended the school. Ho was expelled for political activity.

He left for France just before World War I, working at various jobs in France and Britain, and even visiting the United States. He ended up in France in 1920, and on December 30, 1920, he became a "founding member" of the French Communist Party, 10 years before he helped found the Communist Party of Vietnam. Ho became an editor of the French Communist Party's newspaper and the party's expert on colonial affairs. Later he traveled to the Soviet Union and joined the Comintern. He studied at the University of the Toilers in the USSR and obtained a thorough background in Marxism.

Ho was interpreter for Borodin when he was a Soviet adviser in China. While Ho was in China, he organized Vietnamese refugees. Some of them were trained in Chiang Kaishek's military academy, which the Soviets helped found. Ho managed to infiltrate about 200 of these cadres back to Indochina to organize resistance against the French colonial rule.

Ho traveled extensively for the Comintern. He spoke fluent French, Russian, English, Mandarin, and some German. On one of these trips he founded the Communist Party of Vietnam in Hong Kong in 1930.

During World War II he was in China helping to organize resistance against the Japanese occupation of Indochina. He made contact with the U.S. military intelligence, which gave him arms and ammunition, not knowing his background. With the support of Chinese forces, Ho marched into Hanoi at the close of World War II to liberate it and form a government. The French had official dealings with him at first, but at the end of 1946 fighting broke out, and French troops, which had occupied the southern part of Indochina with the cooperation of the British, were able to take control of Hanoi. They were not able to extend their control over the countryside, however, and Ho's Vietnamese forces fought them with guerilla warfare.

The Korean War of 1950 had a major impact on Asian and Vietnamese history. President Truman saw North Korea's invasion of the South as a step toward the takeover of the rest of Asia following the successful Communist revolution in China. The United States in 1950 began an aid program to the French in Vietnam, and by 1954 was supporting a major part of the French war against Ho's forces. At this point the United States did not provide troops or military advisers.

With guerilla tactics, Ho Chi Minh attacked the French where they were weak and avoided conventional battles. Ho's winning strategy was expressed by General Giap who wrote:

> Our strategy as we have stressed was to wage a long-lasting battle. A war of this nature in general entails several phases; in principle, starting from a state of contention, it goes through a period of equilibrium, before arriving at a general counter offensive. . . .

Only a long-term war could enable us to utilize to the maximum our political trump cards, to overcome material handicaps and to transfer our weakness into strength. To maintain and increase our forces was the principle to which we adhered, contenting ourselves with attacking when success was certain, refusing to give battle likely to incur losses to us or to engage in hazardous actions. . . .

As Marxism-Leninism teaches us: "The history of all societies up till the present day, has been but the history of class struggle." These struggles can take either the form of political struggle or the form of armed struggle—the armed struggle being only the continuation of the political struggle (Giap 1962, 20).

This was the classic version of the Communist guerilla struggle, the one that succeeded in defeating the United States.

In desperation the French tried to lure the Communists into an open fight by challenging them at Dien Bien Phu, an outpost in the middle of the jungle. They isolated some of their best troops there, daring the Communists to fight. The French planned to supply them by air, not dreaming that the Communists would be able to bring in artillery or the troops that could win the battle. Ho's forces received heavy artillery and supplies from their Chinese sanctuaries, and with tremendous effort got them over the mountains and jungles to surround the French. The French General Ely in desperation asked for U.S. air support from aircraft carriers, but President Eisenhower refused to become involved on such a basis. He insisted as a condition of U.S. support that other nations such as Britain join, that the French give independence to the peoples of Indochina, and that Congress approve. These conditions were not met, and Dien Bien Phu fell to the Communists.

The French premier, Mendes France, was elected on a pledge to end the war in 30 days. At an international conference in Geneva, which included the major powers, he agreed to the 1954 Geneva accord, which gave Ho his first major victory—the state of North Vietnam (see Figure 8-2). The agreement provided for elections to form an all-Vietnam government in 1956. South Vietnam and the United States did not sign this agreement, but the Communists later demanded that they carry out its provisions. President Ngo Dinh Diem became premier of South Vietnam after Emperor Bao Dai agreed to give him full powers.

In the period after the 1954 Geneva agreement, Diem confounded observers by being able to consolidate his control over conflicting political factors in South Vietnam. About 1 million refugees fled from the north, fearing to remain there under the Communists. About 90,000 Communist cadres went north for training, whereas perhaps 10,000 remained in South Vietnam to carry on the political struggle and to help win the elections. As noted above, however, Diem refused to hold such elections despite the urging of Ho's government.

Suspected Communists were repressed under Diem's rule; Communists and anti-Diem forces responded with a terrorist campaign, killing local officials, including teachers. It is controversial which tactic started first, repression or terrorism. Ho Chi Minh had a broad view of the struggle as indicated by the following quotation from an article he wrote for the Soviet Union's main Communist newspaper, *Pravda*, on November 3, 1957.

> In a short space of history socialism has become a world system now embracing twelve countries with more than 900 million people. The October revolution like a thunderbolt has stirred the Asian peoples from their centuries old slumbers. It has opened up for them the revolutionary anti-imperialist era, the era of national liberations.
>
> The imperialists seek to sow discord and division in the great family of socialist countries. This is the very nature of their aggression against the Hungarian People's Republic. . . .
>
> As early as 1913 Lenin said, "All young Asia, that is, millions of toiling masses in Asia have a staunch ally—the proletariat of all civilized countries. No force on earth can prevent its victory, which will liberate all the people of Europe as well as of Asia" (Fall 1967, 326–328).

War for South Vietnam

The North Vietnamese continued to call for the elections proposed in Geneva. In the fall of 1956 President Diem announced that he would not agree because there was no way to insure free elections in North Vietnam. Ho Chi Minh would not permit U.N. supervision of the elections, and since under the Communist system the result would be virtually 100 percent support for Ho Chi Minh, Diem saw that his regime would stand no chance in all-Vietnam elections.

Ho continued to call for a "peaceful" solution on the basis of the Geneva agreement. After 1957, and particularly in the period 1959 and after, Communist cadres infiltrated from North Vietnam with military equipment to carry on the revolution against Diem. Officials of the Diem regime were the targets of assassination. In the late 1950s Communist cadres were responsible for killing thousands of village leaders and schoolteachers because they were associated with the Diem regime. By this time South Vietnam had been officially recognized as a sovereign state by most of the states in the United Nations, but not, of course, by the Communist states. Strictly speaking this made North Vietnam's attack an international war, rather than a civil war, although many countries treated the conflict as a civil war.

After 1957 the Diem regime controlled most of South Vietnam through repressive measures against Communists and suspected Communists. Diem's repression and Communist terrorism were a vicious circle. Ho and other Communist leaders never wavered in their determination to take over the South by force (see Figure 8-2).

A major question remains, however, concerning why Ho was so successful. Communist doctrine and ideology call for wars of liberation all over the world; why was there such strong support in South Vietnam? A related question is

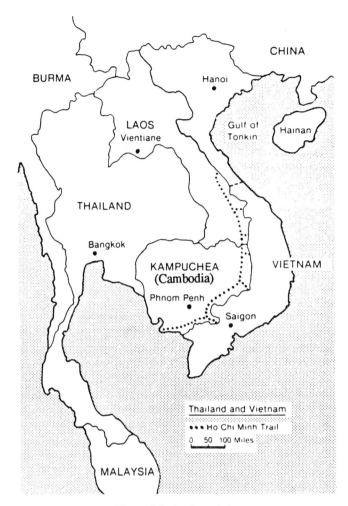

Figure 8-2 Southeast Asia.

whether it was essentially a civil war or an international war supported by the North Vietnamese regime.

Insights into the reasons for the Vietnamese support of the war are provided by a series of interviews carried out by the RAND Corporation, under contract to the U.S. Defense Department. Between August 1964 and December 1968, RAND conducted about 2400 interviews with Vietnamese, mostly Viet Cong and Viet Cong defectors. RAND interviewers were mostly professors aided by interpreters. They tried to disassociate themselves from the South Vietnamese government and to assure privacy to those being interviewed. RAND estimates that privacy was assured in about half of the interviews, but that it was poor in many of the others. RAND also notes that those interviewed were suspicious that the South Vietnam government was involved. Although the interviews were not perfect, there are about 62,000 pages of useful data about the views of those who were leading the rebellion against the Diem government (Davison 1966).

The RAND analysts reported that about 90,000 of the insurgents who fought against the French traveled north after the 1954 Geneva agreement. In North Vietnam, they were "regrouped" under Hanoi's leadership and trained in techniques of insurgency. They later became the "steel frame" of the insurgent organization in South Vietnam. A smaller number remained in the south. They had varying degrees of allegiance to the northern Communist movement, but it was clear from the interviews that they recognized the north's leadership. Their task, at first, was to organize for the elections, and they indicated that they were looking forward to the chance to reunify Vietnam. However, in July 1955 Diem said free elections were impossible. About the same time, he initiated a program of repression against the group that remained in the south. Diem classified people in three categories: (1) the most dangerous Communist Party members, (2) party members of lesser importance, and (3) loyal citizens. Saigon authorities, with the aid of local officials, initiated an active program of repression against the first two categories. Many of the local officials, according to the interviews, abused their power, arresting and even killing some of the group that remained in the south. Those who were interviewed complained particularly about harassments such as stealing their ducks and chickens or forcing them to work on certain projects without pay.

After 1959 Communist leaders in the south increased the pressure on former party members to join in opposition to Diem. Some who were harassed by both Communist leaders and Diem's officials gave up and fled to the jungles with the Communists, where at least they could not be reached by the Diem government. The Communists established base areas in the Plain of Reeds in the south and in other areas between 1955 and 1959. By 1959 the Vietminh Communist insurgents were successfully using coercion to recruit on a larger scale.

The major theme used by the Communists combined nationalism, Communism, and hatred of the Diem regime, which was called a puppet of U.S. imperialists who had taken over "colonial" control from the French. It was alleged that France and the United States had the same goal—"to invade Vietnam, enslave people, and exploit human labor and resources to enrich the totalitarian capitalists in their countries." Another Communist theme was that the U.S. capitalists were interested in subjugating Vietnam to obtain its raw materials. Communist China and the USSR, on the other hand, were pictured as friendly members of the socialist camp. All propaganda pictured Vietnam as one nation (Davison and Zasloff 1966; Donnell 1967; Zasloff 1968; Karnow 1983, 230–239, 256–259, 263).

To sum up, North Vietnam's indirect aggression against South Vietnam during this period was based on a Communist theory that foresaw the ultimate victory over "colonial" forces. It was a struggle between nationalists because

Diem also was an ardent Vietnamese nationalist and was by no means a puppet of France or the United States. Ho, however, had the advantage of a powerful Communist doctrine on colonialism and a powerful Communist apparatus, which generated guerilla support from the people. Thus the burden of blame for the Vietnamese War and the prize for the victory of North Vietnam went to Ho Chi Minh.

President John F. Kennedy inherited the escalating conflict in Vietnam. His administration's position was summarized in a National Security Memorandum (NSM) of April 1961, which restated the goals established by Presidents Truman and Eisenhower and defined the U.S. government policy. The NSM stated as U.S. aims:

> To prevent Communist domination of South Vietnam; to create in that country a viable and increasingly democratic society, and to initiate, on an accelerated basis a series of mutually supporting actions of a military, political, economic, psychological, and covert character destined to achieve that objective (*NYT* 1971, 126).

W. W. Rostow, who was Kennedy's special adviser on Southeast Asia, describes Kennedy's rationale in the *Diffusion of Power* as based on a fear that the Communists would take over if the United States walked away from the crisis and that this would result in a loss of confidence in the United States. He feared that Khrushchev would exploit a shift in the world balance of power that could threaten all of Asia (Rostow 1972, 270–272).

A turning point came in 1963 when Kennedy and his top advisers were horrified by Buddhist monks burning themselves to death in front of television cameras because of their persecution under President Diem, who had ignored U.S. protests. Washington instructed the Saigon Embassy to secretly inform Vietnamese generals that there was no objection to their plans to overthrow Diem. A few months later their coup was carried out, and to Kennedy's dismay, Diem was brutally killed. This laid the basis not only for a succession of military dictatorships, but it also increased the U.S. commitment and responsibility for subsequent events in Vietnam.

A few weeks later Kennedy was assassinated, and his advisors began to prepare plans for the new president, Lyndon B. Johnson, to drastically escalate U.S. participation in the war. Johnson was a leader seasoned by World War II, who saw how failure to stop Hitler early in his aggressions resulted in disaster. It is not surprising that Johnson, therefore, was ready to take a hard line toward Vietnamese aggression.

The Tonkin Gulf crisis reinforced Johnson's hawk tendencies. On August 2, 1964, in the midst of the presidential election campaign, the destroyer *Maddox* came under attack, or thought it was under attack, in the Gulf of Tonkin. It was there on a routine electronic spying mission against North Vietnam. The North Vietnamese apparently thought it was supporting a recent probe of South Vietnamese marines in the general area of the *Maddox* patrol. The president considered that the *Maddox* was in international waters, and in the midst of a storm of

U.S. indignation over the attack President Johnson obtained the resolution from Congress, later known as the Tonkin Gulf Resolution, that authorized him to use armed force in the defense of South Vietnam. During the rest of the election campaign Johnson pictured himself as a peace candidate, although after the elections he took the option of escalating the war that had been planned by his advisers and authorized by the resolution (Johnson 1971, 119–120; *NYT* 1971, 128).

In the summer of 1965 Johnson's top advisers were considering further escalation with a formal declaration of war. President Johnson, however, was afraid that this would provoke retaliation by Communist China, and also stimulate opposition in Congress. Many officials remembered how the attack on North Korea triggered the participation of Chinese troops in that war. Early in 1965, after winning the presidential election, Johnson began sending ground troops a few units at a time, and within a few months the United States took over direction of the war. As draft calls mounted for troops for Vietnam, so did demonstrations in the United States against the war.

The Tet offensive on January 30, 1968, the Vietnamese New Year, was a turning point. Insurgent forces attacked areas throughout Vietnam, including the U.S. embassy in the center of Saigon. The attacks were featured on television, and although the ratio of Vietcong dead to those of South Vietnam was as much as 10 to 1, the Communists won a major psychological-political victory. The U.S. news media, featuring the fact that even the U.S. Embassy in the capital city was not safe, made the Johnson administration's optimistic statements about the war look foolish. The demonstrations against the war continued to mount. Johnson lost so much public support that he announced he would not run for reelection.

Nixon won the presidency on a wave of dissatisfaction with the war. He offered some vague pledges but no specific plan. After taking office, he was convinced by his secretary of defense to Vietnamize the war—let the Vietnamese wage it with U.S. material help. To implement this plan, Nixon announced that he would withdraw troops in stages from Vietnam. The momentum of the antiwar demonstrations continued.

North Vietnam continued attacks, but the South Vietnam government seemed rejuvenated as the United States withdrew troops. It even held elections. Then at the end of April 1970 Nixon announced that U.S. forces would assist South Vietnamese troops in attacking sanctuaries on the border areas in Cambodia where the North Vietnamese had established bases. Militarily the attacks were successful in destroying tens of thousands of rounds of ammunition and hundreds of military vehicles, but protests against the war mounted in the United States. Nixon withdrew from Cambodia as promised at the end of June.

On March 30, 1971, North Vietnam launched a full-scale invasion across the demilitarized zone in the north. Nixon responded by ordering the heavy bombing of North Vietnam and blockading Haiphong harbor. The North Vietnamese offensive was stopped mostly by South Vietnamese forces.

After more bombings, peace negotiations were concluded at the beginning of 1973. They provided for (1) troops in the south not to be reinforced, (2) U.S. prisoners to be returned within 60 days (a primary issue for the United States), (3) U.S. military personnel to be withdrawn in 60 days, (4) Vietnam to be reunified by peaceful means, (5) all foreign troops to be withdrawn from Laos and Cambodia, and (6) a national council to supervise elections and international commissions to supervise the truce.

Under the 1973 agreement, prisoners were returned and the U.S. withdrawal accomplished. Kissinger and Le Duc Tho were awarded the Nobel Peace Prize for the agreement, but Kissinger says that he knew it would not work. Actually, after the agreement North Vietnam continued to reinforce its troops. Nixon was forced to resign by the Watergate scandal. Then in the fall of 1974 the North Vietnamese took Phuoc Long, a provincial capital about 70 miles from Saigon. The U.S. government spokesman noted the build-up of North Vietnamese forces, but the United States made no moves to oppose it.

Meanwhile, Congress was only appropriating less than half of the $1.7 billion that the administration was asking for the war, or $700 million. Both South and North Vietnam noted this reduced U.S. support for the war, which eroded South Vietnamese morale. North Vietnam at this point committed 17 of its 19 *regular* divisions to the attack in the spring of 1975. South Vietnamese morale and resistance crumbled. North Vietnamese forces marched victoriously into Saigon, allowing about 200,000 U.S. and South Vietnamese soldiers to evacuate hurriedly by helicopter and ship. North Vietnam had won the war.

Political observers agreed that the United States attempted too much. It saw its role as a world police force with the duty of stopping the spread of world Communism. Ho Chi Minh's forces responded with guerilla tactics at first, and then as the U.S. will weakened, escalated their attacks to a conventional invasion. With their patience and superior strategy, they won the war and unified Vietnam, but at the cost of devastating their country.

The Socialist Republic of Vietnam

The Democratic Republic of Vietnam had been established in North Vietnam on July 21, 1954, following the conference in Geneva. After the surrender of South Vietnam on April 30, 1975, the army and a provisional committee under the control of the North Vietnamese ran South Vietnam's government until nationwide elections were held on April 25, 1976. They were typical Communist elections with a 98.6 percent turnout and virtually no competition, but a few non-Communist candidates were nominated and actually won office. Hanoi declared formal reunification and the establishment of the Socialist Republic of Vietnam on July 2, 1976. Unbelievably Vietnam actually asked for representatives of both North and South Vietnam to be admitted as two countries to the United Nations. The United States vetoed this request. Later, Vietnam asked for membership as one nation, and this time it was admitted.

The head of the Vietnam Workers Party, Le Duan, gave the policy line for the new government:

> In the south we must abolish the comprador bourgeoise and the remnants of the feudal landlord classes, undertake the socialist transformation of private capitalist industry and commerce, agriculture, handicrafts, and small trade through appropriate measures and steps, and combine the transformation with building an order actively to steer the economy of the south into the orbit of socialism.

But in November 1976 the party, in an action that recalled Lenin's New Economic Policy, for a time allowed private investment.

About 50,000 party officials came in from the north and took positions down to the village level. The suppression of counterrevolutionary activity was carried out by 200,000 North Vietnamese soldiers on garrison in the south. Somewhere between the official figure of 40,000 and other estimates of 200,000 were put into "reeducation" camps. Private commerce was eliminated in March 1978 and one currency was finally established. The USSR provided a stream of Soviet advisers who came to the south and substantial aid of almost $1 billion.

More than 30,000 private businesses were confiscated, mostly owned by Chinese-Vietnamese. Hundreds of thousands of refugees fled from the south including mostly ethnic Chinese who made up the commercial class. Many of these were "boat people" who fled to Thailand and Hong Kong; many perished. By 1989 about 80,000 of these refugees had been admitted to the United States. About 300,000 were supported by the U.N. High Commissioner for Refugees and other refugee organizations in camps in Thailand (*Far Eastern Economic Review* 1989, 28). Again, large-scale flight had followed a Communist takeover.

Vietnam soon began another war in Kampuchea (covered in more detail in the following section on the Cambodian Holocaust). In December 1978 after repeated border clashes, Vietnam invaded Kampuchea and within a few days had captured the capital and set up another government. The bulk of the Khmer Rouge government forces eluded the invaders and continued to fight them. The invasion was opposed by its neighbors. In February 1979 Chinese forces invaded Vietnam's northern provinces "to teach a lesson" to Vietnam for its invasion of China's ally and to end alleged incursions into Chinese territory. China quickly withdrew as promised after a punishing 17-day war.

Vietnam was drained by its continued fighting of the Khmer Rouge and other opposition forces, which were largely supplied from neighboring Thailand. Thailand, along with other Southeast Asian countries, led the condemnation of Vietnam's invasion and cut off trade. The United Nations refused to seat delegates of Vietnam's puppet government while continuing to seat representatives of the old government.

China's attack on North Vietnam was not only aimed at supporting Kampuchea, but it was also a form of shaking its fist at the Soviet Union, which continued to give major economic and military support to Vietnam. The world watched in amazement as the former Communist allies quarreled among themselves. China offered to support Thailand to help protect it from Vietnam. Press reports indicated that Thailand permitted China to supply the resistance forces against Kampuchea through Thailand.

The war and occupation of Kampuchea seriously affected the economy of Vietnam. It reported that 55,000 Vietnamese died from the war in Cambodia including in the initial border attacks (*Far Eastern Economic Review* 1989, 251). This was about the same number as U.S. deaths in the Vietnam War, which obviously took a much higher toll on the smaller Vietnamese population. The indirect costs from the isolation from its neighbors and other nations are impossible to calculate.

In 1988 the Soviet Union reportedly put pressure on Vietnam, to which it had given large amounts of aid, to resolve the Cambodian conflict, although publicly it denied this to save face for Vietnam. Following Foreign Minister Shevardnadze's visit in 1988, Vietnam made such a pledge, conditional on others not providing aid to the resistance. Vietnam also made gestures toward normalizing relations with the United States and China in June 1988 by removing hostile references toward them in its constitution. More importantly, it provided additional information and assistance to the United States in accounting for about 1800 servicemen missing in action from the Vietnam War.

This shift in foreign policy followed a change in leadership. In December 1986 Vietnam underwent the most radical change of leaders since its founding, removing Truong Chinh as the party chief, Premier Pham Van Dong as president, and Le Duc Tho as a Politburo member, along with three other members of the Politburo. These were all close associates of Ho Chi Minh during his lifetime. Truong Chinh admitted to the Party Congress that the party leadership was responsible for many of the economic mistakes, and he called for bold renovations to invigorate the economy.

Seventy-one-year-old Nguyen Van Linh replaced Chinh as party chief. He was credited with encouraging economic decentralization when he was party secretary in Ho Chi Minh City. Also, nine new members were appointed to the 13-person Secretariat. Seventy-five-year-old Pham Hung was appointed premier. Linh purged party members accused of corruption. Of the 22 ministries, 17 received new ministers. In April a new National Assembly was elected; 829 candidates ran for 496 seats.

The Party Congress called relations with the Soviet Union the cornerstone of Vietnamese foreign policy. The Soviets pledged 8 to 9 billion rubles in aid during the 1986–1990 five-year plan. On April 5, 1989, Vietnam unconditionally committed itself to end the occupation of Cambodia by the end of the year. Previously it had said it would withdraw troops only if there were a cutoff of all foreign military aid to the resistance (*NYT* 12/2/88, 8; 1/26/89, 5). The final withdrawal took place in 1991, and the United Nations took over responsibility for Cambodian reconstruction.

The economic situation deteriorated in 1987. Prices in midyear quadrupled from the previous year. Food production dropped in 1987—700,000 tons less than the target of nineteen million. Vietnam appealed for food aid, but most Western countries declined, continuing their policy of economic isolation imposed after Vietnam's invasion of Cambodia. It was estimated that 1.6 million people were unemployed. Exports were only $800 million and imports $1 billion. About 70 percent of the exports of raw materials and agricultural products were sent to the Soviet Union to repay it for economic and military aid.

Linh told a Central Committee meeting in April 1988 that inflation had never increased so fast, and he pressed on with a program for reform. In February 1988 Hanoi introduced measures to encourage private enterprise, such as tax breaks and bank loans. In April the Central Committee instituted a version of China's responsibility system allowing peasants to make contracts for their land for 10 to 15 years and to keep about half the production. It also abolished the check-points that controlled movement of goods across provincial lines. Linh continued to shift operations of government units to cooperatives and to end subsidies. In 1988 foreigners invested more than $300 million in oil exploration.

There were more moves toward relaxation. In September 1988 Vietnam released 6685 prisoners and reduced the terms of another 5320. Journalists were allowed to report on corruption.

Vietnam's June 1991 Seventh Communist Party Congress dropped seven senior party leaders from the ruling Politburo in one of the biggest turnovers at the top of the party since it was founded in 1930. This included President Vo Chi Cong, 78, Foreign Minister Nguyen Co Thach, 68, and Interior Minister Mai Chi Tho, 69, all party leaders for more than a decade. General Vo Nguyen Giap, deputy prime minister and hero of Vietnam's victories over France and the United States, showed his pique at being dropped from the party central committee by leaning back and reading a newspaper during the announcement of the new leadership. Some replacements were from South Vietnam and were considered economic reformers (*UPI* 6/27/91). The party plenum called for market reforms and abolishing subsidies to state enterprises, but it took action on only a few firms. It warned the press to be more cautious in its criticisms of corruption and it reaffirmed the principles of Marxism-Leninism and Ho Chi Minh thought (*Far Eastern Economic Review* 12/19/91, 22).

In 1988 economic reforms had gained momentum, particularly in agriculture. As in China, peasants sold their produce to merchants from the cities and at farmers' markets. More than $300 million of foreign investment was put into oil exploration. Vietnamese in other countries, some of them former boat people, invested in small businesses. Tourism was encouraged, and even former U.S. GIs visited Vietnam. In 1989 inflation fell drastically as a result of monetary reforms and devaluation of the currency to approximately a free market rate.

After this promising beginning the internal reforms stagnated. Vietnamese leaders were alarmed at the Tiananmen rebellion, and they reverted to the Chinese pattern of a hardline political policy that discouraged further market reforms. The economy was still held back by the repressive policies of its Communist bureaucracy. One of the greatest potentials for foreign investment is from the approximately 2 million Vietnamese living abroad, about half of whom live in the United States. More than 50,000 visited Vietnam in 1991, but only a handful were enticed to invest. Those who did visit reported difficulties in getting permits and harassments and arrests by the security police. The Vietnamese visitors were blamed for social problems such as sex scandals and AIDS.

The collapse of the Soviet economy had a major impact in Vietnam, because about half of its trade had been with the Soviets. Moreover, it lost about $1 billion in aid from the Soviets and Eastern Europe. At the beginning of 1992 the foreign exchange market was limited and the value of the local currency fluctuated wildly in the black market. The inflation rate was 3 to 6 percent a month in the spring of 1992 (*Far Eastern Economic Review* 2/23/92, 18; *Far Eastern Economic Review* 2/27/92, 54).

Vietnam made foreign affairs gains by ending the burdens of the war in Cambodia. This, plus Vietnam's gestures to release a few political prisoners, resulted in some countries' relaxation of restrictions on aid to Vietnam. Also Vietnam normalized its relations with China, formally ending the cold war with its powerful neighbor. At the same time it continued efforts to renew relations with the United States, principally by assisting efforts to locate remains of U.S. soldiers killed in the Vietnam War. It made further gestures at market reforms by broadening the market for foreign exchange and by encouraging further foreign investments. (*Far Eastern Economic Review* 2/9/92, 24; *Far Eastern Economic Review* 2/27/92, 54).

Vietnam has a long and difficult road to recovery because of the terrible damage of the Vietnam War and the drain on its resources from supporting the war in Kampuchea. Its Communist bureaucrats permitted only limited economic reform. Officials were alarmed by the Tiananmen incident and the disintegration of the Soviet Union, although their country does not have ethnic problems like those in the Soviet Union. However, limited glasnost in Vietnam, allowing more than 50,000 Vietnamese to visit every year, plus visits by many more other tourists and business representatives, was bound to have an effect. Opening that door will increase pressures for reform. Vietnam's withdrawal from foreign adventure and preoccupation with internal reforms would help to stabilize the balance of power in Asia.

THE CAMBODIAN HOLOCAUST

By the end of 1989 Vietnamese troops completed their promised withdrawal from Kampuchea (Cambodia). This closed what had been one of the most terrible chapters in any nation's history, although the troubles were not over. The tragedy had started during the Vietnam War.

In February 1970 General Lon Nol seized control of the Cambodian government from President (Prince) Sihanouk while he was on a trip abroad. Sihanouk had been a popular ruler, a neutralist; Lon Nol was a hardline anti-Communist. Sihanouk continued as a figurehead with little power.

The Cambodian government did not control the eastern fringe of the country where the Ho Chi Minh Trail was located. This trail, or primitive road, was the major artery for supply to the Communist forces in South Vietnam. In March 1972, therefore, U.S. forces interrupted their withdrawal from Vietnam and mounted a major offensive against the trail in eastern Cambodia. During this campaign the United States destroyed North Vietnam's sanctuaries and many weapons. The campaign was militarily successful for the United States, but it had high political costs. Kent State University in Ohio erupted in antiwar demonstrations, and four students were killed by the state National Guard. The resulting political turmoil in the United States provoked Congress into passing a law cutting off funds to be used in Cambodia after June 30. Nixon came under attack in the Congress and in the news media, although he withdrew U.S. troops on June 30, 1972, precisely when he said he would.

Another political cost was that the U.S. attack contributed to the fall of Lon Nol's government. The U.S. offensive drove the Communists out of eastern Cambodia into the west. There they fought the Lon Nol government, and the same month that Vietnam fell, April 1975, the radical Khmer Rouge Communists took over the government in Cambodia. It was a confused time. There was minimal U.S. presence—no regular forces, only military advisers and the CIA. The Khmer Rouge held "elections" with Communist cadres reading off the names of candidates before a crowd, which vocally approved them.

Cambodia then entered a holocaust that was pictured in the movie, "The Killing Fields," which is a pale reflection of the horror of that time. More than 1 million people were killed out of a population of 7 million as the extremists of the Khmer Rouge tried to destroy all vestiges of bourgeoise culture by forcing people to leave the cities and to obtain their living from the land. At the same time they slaughtered many of the bourgeois or starved them. There are many horrible photographs of piles of human skulls, and many horror stories from the 250,000 refugees who fled to Thailand. In 1989 many still lived in refugee camps along the border, although many were allowed to emigrate to the United States.

Two international wars followed the holocaust. In 1977 and 1978 there were border clashes between the Pol Pot regime and Vietnam. In 1978 Vietnam, the victor over the United States and with one of the strongest armies in the world, invaded little Kampuchea and quickly captured the capital of Phnom Penh. Vietnam claimed that the Kampuchean people had faced extinction by the "monstrous neocolonialist regime " of Pol Pot, "imposed by Peking."

China had helped the Pol Pot government with thousands of advisers and with military aid. On the other hand, there were also thousands of Soviet advisers in Vietnam, and it had continued to receive major amounts of aid from the Soviet Union. The war between Vietnam and Cambodia then developed into a conflict with the Soviet Union and China supporting opposing sides.

Vietnam occupied a virtual wasteland. The Pol Pot forces were forced into the jungles and western part of Kampuchea, where they continued to resist the Vietnamese invasion. The Vietnamese forces put Heng Samrin in power, who was a defector from the Khmer Rouge (the Red Khmers). Vietnam also placed Vietnamese advisers throughout the Kampuchean government, whereas Vietnamese forces did the bulk of the fighting against the Khmer Rouge and its allies including a smaller force loyal to Prince Sihanouk.

The neighboring countries, working together under the Association of South East Asian Nations (ASEAN), and the United Nations refused to recognize the Heng Samrin government, which was obviously dominated by the Vietnamese. The United Nations held their collective noses and continued to accept the representatives of the coalition resistance forces, consisting mostly of the Khmer Rouge but under the nominal leadership of Prince Sihanouk, with only the Soviet Union and its close allies voting to unseat it.

What was the cause of the war? Why did the North Vietnamese invade? In the first place Cambodia invited the war when it challenged Vietnam by incursions along the border. Why did little Cambodia challenge the powerful forces of Vietnam? One explanation is Khmer Rouge were insane. They were obviously crazy to kill 1 million or more people out of their total population of only 7 million. They were also insane to provoke the Vietnamese military, which had just defeated the strongest nation in the world.

Another theory is that Vietnam took the initiative in the war. The Communist Party organized by Ho Chi Minh in the early 1930s had as one of its aims a Communist federation of French Indochina, which included Cambodia and Laos. The Communist Party had split along pro-Vietnamese and pro-China lines. The pro-Vietnamese leaders under Ho won the war against South Vietnam, and, according to some observers, with that momentum spread the war into Kampuchea and opposed China.

China continued to support the coalition headed by Sihanouk. When asked why he allied with the Pol Pot forces, Sihanouk stated that all Cambodians are against being invaded and controlled by Vietnam, their historic enemy.

China and Thailand worked together to support the resistance forces in Cambodia, and there were periodic incidents as Vietnamese forces attacked the Cambodian resistance and even raided camps inside the Thai border. The success of the resistance against the Vietnamese occupation was attributed to support from the local population who resented the Vietnamese invaders. Reportedly the Vietnamese laid more than a million mines along the Thai border to keep the resistance forces out, but without success. Most of the guerilla activity was carried out by the Khmer Rouge, who roamed around the country but did not engage in a major battle with the main Vietnamese military units.

The Soviet Union, which gave strong support to Vietnam during the war, continued to do so. This alarmed China, which did not want to be surrounded with an unfriendly Soviet Union on the north and an unfriendly neighbor on the south. Cambodia then became a pawn in the Communist power politics of Southeast Asia. Reportedly the Soviets provided about $2 billion a year to Vietnam in economic and military aid. The Soviets were permitted to use the big Cam Ranh naval base, built by the United States. The Vietnamese army tied down a large part of the Chinese army along the border where there were continued clashes.

The China–Vietnam War of 1980 grew out of the Vietnam–Kampuchea war and a reaction to the close Vietnam–Soviet alliance. In February 1980 Deng Xiaoping visited the United States and told President Carter in confidence that the Chinese would make a limited attack on the Vietnamese to punish them for their invasion of Kampuchea. The Chinese were also angry about the repression of the Chinese communities in Vietnam, which had forced hundreds of thousands of boat people to flee, many of them to China.

In February 1980 the Chinese, with a force of about 250,000, attacked Vietnam for 17 days. They punished Vietnam, but the Chinese, too, were punished. The Vietnamese were hardened fighters after their experience, and they inflicted high casualties. The Soviets threatened China and airlifted supplies to Vietnam, which further consolidated the split between China and the Soviet Union. On March 16 the Chinese completed their "lesson" and withdrew their troops.

China's invasion would not be called aggression by many observers, since it was coming to the aid of Kampuchea, which had been invaded. China announced from the beginning that it did not intend to march into Hanoi and that it was punishing Vietnam and supporting Kampuchea. It was classic "realpolitik." The Chinese invasion also drew China and Thailand close together.

Only scraps of information are available on the operation of the Kampuchean regime. From the fall of the capital in early 1979 to mid-1981, Kampuchea was ruled by a 14-member People's Revolutionary Council. On May 17, 1981, a 117-member National Assembly approved a constitution. It met rarely if at all after that time. The constitution provided for a cabinet elected from the National Assembly, and Kampuchea was divided into districts, communes, and municipalities.

In 1985 4000 members joined the Communist Party, bringing its number to about 10,000, or about two-tenths of 1 percent. This was about the same as in 1979. There were 50,000 candidate members enrolled. The low number of party members was a reflection of the lack of popular support enjoyed by the Vietnamese-dominated government (Banks 1985, 122; *Far Eastern Economic Review, Asia Yearbook* 1988, 252–254).

In 1989 the government followed the lead of China and Vietnam in instituting a version of the Chinese responsibility system. Land was divided among the peasant families who got the right of long-term tenure including the right to pass it on to their families. The regime also granted private property rights in the capital, which resulted in a surge of housing repairs and construction. In April the National Assembly restored Buddhism as the national religion and even took steps to allow freedom of the press and the formation of political parties. The unlikely architect of the reform was Prime Minister Hung Sen, a former Khmer Rouge guerilla commander with no formal economic or political training. He had defected from the Khmer Rouge because of its brutality. This Gorbachev-type leader liked to travel to remote villages and explain policies on television (*Far Eastern Economic Review* 7/29/89, 16–20).

China's incursion did not stop the resistance forces from continuing to fight the Vietnamese forces and those of the Cambodian regime. The Khmer Rouge were the strongest partners of the anti-Vietnamese coalition. China and Thailand continued to give covert support to the resistance, mostly to Prince Sihanouk's faction. Intermittent peace talks to settle this war were encouraged by the Southeast Asian neighbors of ASEAN (Thailand, Indonesia, Malaya, the Philippines, Singapore, and Burma) with assistance from the United States, the Soviet Union, Britain, China, Australia, Canada, India, Japan, and a representative of the U.N. secretary general. Vietnam, under pressure from the Soviet Union finally withdrew its forces from Cambodia in September 1991. This gave a boost to the U.N.-sponsored negotiations, which finally succeeded in October in bridging the gap between Prince Sihanouk and Hung Sen, the prime minister of the Kampuchean regime.

Just before the agreement was signed the Kampuchean People's Revolutionary Party (Communist Party) changed its name to the Cambodian People's Party. Both it and the Khmer Rouge announced they had dropped the Marxist-Leninist ideology.

The final peace agreement, after more than two years of negotiation, was signed by 19 countries including the 5 permanent members of the Security Council. It provided for the most expensive U.N. peacekeeping operation in history, with about 14,000 military and civilian personnel participating. Initial cost estimates exceeded $2 billion. The U.N. was tasked with disarming about 300,000 troops, helping resettle about 350,000 refugees from Thailand, overseeing government ministries, organizing free elections for a new government in the spring of 1993, and helping clear more than 1 million mines. A new 120-member national assembly would be freely elected and would have the task of drafting a new constitution.

An advance U.N. mission arrived in November 1991, and large numbers of advisers and peacekeeping troops arrived the following spring. Initially Phnom Penh experienced a boom with large amounts of foreign currency being spent by the foreigners. This gave a welcome boost to the economy, which had been heavily dependent on Soviet aid and had suffered from inflation and a depreciating currency when that aid was cut back.

Observers described the task of helping Cambodia recover from economic and political devastation as "mission impossible" (*Far Eastern Economic Re-*

view 2/27/92, front cover). The political hatreds generated by the civil war were dramatically shown on November 27, 1991, when Khieu Samphan, the Khmer Rouge representative, was attacked by a mob in Phnom Penh when he arrived at the airport to participate in the peace negotiations. After several hours government forces intervened to rescue him, and the negotiations were moved to Thailand (*Far Eastern Economic Review* 12/12/91, 10–11).

In the spring of 1992 Prince Sihanouk, heading a coalition of four Cambodian factions, assumed the task of overseeing the government and carrying through on reforms, while the U.N. military and civilian personnel arranged for elections and attempted to recreate a democracy out of the exhausted nation. The question remained whether they could bring peace after the bitterness and horrors arising from the Cambodian holocaust.

LAOS—A VIETNAM SATELLITE

Laos is a backward, landlocked country of about 3.8 million people. It became a pawn of big powers because its location made it the path of the Ho Chi Minh Trail, which was the major artery to supply the Communist forces that fought in Vietnam.

Laos was a part of French Indochina, and when France withdrew in 1954, after being defeated by Ho Chi Minh's forces in North Vietnam, the United States took over support for Laos, as well as South Vietnam. The 1954 Geneva agreement prohibited foreign uniformed soldiers in Laos, so U.S. military aid was directed by CIA civilians.

In 1962 a neutralist government was set up under Prime Minister Souvanna Phouma in accord with international agreements negotiated at Geneva. Nevertheless, North Vietnam continued to support Communist forces under Prince Souphanouvong, which fought the government troops supported by the United States. During the Vietnam War the main opposition to Souphanouvong's Communist forces was from battles with Meo irregular forces supported by the CIA. They managed to keep Souphanouvong from taking over the Royal Lao government, but they did not challenge Communist control of the Ho Chi Minh Trail in southern Laos, which continued down into eastern Cambodia (see Figure 8-2).

In 1975 after the fall of Saigon, Communist forces in Laos moved into the capital and took over the government. In December the monarchy was abolished and a "people's democratic government" was established along the lines of a Communist model.

In 1988 Laos held its first elections for 113 district level committees, and then for provincial committees, and finally for the Supreme People's Assembly. The candidates were selected by the Lao Front for National Construction, which embraced the mass organizations and was dominated by the Communist Party (Lao People's Revolutionary Party).

Lao's "special relationship" with Vietnam was formalized in a 1977 Treaty of Friendship and Cooperation and reaffirmed by the Lao Communist Party Congress in June 1991. Laos repaired its relations with China in that year. Following Chinese Premier Li Peng's visit in December 1990 there was a surge of agreements and visits between the two countries.

It was not a coincidence that Laos followed the Chinese lead on economic and political policies. This involved developing relations with the outside world, coupled with market-oriented reforms. Laos restored close relations with Thailand after a red carpet visit of the Thai princess to Laos in April. The two countries also began negotiations on a border dispute, and established a joint company for transit trade through Thailand, replacing the Thai company that had monopolized that trade. They also reached agreement with the U.N. High Commissioner on Refugees for resettling 60,000 Lao refugees who had fled to Thai camps.

Laos developed relations with the United States by cooperating on the search for remains of soldiers and reducing opium production. In November 1991 the United States restored full diplomatic relations with Laos, and even reached agreement on sending Peace Corps volunteers to work there.

Laos received considerable aid from the Soviet Union and the German Democratic Republic, but aid was severely cut back in 1991. However, Laos developed new sources. In April 1991 the IMF provided Laos with a loan of $12 million, and non-Communist countries provided another $68 million, which were substantial loans for a country with a population of 4 million. IMF advice played an important part in reducing inflation to 10 percent in 1991 and stabilizing the exchange rate. The reform program paid off by permitting Laos to achieve a positive growth rate of about 8 percent annually in 1990 and 1991. The IMF provided another $8 million credit in the spring of 1992 to support its reforms. (*Far Eastern Economic Review* 1992, 142–146; *IMF Survey* 5/11/92, 157).

Laos is a very small country with an economy dominated by agriculture. Since 1986, when economic reforms began, it has replaced collective farms with private farms. Restoring food supply to free markets has had a more positive effect than it would have had if the economy were heavily dependent on industry. Also, opening the door to its large neighbor Thailand and to the rest of the world stimulated the economy. The Communist Party maintained its political controls, but pressures were increasing for further reforms along the lines of those affecting other Communist systems.

THE AFGHANISTAN WAR

Before World War I Britain and Russia competed for influence in Afghanistan, with Britain winning out. The British were forced, however, to grant it independence and sovereignty by 1919. The new Communist government of Russia was the first to recognize the new Afghan state.

In 1953 King Zahir Shah appointed Prince Daoud as prime minister. As a result of friction with Pakistan and lack of interest by the United States, Daoud developed close contacts with the Soviet Union, which provided arms and economic aid. Moscow was Afghanistan's sole arms supplier, and by 1958 the Soviets had provided an estimated $3 billion in aid. At that time this was the largest amount of aid per capita that the Soviets had provided to any nation. The aid projects included roads and airports that later were used when the USSR invaded the country. By 1985 about 70 percent of its trade was with the Soviets (Kamrany 1986, 333–336).

King Zahir removed Daoud in March 1963 and attempted to improve relations with Pakistan and lessen dependence on the Soviets. However, in July 1973 with the help of leftist military officers, Daoud staged a coup and established a republic. In 1978 the local Communists took over in another coup that killed him and his family.

To the outside world there was no obvious Soviet intervention or aggression involved in the 1978 coup, even though it was by Communists. Two local Communist factions had united temporarily to overthrow the government. Taraki, the head of Khalq, or masses party, became president. It was a bloody revolution in which as many as 10,000 were killed. Official U.S. statements indicated no Soviet intervention. After taking over, Taraki soon dismissed Vice President Karmal, the head of the other faction, and sent him to Czechoslovakia as ambassador. He was then dismissed, and the Soviets invited him to stay in Moscow.

Taraki instituted radical reforms alienating the conservative tribesmen. He also drew closer to the Soviets with a 20-year treaty of friendship and increased aid programs from Moscow.

The Soviets had been active in Afghanistan for years training Afghan officers, about 200 a year, and constructing airfields. These soldiers from the backward areas were impressed with the Soviet Union as a modern country. After the 1978 coup the government changed the flag to Soviet red and enthusiastically supported the Soviets in international policies. This was too much for the highly nationalistic Afghani tribesmen, who had fought against foreign domination for over 100 years. About 99 percent of the population are Muslims. Within a few months the Mujahideen, fundamentalist Moslems, were leading a revolt against the Communist government. They objected to Communist atheism, which was anathema to the devout tribesmen, and to Soviet domination of the government, including the 7000 military advisers who came to help put down the rebellion.

In the initial fighting many Soviet advisers were killed, some brutally beheaded. The rebellion and the chaotic civil war set the stage for a September 1979 coup. Reportedly the Soviets backed President Taraki and hoped to make Prime Minister Amin the scapegoat for the rebellion. Amin beat Taraki to the punch, however, and in a shootout in September Amin killed Taraki and took over the government.

A team of Soviet generals visited Afghanistan in the fall of 1979 and apparently recommended replacement of Amin. But Amin did not trust the Soviets, and he demanded that Soviet Ambassador Puzanov be recalled.

In December 1979 the Soviet forces made a surprise move; 50,000 Soviet troops suddenly advanced into key areas of Afghanistan, and by the beginning of 1980 there were 90,000 to 100,000 Soviet troops in place. The Soviets reportedly killed Amin and installed as president his old rival, Babrik Karmal, the leader of the rival Communist faction who had stayed in Moscow after leaving his post as ambassador to Czechoslovakia. The Soviet invasion was quick and ruthless—the first announcement of it came from a transmitter in the Soviet Union (U.S. Department of State 1980).

Soviet officials were placed in senior positions in the Afghan ministries. The Soviet military constructed many permanent military installations, and Afghanistan under Brezhnev took on the appearance of a Soviet satellite. The religious leaders declared a Holy War against the Soviets. The guerilla strategy consisted of sabotage, ambushes, and encouragement of desertions from the Afghan army. The Soviets responded by bombing villages and destroying crops. The war was brutal, and the Soviets were forced to replace their troops from central Asia, who were largely Moslem and felt an affinity with the Afghan Moslems. The troops were replaced by units from non-Moslem republics.

Most observers were surprised and shocked at the invasion. President Carter was unwise enough to admit his surprise, which was seized on by his political enemies as evidence of his naiveté. With hindsight the invasion becomes understandable. Afghanistan is in a strategic position (see Figure 8-3) and presented a target of opportunity. It might even have been a steppingstone to Iran, which has a warm-water port coveted by the Soviet Union for over a century and which has some of the richest oil reserves in the world. By this time Iran had lost the support of the United States because the Iranians had refuses to release diplomatic hostages taken by a radical group of students. Iran was also being threatened by attack from Iraq, which occurred later the following year. Thus Iran was weak and not in a position to oppose the Soviet move even indirectly, and the United States was preoccupied by the hostage crisis.

Another hypothesis is that the Soviets were troubled by militant Islam movements, such as that of Khomeini, and wanted to stabilize the situation in Afghanistan so that the radical movements would not spread into the southern regions of the Soviet Union. This is not a convincing rationale, however, because the Soviet aggression served to unite the Islamic countries of the area into opposition to the Soviets.

A more reasonable explanation proposed by the Chinese is that the invasion was an expression of Soviet hegemonism. The Soviets feared that Amin was wavering in his support of the Soviets and might even ally with China, radical Moslem regimes, or the West. Behind this was an exaggerated concern about the security near Soviet borders. The attack was not triggered by a perception of U.S. weakness. If anything, the Soviets may have been concerned the United States was planning an attack on Iran over the hostage issue (Garthoff 1987).

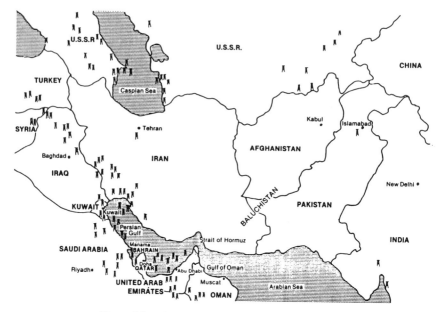

Figure 8-3   Afghanistan and the strategic Middle East.

Perhaps Americans can understand such hegemonism by recalling that the U.S. government was so concerned about Communist influence in Nicaragua, a small Central American country of little more than 3 million people, that it openly supported attacks against the Nicaraguan government. The United States also invaded a small Caribbean country, Grenada, of only 90,000 people, fearing that it might become a base for Communism. The situation is not parallel, since the United States supported self-determination and democracy in Grenada and Nicaragua, but the exaggerated U.S. nationalism that feared Communism in these small countries is similar to the exaggerated Russian nationalism that supported the attack against Afghanistan.

The world was shocked by the brutal invasion, and 52 states called for a Security Council meeting. The United States helped sponsor the Security Council resolution of January 7, 1980, deploring the intervention and calling for the immediate withdrawal of foreign troops from Afghanistan. The vote was 12 to 2 with 5 nonaligned nations joining in the affirmative vote, and with only East Germany, a Soviet satellite, voting with the Soviets, who vetoed the resolution. The Council under the uniting-for-peace procedure sent the issue to the General Assembly, which overwhelmingly, by a vote of 104 to 18, called for the withdrawal of foreign troops from Afghanistan. Cuba, by voting with the Soviet Union, lost the respect of many countries, and failed to get a Latin American seat on the Security Council. The matter stayed on the U.N. agenda, and the

General Assembly year after year passed resolutions calling for withdrawal of foreign forces from Afghanistan.

The United States, to show its disapproval, sharply cut back exports of grain to the minimum specified in its trade agreement with the Soviets, cut back further on exports of high technology goods, and organized a boycott of 65 nations for the Olympic Games in Moscow the following summer. President Carter also withdrew consideration of the SALT treaty from the Senate, and it was never again considered. With President Reagan's inauguration the cold war against the Soviet Union, which Reagan called the "evil empire," intensified. The United States also appropriated hundreds of millions of dollars to help the Afghanistan resistance (*Washington Post* 1/12/85, 1). Aid by the United States, Saudi Arabia, China, and Islamic countries was estimated at about $400 million in 1985.

Indirect talks between the Afghan regime and Pakistan began at Geneva in June 1982 under U.N. auspices. Diego Cordovez managed the talks. At first the Soviets did not attend, and neither did the Afghan guerillas. Moreover, Pakistan would not sit with the Kabul government, so Cordovez arranged for the talks in separate rooms and shuttled back and forth.

In April 1988 Gorbachev reached agreement with the Afghanistan president about the withdrawal of Soviet troops and negotiated a series of agreements under U.N. auspices. This included an agreement between Afghanistan and Pakistan concerning nonintervention, a document on the voluntary return of refugees including guarantees for their rights, and guarantees of the agreements by the Soviet Union and the United States. It was estimated that about 5 million refugees had emigrated to neighboring Pakistan and Iran and that the war caused up to 1 million deaths (*Economist* 3/12/86, 33).

In April 1986 the Soviet-installed Karmal was replaced by Major-General Najibullah, former head of the Afghan secret police. He consolidated his power in October 1987 when he became president of the Revolutionary Council and general secretary of the party. He formally expelled 15 top-ranking members of the Politburo, all supporters of the former president, and named four new members.

The Communist Party structure provided a means for his control from the top, but it did not generate popular support under the Soviet occupation. Desertion rates from the armed forces were so high that the Soviet troops had to do most of the fighting. With the withdrawal of Soviet forces, few observers gave much chance for survival to the Najibullah regime. Rocket attacks from the Mujahiddeen continued during 1989. The security police raided neighborhoods to destroy weapons, helping reduce the attacks. To prevent sabotage the Soviets capped the gas fields, which used to supply about $300 million in energy to its central Asian republics, but this was small savings compared to the $7.5 billion the USSR saved by ending the war (*Far Eastern Economic Review* 7/13/89, 17). The United States, along with Saudi Arabia, also stepped up supplies to the Mujahideen. At the end of 1989 Gorbachev's offer for a mutual cutoff in aid to the opposing sides appeared to be gaining support in Washington as a way to force negotiation instead of war.

Until 1991 Afghanistan was governed by a hardline Communist regime controlled by a military revolutionary council and a Communist-style government. During the war there were widespread human rights violations including tortures, executions, and forced conscription. The government controlled the news media and criticism was forbidden.

In 1991 President Najibullah's Communist Party (Watan Party, formerly the People's Democratic Party of Afghanistan) began to loosen its controls by permitting two-thirds of the cabinet posts to be filled by non-Communists with relatively good records. Najibullah made statements indicating that he was willing to hold elections and negotiate a peace, but the Mujahideen refused to respond. Diplomats from Pakistan and the United Nations intensified their efforts at a settlement.

The ascendancy of Boris Yeltsin in Moscow signalled an end to the former Soviet Union's support for the war. On September 13, 1991, the Soviet foreign minister and U.S. secretary of state agreed to end arms shipments to Afghanistan as of January 1, 1992. On November 10, 1991, 11 Mujahideen delegates led by the Pakistan-based interim government met with the Soviet and Russian foreign ministers in Moscow. Their joint communiqué called for an end to the war, the return of Soviet prisoners, and an Islamic transitional government that would hold elections in two years.

When Soviet troops withdrew in February 1989 observers had expected Afghanistan to be the first domino of the Soviet empire to fall. However, it proved to be the last. On March 18, 1992, Najibullah offered to step down, and on April 16 he was forced to flee as Islamic rebels joined by rebellious government forces surged toward the capital. The vice president, a non-Communist, took control of the interim government. The rebel groups temporarily agreed on a provisional government but soon began fighting among themselves for control of the capital. In the early fall of 1992, they had not reached an agreement and fighting continued.

Press reports indicated that the war had caused as many as 2 million deaths out of a population of 17 million (*AP* 4/16/92) and that about 5 million refugees had fled to neighboring Pakistan and Iran. In September 1992, the capital was without electricity and piped water. The United Nations was assisting the return of refugees, but it was trying without success to mediate a settlement among the rebel groups.

MONGOLIA—A FORGOTTEN SATELLITE

Mongolia is an isolated, pastoral country with China on the south and the Soviet Union on the north. It has a population of about 2 million. Except for a few years it was under Chinese suzerainty in the 200 years before 1921. At that time, with Soviet assistance, it became independent, only to become a Russian satellite in 1924. It was the first Communist state established outside the Soviet Union.

Soviet troops withdrew in 1925, but Mongolia continued to be dominated by the Soviet advisers who remained. Soviet troops returned and they were stationed there after 1966, outnumbering the Mongolian forces. Both the People's Republic of China and the Republic of China on Taiwan recognized the independence of Mongolia, thereby renouncing any claim to it.

The economy is based on livestock with the exception of a Soviet-built copper-molybdenum plant, which is one of the ten largest in the world.

Until the late 1980s the government was a standard Stalinist model. The economy had been integrated into that of the Soviet Union, and foreign trade was mostly with the Council for Mutual Economic Assistance (CMEA) countries. Beginning in 1987, modest economic reforms were implemented (*IMF Survey* 4/29/91).

In March 1990 pressures for reform brought about the resignation of the leadership of the Communist Party (Mongolian People's Revolutionary Party) and multiparty elections. The electoral system kept the Communist Party in control, but the opposition was able to win major representation in the bicameral legislature.

Freedom House graded the government as "free" stating that Mongolians are able to change their government democratically and that the 1990 elections were generally free. It adds that fundamental freedoms are generally respected by the government and that there are no political prisoners (Freedom House 1991–1992). In the June 1992 elections, the former Communist Party, which formally abandoned Communist ideology, won over 90 percent of the seats (*NYT* 7/1/92).

This newfound freedom was enough for reformers to assert independence from Soviet influence and start market reforms, including freeing prices and privatization of the state-controlled livestock cooperatives and industrial enterprises. This encouraged 14 nations, along with the World Bank and the IMF, to pledge $150 million for credits to small enterprises. The government, however, kept control of the most important sectors, such as transportation, mines, and electric power. As in other Communist states the shock of restructuring, the reduction of aid, and purchases from the former Soviet bloc led to a sharp decrease in output, estimated at 18 percent in 1991 (*IMF Survey* 5/25/92).

Mongolia was asserting its sovereignty in 1991. In January 1991 President Ochirbal met with President Bush and with the U.N. Secretary General. Soviet troops withdrew. Mongolia opened more border crossing points with China, which had been discouraged while it was under Soviet tutelage. Mongolia quickly recognized the independence of Latvia, Estonia, and Lithuania.

Mongolian nationalism supported the new leaders in seizing the opportunity to assert independence from Soviet domination. The process was aided by the general détente between the Soviet Union and China, which downgraded Mongolia's strategic importance as a threat to China. In this sense, the process was similar to Soviet détente with Western Europe and the ending of Soviet domination in Eastern Europe. Mongolia's opening up to the outside world also gave impetus to political groups calling for democratic and market reforms. The opening was followed by hardships of economic adjustment to market prices, but the majority of the Mongolian people who depended on livestock for a livelihood were not seriously affected.

PATTERNS OF COMMUNIST WARS IN ASIA

After World War II Communist wars kept Asia in a turmoil. North Korea's attack on South Korea, supported by the Soviet Union and China, gave the cold war a worldwide dimension. The war was initiated by Kim Il Sung to unify Korea and spread Communism in defiance of the United Nations and its attempts to establish a peaceful world order. The United States led the U.N. in fighting back against the challenge. Kim Il Sung consolidated control of a hostile, Stalinist-type of government that fell behind the development of the regime in the south.

Ho Chi Minh won his wars against French colonialism. North Vietnam then defeated South Vietnam and the United States, which were supported by a few Asian allies. The anti-imperialist elements of the Communist doctrine, joined with Vietnamese nationalism, fueled the guerilla warfare that exhausted the United States and caused it to withdraw. North Vietnamese forces gave the coup de grace by a conventional military offensive.

The Cambodian war, which made a wasteland of the country, was a case of Communist ideologues gone mad in their attempt to erase bourgeoise culture. The Khmer Rouge under Pol Pot were also insane to challenge the victorious North Vietnamese. They retaliated by installing a puppet regime under Vietnamese control. Vietnam and Cambodia then became pawns in the contest between China and the Soviet Union. Vietnam finally withdrew in exhaustion in 1989. The growing détente between the Soviet Union and the West played a part in this withdrawal as the Soviet Union cut back on aid to Vietnam. After extensive negotiations aided by the conciliatory policy of Gorbachev, the United Nations agreed to assist in political and economic reconstruction of Cambodia with the most expensive peacekeeping operation in history. It was a formidable task to heal the wounds caused by one of the cruelest governments in history.

Laos's wars were a byproduct of Vietnam's wars. After Vietnam was settled, Laos became Vietnam's satellite. The Communist system also failed to take hold in Laos, and the movement for reform in other Communist nations encouraged reformers in Laos. Its economic reforms showed encouraging results by 1992, but it was still following the Chinese example by keeping the Communist Party in control.

The Soviet attack on Afghanistan astounded the world. The violent resistance of the Afghanis to Communist atheist domination succeeded in exhausting the Soviet invaders. The Afghanis were assisted by weapons from the United

States, China, Saudi Arabia, and other countries, as well as the general condemnation of most of the world. The United Nations helped negotiate a withdrawal of Soviet forces by 1989. The Soviets and the United States terminated aid at the beginning of 1992, and by March the Afghan regime was exhausted. In the spring of 1992 the United Nations continued to assist in setting up a democratic government and coordinating aid. It was able to operate much more effectively with the cooperation of Gorbachev and Yeltsin.

The Communist-led wars in Korea, Vietnam, Cambodia, Laos, and Afghanistan, caused upward of 9 million deaths and countless nonfatal casualties, millions of refugees, and widespread destruction. Nationalism, allied with Communism, had fueled the attacks to unify Korea and Vietnam. In these wars Communists aimed at "liberating" people from Western "imperialism." By the early 1990s, their sacrifices appeared to be in vain. South Korea was free and prosperous in contrast to the poverty in the Communist north, while Vietnam was beginning market reforms and welcoming Western foreign investment and aid.

Communist regimes were the aggressors against other Communist regimes in the wars of Cambodia and Afghanistan. After the Khmer Rouge Communists ran amok killing over 1 million of their own people, Vietnam attacked and made Cambodia a satellite. Vietnam withdrew under international pressure, and the United Nations began major democratic and market reforms in Cambodia. Afghanistan was in chaos in 1992 after the Soviets withdrew. These wars in Afghanistan and Cambodia also were in vain and proved little except that the Communist regimes were aggressive, and that nationalisms of the Cambodian, Laotian and Afghanistan people proved to be stronger ideologies than Communism.

Chapter 9

Communist Challenges in Latin America

Many Americans saw Communism in Central America as a challenge to the Monroe Doctrine, which President James Monroe set forth in his annual message to Congress on December 2, 1823. In essence, he said that the United States would regard as unfriendly any effort by a European power to interfere with the political systems on the American continents. By that time Latin Americans had successfully revolted against Spanish colonial controls and established many of the present states. Moreover the Russians had been moving to extend control southward from Alaska along the California coast (Bemis 1942, 196–209).

The Monroe Doctrine became part of American tradition and was even used to excuse U.S. intervention in Latin America in the first part of this century. Before World War II the United States cooperated with Latin American countries to prevent Nazi Germany from taking over colonies in this hemisphere from the European countries it had conquered. It was natural, then, for U.S. leaders to apply the Monroe Doctrine to the Communist challenge after World War II as Castro moved Cuba toward Communism and an alliance with the Soviet Union, and as Nicaragua aligned with Cuba in the 1980s. On the other hand, Latin American countries had negotiated treaties with the United States that forbid its intervention in their affairs.

This helps explain why the United States took such a serious view of the Soviet Union's relations with Cuba and Nicaragua. The Soviet Union's challenge to the United States by moving missiles into Cuba in 1962 was one of the most serious crises that the United States and the world has faced.

CASTRO'S CUBA

The United States has long been concerned about Cuba not only because of its close geographic position, but also because of the ties stemming from the Spanish-American War of 1898. That war grew out of U.S. outrage over the suppression of Cubans by Spanish colonial masters. The United States defeated Spain easily. During the U.S. military occupation that followed, Cuba obtained special arrangements to sell its sugar in the United States, which, depending on market conditions, eventually amounted to a subsidy of $100 million a year or more. The United States invested a great deal in Cuba. Moreover, the United States navy obtained the right to develop Guantanamo Bay on the island as a major naval base. U.S. troops withdrew a few years after the war, but Congress passed the Platt Amendment in 1901 stating that the United States might intervene in Cuba to maintain law and order. The United States intervened frequently in Cuba and other Latin American countries as well, until the Good Neighbor policy of President Franklin D. Roosevelt in the early 1930s renounced interventionism there.

A series of dictatorships in Cuba preceded Batista's rule in 1952. In 1957 Fidel Castro began a revolution by landing in Cuba and establishing a base in the mountains with the help of a few intellectuals, professionals, and two leading Communists, Che Guevara and Castro's brother Raul. Castro issued a Manifesto of Sierra Maestra in 1957 calling for freedom of the press and other democratic freedoms. The Batista dictatorship by that time had become so oppressive that President Eisenhower in March 1958 stopped shipping arms to that government. In 1958 the U.S. ambassador reported that stopping arms had a crippling psychological effect on the Batista regime. In August 1958 Castro started marching on the capital with less than 2000 men. Batista's army of 40,000 evaporated for lack of support, and Castro took over the government in an almost bloodless revolution.

Castro's first announcements indicated that he would establish a left-wing, but not Communist system, and apparently even the Soviets did not regard him as a Communist at first (Khrushchev 1970, 580–583). Initially, the Communist Party did not support Castro's revolution, although a few Communists including his brother were in the movement. By early 1959, if not earlier, Castro was a convert—by March 1959 making speeches that sounded Communist. By October and November the moderates who had helped him with his revolution had been arrested or had resigned. By the end of 1959 several of the non-Communist members of his cabinet fled to the United States along with about 100,000 other refugees. Eventually there were about 1 million Cubans living abroad. By 1960 the government was taking over newspapers and establishing a Communist-type regime. Castro also made arrangements with the Soviet Union for a large-scale import of arms, scheduled for delivery in the summer of 1961. The dramatic events of the next two years consolidated his Communist ties and the confrontation with the United States.

The Soviet Missiles

The Cuban missile crisis brought the United States and the Soviet Union close to nuclear war. After Kennedy and Khrushchev faced this horror, they initiated an era of nuclear arms control and détente. Most observers believe Kennedy's wise and firm policy brought about a victory for the United States. However, the crisis and its aftermath raises serious issues—questions about how fragile peace was in the nuclear era, how Americans misread Kennedy's policies, and whether a hard line against Cuba succeeded.

The United States had given Castro's new government prompt recognition in 1958, sending Ambassador Philip Bonsal. Castro refused to see him during the first few months. When Castro visited Washington in April 1959, the State Department set up meetings to discuss an aid program, but the Cuban instructed his officials not to discuss aid. Castro himself did not use the argument of his sympathizers that rejection in Washington drove him to Moscow. Up until March 1960 the United States was trying to make reconciliation with Castro, but it was rejected. At that time President Eisenhower agreed to a CIA recommendation to start training Cuban exiles for a possible overthrow of Castro (Schlesinger 1965, 209).

On January 3, 1961, Castro ordered the U.S. embassy staff to be reduced to 11 people in 24 hours. Why? The U.S. Senate report on assassination plots, published in 1975, throws light on this question. In August 1960 CIA officials in Havana offered $10,000 to a new Cuban contact if he would kill Castro. In line with Washington instructions, the CIA later dropped the matter. On August 16, 1960, however, the CIA in Havana received a box of Castro's favorite cigars with a botulism toxin so potent that anyone would die if he put one in his mouth. It was ready on October 7, and presumably the CIA was discussing with some contact in Cuba how to get these cigars to Castro. In October 1960 a Chicago gangster named Giancana bragged that he had a contract with the CIA to kill Castro in November. This report was picked up by the FBI, which knew nothing of the CIA plot.

Meanwhile, early in 1960 the Eisenhower administration had authorized the CIA to begin training and arming of a Cuban Exile Liberation Army in Guatemala. By October 30 a Guatemalan city newspaper broke the story saying that the army was training to invade Cuba, and it hinted at U.S. collusion. In the following months, U.S. periodicals and newspapers picked up the story, and by April there were numerous news stories telling about recruitment in the United States for the invasion efforts.

In retrospect, the U.S. plots for Castro's death and overthrow seemed so widespread that it is obvious Castro had received word of them by the time he demanded reduction of the U.S. embassy staff. Later Castro asserted that there were 26 U.S. attempts to assassinate him. If he did not know of such efforts at the time, he certainly read the reports in the news media about CIA support for the invasion army of Cuban dissidents. Either one of these endeavors would have justified his action to severely cut back the embassy staff.

President Kennedy at his inauguration in January 1961 inherited the invasion plot from Eisenhower. After discussing it with top intelligence and military officials, Kennedy decided to go ahead on the condition that the United States would not provide direct support by its forces. On April 17, 1961, the Cuban exiles landed at the Bay of Pigs with disastrous results. About 1400 Cubans failed to maintain a beachhead. Instead of fading into the jungle as planned, almost all of them were captured by Castro. By the time the fiasco ended, a few U.S. pilots had helped in raids with B-26s, and the U.S. navy and aircraft had escorted vessels close to the Cuban coast.

President Kennedy publicly took full responsibility for the failure. Although the attack did not come close to success, his popularity in U.S. polls increased for trying to do something about Castro. It was clear to Castro and the rest of the world that the United States was making determined efforts to attack his regime.

Before judging whether the U.S.-sponsored efforts to attack Cuba and kill Castro led to Khrushchev's decision to place nuclear missiles in Cuba, it is useful to review how the crisis unfolded and to examine Khrushchev's account. On the morning of October 16, 1962, President Kennedy was shown pictures of missile sites in Cuba where between 16 and 32 intermediate-range Soviet ballistic missiles were being emplaced. It was estimated that they would be operational in about two weeks. Kennedy immediately appointed a committee of top officials (EXCOM) to recommend what action the United States should take.

During the week after the initial discovery of the missile sites, the president carried on business as usual while the committee debated various options. On Friday, October 19, after listening to the conclusions of EXCOM, the president decided on the limited blockade option, to be called a quarantine. During discussion of this option, Adlai Stevenson, ambassador to the United Nations, suggested that this demand be coupled with an offer to withdraw U.S. nuclear missiles from Turkey. The president replied that some time ago he had asked the State Department to negotiate the removal of these Jupiter missiles since they were obsolete, liquid-fuel weapons. Kennedy was irritated to learn that the State Department had not carried out this task. The president was informed that the missiles were tied to NATO defenses, and the State Department had gone on the assumption that removal required approval from NATO and Turkish authorities, and this approval had not yet been forthcoming. The president believed that backing down and withdrawing the missiles from Turkey at that point would have undermined the confidence of our European allies and our willingness to help defend them (Sorenson 1966, 770).

Later, at American University in Washington, DC, the president explained his choice of the quarantine strategy: "Above all while defending our own vital interest, nuclear powers must avoid those confrontations which bring an adversary to a choice of either humiliating retreat or a nuclear war." He wanted to leave some options for Khrushchev and some options for saving face that a direct invasion would not permit. Khrushchev, as late as September 11, had indicated that a military invasion of Cuba would unleash a nuclear war. In the face of such a threat, Kennedy decided to picture the blockade option as "a quarantine" that would only block shipments of additional missiles and missile components, and it was not a full-scale blockade of petroleum and other civilian products. A blockade traditionally is considered an act of war.

On Monday, October 22, after consulting with congressional leaders, Kennedy announced the quarantine. That evening in reporting to the U.S. people he said that the Soviets' "sudden, clandestine decision to station strategic weapons for the first time outside of Soviet soil, is a deliberately provocative and unjustified change in the status quo which cannot be accepted by this country, if our courage and commitments are ever to be trusted again by either friend or foe." He added that "the 1930s taught us a clear lesson: aggressive conduct, if allowed to go unchecked and unchallenged, ultimately leads to war." He then outlined the steps that would be taken including the quarantine on shipment of additional missiles and missile parts (Sorenson 1966, 780).

The following week was a period of high tension as the world waited for the Soviet response. The president, with concern for international law and the Monroe Doctrine, took the matter to the Organization of American States (OAS), which gave him unanimous support. Cuba did not attend the OAS meeting. An important action in the minds of the U.S. Executive Committee during that week was the unanimous endorsement by the OAS of the quarantine in a broad, authorizing resolution. The United States also presented its case to the U.N. Security Council. The following Tuesday and Wednesday, October 23 and 24, 16 of the 18 Soviet ships sailing toward Cuba reversed course in the face of the U.S. navy. The tension continued, however, because daily U-2 flights over Cuba indicated that the emplacement of the missiles was being rushed, and reports indicated that Soviet diplomats in New York were burning their secret messages and getting ready to evacuate.

On Friday, October 26, President Kennedy received a rambling letter from Khrushchev stating that the missiles were being emplaced only to defend Cuba and that if he had assurance that the United States would not attack Castro, he would withdraw them. The Executive Committee immediately went into session to consider how to reply. On Saturday, October 27, another letter from Khrushchev added the condition that the Jupiter missiles in Turkey be withdrawn. After intensive consideration with the Executive Committee, Kennedy decided that the United States would not withdraw the Jupiter missiles under pressure and that he would finesse the second letter by replying only to the first one.

In the reply, which was okayed by the Executive Committee, the president agreed to the conditions set by Khrushchev in his October 26 letter, saying that the United States would give a commitment not to invade Cuba if work on the missile sites would cease. The withdrawal of missiles would be confirmed by U.N. observations. He ignored the question of the Jupiter missiles in Turkey. Nevertheless, the Joint Chiefs of Staff continued to favor an air strike. One of the Joint Chiefs, Air Force General Curtis LeMay, wanted a nuclear strike against Cuba.

The next day, October 28, Khrushchev publicly announced that the missiles would be withdrawn since the United States had pledged not to invade Cuba. This was the climax of the missile crisis, and most accounts of it end with this decision, noting that the missiles were withdrawn as promised by the Soviets. Although the U.N. did not supervise their withdrawal because of strong objec-

tions by Castro, the Cubans did permit daily U-2 flights to monitor the dismantling of the Soviet missiles, and U.S. navy ships and U-2s from a distance
checked on their return as the ships sailed back to the Soviet Union.

There is little agreement, however, on the motives for the Soviet move. The
most obvious conclusion was that the Soviets, in one stroke, would have greatly
reduced the strategic missile advantage of the United States. At that time, the
U.S. arsenal of intercontinental missiles far exceeded that of the USSR by
probably a ratio of 5 or 10 to 1. Placing intermediate-range missiles in Cuba,
which the Soviets had in greater numbers, would have reduced the strategic
advantage of the United States. Other reasons seriously considered by Kennedy
for the Soviet move were: (1) that it was a probe or test of U.S. will, (2) that it
was a trap to divert U.S. attention from another power move, (3) that it was
designed to defend Cuba against attack, and (4) that it was a bargaining move to
exchange for a U.S. withdrawal from Berlin. The president tended to lean
toward the first reason, that it was a test of U.S. will, with the defense of Cuba
and a move to catch up with U.S. missile strength as secondary motives (Sorenson 1966, 747–749).

Kennedy made a diplomatic move during the crisis that initially escaped the
attention of many commentators. After the EXCOM decided not to offer to
withdraw the missiles from Turkey, he secretly sent Bobby Kennedy, his brother
who was attorney general, to discuss the issue with Ambassador Dobrynin. In
this discussion, the attorney general assured Dobrynin that the president would
remove the missiles from Turkey, but that he could not make such a commitment in public at this time. Bobby also indicated that there was a great deal of
pressure being exerted by the U.S. military command for an invasion, but that
the president was resisting such pressures (Kennedy 1969, 13–14, 38–39). The
assurance about the missile sites in Turkey, off the record, did meet the important condition laid down in the second Khrushchev letter and at least added
more room for the Soviets to maneuver.

Also, the president prepared another conciliatory move that should go on the
record, but that has been largely overlooked. Toward the end of the crisis
Kennedy secretly arranged to have the U.N. secretary general propose that the
Soviets withdraw their missiles from Cuba and that the United States withdraw
its missiles from Turkey (Garthoff 1987, 59–60; Schoenbaum 1987, 323–325).
The ploy of having the U.N. secretary general suggest this solution would have
saved face for Kennedy in relation to NATO. Khrushchev yielded before this
was put into effect.

Before making a final assessment on the causes of this major crisis and the
lessons to be learned from it, it is helpful to look at it from the point of view of
Khrushchev and Fidel Castro. Fortunately, we have Khrushchev's account in
his memoirs.

Khrushchev notes that at the beginning of the revolution he had no idea that
Castro would establish a Communist regime, although he knew that Raul Castro, Fidel's brother, was a Communist and that Che Guevara, the leader of

Fidel's military, was also a good Communist. Then, before the Bay of Pigs invasion, Castro declared that Cuba would follow the Communist course. Khrushchev stated that this puzzled Soviet leaders, since from a tactical standpoint it did not make sense to invite U.S. opposition. Khrushchev believed that the Bay of Pigs was only a beginning of the assaults against Castro. To Khrushchev, Cuba appeared like a "sausage" that was vulnerable to U.S. attack.

Khrushchev then asserts that the Soviet Union had to confront the United States with more than words. The logical answer was missiles, and his major motive, he said, was to restrain the United States from attacking Castro. He added, "In addition to protecting Cuba, our missiles would have equalized what the West likes to call the balance of power." It was high time, he said, that the United States knew what it felt like to have its own land and people threatened. The idea came to him on a visit to Romania after he read about the installation of intermediate-range missiles in Turkey. Therefore, Khrushchev decided to install intermediate-range missiles and the medium-range IL-28 bombers in Cuba, which, although they were becoming obsolete, could reach American cities with nuclear warheads.

He noted that U.S. citizens became frightened, so the Soviets stepped up their shipments to get the missiles in place. Then, he said, Kennedy issued a warning, and the United States began to make a belligerent show of strength including blockading the island. By that time, Khrushchev said, the Soviets had installed enough missiles to destroy New York, Chicago, and other huge industrial cities, as well as Washington, DC. Then President Kennedy issued an ultimatum about withdrawing the missiles. Robert Kennedy went to see Ambassador Dobrynin, and, according to Khrushchev, Kennedy said that if the situation continued much longer, the military could seize power. According to Khrushchev, Robert Kennedy said, "We don't know how much longer we can hold out against our generals" (Khrushchev 1974, 580–584).

Khrushchev spent the night at the Council of Ministers office, and, upon receiving the president's assurance that there would be no invasion of Cuba by the United States, and after consultation with his comrades, the Soviet leader agreed to remove the missiles. Khrushchev reports that Castro was furious and even refused to receive the Soviet ambassador. Nevertheless, despite the Soviet withdrawal of missiles under pressure from the United States, Khrushchev states in his memoirs that he remembers Kennedy with "deep respect" because he was soberminded and determined to avoid war. Moreover, Khrushchev says, Kennedy left himself a way out of the crisis and showed real wisdom in turning his back on the right-wing forces that were trying to goad him into military action. Khrushchev concludes that it was a great victory for the Soviets because the United States had to pledge not to invade Cuba. He adds that "the American imperialist beast was forced to swallow a hedgehog, quills and all" (Khrushchev 1974, 580–584).

Kennedy conditioned his commitment not to invade Cuba on the United

Nations supervising the withdrawal of the missiles. However, Castro refused to admit U.N. officials to supervise their withdrawal.

In 1992 American and Soviet participants compared notes and revealed further alarming information. During the crisis both sides were prepared to use nuclear weapons, if the United States had invaded Cuba to destroy the missile sites, and American advisers were urging an invasion. During the crisis Castro had sent a telegram to Moscow urging it to launch an immediate nuclear strike. This frightened Khrushchev, and he backed off. (*NYT* 10/23/92, 17; 10/14/92, 19). Khrushchev lost the political support of the military as a result of his actions during the crisis. (Garthoff 1978, 41–43).

It is also disturbing that most U.S. citizens backed the hard line and would have gone into nuclear war without agreeing to remove the missiles from Turkey. In fact, Kennedy secretly did meet Khrushchev's reasonable demand to remove these missiles. Americans tend to trust their leaders and back them in a crisis even if their positions are unreasonable. Moreover, the United States continued to back a hard line against Castro's government, while Cuba has refused to stop much of its revolutionary activity.

After the crisis, the United States honored the pledge not to invade Cuba, but the CIA supported probes and small-scale attacks of Cuban refugees from bases along the Florida coast. President Johnson ended those raids (Schlesinger 1978, 472–474; Garthoff 1987, 91). Castro continued to give material and propaganda support to revolutionary movements in Latin America.

Before the Cuban missile crisis, Castro had supported raids against Haiti, Panama, Nicaragua, and the Dominican Republic (Higgins 1987). After the crisis Cuban personnel and urban terrorists unsuccessfully tried to overthrow the Venezuelan government. As a result the Organization of American States (OAS) in 1964 imposed economic and political sanctions on Cuba. In 1967 Che Guevara, a close Castro associate, failed to promote revolution in Bolivia, and he was captured and killed.

Cuba cooperated closely with the Soviet Union in supporting Marxist regimes in Africa, including sending over 20,000 troops to support the Marxist government of Angola against insurgents, and large contingents to a Marxist-military regime in Ethiopia. In December 1981 the U.S. State Department reported that Cuba had sent 1500 to 2000 military and security advisers to Nicaragua, and that Cuba had been a funnel of $28 million in aid for military equipment (U.S. Department of State 1981, February 23 and December 14). The advisers had a great deal of influence in Nicaragua (Aguila 1987, 425–428).

Cuba lost credit in the eyes of the world because of its dependence on the Soviet Union. It had been active in the nonaligned movement of about 100 countries that asserted they were not tied to either of the superpower alliances. In the 1979 Sixth Summit Conference of the nonaligned nations, Cuba was criticized for sending troops to Africa, and 30 countries threatened to boycott the Havana meeting because of Cuban activities. President Tito of Yugoslavia led the opposition on the basis that Cuba was not truly nonaligned because of its alliance with the Soviet Union. He did not succeed in getting a formal condemnation. In 1980, however, after Cuba supported the Soviet Union in the United Nations on the invasion of Afghanistan, Castro's government was soundly defeated in trying to get a seat on the Security Council, although it had been in line for one before the invasion.

Before 1988 Castro's overtures to the Carter and Reagan administrations to end the confrontation foundered on U.S. demands that he stop supporting revolutionary movements and withdraw troops from Angola. In 1988, however, there were signs of an interest in a détente with the United States. Castro agreed to withdraw troops from Angola in connection with arrangements for neighboring Namibia to hold elections under U.N. auspices and attain independence from South Africa. In the summer of 1989 Castro brought General Elizardo Sanchez, number three in the Cuban hierarchy, to trial along with other officers and condemned him to death for helping smuggle drugs to the United States. This confirmed U.S. charges of Cuban complicity in the drug trade and was an important move toward discouraging such trade. There also was a minor relaxation of suppression of dissidents in Cuba (*CSM* 4/5/89).

Meanwhile Castro's relations with the Soviet Union cooled. At the end of March 1989 Gorbachev visited the island. Although on the surface relations were cordial, in the background was Castro's criticism of perestroika, Gorbachev's admonitions for Castro to reform, and reports that Soviet subsidies to Cuba were cut (*NYT* 4/3/89, 1; *Economist* 7/8/89, 45–46).

The United States continued to take a hard line by intensifying the embargo in 1992. President-elect Clinton approved. The embargo was popular among Cubans who had settled in Florida, a pivotal state in elections. The U.S. embargo was condemned by the U.N. General Assembly and by pundits who believed Castro would be weakened by open commercial and travel relations with the United States (*NYT* 11/25/92, 1). Castro continued his propaganda attacks against the United States, using the embargo as a means of rallying support, and even paid an agent in America to support raids against Cuba (*Economist* 11/21/92, 28). Examining Castro's society helps shed light on these issues.

Castro's Communism

Castro's government was based on a strict Communist model. His revolution was supported by an alliance of intellectuals with some participation by Communists but not from the Communist Party. In the first 20 years he established a personal dictatorship with a Communist ideology rather than a standard Communist system controlled by a party elite. The Communist Party did not hold its first congress until 1975, almost 20 years after Castro's seizure of power. The purpose of the congress was to consolidate the one-party "Caudillo" (military dictator) system dominated by Castro.

Before the 1975 Cuban Communist Party Congress, the party had no formal rules and regulations, and the party bodies met sporadically, if at all. In 1969 the Communist Party had only 55,000 party members, among the smallest per capita in the world. Before the Party Congress, it expanded to 203,000 based on only half the workplaces in Cuba; it still was one of the smallest Communist parties. By 1980 it doubled again. The great mass of members were officials and military. From 1975 to 1989 the Central Committee met only every six months for one day to ratify decisions of the Politburo and Castro.

The legislative facade of the government consisted of local, provincial, and national bodies called Organs of People's Power and Assemblies of People's Power. Party members dominated these assemblies with their recommendations and decisions. Almost all the Council of State and more than 90 percent of the national assembly consisted of party members. The National Assembly of People's Power was elected indirectly by the Assemblies of People's Power.

The major mass organization, the Committee for the Defense of the Revolution, was an auxiliary to the armed forces and militia to which over half of the population belonged. They tracked down counterrevolutionaries, corrupt officials, and black marketeers. The confrontation with the United States and the past CIA attacks helped to keep up the morale of this organization.

Castro's party coalition was officially the Communist Party of Cuba in 1965. Castro was first secretary of the Communist Party and also served as head of state and prime minister. Castro's brother, Raul, was second in command as first vice president of the Council of Ministers. Castro and his family were in key party and key government positions. Castro's speeches were laced with Marxist language and attacks against U.S. imperialism. There were periodic purges to remove opposition. The old guard revolutionaries occupied the top positions in the tradition of the Latin American caudillo.

In 1991 Freedom House gave Cuba the lowest ratings in terms of political rights and civil liberties for a number of reasons. It cited the high proportion of prisoners per capita and the tight controls over social organizations. There were severe crackdowns on human rights activists and reports of torture in the prisons. Political opposition was severely repressed. The ratings were controversial in the intellectual community for several reasons. Some intellectuals had sympathy for Castro and his government. On the positive side, Castro's program to remove illiteracy had been successful. Reportedly medical care was among the best in Latin America (Ozinga 1987, 202). Castro was a populist type of leader and seemed to enjoy popular support as he traveled around Cuba. The rich and powerful United States maintained an embargo, and in the past the CIA had supported attempts to overthrow him. The most extensive attempt was at the Bay of Pigs. Castro in past decades allowed dissidents and criminals to emigrate. The United States attempted to be selective in granting immigration visas to these people.

By the time of the anti-Communist revolutions in Europe, pressures were building up in Cuba. The strict government controls over the economy were causing major problems. Cuba had accumulated a foreign debt of about $10 billion, or $1000 per capita, the largest per capita in Latin America, with the bulk of the debt to the Soviet Union. However, by 1992, with the depreciation of the ruble, repayment would be much less burdensome. Soviet subsidies and aid, estimated at as much as $5 billion a year, including military support, which would be about $500 per capita, were cut off. However, this figure may have been greatly overstated, since prices of Soviet goods included in that figure often were highly overpriced.

The Cuban economy was jolted by the revolution in the Soviet Union. About 85 percent of Cuba's trade was with the Eastern bloc, and much of that trade was subsidized. Castro declared a state of emergency and vowed "socialism or death." He warned against political experiments (moves toward democracy) and difficulties coming from the camp of Cuba's friends (the Soviet Union and Eastern Europe). The drastic cutback in aid and trade from former Communist countries caused Cuba to ration food. Since farmers' markets were banned, black markets developed. Special reaction squads of Communist Party members were organized to cut down protests or debate (*Economist* 5/16/92, 51–52). Cuba's sugar crop was expected to drop 25 percent in 1992, and foreign trade to be less than half of that in 1989 (Dispatch 4/20/92, 312–314).

By 1992 Castro had begun to adjust economic policy to the winds for change, but not his hardline politics. In 1989 he had said if capitalism returned to Cuba, it would become "an extension of Miami" (Gunn 1990, 140). In November 1991, however, he was saying that Marx, Engels, or Lenin never said it was possible to construct socialism without capital, technology, and markets, particularly in the case of a small island like Cuba. He added that we are dealing with a world "where a large part of the socialist system has collapsed." Cuba, by that time, was encouraging foreign private investment with guaranteed repatriation of profits and tax holidays. However, in the critical food sector, where food was severely rationed, Castro himself emphatically rejected the idea of permitting free farmers' markets (Gunn 1992, 59–64). In the political sphere, those who dared to speak out against Castro were imprisoned. In 1992 he dismissed some top officials, including his son (*NYT* 9/7/92).

To sum up, Castro was a psychological thorn in the side of the United States because of his support for radical movements in Latin America and elsewhere. Confrontation almost caused a nuclear war in 1962 when the Soviets moved nuclear missiles into Cuba. The crisis was solved when Khrushchev withdrew the missiles after Kennedy threatened to attack Cuba while secretly yielding to Khrushchev's conditions. Kennedy was backed by political support from Latin America and U.S. allies.

Castro based his hardline Communism on national pride and opposition to the United States. He continued to use Cuban nationalist resentment of the U.S. embargo as a psychological prop to his regime, which was having serious economic and political problems. Democratic opposition was suppressed and arrested.

THE COMMUNIST THREATS TO NICARAGUA AND PERU

In 1937 Anastosio Somoza took control of Nicaragua and his family continued dictatorial rule until the regime was overthrown by the Sandinista National Liberation Front. The Sandinistas took their name from an early guerilla hero, Augusta Sandino, who had opposed the occupation of Nicaragua by U.S. marines in the early 1930s.

A few days before President Reagan took office, the Carter administration suspended disbursement of aid to the new Nicaraguan Sandinista government because it was helping El Salvadoran rebels to obtain aid. The cutback of U.S. aid was followed by a large inflow of Cuban and Soviet arms to Nicaragua along with 1500 Cuban advisers.

By 1981 the Sandinista government pointed to press reports of a U.S. military training camp near Miami, Florida, for Nicaraguan exiles planning to overthrow the Sandinistas and to CIA-supported raids from Honduras. *Newsweek* and other news media featured reports of CIA assistance in Honduras to groups raiding Nicaragua. This pressure was reinforced by major U.S. military exercises carried out in Honduras.

Despite the 1982 Boland Amendment, which prohibited covert aid designed to overthrow the Nicaraguan government, the Reagan administration continued indirect U.S. aid to the contras with the rationale that it was designed to cut off aid to the rebels in El Salvador that was channeled through Nicaragua. In April 1984 the news media featured reports of the mining of Nicaraguan harbors that had been supported by the CIA. In the ensuing uproar Congress cut off funds to finance covert attacks against Nicaragua, which pressed a claim in the International Court of Justice that U.S. intervention and support of the contras violated international law. On May 10, 1984, the court gave an initial order that the United States respect Nicaragua's sovereignty. In January 1985 the United States refused to participate further in the court proceedings. After Reagan's reelection in November, he obtained congressional approval for $27 million in aid to the contras, but Congress limited it to "nonlethal" aid.

Meanwhile, Guatemala, El Salvador, Costa Rica, Nicaragua, and Honduras negotiated a plan for peace that included removing foreign military advisers from the area and bringing to an end the use of one country as a base for an attack against another. The United States refused to accept the plan, alleging that it did not provide for adequate enforcement. The five nations made supplementary pacts in the Esquipulas II agreement of August 5, 1987, and the El Salvador agreement of February 15, 1989. These agreements provided for Nicaragua to guarantee "free functioning of communication media" and for free elections to take place no later than February 25, 1990, for its National Assembly, president, vice president, municipalities, and for a Central American parliament. In return the Central American presidents committed themselves to formulate a plan for voluntary repatriation in Nicaragua of the contras. The presidents also undertook necessary steps to work out a cease-fire.

After complicated negotiations in the U.S. Congress, it passed further non-lethal aid for the contras. Meanwhile the OAS and the U.N. secretary general arranged to monitor the repatriation of the contras and the 1990 free elections in Nicaragua. The United States, faced with overwhelming support for the Central American plan, did not block the arrangements. The net effect was to bring the civil war to an end at the end of 1989 except for a few isolated raids, which Nicaragua blamed on the contras.

There was hope the cease-fire would hold and that Nicaragua would carry out its commitments for democratic elections. Nevertheless the tensions in the area did not abate as the United States continued to supply the contras with nonlethal aid and as the Soviet Union continued to provide an estimated $1 billion a year in aid. The aid tapered off when the Soviets reached agreement with the United States in the summer of 1989 to stop direct aid to Nicaragua, but Cuba continued to provide aid.

Table 9-1 indicates that the major issue was political-psychological rather than a military threat of aggression. Nicaragua's neighbors, with the help of the United States and with their superior population and armed forces, could easily defeat aggression by Nicaragua. The real fear was the spread of Cuban-type Communism through Nicaragua's support of revolution in its neighbors. The United States, moreover, appeared to fear this spread more so than the Central American countries themselves, which were able to sit down with Nicaragua and negotiate guarantees that would allow an opposition to express itself in elections. In other words they were negotiating away a tendency toward Communism in Nicaragua. With this as a background, we now examine the Nicaraguan political system to determine if it was, in fact, close to Communism and what kind of political challenge it presented.

The Sandinista National Liberation Front (FSLN) took control of the country

Table 9-1
Comparison of Population, Armed Forces, and Defense Spending in Central America, 1987

Country	Population (millions)	Number in armed forces (thousands)	Defense spending ($ millions)
Nicaragua	3.5	77	436 (1986)
El Salvador	5.9	47	177
Guatemala	8.6	40	266
Honduras	4.8	19	68
Costa Rica	2.7	31 (1986)	9.5

Source: International Institute for Strategic Studies, *The Military Balance 1988–1989* (London: International Institute of Strategic Studies, 1989), 189–197.

from the Somoza dictatorship in 1979. The FSLN was a coalition that included the Nicaraguan Socialist Party, a pro-Soviet Communist Party that later broke away from FSLN. The revolution succeeded because a broad spectrum of people helped overthrow the Somoza dictatorship.

There is no doubt about the socialist (Marxist) orientation of the controlling faction of the FSLN. Although the government adopted Marxism-Leninism as its ideology, it did not completely suppress political opposition. The FSLN leaders talked about their party being the vanguard, but internal opposition, as well as external pressures, forced it to permit elections with some degree of political opposition. Also, it nationalized only a small proportion of the economy due in part to the economic problems it faced. Moreover, in early 1991, as a result of pressure from the United States and its neighbors, it stopped funneling arms to the revolution in El Salvador (U.S. Department of State 1981; Fagen 1983; Krumwiede 1984; Gilbert 1986).

In 1984 Nicaragua had held elections for the legislature and the presidency. Daniel Ortega won the presidency by a two-thirds vote, and the FSLN won control of the legislature in a similar vote. Opposition parties were harassed and some opponents refused to participate, but observers reported that otherwise the balloting was fair.

In February 1990 Nicaragua held the elections negotiated by its Central American neighbors. They were monitored by hundreds of observers including a 200-member U.N. team. In the campaign the Sandinistas blamed their economic distress on the U.S. boycott and accused the opposition of being a stalking horse for Yankee imperialism (*NYT* 1/28/90, 3). The elections were fair and to observers' surprise, Violeta Chamorro, wife of an editor who had been killed after he courageously opposed the Sandinistas, won over Ortega. After the elections Ortega accepted the opposition role after he negotiated with the new president to preserve Sandinista influence in the armed forces and the police.

The government of Violeta Chamorro operated under intimidation of the armed forces and the police, which were controlled by the FSLN. For example, the legislature passed a bill taking back government property expropriated by the FSLN, but under pressure from Ortega the bill was vetoed. Reports persisted of false arrest, torture, and executions by the FSLN-dominated police.

The economic situation in Nicaragua in 1992 was grim. The per capita GDP was estimated to be well below that of 1974, and declining. Exports could finance only a small part of import needs. The foreign debt was one of the highest *per capita* in Latin America.

Although the Nicaraguan government had drifted toward a Cuban-type of Communist government, it permitted elections and an opposition. The FSLN was not organized like a Stalinist-type of Communist Party. A large proportion of business remained in private hands and Ortega's military junta had permitted elections. If Ortega had regained power, however, he might well have reestablished an authoritarian government. In 1992 there seemed to be a risk of further erosion of democracy but little risk of establishment of a Marxist-Leninist, Communist system.

Peru in the 1980s was infected by a rapidly increasing cocaine trade with the United States along with a Maoist-Communist rebellion. The leader of the rebellion, Abimael Guzman Reymoso, a former philosophy professor, after studying in China founded the Shining Path movement. He built up the Shining Path movement at the time the drug mafia was developing a highly profitable cocaine trade. By 1991 the Shining Path controlled 20 to 40 percent of Peru. It reportedly financed its movement with $40 million of levies on the cocaine trade (Freedom House 1991–1992).

In 1991 and 1992 Shining Path was gaining ground and recruiting followers in the capital. It murdered elected leaders and police and it attacked U.S. officials and drug enforcement agents who had come to Peru to help it eradicate cocaine plantations and factories.

Peru's army could not act effectively against the Shining Path or drug dealers because it was corrupted by profits from the cocaine trade. The economic situation was grim. Although the president managed to control runaway inflation in 1991 and institute market reforms, he faced an economic depression, paralyzing strikes, and an exodus of professionals (*NYT* 4/7/92, 1).

In April 1992 President Alberta Fujimoro in frustration dissolved Congress, suspended the constitution, and arrested politicians in what he called an offensive against the Shining Path rebels and the drug dealers. Fujimoro was criticized by the United States and the Organization of American States for this authoritarian action.

In September 1992 Fujimoro's government scored a major breakthrough when it arrested Guzman Reymoso, the leader of the Shining Path, along with its top leaders. Overconfident, they had secretly been directing the movement from the capital. However, not all the leaders were arrested, and the movement could still extort financial support from the drug producers and traders in the provinces. The Maoist Shining Path movement was crippled but still not dead.

To sum up, it is not surprising that the turn toward Communism in Cuba and the threat of the growth of Communism in Nicaragua and Peru caused major military and political crises. The Monroe Doctrine had long been accepted as a foundation of U.S. foreign policy, and this was reinforced during World War II when the United States helped Latin America defend against German-Nazi influence. Before the Roosevelt era, moreover, the United States had regarded Latin America as its sphere of influence for investments and trade, and had often intervened to protect economic interests in Latin American countries.

At first many U.S. citizens welcomed Castro's revolution overthrowing the harsh Batista dictatorship. Castro did not show his Communist sympathies at first, but within a few years he was establishing the Communist model as an instrument to control Cuba. The system allowed him to dominate Cuba like

Stalin did in the USSR, Mao in China, Ho Chi Minh in Vietnam, and Kim Il Sung in North Korea. Cuba also developed a close alliance with the Soviet Union, which was glad to provide military equipment to protect against the threat of an attack by the United States.

Eisenhower approved planning by the CIA to support Cuban refugees to form a force to overthrow Castro, hoping for a replay of Castro's overthrow of Batista. Castro's forces easily overcame the poorly trained Cubans, many of whom had hoped for direct U.S. military support. This set the stage for the Cuban missile crisis, where for a while the world was on the brink of a nuclear war. Kennedy publicly played it tough, but privately compromised, and Khrushchev withdrew the missiles. Khrushchev received an assurance that the United States would not attack Cuba, although the CIA continued to support probes and even attempts to assassinate Castro.

In 1992 Castro's Communist government continued to carry the banner of Marxism-Leninism. The banner was tattered by severe economic problems in Cuba that occurred after the drastic cutoff of aid and political support from the Soviet Union, and later Russia.

Castro had provided considerable support to the FSLN revolution in Nicaragua, which veered toward Marxism-Leninism at the end of the 1980s. President Reagan used an embargo and the CIA to try to unseat its government. By the end of 1988 the efforts of the CIA-supported contras were faltering, in part due to lack of U.S. congressional support. The Soviet Union cut back its support to the Nicaraguan government after 1989, but Cuba continued to support the FSLN.

Nicaragua's neighbors were concerned about the influence of the Communists in Nicaragua and the actions of the contras. They negotiated the Arias Plan, which committed Nicaragua to permit democratic elections by February 1990. After the elections, which were monitored by the United Nations, a non-Communist government was established. The FSLN still controlled the military and police, so the government was intimidated, as was opposition to the FSLN.

The other major Communist challenge in South America was by the Shining Path movement in Peru. Its anti-imperialist slogans struck a response among poor farmers who had made profits from the cocaine trade and resented U.S. advisers and military equipment in their country. Communist organizers made headway among the poor in the cities, who suffered from a legacy of corruption from the previous government and disruption caused by the government's anti-drug campaign. However, the government's capture of its leaders seriously crippled the movement in September 1992.

In the final chapter, the Communist challenges in Latin America are viewed in perspective to Communist failures in other parts of the world.

Chapter 10

Communism and Its Prospects

THE GRAND EXPERIMENT

In the introduction it was noted that in this era a unique chance exists to evaluate trends and really predict the future of more than 30 Communist and former Communist societies that are beginning democratic and free market reforms. Figure 2-7 (see p. 47) shows a dramatic similarity in the reforms that have moved the great majority toward democracy and a free market starting in 1989. This grand experiment challenges social scientists to evaluate the process and predict outcomes—to validate their theories by predicting the chances of success before the experiments are finished. Social scientists in the past have not been able to experiment with societies, but leaders of these societies, in effect, now are performing a historic experiment in political and economic policies.

Initially there were 16 regimes involved in this grand experiment: the Soviet Union, Hungary, Czechoslovakia, Poland, East Germany, Yugoslavia, Romania, Bulgaria, Albania, China, North Korea, Vietnam, Cambodia, Laos, Mongolia, and Cuba. In 1992 reforms were also beginning in the 15 former provinces of the Soviet Union, now recognized as independent states, and in two to five of the former provinces of Yugoslavia. This makes over 30 regimes in total. In terms of population in 1992 the Communist system still prevailed in most of the political systems which could serve as a control group for the experiment (China, Vietnam, North Korea, Cuba, and Laos).

Only a few years ago, the previously mentioned countries and provinces had standard Communist governments where the Communist Party controlled the society and indoctrinated its people in Marxism-Leninism. Today, most of these countries have discarded that ideology and begun democratic and market reforms. In three of them, the Communist Party kept control but has begun market-oriented reforms (China, Vietnam, and Laos).

It is true there are important cultural and historic differences among these countries. However, the fact that the reforms came to a climax shortly after 1989 suggests that there were underlying forces acting in common to bring about change. Most of these countries are continuing reforms despite the hardships involved. Also, it is significant that East European and other former Communist countries are accepting Western definitions of political and economic reform. That is, they accept the idea that reform means more political freedom in terms of permitting opposition parties, protecting basic human rights, discarding pervasive government controls, and also moving toward a market-oriented economy. Decades of Communist indoctrination had not succeeded in imposing tenets and mechanisms of Communism, and they were being discarded.

This chapter draws together conclusions from the previous chapters. It analyzes the growth and decline of Communism, the problems of reform strategies, and the implications for the future of international relations. The conclusions will be confirmed or proven invalid over the years by the outcome of the grand experiment.

PATTERNS OF COMMUNIST PARTY DOMINATION

The Communist systems, as usually defined, were based on the Marxist-Leninist ideology and a totalitarian government. The ideology asserted history was moving through stages in which capitalism would be replaced by a higher form of society. Communists believed the historical process would cause workers to revolt against economic oppression and establish a government dominated by a Marxist-Leninist party. It would abolish private ownership and establish state control of the economy and social system.

The Communist doctrines were persuasive, particularly in areas that had experienced imperialism. They blamed backwardness on the rich nations that had exploited colonies for cheap labor, raw materials, and markets. The Communist ideology, as Ho Chi Minh stated, gave the Communists in Vietnam "the miraculous weapon" to win the war against France and the United States. In Vietnam Communism was tied to Vietnamese nationalism and brought about the defeat of the strongest military power in the world.

The Communist ideology naturally gave birth to totalitarian governments even though it seems Marx did not have that in mind. Lenin's main contribution to Communism was forming a tightly disciplined party that would grasp history by the forelock and carry out the revolution. He persuaded or purged opponents, intensifying these efforts after his party seized power. Communist leaders became corrupted by power, and their suppression of opposition became a characteristic of the Communist systems.

In analyzing the transition of Communist governments it is useful to review Figure 1-1 from Chapter 1 (reproduced as Figure 10-1 on the following page) that pictured governments as being on two tracks, political and economic. The totalitarian government controls important political and economic aspects of life. The democratic governments, on the opposite end of the spectrum, guarantee freedoms, including free speech, freedom for political opposition groups to organize, and free elections, plus varying degrees of economic freedom. Marx believed revolution would cause rapid transition from one form of society to another. Figure 1-1 shows how new democracies of Eastern Europe can move

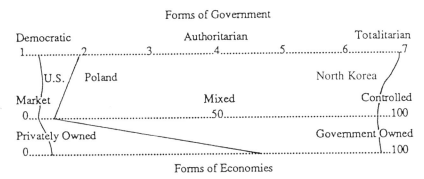

Figure 10-1 A model for comparing governments and economies.

gradually as they adjust their laws to freer political and economic life. The chart also reflects how Poland was able to free prices rapidly, but found it difficult to privatize government-owned property. This was the typical experience of other East European countries.

Communist movements relatively independently of each other seized control of two of the largest world powers, Russia and China. In both cases the Communist parties were disciplined and organized by strong leaders. They took advantage of the chaos following world wars, and not economic crises of capitalism as predicted by Marx. Lenin's Communist propaganda undermined the tsar's armies, and his party. With the help of soldiers and sailors, Lenin seized control of the government. In China, Mao's Communist Party and revolutionary army were virtually the same, and the Communists defeated Chinese government forces after long and fierce battles. Military strength determined the outcome more than class struggle.

Mao's dictum that power comes out of the barrel of a gun is more useful than Marx's theories in explaining these events and subsequent developments in the Communist world. Communism in Cuba, Yugoslavia, Vietnam, and Albania also achieved power through movements with strong military leaders—Castro, Tito, Ho Chi Minh, and Hoxha. Each used the Communist system to control revolutionary movements and maintain control of the governments. Vietnam's and Yugoslavia's leaders were Soviet-trained Communists. Although Castro was not a Communist in the beginning, he became a Communist when he saw how the Communist model provided him with an instrument of control and a way to get Soviet aid to make him independent of the United States.

Why did the above revolutions succeed? In each case there was (1) a close association of the revolutionary movement with the military, (2) a strong leader against a country weakened by war, except in the case of Cuba, (3) a disciplined party, and (4) a strong ideology with easy answers including anticapitalist and anti-imperialist doctrines.

The other Communist countries had Communist governments imposed by

Soviet occupation troops, or by Vietnamese troops in the cases of Cambodia and Laos. Imposing complete Communist control took several years. The Communist parties forced other parties into fronts, or alliances of parties, that were facades for Communist domination. These fronts would also embrace mass organizations and would control elections by nominating only one candidate for election.

The realization that Communist systems failed to keep up with the West in their standards of living stimulated major economic reforms in Communist countries. The most successful reforms were those freeing agricultural prices and allowing farmers to take out long-term contracts with the state to farm certain parcels of land. This resulted in higher prices for farmers and greater supplies of food, particularly under China's responsibility system. Hungary, Yugoslavia, and Vietnam also had some successes with these policies. The Soviet Union began a similar reform that started to take effect in 1992.

How did these revolutionary governments maintain power? The group of Communist leaders who came to power through a revolution kept the military under control. The Stalinist model had Communist Party officers attached to military units to ensure their reliability. Moreover, Stalin carried out massive purges of the military in the 1930s. In crises the military played a crucial role. Tanks patrolled the streets after Stalin's death. A few years later, Khrushchev came to power with military support after he persuaded generals to arrest Beria, the head of the security police. Gorbachev consolidated control by replacing military officers who would not back him in his dramatic proposals to reduce armaments.

The map of Europe after World War II reflected the areas Soviet armies occupied in defeating the German armies. Communist governments were established in Eastern Europe by Soviet armies. The Soviet forces then intervened to suppress rebellions against the Communist systems of East Germany, Hungary, and Czechoslovakia.

Mao used military backing in the Great Leap Forward. Lin Biao, the commander of the Red Army, backed the Cultural Revolution, and then Mao called on him to bring an end to the chaos that resulted. The military arrested the Gang of Four, and then Deng got their backing when he maneuvered to replace Hua Guofeng. When the students and masses threatened the government in Beijing's Tiananmen Square, Deng called on loyal troops to brutally suppress the demonstrations.

After Gorbachev indicated the Soviet military would not intervene in Poland and Hungary, they discarded the Communist system. A revolution then erupted in East Germany in November 1989 as President Honecker was forced to step down in the wake of demonstrations for democracy. Reverberations of the reform spread into Bulgaria, and a Gorbachev-type of leader took control and promised free speech and a parliamentary system.

The security police also played a key role in maintaining control. Lenin used the Cheka and Stalin used its successors to suppress opposition. Millions were sent to labor camps under Stalin. The first target of Communists was to take control of the military and the security police. The Soviets also maintained control in Eastern Europe in part by having the KGB work closely with the local security police. In China and in other Communist countries there still is a pervasive fear of being arrested and punished for opposition to the Communist-controlled governments.

The Communist model for organizing the party and the government proved to be an effective instrument of control. Following are the essentials of that model that have been applied to the party and the Communist governments examined here. Lenin's main contribution to Marxism-Leninism was the establishment of a disciplined, authoritarian party that would control the government. Under Lenin, Marx's idea of dictatorship of the proletariat became the dictatorship of the party. Democratic centralism was used to have lower bodies elect delegates to higher bodies. In practice the secretariat and Communist leaders would select nominees and control policies of lower echelons of the party and the government.

In Communist systems the general secretary, who controlled key appointments to the Communist Party and the government, usually dominated the government. Stalin as general secretary built up the Communist Party bureaucracy to control the economy and society. The heads of the party in Korea (Kim Il Sung), in Romania (Nicolai Ceausescu), and in Cuba (Fidel Castro), were also the heads of government, heads of state, and commanders of the armed forces. They developed a personality cult like Stalin's, and they installed family members in key positions.

The Politburos, which usually were the supreme organs of control, met at least weekly. The general secretary and the secretariat saw that party decisions were carried out. Each member of the secretariat was in charge of large departments or specialized in certain policy areas. Party leaders were normally the highest officials in their country, although not formally heads of agencies. In the Soviet Union Gorbachev, when he was the party secretary, had more power than Gromyko, the head of state. This was generally true in other Communist countries. In the 1989 reforms Gorbachev made the presidency the most powerful position, but he retained his role as head of the party. He realized the inefficiency of having a powerful Communist Party bureaucracy intervene in decisions of the government and economic enterprises, and he and Deng Xiaoping attempted to reduce the party intervention, particularly in economic decisions.

In the Soviet Union, the Central Committee, ranging from 100 to 300 or more people in size, directed the activities of the party, selected leading personnel, and endorsed major policies. In the early 1980s about one-third of the members were party secretaries from territorial party organizations. The next largest bloc included heads of ministries and departments. Sometimes the military was heavily represented in the Central Committees of Communist countries, but party leaders resisted military control. Members of the Central Committee with a military background were more common outside Eastern Europe, since many party leaders were in the military units that led the revolutions. In China the career military was heavily represented when it restored order after the Cultural Revolution, but many of these military leaders were purged as the party resumed control.

The Party Congress usually met for a few days every four or five years. Under the Stalinist system it ratified major policies and the slate of candidates prepared in advance by the secretariat for the new Central Committee.

The cells were the lowest units of organization of the Communist Party, and they were established in local factories, farms, or other work units. Large party organizations had a full-time secretary. Membership in the Communist Party ranged from a high of about 15 percent in North Korea to less than 1 percent of the population in Cuba and Laos. Party membership generally was mandatory for a successful career in politics or government. Candidates would be recommended for membership by party members who knew the candidate well for at least one year. Usually members graduated into the party from the Communist youth organization.

Communist countries had problems with designating a successor to the top party leader. Generally the leader was replaced only after death or with violence. Major Communist leaders who were removed by death include Tito in Yugoslavia; Stalin, Brezhnev, Andropov, and Chernyenko in the USSR; Mao in China; and Ho Chi Minh in Vietnam. Stalin used the position of general secretary to control the Soviet Union. After Lenin, Stalin kept his position for about 40 years until his death in 1953.

The politics of the Chinese Communist Party were unique. Mao gave up the head of state role in 1959 but remained as chairman of the Chinese Communist Party. When the party took positions away from him and tried to make him a "Buddha on the shelf," he responded by appeals to students to demonstrate in the Cultural Revolution. After Mao's death and after a period of political turmoil, Deng Xiaoping, a popular party leader, took over leadership of the party. He voluntarily stepped down from formal positions of responsibility while maneuvering his protégé Zhao Ziyang, a reformer, to replace him. Deng continued to dominate China's government, however, because of his friendships and personal influence as chairman of the Military Affairs Committee. This was demonstrated when he removed Zhao Ziyang and got the military to suppress the mass demonstrations of June 1989.

In the Stalinist system, the bureaucracy was compounded by conventional government bodies that were subordinate to the party. The government bodies included

1. Assemblies as representative bodies: They seldom had real authority although the constitution asserted their primary authority.
2. A Presidium of the assembly: This small body drafted legislation desired by the Politburo. Some constitutions designated it as a collective head of

state, but the president or chairman of the assembly performed that function, which to a large extent involved meeting with foreign dignitaries.

3. A Council of Ministers or cabinet.
4. A large executive branch bureaucracy: Under Stalin there were about 100 commissions, councils, and ministries as part of the Soviet Council of Ministers.
5. A large and influential military element: The military played a key role in Communist societies and received a large part of the government budget. In China during the early years the People's Liberation Army was hard to distinguish from the Communist Party.
6. A strong secret police: In China the police were powerful but unobtrusive. The KGB often controlled the police of the Soviet Union.

The size and number of control structures resulted in a tremendous bureaucracy. State control of economic and social life required many officials. Also the party apparatus tended to duplicate the state apparatus both in the legislature and executive branches, which led to delays and passing of the buck. The bureaucracy for mass organizations of labor, youth, women, and other groups in society created even more red tape.

The totalitarian structure pervaded society. Power concentrated at the top in a leader with dictatorial powers. To varying degrees he abused these powers. The Communist ideology called for the use of force to eliminate opponents and to transform the political system. Some Communist leaders ran amok as power corrupted them. Pol Pot's holocaust in Cambodia, Stalin's great purges of the 1930s, Mao's Cultural Revolution, as well as the aggressive wars started by Communist leaders, grew out of the Communist ideology of no compromise and the lack of democratic checks and balances on the leaders.

Communist Party members supported the systems because of their positions of power and the perks they received. City elites benefited from subsidies on food, rent, and transportation. The people were indoctrinated by the educational system and pervasive propaganda. All were intimidated by the secret police.

Yet anti-Communist forces with the help of mass demonstrations threatened the Chinese government and overthrew the Soviet Communist government. Following is a summary analysis of the policies of undermining and reforming Marxism-Leninism and of the ways they affected the foreign policy contest with democratic societies.

STRATEGIES OF POLITICAL REFORM

The reasons for the success of the democratic revolutions in Eastern Europe and the breakup of the internal Soviet empire were listed at the end of Chapter 5. Some observers have suggested that the Soviet Union might have been able to hold together its internal and external empires if it had started with economic

reforms like China did instead of with political reforms. Although two examples are not sufficient for proof, comparing their experiences provides insights
to the failures of the Communist system and the problems of reform.

Many pundits previously thought that Communist systems were developing a
new type of human being who would be conditioned to accept the doctrines and
policies of Communist leaders. It followed that a major challenge posed by
Communist systems would depend on the extent to which they conditioned their
subjects to support the system. Chinese Communists were famous for thought
reform and self-criticism, which were designed to purge the Chinese of bourgeois tendencies. Mao's little Red Book was a part of this effort, and almost
every adult Chinese had a copy. Later the Red Book disappeared as did many
pictures and statues of Mao.

The socialization process, moreover, was not successful in Eastern Europe
evidenced by revolts and demonstrations there. Polls gathered by Radio Free
Europe from large numbers of East Europeans—millions traveled to the West
every year—showed that the Communist Party in a free election would get
less than 10 percent of the vote (Radio Free Europe 1981; Hart 1984). This
failure of the Communists to win the hearts and minds of the people was
confirmed when the Polish Solidarity movement defeated the Communists by
winning 99 out of 100 seats for the Senate in the first free election in Poland in
1989.

One of the most dramatic demonstrations against Communism occurred in
China in June 1989 when hundreds of thousands of Chinese students and Beijing residents defied the authorities and soldiers and demonstrated with democratic slogans. This demonstration was brutally suppressed by the military with
many hundreds being killed. It was evident in China that power came out of the
barrel of the gun, as Mao had said, and that the military was in charge.

A dynamic element that generated demonstrations in China and brought
about the revolution in the Soviet Union was openness (the open door policy
and glasnost). Note that in some respects China had more openness in a political sense than the Soviet Union. In the Soviet Union under Gorbachev there
was a great increase of frank media coverage of the reports of corruption and
weaknesses in the Communist system. There was even good reporting of the
strikes and nationalist demonstrations, which helped them feed on each other.
This was also true in China, until the reaction after the Tiananmen Square
demonstrations in June 1989, when the controlled Chinese news media attempted to suppress and distort the truth.

In China a major element of openness was students' exposure to foreign
influences. In 1989 there were 40,000 students from China studying in U.S.
universities and by that time many had returned. In contrast, in September 1989
the first student ever from the Soviet Union to study for a degree came to the
United States. The Chinese students' call for democracy and freedom sparked
the 1989 Tiananmen Square demonstrations. Many of the students wanted the
material benefits they had seen or heard about in the West. They also saw the

weaknesses of their Communist system and, probably, as young people might, exaggerated the deficiencies of their own system and the advantages of others. It is true that many wanted material benefits they had heard about in the West, but they were demonstrating for the democratic rights to speak freely, to travel freely, and to organize a political party. The statue of liberty of Tiananmen Square symbolized their demands.

Why were they joined by many from the urban population? Party members had not been able to conceal the fact that they got special privileges in housing, special stores, vacations, chauffered cars, and so on. This became more evident in China and other Communist countries in the era of glasnost and the open door. The Communist news media printed many reports of party officials' corruption. "Power corrupts and absolute power corrupts absolutely" applies to Communist as well as bourgeois societies. Moreover, the open door in China revealed that the Communist systems had fallen behind the West in providing housing, food, and modern conveniences. The informed people of Communist societies knew that the excessive bureaucracy and lack of incentives were responsible, and if they did not already know this, speeches of Gorbachev, Deng Xiaoping, and others told them so.

China stressed economic reforms and only incidentally political reform. Its economic reforms began with the responsibility system for agriculture—a dominant sector of the economy. China also allowed market forces to stimulate production of consumer goods such as televisions, washing machines, and radios. Deng retired old Communists and ended some bureaucratic interference in decisions at the enterprise level. These reforms greatly increased the availability of food and other consumer goods. The rapid expansion of the economy did not forestall the Tiananmen demonstrations, which as already noted demanded political reforms. Most economic reforms were not reversed during the hardline political reaction following Tiananmen.

Reformers in Communist systems faced the classic dilemma of whether to maintain tight control or to relax controls and let the pressures for reform dissipate before they exploded. Gorbachev permitted many demonstrations by workers and dissatisfied ethnic groups in the Soviet Union. In China the government weathered the storm in 1986–1987 by allowing demonstrations, but it brutally suppressed them in 1989. Egon Krenz took a tremendous gamble in November 1989 by opening the Berlin Wall to reduce the pressure to flee from East Germany, and he succeeded in that limited respect.

These examples underline the importance of leadership. In Gorbachev's case it was simple. After Brezhnev, Andropov, and Chernyenko died, Gorbachev was in line for party leadership. If any one of them had still been living, the dramatic Gorbachev reforms probably would not have occurred. In the Chinese case, Deng Xiaoping lived longer than even he expected, and he stepped in from behind the scenes to remove Zhao Ziyang as head of the party. Zhao was the reformer who was prepared to negotiate the student demands for reforms. If Deng had died, the violent suppression of the Tiananmen demonstrations might well have been avoided by Zhao. Most observers believe Deng's success in stopping the reform movement is only temporary.

Ironically, there was an Achilles' heel built into the government structures of the satellites, particularly those of Eastern Europe. Governments established there at the end of the war had a structure of democracy including the existence of minority parties. Legislatures were retained in name, although they were not allowed to legislate. As the Communist Party took control in the "salami" process, existing political parties were forced to join fronts or alliances that the Communists were able to control by taking over leading positions. Many of these parties still existed in name in Eastern Europe in these coalitions. In the Polish moves toward democracy in 1989 the Peasant Party and the Democracy Party, to the surprise of the Communists, broke away from the front and joined with Solidarity to back the selection of a non-Communist prime minister. This meant that democracy could be established in other satellites and in other Communist countries without a constitutional change by allowing the legislature to meet long enough to legislate and the parties to break away from the Communist Party.

It would take more than all this to establish democracy because Communists still filled important positions throughout society. Anti–reform officials would have to be removed from positions of power where they controlled permits and materials for building a new society. East European countries only started reforms with their free elections and parliaments. After 1989 the world watched with fingers crossed as the northern European tier of former satellites pressed forward with reforms in a great experiment to transform Communist systems.

The Marxist-Leninist ideology had predicted that the Communist system would prevail and that nationality issues would be submerged in class conflict. However, after Lenin's death Stalin had pragmatically turned toward establishing Communism in one country as the first priority, and he had glorified Russian nationalism. At the same time he had allowed the many nationalities to have their own language and cultural traditions, while controlling their political and economic life through the Communist Party. Gorbachev's reforms led to an end of that system of control.

Russians made up about 50 percent of the Soviet Union. It had 15 republics, that nominally were autonomous. Next to the Russians, the largest ethnic groups were Ukrainians, Uzbeks, and Byelorussians. The Soviet Union had the fifth largest Moslem population in the world, which caused problems during the Afghanistan war.

In 1989 the largest ethnic demonstrations in the Soviet Union were in the Baltic provinces—Latvia, Lithuania, and Estonia—which were independent before World War II. In August 1989 on the 50th anniversary of the Nazi-Soviet pact, which included provisions for the Soviet Union to take over these states, as many as 2 million people joined hands across state boundaries in a demonstration for independence. Gorbachev initially acknowledged that such demonstrations were to be expected as more autonomy was granted under perestroika and called for their leaders to negotiate the issues. Demonstrations continued and were suppressed by the Soviet military. In August 1991 the first act of the Soviet parliament after the attempted coup was to grant the three republics their independence.

In 1992 the Commonwealth of Independent States of 11 of the 15 former republics of the Soviet Union were only loosely held together in a federation agreement. Ethnic pressures had kept Georgia from joining the CIS, and brought about decisions by the Ukraine, Azerbaijan, and Moldova to form separate armies. In 1992 the extent to which the former Soviet republics would permit a unified economy, military force, and foreign policy was still very much in doubt.

Yugoslavia had the most serious nationality problem in Eastern Europe. For many years Tito, as a powerful leader, kept the country together. After his death a system of rotating presidencies among the various nationality groups helped hold the country together. However by 1991 Croatia and Slovenia had broken away after a bitter conflict with Serbian-dominated forces of the central government. The United Nations mediator, Cyrus Vance, managed to negotiate a truce after the European Community failed to end the conflict. In the spring of 1992 a new conflict broke out in Bosnia-Herzegovina as Serbian units supported by central government forces tried to incorporate Serbian territories into what remained of Yugoslavia.

Eastern Europe is a patchwork of nationalities. For example, large Hungarian communities in the Ukraine, Slovenia, Slovakia and Romania consider themselves Hungarian first rather than Ukrainians, Slovenians, Slovakians or Romanians. However, the deaths and destruction from the conflict in Yugoslavia had a sobering influence on the national groups, and cease-fires were negotiated in Yugoslavia with Croatia and Slovenia and in conflicts in some of the former republics of the Soviet Union.

China's leaders observed the breaking up of the Soviet Union and Yugoslavia with fear, although statistically the Chinese problem was much less serious. The Han people make up about 94 percent of the Chinese population, but there were 98 autonomous areas, each with its own language and culture. China's main concern was Tibet, where in the 1980s Tibetan demonstrations were repressed with violence. Tibetans obtained no important international support for their demands, but U.S. congressmen, including those never reconciled to U.S. détente with China, supported Tibetan independence. Legislation objecting to Chinese suppression of human rights was vetoed by President Bush, so an open break on the Tibetan and human rights issues was avoided.

Contrary to Marx, nationalist ideologies proved to be stronger than the Communist ideology after the forces of glasnost and democracy began to work. In the Soviet Union there was strong resentment of Great Russian domination of the central government and the influx of Russian officials into the various republics. In Yugoslavia there was a similar resentment of Serbian domination of the central government. Associated with demands for national identity was the pent-up resentment of Communist controls that had held back political and economic development.

Before 1989 observers marveled at the success of the Communist system in maintaining the integrity of the Soviet Union and Yugoslavia with their different cultures. Since 1989, after the pent-up pressures of many decades exploded, the pundits feared new wars as new nations demanded recognition. Democracy proved to be a double-edged sword permitting new nations to assert their identity, but also removing controls against wars between competing ethnic groups. In the 1990s there were revolts by extreme nationalists—not Marx's proletariat.

To sum up, whether economic or political reform came first did not determine the outcome of Communist revolutions. Politics and economics were intertwined, and many factors, such as leadership and ethnic rivalries, were at work.

ECONOMIC FAILURES AND STRATEGIES OF REFORM

Economics is at the heart of Marxist ideology. Marx predicted that the revolution would occur from the industrial proletariat oppressed by the low wages and poor working conditions of the capitalist system. However, the Communist revolutions actually occurred in countries that were mostly agricultural—around 80 percent—whereas the most industrialized countries remained capitalist. Marx's theory also stated that after the state controlled the economy under socialism, the state would wither away and people would work according to their ability and receive according to their needs. But under Stalin a huge bureaucracy was established to control the economy, and the state expanded instead of withering away. Marx claimed that under capitalism the workers had become estranged or alienated from their work, and therefore their productivity was very low. However, under the bureaucratic Communist systems workers have little incentive to work hard and their productivity is low compared to capitalist countries. Strikes in the Soviet Union in 1989 protested against privileges of the Communist elite, and Gorbachev supported such complaints.

The flaws in the theory have had a minor effect on its popularity in comparison with the poor economic record of Communism. Mao's Great Leap Forward was an extreme application of Communist theory that tried to achieve development by exhortations instead of incentives. It failed as it overstrained the Chinese economy, and the Chinese Communist leaders kicked him upstairs. Mao struck back rallying the masses in the Cultural Revolution, but as he aged, party leaders, with the aid of the military, resumed control. The major ideological dispute in the Great Leap Forward and the Cultural Revolution centered on economic policies—whether to force development by government commands or by incentives to peasants and others to produce goods for free markets. Eventually the promarket pragmatists led by Deng Xiaoping won out. A main element of his programs was to open the door to the West and invite Western concerns with their modern technologies to trade and invest in China. During the 1980s the Chinese economy expanded rapidly with these new policies. Deng was "ahead of the game" until the 1989 Tiananmen demonstrations.

Communist officials in the USSR and Eastern Europe who had applied the Stalinist economic model of controls ran into problems in the 1980s as their economies lagged further behind those of the Western democracies demonstrated by the lack of food on the shelves of Communist stores.

Table 10-1 makes rough comparisons between levels of GNP of Communist and non-Communist countries before the revolutions, and gives a few clues as to reasons for differences.

The figures showed West Germany far ahead of East Germany, and South

Table 10-1
Comparison of Per Capita GNP with Education and Foreign Trade

Region	1984 GNP (dollars per capita)	% Kids in in school (ages 5-19)	Military as percent of GNP	Percent of trade with Communist bloc
Bulgaria	5018	64	4	75
Czechoslovakia	6267	61	4	80
East Germany	7995	59	5	33
Hungary	5915	62	2	54
Poland	4634	59	3	61
Romania	3571	54	1	60
Soviet Union	7095	62	15–20	61
Warsaw Pact	6580	61	10	
Yugoslavia	2990	59	1	41
Albania	1655	61	4	
NATO Europe	7477	63	4	11
West Germany	10,985	60	3	4
Mongolia	1026	59	11	
Cambodia		31		
Vietnam		55		86
China	304	55	7	
Taiwan	3140	60	6	
South Korea	2126	70	5	1
North Korea	1134	—	10	79
Laos	288	46	—	
Far East (avg.)	1250	57	5	2
Nicaragua	1044	53	12	
Cuba	1911	64	7	89
Latin America (avg.)	1907	60	3	
United States	15,541	77	6	2

Sources: Ruth Leger Sivard, *World Military and Social Expenditures 1987-1988*; International Bank, *World Development Report 1987*; East German figures from U.S. Congress, Joint Economic Committee, *East European Economic Assessment* (Washington, DC: U.S. Government Printing Office, 1981); *Handbook of International Trade and Development Statistics 1987*, United Nations; National Trade Data Bank.

Korea far ahead of North Korea in per capita GNP. Before these countries were split, the standards of living throughout were about the same, so the differences reflect, at least in part, the superior efficiency of capitalist market systems in comparison with Communist-controlled economies. Moreover, the Warsaw Pact countries as a whole were below the NATO countries in per capita GNP, which supports the above conclusions.

These figures reinforce what was well known even among the Communist leaders—they had fallen behind the West in technology and productivity, and therefore in the production of consumer goods and standards of living.

One reason for the gap in living standards was that Communist countries channeled a large proportion of their resources to the military. The Soviet Union and the Warsaw Pact spent much more on the military than did the NATO countries. North Vietnam and North Korea also had high military spending in relation to other countries. North Vietnam easily defeated South Vietnam despite its larger population. North Korea successfully invaded South Korea despite its much larger population and was turned back only with the support of U.S forces. The Soviet Union matched the military spending of the United States despite the much lower Soviet GNP. This greater emphasis of Communist systems on military spending and military strength undermined the Communist theories that the Western nations promoted the arms race because they were controlled by business interests of the military-industrial complex.

It is interesting to note that East Germany had a higher per capita GNP than that of the Soviet Union. This in part reflected the energy and work ethic of the Germans and probably the quality of their education, which does not show up in the table. East Germany also had a more competitive economy as reflected in its high percentage of foreign trade, which included a much higher volume of trade with the West. The less developed Communist countries were handicapped in educational levels with a low proportion of their school-age children in school.

The realization by leaders and the people of the Communist countries that they were falling far behind the standard of living of their neighbors stimulated major economic reforms in some Communist countries. The Chinese farms and industries were far behind those of Japan, Taiwan, Korea, and others. Eastern Europe was far behind the productivity of Western Europe. The most successful reforms initially were those freeing prices and allowing farmers to make long-term contracts with authorities for farmland. China's responsibility system reforms along these lines boosted its economy for more than 10 years. The Soviet Union belatedly began such reforms and increased land transfers at the beginning of 1992.

Even these economic reforms were a type of tenancy with government as the landowner. Land reforms of South Korea, Japan, and Taiwan abolished most tenancy under private owners after World War II. The success of these land reforms was widely recognized, and Communist countries could reform further by allowing genuine private ownership of farmland.

Encouraging tourism was another type of economic reform. Countries such as China, Yugoslavia, Hungary, and the Soviet Union found that luxury accommodations for tourists from capitalist countries were a lucrative source of foreign exchange. Joint ventures with foreign investors were almost essential to attracting tourists in large numbers.

Reform of Communist industrial systems is proving to be much more difficult. The key to such reform is realistic prices, as Adam Smith pointed out two centuries ago. This involves competition, including a convertible currency to allow imports to compete, reform of laws to permit private enterprises, and an end to bureaucratic controls (*Economist* 1/13/90, 21–26). These reforms eventually lead to hard decisions about whether to close plants and start new ones—implying bankruptcies and unemployment—that are relatively easy for private owners to make compared to governments. The outcome is privatization, which is proving to be the most difficult reform program to implement. It takes years to find investors and managers to organize new enterprises. Major opposition to privatization arises from entrenched bureaucracies led by former Communists. Abolishing subsidies is another painful process in achieving market prices. Urban dwellers had became used to subsidized food, rents, education, medical care, and transportation. Thus even if the Communist economic systems could endure the pain of economic adjustments, it was questionable whether political systems would bear up under the strain.

Four general strategies were used to attack the problem of economic reform: state ownership with market prices, rapid or "Big Bang" conversion to a market economy, gradual change, and the special case of East Germany joining with capitalist West Germany.

China, Vietnam, and Gorbachev's perestroika in the former Soviet Union illustrate attempts to join state ownership with slow moves toward market prices and ending subsidies. China had the most success by freeing farmers to sell their goods for profit and to take long-term leases on farmland. Because the Chinese economy was based on agriculture, because the farmers were enterprising, and because farms were close to city markets, the farmers and the economy as a whole still prospered after more than a decade of such reforms. This reform was joined with the open door policy of welcoming foreign investors into the business and industrial sectors, although the state still owned important industries and controlled the financial system. The major problem with the open door policy was that it let in winds of reform that fanned fire into the Tiananmen demonstrations, which led to a severe political reaction. In the Soviet Union Gorbachev made stunning political changes, but he failed after his policies did not put additional goods on the shelves.

In the fall of 1992 the CIS was in jeopardy as members tried to write a weak charter for its sovereign republics. Moreover, there were serious conflicts involving Russia, Georgia, Azerbaijan, Armenia and Tajikistan. Russia's economic reforms sped up after Yeltsin took over. Inflation was accelerating and people faced another hard winter, but economic reforms, including control of the money supply, were starting to take effect. The major problem was to mobilize enough political support while the economy suffered through inflation, unemployment, and corruption.

Poland was the first to go for the big bang conversion in 1990. It was assisted by advice and generous financial help from the West and from the IMF. In the spring of 1992, after an election that divided parliament into many parties unwilling to support the program, the Polish big bang was faltering. Romania's big bang experiment rivaled that of Poland's but received much less attention.

Before 1992 Hungary and Czechoslovakia were examples of gradualism that appeared to work, at least until 1992. Their reforms had begun between 10 and 20 years earlier. The abundance of goods on the shelves with people to buy them contrasted with the empty shelves across the border in the former Soviet Union. Czechoslovakia's experiment faltered at the end of 1992 as the country prepared to split apart.

East Germany seemed to have the best chance of success. After it joined with West Germany, the East received hundreds of billions of dollars in aid with financial and technical support. However, even this effort ran into political trouble as the West German economy groaned under the burden and the West German people complained about paying for it.

REVOLUTIONS IN COMMUNIST FOREIGN POLICIES

During the turmoil at the end of World War I a violent contest began between the new Communist government of the Soviet Union and Western democracies. In the 1930s fascist movements rose to power exploiting the fear of Communism, extreme nationalism, and the failure of democracies and the market system to prevent the Great Depression. In the late 1930s two fascist governments, Germany and Japan, threatened the entire world, and fascism was seen by some as the wave of the future. Hitler's fascism died in a vain attempt to add the Soviet Union to its European empire. His forces were defeated in World War II by the Soviet Union in alliance with democracies.

After that war the Soviet Union established Communist governments in Eastern Europe as a buffer against a revived Germany. Chinese and Korean Communists also established Communist governments with the help of the Soviets in the wake of Japanese aggression in World War II. Then Communism with its momentum of victories and powerful propaganda spread into Vietnam, and it was seen as the wave of the future by some leaders of Asia and the developing world. The cold war, based on the antagonism of Communism and democracy, continued to dominate world politics after World War II. Until 1989, with few exceptions, the Eastern European satellites followed the lead of the Soviet Union on foreign policy issues.

Although the Communist system had similar ideologies and structures, outside of Eastern Europe there were striking differences in foreign policies. The conventional wisdom is that this was due to different national interests. However, did China's national interest change drastically in 1977 when Deng Xiaoping took the reins in China and opened the door to the West? Did the Soviet Union's national interest change suddenly after 1984 when Gorbachev took over and made major concessions on arms control and withdrew Soviet troops from Afghanistan? If such changes reflected national interests, why were they not foreseen by analysts?

By the late 1980s the peaceful ideals of democracy and economic and political successes of the European Community had eroded the militant, totalitarian ideas of Communism in Europe. From 1989 to 1991 Communist regimes collapsed in Eastern Europe, and the Soviet Union broke apart. This opened a new era in foreign policy. We will analyze these changes and why the experts failed to anticipate them. In conclusion we will evaluate how the growing cooperation with Russia and former satellites opened new vistas for international relations.

The End of the Soviet Empires

A fear of invasion from the West and the desire to promote Communism undergirded Soviet foreign policy until recent years. Soviet leaders remembered how German armies in World War I and again in World War II devastated their country. Soviet histories stressed intervention by British, French, and U.S. troops after World War I, glossing over the fact that the Soviet Union was trying to promote revolutions in Europe and Asia. These events started the cold war.

After World War I Moscow considered the Soviet Union as the model for Communist movements throughout the world. The Soviet-dominated Comintern supported revolutionary Communist parties throughout the world. The seeds bore fruit in China and Vietnam, and in many other Communist parties. They also helped generate anti-Communist ideologies, such as fascism, and the cold war that prevented an alliance against Hitler. The fascist movement won out in Germany during the 1930s aided by the Great Depression.

Many Communists were disillusioned by Stalin's purges during the 1930s. Others became disillusioned by Soviet foreign policy, which put Soviet interests ahead of the Communist doctrine. The Soviet Union's cynical alliance with Hitler and joint attack on Poland, in particular, caused many defections from the world Communist movement. The Soviet attack on Finland added to distrust of the Soviet Union.

After the defeat of Hitler in World War II by the Soviet Union in alliance with the West, the Soviets entered the United Nations. They feared a revival of Germany and also the nuclear power of the United States. While the Soviets ruthlessly consolidated control over their new empire in Eastern Europe, the Communist parties promoted a peace movement throughout the world. The Soviet Union's initial exploitation of East Germany and of their new empire contrasted with the actions of the United States. It demobilized most of its troops and instituted a major aid program to restore Europe to economic health. The Soviet Union's consolidation of control of Eastern Europe and support to the Korean War encouraged the formation of NATO, the rearmament of Germany, and the growing unity of Western Europe.

The two superpowers came close to a nuclear war in 1962 during the Cuban missile crisis. This cleared the air, and the United States and Soviet Union, after facing utter destruction, concluded both the Hot Line agreement, to keep better communications during a crisis, and the partial-nuclear-test-ban treaty. Détente, the opposite of cold war, grew out of such nuclear arms agreements, which reflected a pragmatic policy of avoiding nuclear war. In 1972 President Nixon signed the landmark SALT I agreement, which limited strategic nuclear missiles, and the Antiballistic Missile Treaty (ABM).

The developing détente with the Soviet Union was shattered by its invasion of Afghanistan at the end of 1979, which also further alienated China. Relations between the United States and the Soviet Union deteriorated further during the first part of President Reagan's administration, with CIA attacks against the leftist government of Nicaragua, which was supported by the Soviet Union and Cuba.

In the late 1980s Gorbachev made a historic shift in Soviet foreign policy toward détente. He withdrew Soviet forces from Afghanistan and made major concessions under the Intermediate Nuclear Forces agreement. This allowed military units of the two superpowers to help destroy each other's nuclear missiles on hitherto secret military bases.

Gorbachev's commitments of nonintervention in Eastern Europe brought about a collapse of the Soviet empire. In November 1989 after a visit to Moscow, Egon Krenz, the new Communist leader of East Germany, brought down the Berlin Wall, the symbol of the cold war. In the first few days 3 million East Germans surged into West Germany to see what had previously been closed to them. Soviet officials indicated their approval. Krenz's gamble paid off initially, with only a fraction of 1 percent of the East Germans staying in the West. The jubilation of millions of Germans as well as millions in Poland and Hungary over these reforms indicated that it would be dangerous for the Communist elite to restore strict Stalinist controls.

Poland, Czechoslovakia, and Hungary then successfully negotiated arrangements for Soviet troops to withdraw, and they were free at last. In 1990 Gorbachev negotiated U.S., U.K., and French approval to end the occupation of Germany and to unify East and West Germany. Negotiations included their withdrawals of troops from Germany and major reductions in nuclear arms. With the end of the cold war, the world entered a new era of international politics.

Yeltsin then grasped the baton of reforms. He had become convinced that the Communist Party was corrupt and should be abolished. His strategy was to use ethnic pressures in the republics for independence to destroy the party so that he could carry out reforms. He was at the forefront of the movement to obtain elections and independence for the republics, and he was elected president of the Russian Republic in 1991. After he used his popular support to foil a coup against Gorbachev, his strategy worked. The examples of freedom in Eastern Europe helped the Baltic republics break free from the Soviet Union, and the internal Soviet empire then unraveled. The Communist Party was dissolved, and political and economic reforms accelerated.

After the Soviet Union broke apart and Gorbachev resigned, Yeltsin successfully negotiated a loose agreement among former republics. With the Soviet Union having about one-half the population of the former Soviet Union, he was able to dominate that loose association and speak for the former Soviet Union in the United Nations and elsewhere. In June 1992 he signed an agreement with President Bush for cuts of about two-thirds in strategic nuclear warheads.

He followed this with a speech before the U.S. Congress pledging further democratic and free market reforms and cooperation with the United States. Congress responded with 13 standing ovations. It later endorsed U.S. participation in a $24 billion aid program for Russia. The end of the cold war had brought about as dramatic changes in relations between Russia and the United States as the end of World War II did in U.S. relations with Germany and Japan.

Gorbachev and Yeltsin, as messiahs of reforms, had released democratic pressures not only in the Soviet Union but also in Eastern Europe. The new East European governments moved ahead transforming their societies into democracies and market economies. There were still many obstacles ahead, however. Former Communists held most of the important positions in the governments and in the economies. The military still had the guns, and there was the threat of its taking over. There would be plenty of excuses for this. Governments had to make painful adjustments of abolishing price controls and ending subsidies. Workers had rebelled against hardships under the Communist systems. Now they faced not only inflation but large-scale unemployment from reforms toward a market system. The Soviet Union and Yugoslavia, in particular, also faced ethnic conflicts that unraveled their federations.

In addition to the historical and ideological roots of foreign policy, the institutional factor is important. The original Soviet leaders were trained in a secret revolutionary conspiracy, and their domestic as well as international policies were based on power politics with no influence of the internationalist idealism that at times affected the policies of the Western powers. Soviet Communists were ruthless, and after World War II the Soviet Union did not hesitate to take over border territories and establish a buffer of satellites in Eastern Europe, even though these policies violated the U.N. Charter and other agreements. The Soviet leaders suppressed opposition in their buffer zone by invading Hungary in 1956 and Czechoslovakia in 1968. This action later was called hegemonism by their Chinese comrades. The Soviet Union's actions stimulated the growth of the Eurocommunist movement, which denounced Soviet aggression. The movement was particularly strong in Italy, France, and Spain.

These historical, ideological, and institutional factors help explain the reasons for Soviet foreign policy up to the era of Gorbachev beginning in 1985. Why was there a radical change under him from confrontation to cooperation, or from the cold war toward détente? One explanation is pragmatism. Gorbachev must have realized that the West had prevented Germany from developing atomic, bacteriological, or chemical weapons in the 1955 ABC agreement. Germany was no threat without these weapons, and there was no evidence that other countries would join in an aggressive adventure.

Gorbachev and other world leaders recognized that neither NATO or the Warsaw Pact would win a nuclear war, and that both were burdened by the weight of armaments. The firm line of the Carter and Reagan administrations in installing Pershing and cruise missiles in Europe, which with but a few minutes' warning could destroy Soviet cities and command centers, helped to bring the Soviets to the bargaining table to destroy their intermediate-range missiles. Gorbachev admitted that the Soviet economy had stagnated and needed more stimulation and trade with the West. The cold war policies of the Soviet leaders had generated a defense burden twice as high in percentage of GNP as that of the West, and this also acted as a drag on Soviet economic development. Yet these factors had also been present before Gorbachev. What motivated him?

It is very speculative to try to assess motives, even in an open society where lots of data are available. Only a few facts are known that might help. These include the fact that Gorbachev's relatives and friends had suffered from Communist repression in the 1930s and 1940s. He had the opportunity to study Western democratic thought during his law studies in Moscow. During this formative period he and his friend, Shevardnadze, had been impressed by Khrushchev's frank criticism of Stalin and his repressive system. Gorbachev had traveled in the West and seen freer and more prosperous democratic systems. Whether he wanted to establish a multiparty system is doubtful, but once he unleashed the forces of glasnost, political forces got out of control. After the coup, when Gorbachev lost his political punch, Yeltsin willingly took the reform baton, and in 1992 he was carrying out drastic economic and political reforms along democratic and market lines.

Some observers have suggested that economic reasons dominated in bringing about a moderation of Soviet foreign policies. However, after World War II when the Soviet Union was most strapped economically, it did not moderate its policies or seriously offer to disarm.

The Soviet political system finally permitted a personable, pragmatic leader in Gorbachev to conclude a historic agreement with the United States to destroy all intermediate nuclear missiles and to permit U.S. military inspections of Russian military bases. He also pressed forward with a radical agreement to reduce drastically long-range nuclear missiles. He withdrew Soviet troops from Afghanistan and ended the aggression there that had destroyed the moves toward détente during the Carter administration. He began unilaterally reducing Soviet troops by 500,000. He encouraged democratic reforms in Eastern Europe and renounced the Brezhnev policy of intervention.

The glasnost or openness within the Soviet Union was accomplished by its glasnost toward the West in a new era of détente to replace the cold war. This change came as a shock after decades of hostility and suspicion. The idea that Gorbachev's leadership was of critical importance in changing Soviet foreign policy is an easier explanation to defend than one that asserts that the Soviet Union's national interest suddenly changed after 40 years, or that economic factors were responsible for the change. In the long run, the real national interests of all countries are in peaceful cooperation rather than the wars, violence, and arms races of past centuries.

The restive nationalities of the Soviet Union seized on the logic of the breakup of the external Soviet empire to demand independence. As indicated above, Latvia, Lithuania, and Estonia took the lead. They demanded sovereignty since they had been conquered in World War II like the East European empire. Their demands were granted in the wake of the August 1991 coup, and the Soviet parliament and even the Soviet people agreed.

The Ukrainians overwhelmingly asserted their independence in a referendum and the game was over. Gorbachev and later Yeltsin were not willing to hold the internal empire together by force, and in the following months it split into a loose association of independent states. The rest of the world was quick to recognize their independence and to rejoice at the end of the superpower confrontation that had threatened a world catastrophe. The disintegration of the internal empire continued, and even the continuation of the loose Commonwealth of Independent States seemed doubtful at the end of 1992.

Ironically Marx was 180 degrees wrong. The political repression of the rigid Marxist-Leninist empires had been shattered at the same time the economic logic of a common market had pulled the capitalist European Community closer together. Perhaps democratic and capitalist reforms in the new republics of the former Soviet Union would someday let them create Gorbachev's dream of a Europe House—the European Community and the CIS.

Former Communist Countries

The East European Communist countries had the Communist system imposed on them by the Soviet occupation troops after World War II. Most had the misfortune to be located in a strategic position relative to Germany, so the Soviets insisted on keeping friendly Communist regimes in power. The East Germans, Hungarians, Poles, Romanians, and Czechs resisted this domination. The Soviet Union used war or the threat of war against Communist satellites that tried to assert independence.

Yugoslavia openly broke with the Soviet Union in 1948, and it did not hesitate to take issue with the Soviets. Tito's, and later Mao's, split from the Soviet Union, buried illusions concerning monolithic Communism and the Soviets' ability to lead a worldwide commonwealth of Communist nations. Tito became one of the leaders in the nonaligned movement, and he challenged Cuba because of its alliance with and subservience to Soviet foreign policies. Romania cautiously asserted itself by not participating in Warsaw Pact maneuvers, and by the 1970s it had cautiously separated itself from some of the hardline Soviet foreign policies.

The other East European satellites followed the Soviet lead in foreign policy until the 1989 revolutionary movements undermined its control. Their participation in the Warsaw Pact and its threat to Western Europe was used by NATO powers to support the NATO alliance. After the 1989 revolutions it became apparent that the satellite armies had been a paper tiger. After the humiliating defeat of Iraq by the U.N. coalition led by U.S. forces it was apparent also that Soviet military equipment was inferior. The threat of the Warsaw Pact completely evaporated after Gorbachev's democratic reforms, arms control agreements, and the West's generous response to help the Soviet Union disarm nuclear weapons and change to a market economy. This ended the cold war and opened new vistas for international relations.

China Leaves the Door Ajar

China's leaders have also been influenced by Marxist-Leninist ideology and by Communist institutions, but historical factors put its foreign policy on a different course. Soviet leaders advised and helped train the Chinese Communist leaders after World War I. The anti-imperialist elements of Marxist-Leninist ideology appealed to Chinese reformers in explaining the attempts of the Western powers to colonize China. They did not worry about the fact that the theory did not explain the open door policy of the United States after 1900 to oppose colonization of China.

The split with the Soviets helped bring about a drastic change in Chinese foreign policy toward the West. The split had a long history. Mao Zedong in the 1920s clashed with Soviet Communist leaders, who supported an opposing faction in the Chinese Communist Party. The Soviet advisers opposed Mao because he generated his revolution from the peasants instead of from the proletariat of the cities. Mao resented the Soviets' domineering attitude. In the 1930s he was further alienated when the Soviets pressured China to ally with Chiang Kaishek against the Japanese in an obvious move to strengthen the USSR against Japan. This policy subordinated the interests of the Chinese revolution.

After World War II the Soviet Union bargained with the Chiang Kaishek government to get concessions in Manchuria, whereas the Soviet Union did not openly support Mao's forces. Ideological and historical factors, nevertheless, drew the two Communist giants together for almost a decade after Mao's forces took control of the Chinese mainland. The Soviet Union was the first to recognize the new Communist government. In 1950 the Soviets' support for Kim Il Sung's attack on South Korea backfired when U.N. forces under the leadership of the United States threatened to destroy that regime. China was alarmed at the prospect of a U.S.-dominated regime on its border, so it threw hundreds of thousands of soldiers called volunteers into the battle to save North Korea. This incidentally prevented a humiliating defeat for the Soviet-backed North Koreans and drew the Soviet Union and China closer together, with the Soviets providing technicians and loans to develop China's heavy industry. However, old suspicions remained, and the break occurred after Mao made some reckless statements about nuclear weapons that frightened Soviet leaders. This included Mao's statements about China building an ideal society after a nuclear war and about using nuclear weapons to destroy U.S. forces after they were enticed to invade China. The Soviet Union broke off nuclear cooperation, which included a promise to provide China with a sample nuclear weapon.

Shortly thereafter, in frustration over China's reckless Great-Leap-Forward policies, which were ruining Soviet-provided equipment, Khrushchev withdrew his technicians and cut back on trade, which widened the growing split. Within a few years the two Communist giants were attacking each other in propaganda, and by the end of the 1960s the Soviets were even considering a preemptive attack to wipe out Chinese nuclear weapons installations. This split, along with the U.S. withdrawal from the Vietnam War, prepared the way for Nixon's beginning normalization of relations with China.

This normalization with the capitalist United States helped cause political crises in China, which involved the removal or assassination of Lin Biao, the military head, and the arrest of the radical Gang of Four, who opposed détente with the West. President Carter went forward with full diplomatic recognition of China, which involved terminating the alliance and diplomatic relations with Taiwan. The United States and China then developed close economic cooperation and even military cooperation, which reinforced China's open door policy and its economic reforms. During this period, however, there was no serious consideration of an alliance with the United States, and China kept its options open.

China's pragmatic economic and foreign policies preceded those of the Soviet Union by almost 10 years, and encouraged it to follow China's example. Also, China demanded that the Soviets withdraw from Afghanistan, get Vietnam to withdraw from Kampuchea, and reduce troops along China's border. These conditions were met by the summer of 1989, and Gorbachev met with Deng to restore the diplomatic ties that had been strained by Soviet "hegemony." Ironically the visit occurred during the Beijing demonstrations and helped keep them alive.

A few weeks later China's brutal suppression of Beijing demonstrations at Tiananmen cooled relations with the United States. Both sides went through the motions of minor sanctions and reprisals, but kept the door open. In the heat of the 1992 political campaign, President Bush approved a massive arms sale of fighter jets to Taiwan, which China regards as a rebel regime and a critical political problem. Bush's decision broke a 1982 agreement with China that had been an important part of normalization of relations. This new cloud on the U.S.–China détente threatened to close the door to commerce and to further entry of tens of thousands of students to study in the United States. Because of the Chinese veto in the U.N. Security Council, the sale could also end the cooperation in the Security Council that had allowed it to operate effectively in the years after Gorbachev came to power.

Vietnam

Examining the foundations of Vietnam's foreign policy throws light on why the United States blundered into a war and was defeated by that small country. President Johnson and top advisers tended to believe that Vietnam was an arm of the Asian revolution controlled by Moscow and Peking. Actually Ho Chi Minh, the father of the revolution, was both a Communist and an ardent Vietnamese nationalist. He worked for the Comintern for many years before instituting the revolution against France. He was a patient revolutionary, and his patience paid off after about 10 years of revolt against the French colonialists when the 1954 Geneva Conference awarded him North Vietnam. He bided his time for another five years before escalating the drive to take over South Vietnam.

The Communist ideology was ideally designed to mobilize Vietnamese against France and then the United States, which was pictured as a colonial power that took over from the French after they were defeated in 1954. The overwhelming U.S. military and civilian presence in Hanoi and other cities helped give credence to Communist propaganda. By 1965 the United States was fielding large armies to try to save South Vietnam, but in another 10 years North Vietnam with its persistence won the war in a conventional blitzkrieg after the United States withdrew.

The ideological pattern, then, is that Ho, as a convinced Communist, was determined to end French colonial rule, and he believed that the United States would impose an indirect colonial rule unless driven out. He appealed to Vietnamese nationalism to unify the country and set up a government free of Western control. Institutionally, the Communist ideology and government model were powerful instruments for Ho to promote the revolution and control the country. The historical pattern was that as a Vietnamese nationalist he feared the Chinese would exert their control over Vietnam as they had in previous centuries, so he also resisted Chinese influence and he exploited the Chinese rift with the Soviet Union to get more Soviet support. The Soviet Union was glad to have a powerful military ally such as Vietnam, which allowed the USSR to project its power in that part of the world.

After the Vietnam War ended in North Vietnam's victory, Vietnamese troops attacked Kampuchea, an ally of China, to which China responded with an attack against Vietnam's northern border. The world watched in amazement as these two former Communist allies warred against each other, and as the Soviet Union gave indirect support to Vietnam.

How can we explain Vietnam's attack against Kampuchea? One explanation is that Ho's Communist Party was carrying out its goal of unifying the area of former French Indochina, which was an aim expressed at its founding in the early 1930s. Another explanation is that Pol Pot's radical, terrorist regime challenged Vietnam with attacks along its border, and Vietnam moved in to end this provocation. The first explanation carries more weight since Vietnam installed a former Khmer Rouge leader Heng Samrin, who permitted Vietnam to dominate the country with advisers and military units that tried to eliminate the Pol Pot forces. Pol Pot's resistance forces joined two other Cambodian groups including one headed by the former president, Prince Sihanouk. Their resistance, supported by China, continued the war. In 1988 and 1989, however, Vietnam finally announced that it would withdraw all its troops from Kampuchea in 1989.

Ho Chi Minh died in 1971. Years later, after the battle against the United States was won, there was a radical change in leadership. The new leaders consciously or unconsciously followed the lead of China and the Soviets in experimenting with economic and political reforms. They also made arrangements with the United States to return the remains of U.S. soldiers killed in the war. A major motive in these approaches was probably similar to that of the Soviets and the Chinese—access to Western technology and economic aid. The major obstacle to their open door policy was their occupation of Kampuchea. The Southeast Asian countries took the lead in negotiations that bore fruit in the withdrawal of Vietnamese troops and arrangements for the U.N. to supervise elections and to establish a new government. In the spring of 1992 14,000 U.N. troops, in its largest peacekeeping operation, began this task.

North Korea

North Korea's foreign policy has some elements in common with that of North Vietnam. Both fought the United States in wars to unify their country. Both have been close allies of the Soviet Union and have received extensive military and economic aid and advice from the Soviets. They, therefore, based their government and economy on the Soviet model. However, Kim Il Sung of North Korea used the Communist model to create a dictatorship dominated by him, his son, and relatives. This is what Communists criticize as the "cult of the personality" comparing it to Stalin's. Kim's pictures and statues were all over the north. His policy of *chuch'e* or self-reliance was a strong nationalist ideology that was isolationist, but he was also ambitious to take over the south. He refused to accept the humiliating defeat in the Korean War by U.S.-U.N. forces.

North Korea was occupied and dominated by the Soviet Union in its early years, but it achieved independence, in part by playing off China against the Soviet Union. Kim Il Sung's brand was a dangerous, aggressive Communism that was not strong enough to resume the war against the south, particularly with U.S. troops there. In frustration the north generated terrorist attacks against the south. In 1987 North Korean agents destroyed South Korea's Airline (KAL) flight 858, causing the death of 115 civilians. Japanese authorities traced the terrorist's connection to a North Korean agent. North Korea also was responsible for another major terrorist act in 1983 when a bomb planted in Rangoon killed 17 members of the visiting South Korean official party as well as four Burmese (U.S. Department of State 1988). One of North Korea's aims was to frighten people from attending the 1988 Olympics in Seoul. This was its answer to the Olympic Committee's offer to allow North Korea to host only four of the Olympic events in that country.

It is hard to provide rational reasons for these violent terrorist acts. They were a reflection of extreme nationalism. In addition, Kim Il Sung's dictatorship reflected the corruption that comes with excessive power. Historically, he harbored resentment over the defeat in the Korean War. His policy of *chuch'e* isolated North Korea from the modern influences of the outside world and held back development. The failure of North Korea's policies was obvious in 1988 when South Korea showed off its economic success as it hosted the Olympic Games.

One of the successes of the developing cooperation between the new Soviet Union and the West was to force North Korea to recognize the reality of South Korea. In 1991 both China and the Soviet Union told North Korea they would no longer veto admission of South Korea into the United Nations (*Far Eastern Economic Review*, 1992, 135–136). North Korea, along with South Korea, then joined the U.N., implicitly recognizing South Korea. Under further pressure from these powers and from Japan and the United States, North Korea agreed to implement its joining the Nuclear Nonproliferation Treaty by allowing inspections by the International Atomic Energy Agency. In the spring of 1992 it was still stalling, however, on opening up all its installations. It agreed to a vague confederation of North and South Korea, but there were little prospects for reunification, because a new Korea would be completely dominated by the south, which has twice the population and a much more powerful economy.

Latin America

Cuba, like North Korea and North Vietnam, also had a major confrontation with the United States. The Cuban missile crisis threatened but did not result in a nuclear war.

The historical and ideological origins or Castro's conversion to Communism can be surmised. He started out claiming that he wanted a democratic revolution against the Batista dictatorship, and he attracted moderate democrats to his cause. According to Khrushchev's memoirs, even he did not know that Castro was a Communist at that time. His brother Raul and his close associate Che Guevara were Communists, and they probably had a major influence on Castro. As a nationalist, Castro resented the economic influence of U.S. investors and traders in Cuba. The radical, anticolonial elements of the Communist ideology appealed to Castro, and the Communist model provided a convenient instrument for his political and economic control of Cuba. So within two years Castro was talking and acting like a Communist to the degree that he arrested former democratic associates who had helped in the revolution, and he forced others to flee the country.

President Kennedy carried through on Eisenhower's plan for the CIA to support a small invasion by Cuban refugees, but the invasion at the Bay of Pigs was easily broken up by Castro's armed forces. Then in 1962 Khrushchev got the idea of moving medium-range nuclear missiles into Cuba. He indicated in his speeches at that time that he was disturbed about reports that the United States had installed nuclear missiles in Turkey aimed at the Soviet Union. His aims, he said, were to protect Cuba from U.S. attacks, like the Bay of Pigs in the previous year, and to correct the balance of power in which the United States had about 10 times more long-range missiles than the Soviets had. Castro was delighted, since the United States had shown it was willing to use force to overthrow him, and he welcomed a strong ally.

When Kennedy learned of the secret movement of missiles to Cuba, he imposed a partial blockade called a quarantine. During the crisis that threatened nuclear war, Kennedy began preparations to invade Cuba and persuaded Khrushchev to withdraw the missiles in return for a U.S. pledge not to invade. This bargaining was done without Cuba's participation, and it infuriated Castro, but it saved face for Khrushchev. Strangely this was followed by a détente between the USSR and the United States. However, the CIA continued attacks against Cuba including assassination attempts on Castro.

The confrontation continued between Cuba and the United States after that crisis. Apparently the assassination attacks stopped, but CIA help to Castro's opponents did not cease. The main problem was that Cuba provided training camps or a staging area for insurgencies in El Salvador, Nicaragua, and other countries in Latin America. Moreover, Cuba openly acted as a client of the Soviet Union, providing troops to Angola, Ethiopia, and other Marxist African countries to help protect them from attacks by insurgents. These insurgents were supported by hostile neighbors, such as South Africa, and the CIA. The Marxist countries of Africa supported revolutionary movements, whereas their opponents supported insurgencies against the Marxist regimes. The armed forces of the African countries were small, so the relatively well-trained Cuban forces exercised a great deal of leverage in these conflicts.

In the process of acting as the Soviet Union's cat's paw in Africa, Cuba received a tremendous amount of military and economic aid, estimated at the equivalent of between $3 and $5 billion a year, or almost one-third of its GNP. Much of the aid consisted of high prices for buying Cuba's sugar exports.

Cuba's covert and propaganda support for revolution and its opposition to the United States made it popular among Marxist groups in Latin America, but Cuba paid a high price for its revolutionary activity. The United States prevented trade and investment in Cuba, which is a natural trading partner. Cuba's dependency on the Soviet Union for aid and trade was galling to a nationalist such as Castro. In secret conversations with representatives of Presidents Carter and Reagan, Castro made known his desire to end this dependency and normalize relations with the United States. He was not willing to give up revolutionary aims, however, so the confrontation continued.

The possibility of détente exists between Cuba and the United States if both sides would stop the use of covert and overt violence against other countries. Perhaps Cuba, like North Korea and Vietnam, could begin to follow the examples of Russia and China and try to normalize relations with the United States. Cuba was faced with similar economic problems, and its proximity to the United States could probably attract even a higher proportion of investment if a political détente prepared the way. In the spring of 1992 pressures on Castro increased as the Cuban economy reeled from the cutting off of subsidies it formerly had received from the Soviet Union.

In Nicaragua, contra forces supported by the CIA attacked the government, which was more of a military authoritarian regime than a Communist model. It harassed but did not suppress other political movements. Under pressure from Central American neighbors, the Nicaraguan government headed by Daniel Ortega, the head of the Marxist military junta, agreed to elections. The Organization of American States assisted by the U.N. monitored disbanding the contras and the holding of free elections in February 1990. The non-Marxist party won the elections, and Ortega stepped down to head the political opposition. By agreeing to the system of elections, albeit under pressure from the United States, the Marxist government was ousted and Nicaragua turned away from a Communist (Marxist-Leninist) form of government.

In Colombia, the Colombian Shining Path movement, which was built alongside a profitable trade in cocaine, mounted terrorist attacks on the government during the late 1980s and early 1990s. There was no apparent support from Cuba or other Communist states, and Marxism-Leninism appeared to be overshadowed by the disruption caused by the drug trade and its mafia. The movement was weakened by the government's capture of its leaders in 1992.

Summary

To sum up, after World War I the reactions and counterreactions to the Communist threat set the stage of international politics for most of the twentieth century. The Communist ideology created hostility and suspicions of the Western democracies. The ideology was a particularly powerful instrument to support wars in areas formerly threatened by Western colonialism. In Asia, Vietnamese nationalists and Communists were able to picture their aggression against South Vietnam as an anti-colonial war even after the French withdrew, and they were able to defeat the powerful forces of the United States and its allies trying to prevent the spread of Communist aggression in Asia. North Korean aggression was defeated by these forces under the banner of the U.N.

The Communist ideology was not strong enough, however, to keep Communist nations from fighting among themselves. The Soviet attacks on its East

European satellites, the Sino-Soviet split, the Soviet attack on Afghanistan, and the Vietnamese war against Cambodia, revealed the inherent aggressive nature of the Communist systems. The democratic reform movements after 1989 further weakened Communism, shattered the Soviet Union's East European empire, and destroyed the Soviet Union itself as a superpower. The world's leaders then reversed the directions of their foreign policies.

A NEW ERA OF INTERNATIONAL RELATIONS

After World War I, generations were influenced by the conflicts of the cold war. Pundits accepted, as a fact of life, conflicts between Communists and their opponents. It affected pundits' habits of thought to the extent that they were caught by surprise at the collapse of the Soviet Union and its Eastern European empire. With the end of the cold war new vistas in international relations opened. It is important to analyze the forces at work and why the experts on Communism did not foresee its collapse.

Many of those who were wrong assumed that international politics is determined by power factors—such as military and economic factors. Pundits and diplomats have been influenced strongly by the philosophy of power politics. Many accepted as given that leaders of nations promote the national interests by trying to increase their military and economic power. If this were true, why would Gorbachev and Yeltsin disarm the Soviet Union unilaterally and carry out policies resulting in the weakening and finally the demise of the Soviet Union?

The other major philosophy that influenced analysts is Marxism-Leninism. For many decades it dominated the thought of the Communist world. Also, in the West, Marxism and neo-Marxism had an influence on ideas of intellectuals. Such ideas included the concept of "economic imperialism," in which industrial nations, through multinational corporations with their economic power, created "dependency" of weaker Third World nations through trade and investment. Related with this was the idea that the military-industrial complex of industrial nations prospered through world tensions and the sale of military goods. Marxists believed that politics is dominated by the ruthless use of power motivated by economic factors.

Marxists and intellectuals believed that if the state controlled the economy, the government, the news media, and schools, as well as the police and the military, the state's power was unassailable. Before 1989 even conservative pundits, such as Professor Jean Kirkpatrick, our former U.N. representative, pointed out that no Communist dictatorship had ever been overthrown. She concluded it was better to try to change right-wing dictatorships than to work with entrenched Communist dictatorships. Conservatives were as surprised as anyone at the rapid collapse of the Soviet empire.

Power factors, of course, are important. There was enough truth in the above theories to make them convincing. However, if they alone are not adequate to explain the growth and collapse of political systems and their empires, then what other factors are important?

Ideas of leaders and of people are even more fundamental than power factors. What were the ideas of leaders and the people that pundits did not take seriously, and how did these ideas influence actions in Eastern Europe and the Soviet Union?

Many observers realized before 1989 that Communists were not popular and that they would not win in a free election. Radio Free Europe regularly evaluated and published polls of visitors from Eastern Europe to the West that showed in a free election the Communists would not get more than 3 to 14 percent of the vote. Writings of Hedrick Smith, former reporter of the *New York Times*, academic studies, and even speeches of Gorbachev and Yeltsin indicated that the Communists themselves did not take their ideology seriously, and some Communists even ridiculed it in unguarded moments. If the pundits had realized that this erosion of ideology and of Communist support was of major importance, they would have realized that the Soviet empire in Eastern Europe and in the Soviet Union was like an explosive charge waiting for dynamic younger leaders like Gorbachev or Yeltsin to detonate it. In Eastern Europe anti-Communists like Lech Walesa of Poland and Vaclav Havel lit the matches, but converted Communists like Imre Pozsgay of Hungary, Egon Krenz of Germany, and General Jaruzelski of Poland also helped destroy the empire.

What were the specific ideas that were underestimated and that influenced these revolutionaries and reformers? Their ideas included the following:

1. Hatred of Soviet domination and pride in their national cultures and heritage. In a word, nationalism.
2. Admiration of the relative prosperity and well-being of Western European democracies and market systems.
3. Ideals of freedom. The people wanted freedom and democracy.
4. Resentment of the special privileges and corruption of the Communist elites.
5. Resentment of being manipulated by Communist propaganda.
6. Hatred of the security police. The military, on the other hand, after the revolutions started, supported revolution and change in Poland, Romania, the Soviet Union, and Czechoslovakia and did not intervene to preserve Communism in other Eastern European countries.

What was different about Eastern Europe that accounts for its relatively rapid rejection of Communism compared to other Communist countries?

1. Eastern Europe's Communism was imposed rather than homegrown like that of the Soviet Union, China, Vietnam, North Korea, and Cuba. Although China began with the Soviet model, their dispute of the 1960s and 1970s included different ideas of Communism—whether to depend on the

proletariat or on the peasants—and China's opposition to Soviet hegemonism—including its domination of Eastern Europe and its attack on Afghanistan. Also, the Soviets had a close alliance with Vietnam, an enemy of China. Chinese government propaganda created a god out of Mao, so that its following of the Communist ideas was not considered subservient to the Soviet Union. In Eastern Europe, on the other hand, the Communist doctrine was associated with Soviet domination, which offended the nationalists in Eastern Europe.

2. There was more interaction with the West from Eastern Europe, particularly by the northern tier of East European states, which could observe the economic and political success of the European Community. China's interaction with the West was substantial in terms of students, but this will take longer to take effect because of their relative youth. Also factors of distance, language, and cultural barriers lessened the impact of the West on China. This is even more true of North Korea, which has had almost no contact with the West. However, North Korea is beginning to open up. Vietnam has had more contacts with the West than North Korea, and it is further along toward trade and normal relations than Korea.

How did anti-Communist ideas bring about revolutions? Leadership was the factor that precipitated the process. Obviously, the following leadership factors were important to 1989's revolutions:

1. Gorbachev's leadership. When it became clear he would not order the Soviet troops to suppress reform, the pressures exploded in Eastern Europe and the Baltic states.
2. Virtually all of the Communist reformers had travelled in the West and had contacts with it. They were impressed by the relative prosperity and freedom that contrasted with the economic stagnation and political repression in the East. Yeltsin said his views of the United States changed 180 degrees during his visit.
3. As older hardline Communist Party members retired, and as younger activists had a chance to make policy, the movements for change took place and detonated larger reservoirs of resentment and pressures for change. Older cadres and opponents of Communism had been intimidated by the repressions of 1956 (Hungary), 1968 (Czechoslovakia), 1980s (Poland), and the Afghanistan invasion. Younger activists with no experience and with an energetic spirit were willing to risk much more than their elders. When the movement was underway, elders joined.
4. Another factor that encouraged expression of opposition to the Communists was that the East European countries had a democratic framework of a parliament and opposition parties, although the opposition views could not be expressed under a repressive Communist system. Some leaders who had been repressed in these institutions were able to play

important roles when they were given a chance to assert themselves in 1989 and after.

What does the above mean for the future of remaining Communist systems? Modern communications and the power of ideas will continue to build pressures for changes. The great electronic revolution in the latter part of this century was based on rapid processing of information. If the Communists modernize their enterprises and their economy, they will need computers, faxes, modums, and telecommunication contacts with the outside world. They will need to expose their people to foreigners to learn the new technologies. This would be dangerous because this would reveal how distorted the Communist picture of the world has been.

1. In China the movement for freedom was barely suppressed at Tiananmen. Zhao Ziyang, the prime minister, almost prevailed over the hardliners. The Beijing garrison troops were fraternizing and sympathizing with the demonstrators. Deng Xiaoping had to call in troops from outside the Beijing area to suppress demonstrations. The younger Communist cadres and the tens of thousands of Chinese who have studied in the United States and who will be future leaders, resent Communism and will gain strength as the old leaders die off in the next few years.

2. Castro's economy is deteriorating, and his revolution has lost momentum. Over 25 regimes have already been influenced to a greater or lesser degree by the democratic revolutions against Communism in Europe. Today, "A specter is haunting" the remaining Communist regimes, and that specter is democracy, not Communism as Marx asserted. Castro appears worried as he faces a battle (Gunn 1992, 62). His regime and other Communist regimes are vulnerable, particularly if the new democracies start to succeed economically.

3. In the past, Vietnam and Laos consciously or unconsciously have followed the lead of their powerful neighbor, China. If China does carry out political reforms in addition to its economic reforms, as suggested above, Vietnam and Laos are likely to follow suit. Moreover, their other neighbor, Cambodia, is carrying out democratic and market reforms under the tutelage of the United Nations. This leaves North Korea, which is already beginning to loosen up its strict isolationism and totalitarian controls.

It is naive to conclude that people are finally forcing governments to become democracies because it is the most effective system? Is it being overly optimistic to assume that democratic values on an international scale, such as human rights and peace, are a self-reinforcing, winning combination? It is revealing about this century to realize that pundits must strain their imaginations to explain why leaders make peaceful, reasonable decisions. In a century dominated by two wars, the Holocaust, and terrorism, it was assumed that international politics will continue to be controlled by the darkest side of human nature. We should at least recognize the possibility that after facing the abyss of mass destruction, leaders can make peaceful, rational decisions. Gorbachev and Yeltsin could have as much influence toward rationality in this century as Lenin and Stalin did toward revolutions and repression.

Intellectuals underestimated the power of progressive ideals in bringing about the revolutions in Eastern Europe that ended the cold war. They should not underestimate the continuing strength of these ideas. Ideas of politics can act as vicious circles or spirals for progress. If diplomats believe foreign affairs are governed by military and economic power, they will carry out policies of power politics. If they believe international law and human rights are important, they will adjust their policies to those restraints. It would be a tragedy, when the world is in flux, if educators, pundits, and leaders are preoccupied with the horrors of the past century and delay reforms by downgrading the power of progressive ideas.

As the world approaches the end of the twentieth century, it seems the winning system would not be the one with the greatest inventory of arms, but the system that would produce the most for its people and provide personal freedoms. The democratic systems had proven to have the advantage in this race, and they had built-in glasnost and democratic institutions to correct their faults.

In 1992 pessimists expected hardliners in former Communist countries to reverse movements toward democracy and to establish authoritarian governments or Communist dictatorships. At the end of 1992 the great majority of the democratic reforms had been maintained despite economic hardships of adjusting toward market economies. The power of the people who overthrew Communists continued to prevail. In Russia initial attempts of the Congress of People's Deputies to end Yeltsin's rapid market reforms were narrowly defeated. Significantly, attempts were made by voting, under the constitution, and not by guns. The major problem of the new democracies was not how to reform but how to maintain political support for economic reforms. However, assuming the democratic reforms continue to generate political support, most of the new democracies will survive as democracies.

There are positive ideals, in addition to democracy, at work in the former Communist countries of Eastern Europe, and they are an antidote to the ideas of conflict in Eastern Europe. One is the idea of the European Community. Jean Monnet's main aim was political and not economic—he wanted to integrate Germany and France so closely that this would end the vicious cycle of hatred and wars between the two nations. He succeeded many years ago in this primary aim of promoting the European unity ideal among the people and leaders of Germany and France, so that war between them is virtually inconceivable.

Eastern European governments have put joining the European Community as a top priority. Just as the European Community and its ideals brought Germany and France closer together, such a process could help sublimate the nationlist conflicts in Eastern Europe. This involves promoting policies of open borders and broader loyalties. If people could travel freely across borders to visit relatives and friends or seek new jobs, if they could easily purchase goods in other countries, and if they could work toward common goals with other nationalities, the dangers of wars over boundaries would evaporate.

Such a process could help the new Commonwealth of Independent States. At one point Gorbachev held forth the ideal of a Europe House. Even the beginning steps of lowering tariff barriers between France and Germany coupled with the European Community ideal ended the dangerous frictions between them. The European Community's promotion of those policies and the all-Europe ideal among the republics of the former Soviet Union and in Eastern Europe could alleviate tensions there.

In a grand experiment to establish democracy and the market system in over 25 sovereign states, leaders are risking their careers on their belief that these systems will work. Academics also should test their theories by predicting chances for success before the experiment is over. I predict that by the end of the century the great majority of the new democracies will survive and most remaining Communist countries will follow their lead.

Related positive ideas are embodied in the United Nations. U.N. forces defended South Korea from aggression in 1950 in the first major enforcement action of the U.N. Mediators and peacekeeping forces under the authority of the U.N. Security Council helped negotiate truces in the terrible Yugoslav civil wars and were continuing these efforts in 1992. In 1992 the largest U.N. peacekeeping force in history was arranging for free elections and the setting up of a democratic government in Cambodia after Vietnam withdrew its troops. U.N. mediators helped negotiate a truce and made arrangements for elections to phase out the Marxist government in Nicaragua. U.N. mediators helped bring about a withdrawal of Soviet troops and peace to Afghanistan. The International Atomic Energy Agency helped clean up the radioactive emissions of Chernobyl, and inspected installations of North Korea. The above activities were carried out under international law and with the authority of the U.N. Security Council. The International Monetary Fund, a specialized agency of the U.N., played a central role in promoting economic reforms and providing credits to help restructure Communist economies of Eastern Europe, former Soviet republics, and also former Communist countries of Asia.

The growing cooperation in the United Nations between Russia and former Communist countries and Western democracies promised to permit the United Nations to achieve the main purpose of its founders "to maintain international peace and security." At the end of 1992, the strained relations between China and the United States threatened to complicate matters. Nevertheless, with the end of the cold war, states could shift their focus to problems of the economy, environment, and health, as well as the remaining security problems of an interdependent world. The 21st century promises to be one of hope without another world war.

Appendix 1

Excerpts from the *Communist Manifesto*–1848

A specter is haunting Europe—the specter of communism . . .

Two things result from this fact:

I. Communism is already acknowledged by all European powers to be itself a *power*.

II. It is high time that Communists should openly, in the face of the whole world, publish their views, their aims, their tendencies, and meet this nursery tale of the *specter of communism* with a manifesto of the party itself . . .

I. BOURGEOISIE AND PROLETARIANS*

This history of all hitherto existing society is the history of class struggles.

Freeman and slave, patrician and plebeian, lord and serf, guildmaster and journeyman, in a word, oppressor and oppressed, stood in constant opposition to one another, carried on an uninterrupted, now hidden, now open fight, a fight that each time ended, either in a revolutionary reconstitution of society at large, or in the common ruin of the struggling classes . . .

The modern bourgeois society that has sprouted from the ruins of feudal society has not done away with class antagonisms. It has only established new classes, new conditions of oppression, new forms of struggle in place of the old ones.

Our epoch, the epoch of the bourgeoisie, shows, however, this distinctive feature: it has simplified the class antagonisms. Society as a whole is more and more splitting up into two great hostile camps, into two great classes directly facing each other: *bourgeoisie* and *proletariat* . . .

Each step in the development of the bourgeoisie was accompanied by a corresponding political advance of that class. . . . The executive of the modern state is but a committee for managing the common affairs of the whole bourgeoisie . . .

---

*By bourgeoisie is meant the people in the class of modern capitalists, owners of the means of social production and employers of wage labor. By proletarians, the people in the class of modern wage laborers who, having no means of production of their own, are reduced to selling their labor power in order to live.

The bourgeoisie has stripped of its halo every occupation hitherto honored and looked up to with reverent awe. It has converted the physician, the lawyer, the priest, the poet, the man of science, into its paid wage laborers . . .

The need of a constantly expanding market for its products chases the bourgeoisie over the whole surface of the globe. . . . All old-established industries have been destroyed or are daily being destroyed. They are dislodged by new industries, whose introduction become a life and death question for all civilized nations, by industries that no longer work up indigenous raw material, but raw material drawn from the remotest zones; industries whose products are consumed, not only at home, but in every quarter of the globe. . . .

The bourgeoisie, by the rapid improvement of all instruments of production, by the immensely facilitated means of communication, draws all, even the most backward nations into civilization. The cheap prices of its commodities are the heavy artillery with which it batters down all Chinese walls, with which it forces the underdeveloped nations' intensely obstinate hatred of foreigners to capitulate. It compels all nations, on pain of extinction, to adopt the bourgeois mode of production; it compels them to introduce what it calls civilization into their midst, i.e. to become bourgeois themselves. In one word, it creates a world in its own image . . .

The bourgeoisie, during its rule of scarcely one hundred years, has created more massive and more colossal productive forces than have all preceding generations together . . .

But not only has the bourgeoisie forged the weapons that bring death to itself; it has also called into existence the men who are to wield those weapons—the modern working class—the proletariat. . . . These laborers, who must sell themselves piecemeal, are a commodity, like every other article of commerce, and are consequently exposed to all the vicissitudes of competition, to all the fluctuations of the market.

Owing to the extensive use of machinery and to division of labor the work of the proletarians has lost all individual character, and, consequently, all charm for the workman. He becomes an appendage of the machine, and it is only the most simple, most monotonous, and most easily acquired knack that is required of him . . .

But with the development of industry the proletariat not only increases in number, it becomes concentrated in greater masses, its strength grows, and it feels that strength more. . . . Thereupon the workers begin to form combinations (trade unions) against the bourgeoisie; . . . This union is helped by the improved means of communication that are created by modern industries and that places the workers of different localities in contact with one another. It was just this contact that was needed to centralize the numerous local struggles, all of the same character, into one national struggle between classes. . . . Further as we have already seen, entire sections of the ruling classes are, by the advance of industry precipitated into the proletariat, or are at least threatened in their conditions of existence. These also supply the proletariat with fresh elements of enlightenment and progress. . . . Of all the classes that stand face to face with the bourgeoisie today, the proletariat alone is a really revolutionary class . . . the violent overthrow of the bourgeoisie lays the foundation for the sway of the proletariat . . .

What the bourgeoisie, therefore, produces, above all, is its own gravediggers. Its fall and the victory of the proletariat are equally inevitable . . .

II. PROLETARIAN AND COMMUNISTS

The Communists, therefore, are on the one hand, practically, the most advanced and resolute section of the working-class parties of every country. . . . The immediate aim of the Communists is the same as that of all the proletarian parties: formation of the proletariat into a class, overthrow of the bourgeois supremacy, conquest of political power by the proletariat . . .

All property relations in the past have continually been subject to historical change consequent upon the change in historical conditions. . . . But modern bourgeois private property is the final and most complete expression of the system of producing and appropriating products that is based on class antagonisms, on the exploitation of the many by the few.

In this sense, the theory of the Communists may be summed up in the single phrase: Abolition of private property . . .

The workingmen have no country. . . . National differences and antagonisms between peoples are daily vanishing, owing to the development of the bourgeoisie, to freedom of commerce, to the world market, to uniformity in the mode of production and in the condition of life corresponding thereto. . . . In proportion as the exploitation of one individual by another is put to an end, the exploitation of one nation by another will also be put to an end. In proportion as the antagonisms between classes within the nation vanishes, the hostility of one nation to another will come to an end . . .

We have seen above that the first step in the revolution by the working class is to raise the proletariat to the position of ruling class to win the battle of democracy.

The proletariat will use its political supremacy to wrest, by degrees, all capital from the bourgeoisie, to centralize all instruments of production in the hands of the state, i.e., of the proletariat organized as the ruling class; and to increase the total of productive forces as rapidly as possible.

Of course, in the beginning this cannot be effected except by means of despotic inroads on the rights of property . . .

Nevertheless in the most advanced countries, the following will be pretty generally applicable:

1. Abolition of property in land and application of all rents of land to public purposes.
2. A heavy progressive or graduated income tax.

3. Abolition of all right of inheritance.
4. Confiscation of the property of all emigrants and rebels.
5. Centralization of credit in the lands of the state, by means of a national bank with state capital and an exclusive monopoly.
6. Centralization of the means of communication and transport in the hands of the state.
7. Extension of factories and instruments of production owned by the state; the bringing into cultivation of wastelands, and the improvement of the soil generally in accordance with a common plan.
8. Equal liability of all to labor. Establishment of industrial armies, especially for agriculture.
9. Combination of agriculture with manufacturing industries; gradual abolition of the distinction between town and country, by a more equitable distribution of the population over the country.
10. Free education for all children in public schools. Abolition of children's factory labor in its present form. Combination of education with industrial production, etc., etc. . . .

In short Communists everywhere support every revolutionary movement against the existing social and political order of things . . .

The Communists disdain to conceal their views and aims. They openly declare that their ends can be attained only by the forcible overthrow of all existing social conditions. Let the ruling classes tremble at the Communistic revolution. The proletarians have nothing to lose but their chains. They have a world to win.

WORKINGMEN OF ALL COUNTRIES, UNITE!

Appendix 2

Excerpts from Speech by Vaclav Havel

former President of Czechoslovakia
January 1, 1990
(*Source*: *New York Times*, January 2, 1990)

PRAGUE, Jan. 1—Following are excerpts from President Vaclav Havel's New Year's Day address, as translated by the *New York Times*:

For 40 years you have heard on this day from the mouths of my predecessors, in a number of variations, the same thing: how our country is flourishing, how many more millions of tons of steel we have produced, how we are all happy, how we believe in our Government and what beautiful prospects are opening ahead of us. I assume you have not named me to this office so that I, too, should lie to you.

Our country is not flourishing. The great creative and spiritual potential of our nations is not being applied meaningfully. Entire branches of industry are producing things for which there is no demand while we are short of things we need.

The state, which calls itself a state of workers, is humiliating and exploiting them instead. Our outmoded economy wastes energy, which we have in short supply. The country, which could once be proud of the education of its people, is spending so little on education that today, in that respect, we rank 72d in the world. We have spoiled our land, rivers and forests, inherited from our ancestors, and we have, today, the worst environment in the whole of Europe. Adults die here earlier than in the majority of European countries. . . .

The worst of it is that we live in a spoiled moral environment. We have become morally ill because we are used to saying one thing and thinking another. We have learned not to believe in anything, not to care about each other, to worry only about ourselves. The concepts of love, friendship, mercy, humility or forgiveness have lost their depths and dimension, and for many of us they represent only some sort of psychological curiosity or they appear as long-lost wanderers from faraway times, somewhat ludicrous in the era of computers and space ships. . . .

The previous regime, armed with a proud and intolerant ideology, reduced people into the means of production, and nature into its tools. So it attacked

259

their very essence, and their mutual relations. . . . Out of talented and responsible people, ingeniously husbanding their land, it made cogs of some sort of great, monstrous, thudding, smelly machine, with an unclear purpose. All it can do is, slowly but irresistibly, wear itself out, with all its cogs.

If I speak about a spoiled moral atmosphere I don't refer only to our masters. . . . I'm speaking about all of us. For all of us have grown used to the totalitarian system and accepted it as an immutable fact, and thereby actually helped keep it going. None of us are only its victims; we are all also responsible for it.

It would be very unwise to think of the sad heritage of the last 40 years only as something foreign, something inherited from a distant relative. On the contrary, we must accept this heritage as something we have inflicted on ourselves. If we accept it in such a way, we shall come to understand it is up to all of us to do something about it.

Let us make no mistake: even the best Government, the best Parliament and the best President cannot do much by themselves. Freedom and democracy, after all, mean joint participation and shared responsibility. If we realize this, then all the horrors that the new Czechoslovak democracy inherited cease to be so horrific. If we realize this, then hope will return to our hearts.

Naturally we too had to pay for our present-day freedom. Many of our citizens died in prison in the 1950s. Many were executed. Thousands of human lives were destroyed. Hundreds of thousands of talented people were driven abroad. . . . Those who fought against totalitarianism during the war were also persecuted. . . . Nobody who paid in one way or another for our freedom could be forgotten.

Independent courts should justly evaluate the possible guilt of those responsible, so that the full truth about our recent past should be exposed.

But we should also not forget that other nations paid an even harsher price for their present freedom, and paid indirectly for ours as well. All human suffering concerns each human being. . . . Without changes in the Soviet Union, Poland, Hungary and the German Democratic Republic, what happened here could hardly have taken place, and certainly not in such a calm and peaceful way.

Now it depends only on us whether this hope will be fulfilled, whether our civic, national and political self-respect will be revived. Only a man or nation with self-respect, in the best sense of the word, is capable of listening to the voices of others, while accepting them as equals, of forgiving enemies and of expiating sins . . .

Perhaps you are asking what kind of republic I am dreaming about. I will answer you: a republic that is independent, free, democratic, a republic with economic prosperity and also social justice, a humane republic that serves man and that for that reason also has the hope that man will serve it . . .

My most important predecessor started his first speech by quoting from Comenius. Permit me to end my own first speech by my own paraphrase. Your Government, my people, has returned to you.

References

Allison, Graham. 1971. *Essence of decision*. New York: Little, Brown.

Banks, Arthur S. 1985. *Political handbook of the world*. Binghamton, NY: SUNY.

Bell, John D. 1990. Post-Communist Bulgaria. *Current History* (December), 417–420.

Bemis, Samuel. 1942. *A diplomatic history of the United States*. New York: Holt, 196–209.

Bertsch, Gary K. 1985. *Power and policy in communist systems*. New York: Wiley.

British Embassy, Prague. (1991, 1992) Press reviews.

Byrnes, James F. 1947. *Speaking frankly*. New York: Harper & Row.

Butterfield, Fox. 1982. *China: Alive in the bitter sea*. New York: Bantam.

Chou, Ching-wen. 1960. *Ten years of storm*. New York: Holt.

Christian Science Monitor (*CSM*). Various issues.

Childs, David. 1988. East Germany: Glasnost and globetrotting. *The World Today* (October 1987) In *Global studies. The Soviet Union and Eastern Europe*. Guilford, CT: Dushkin Publishing Group.

Churchill, Winston. 1953. *Triumph and tragedy*. Boston: Houghton Mifflin.

Clubb, Edward. 1964, 1972, and 1978. *Twentieth century China*, 3 vols. New York: Columbia University Press.

Connor, Walter. 1979. *Socialism, politics, and equality*. New York: Columbia University Press.

Davison, W. P., and J. S. Zasloff. 1966. A profile of Viet Cong cadres. Memorandum RM-4983-1-ISA/ARPA (June). RAND Corporation.

del Aguila, Juan M. 1987. Cuba's declining fortunes. *Current History* (December), 424–428.

Dienstbier, Juri. 1991. Central Europe's Security. *Foreign Policy* (Summer).

Dispatch. Published by U.S. Department of State, Bureau of Public Affairs.

Eklof, Ben. 1989. *Soviet briefing: Gorbachev and the reform period*. Boulder, CO: Westview Press.

Fagen, Richard R. 1983. Revolution and transition in Nicaragua. In *Stanford Central American Action Network, revolution in Central America*. Boulder, CO: Westview Press.

Fall, Bernard B. 1967. *Ho Chi Minh on revolution*. New York: Praeger.

Far Eastern Economic Review. (1988, 1989, 1991, and 1992). *Asia Yearbook*.

Freedom House 1991–1992. 1992. *Freedom in the world*. New York: Freedom House.

Freedom House 1990–1991. 1991. *Freedom in the world*. New York: Freedom House.

Freedom House 1987–1988. 1988. *Freedom in the world*. New York: Freedom House.

Furtak, Robert. 1986. *The political systems of the socialist states*. New York: St. Martin's.

Garthoff, Raymond. 1987. *Reflections on the Cuban missile crisis.* Washington, DC: Brookings.

Garthoff, Raymond. 1990. *Détente and confrontation.* Washington, DC: Brookings.

Giap, Vo Nguyen. 1962. *People's war, people's army.* New York: Praeger.

Gilbert, Dennis. 1986. Nicaragua. In *Confronting revolution*, Morris J. Blackman et al. eds. New York: Pantheon.

Ginsburg, George. 1978. *The Sino-Soviet territorial dispute 1949–1964.* New York: Praeger/Holt.

Gorbachev, M. 1987. *Perestroika.* New York: Harper & Row.

Griffith, William E. 1964. *The Sino-Soviet rift.* Cambridge: MIT Press.

Gunn, Gillian. 1992. Cuba's search for alternatives. *Current History* (February).

Gunn, Gillian. 1990. Will Castro fail? *Foreign Policy* (Summer).

Hart, Henry. 1984. *If East Europeans could vote.* Washington, DC: Ethics and Public Policy Center.

Haseler, Stephen. 1978. *Eurocommunism.* New York: St. Martin's.

Higgins, Trumbill. 1987. *The perfect failure.* New York: Norton.

Hinton, Harold. 1982. *Government and politics in revolutionary China.* Wilmington: Scholarly Resources.

Hull, Cordell. 1948. *The memoirs of Cordell Hull*, 2 vols. New York: Macmillan.

Hunt, R. N. Carew. 1963. *The theory and practice of communism.* Baltimore: Penguin.

International Monetary Fund, *IMF Survey.*

International Monetary Fund, *World Economic Outlook May 1992.* Washington, DC.

International Monetary Fund, *World Economic Outlook, October 1992.* Washington, DC.

Johnson, Lyndon B. 1971. *The vantage point.* New York: Holt.

Jones, Christopher D. 1981. *Soviet influence in Eastern Europe.* New York: Praeger.

Kamrany, Nake M. 1986. The continuing war in Afghanistan. *Current History* (October), 333–336.

Karnow, Stanley. 1983. *Vietnam: A history.* New York: Penguin.

Kennan, George. 1960. *Russia and the West under Stalin.* New York: Little, Brown.

Kennedy, Robert F. 1969. *Thirteen days.* New York: Signet.

Khrushchev, Nikita. 1970. *Khrushchev remembers.* Boston: Little, Brown.

Khrushchev, Nikita. 1974. *Khrushchev remembers—The last testament.* Boston: Little, Brown.

Kissinger, Henry. 1979. *White House years.* Boston: Little, Brown.

Klosowski, Julius. 1991. *The Warsaw Voice.* August 4, 1991.

Krumwiede, Heinrich-W. 1984. Sandinist democracy: Problems of institutionalization. In *Political change in Central America*, Wolf Grabendorff et al., eds. Boulder, CO: Westview Press.

Leonard, Wolfgang. 1978. *Eurocommunism: Challenge for east and west.* New York: Holt.

Lowenthal, Richard. 1964. *World communism.* New York: Oxford University Press.

McColm, Bruce R. et al. (Freedom House Survey Team). 1991. *Freedom in the world: Political rights and civil liberties.* New York: Freedom House.

McNeal, Robert H. 1963. *The Bolshevik tradition.* Englewood Cliffs, NJ: Prentice-Hall.

Mackintosh, J. M. 1963. *Strategy and tactics of Soviet foreign policy.* New York: Oxford University Press.

Macridis, Roy C., ed. 1987. *Modern political systems: Europe*. Englewood Cliffs, NJ: Prentice-Hall.

Meisner, Maurice. 1989. *Mao's China*. New York: Free Press, 365–370.

Michielsen, Peter. 1988. The world and I (June 1987). In *Global studies. The Soviet Union and Eastern Europe*. Sluice Dock, Guilford, CT: Dushkin Publishing Group.

Morrison, John. 1991. *Boris Yeltsin*. New York: Dutton.

Naughton, Barry. 1991. The economy emerges from a rough patch. *Current History China* (September), 259–263.

Nelkrich, Alexander. 1978. *The punished peoples*. New York: W. W. Horton.

New York Times (*NYT*). Various issues.

New York Times. 1971. *Pentagon Papers*. New York: Bantam Books.

Nethercut, Richard D. 1983. Leadership in China: Rivalry, reform and renewal. *Problems of Communism*. U.S. Department of State.

Oksenberg, Michael. 1991. The China Problem. *Foreign Affairs* (Spring), 1–16.

Ozinga, James R. 1987. *Communism: The story of the idea and its implementation*. Englewood Cliffs, NJ: Prentice-Hall.

Peking Review. Various issues.

People's Republic of China Yearbook. 1988–1989.

Pollack, Maxine. 1988. Insight (November 23). In *Global studies. The Soviet Union and Eastern Europe*. Sluice Dock, Guilford, CT: Dushkin Publishing Group.

Pye, Lucian W. 1984. *China: An introduction*. Boston: Little, Brown.

Radio Free Europe. 1981. East European area audience and opinion research.

Remington, Robin Allison. 1990. The federal dilemma in Yugoslavia. *Current History* (December).

Rice, Edward E. 1974. *Mao's way*. Berkeley: University of California Press.

Roskin, Michael. 1991. *The Rebirth of East Europe*. Englewood Cliffs, NJ: Prentice-Hall.

Rossi, Peter H., and Alex Inkeles. 1957. Multidimensional ratings of occupation. *Sociometry* (March).

Rostow, W. W. 1972. *Diffusion of power*. New York: Macmillan.

Rubinstein, Alvin E. 1985. *Soviet foreign policy since World War II*. Boston: Little, Brown.

Schlesinger, Arthur. 1965. *A thousand days*. New York: Fawcett Crest.

Schlesinger, Arthur. 1978. *Kennedy and his times*. New York: Fawcett Crest.

Schmid, Alex P. 1985. *Soviet military interventions since 1945*. New Brunswick, NJ: Transaction Books, 26–29.

Schram, Stuart. 1969. *Poltical Thought of Mao*. New York: Praeger.

Seton-Watson, Hugh. 1961. *The East European revolution*. New York: Frederick A. Praeger.

Sivard, Ruth. 1991. *World military and social expenditures*. Washington, DC: World Priorities.

Snow, Edgar. 1971. Conversations with Mao Tse-tung. *Life* (April 30), 46–48.

Sorenson, Theodore. 1966. *Kennedy*. London: Pan Books.

Starr, Richard F. 1982. *Communist regimes in Eastern Europe*. Stanford, CA: Hoover Institution Press.

Szoboszlai, Georgy. 1991. Political transition and constitutional change. In *Democracy and political transformation: Theories and East-Central European realities*, Georgy Szoboszlai, ed. Budapest: Hungarian Political Science Association.

Tannahill, R. Leonard. 1978. *The Communist parties of Western Europe*. Westport, CT: Greenwood Press.

Tokes, Rudolf. 1978. *Eurocommunism and détente*. New York: New York University Press.

Tokes, Rudolf L. 1991. Hungary's new political elites: Adaptation and change, 1989–1990. In *Democracy and political transformation: Theories and East-Central European realities*, Georgy Szoboszlai, ed. Budapest: Hungarian Political Science Association.

United Nations. 1968. *Everyman's United Nations*. New York.

U.S. Department of State. 1980. Soviet invasion of Afghanistan. Special Report No. 70 (April).

U.S. Department of State. 1981. Communist interference in El Salvador. Special Report No. 80 (February 23).

U.S. Department of State. 1981a. Cuba's renewed support for violence in Latin America. Special Report No. 90 (December 14).

U.S. Department of State. 1987. Treaty between the United States of America and the Union of Soviet Socialist Republics on the elimination of their intermediate-range and shorter-range missiles. (Washington, DC, December). Transcript of hearings before the Committee on Armed Services of the House of Representatives, March 10, 15–16.

U.S. Department of State. 1988. U.S. condemns North Korean terrorism. Current Policy Paper 1042 (March).

U.S. Embassy, Budapest. 1992. FY92 Country marketing plan: Hungary.

van Tuyll, Herbert. 1989. *Feeding the bear*. New York: Greenwood Press.

Wang, James C. F. 1989. *Contemporary Chinese politics*. Englewood Cliffs, NJ: Prentice-Hall.

Washington Post. Various issues.

Wesson, Robert G. 1978. *Communism and communist systems*. Englewood Cliffs, NJ: Prentice-Hall.

Yoder, Amos. 1961. Communist China's economic growth in perspective. *American Journal of Economics and Sociology* (July).

Zasloff, J. J. 1968. Origins of the insurgency in South Vietnam, 1954–1960. RAND memorandum Rm-5163/1-ISA/ARPA (May).

Zoltan Abadi-Nagy. Dean, Faculty of Arts and Social Sciences. L. Kossuth University, Debrecen, Hungary. Letter. 10/10/92.

Zweig, David. 1989. Slowly North Korea begins to stir. *New York Times*, July, editorial page.

Selected Bibliography

The following books are recommended reading in addition to those cited in text (see References).

Acheson, Dean. *Present at the Creation*. New York: Harcourt Brace, 1967.

Adelman, Jonathan R., and Deborah Palmieri. *The Dynamics of Soviet Foreign Policy*. New York: Harper & Row, 1989.

Banac, Ivo. *The National Question in Yugoslavia*. Ithaca, NY: Cornell University Press, 1992.

Bialer, Seweryn. *Inside Gorbachev's Russia*. Boulder, CO: Westview Press, 1989.

Brzezinski, Zbgniew. *Power and Principle*. New York: Farr, 1983.

Carter, Jimmy. *Keeping Faith*. New York: Bantam, 1982.

Chanda, N. "Suddenly Last Spring," *Far Eastern Economic Review*, September 12, 1975.

Chayes, A. *The Cuban Missile Crisis*. New York: Oxford, 1974.

Churchill, Winston. *The Aftermath*. London: Macmillan, 1929.

Churchill, Winston. *The Gathering Storm*. Cambridge: Houghton Mifflin, 1948.

Cohen, Warren. *America's Response to China*. New York: Wiley, 1971.

Davies, J. E. *Mission to Moscow*. New York: Pocket Books, 1943.

Devine, R. *The Cuban Missile Crisis*. Chicago: Quadrangle, 1971.

Donnell, John C. "Vietcong Recruitment: Why and How Men Join," RAND, Memorandum RM-54-86-1-ISA/ARPA, December 1967.

Dreyer, June Teufel, ed. *Chinese Defense and Foreign Policy*. New York: Paragon, 1989.

Eisenhower, Dwight. *Mandate for Change*. New York: Doubleday, 1963.

Eisenhower, Dwight. *Waging Peace*. New York: Doubleday, 1965.

Fischer-Galati, Stephen. *Eastern Europe in the 1980s*. Boulder, CO: Westview Press, 1981.

Gravel, M. *The Pentagon Papers*. Boston: Beacon Press, 1971.

Griffith, William E., ed. *Central and Eastern Europe: The Opening Curtain?* Boulder, CO: Westview, 1989.

Halperin, Morton H. *China and the Bomb*. New York: Praeger, 1965.

Hendel, Samuel. *The Soviet Crucible*. Belmont, CA: Brooks Cole, 1981.

Herring, George C. *America's Longest War*. New York: Wiley, 1979.

Higgins, Trumbull. *The Perfect Failure*. New York: Norton, 1987.

Hill, Ronald J., and Peter Frank. *The Soviet Communist Party*. Boston: Allen & Unwin, 1986.

Holmes, Leslie. *Politics in the Communist World*. Oxford: Clarendon Press, 1986.

Kattenburg, Paul. *The Vietnam Trauma*. New Brunswick, NJ: Transaction, 1980.

Kane, Anthony J. *China Briefing, 1988*. Boulder, CO: Westview Press, 1988.

Kissinger, Henry. *Years of Upheaval*. Boston: Little, Brown, 1982.

Medvedev, Roy, and Giulietto Chiesa. *Time of Change: An Insider's View of Russia's Transformation*. New York: Pantheon, 1989.

Moorehead, Alan. *The Russian Revolution*. New York: Harper, 1958.

Morrison, John. *Boris Yeltsin—From Bolshevik to Democrat*. A. Dutton, 1991.

Mosley, Philip. *The Kremlin and World Politics*. New York: Random House, 1959.

New York Times. *Pentagon Papers*. New York: Bantam Books, 1971.

Nogee, Joseph L., and Robert Donaldson. *Soviet Foreign Policy*. New York: Pergamon, 1988.

Pachter, H. M. *Collision Course*. New York: Praeger, 1963.

Paterson, T. G. *The Origins of the Cold War*. Lexington: D. C. Heath, 1970.

Paterson, T. G. *Soviet-American Confrontation*. Baltimore: Johns Hopkins, 1973.

Rose, L. A. *After Yalta*. New York: Scribner's, 1973.

Selden, Mark, and Victor Lippit, eds. *The Transition to Socialism in China*. Armonk, NY: M. E. Sharpe, 1982.

Sherwood, Robert. *Roosevelt and Hopkins*. New York: Harper, 1948.

Stankovic, Slobodan. *The End of the Tito Era*. Stanford: Hoover Institute, 1981.

Talbott, Strobe. *Deadly Gambit*. New York: Knopf, 1984.

U.S. Arms Control and Disarmament Agency. *Arms Control and Disarmament Agreements*. Washington, DC: GPO, 1980.

U.S. Central Intelligence Agency and Defense Intelligence Agency. *The Soviet Economy Stumbles Badly in 1989*. Washington, DC: U.S. Congress, Joint Economic Committee, 1989.

U.S. Congress, Joint Economic Committee. *China's Economic Dilemmas in the 1990s*. Washington, DC: U.S. GPO, 1991.

U.S. Senate, Select Committee. *Alleged Assassination Plots Involving Foreign Leaders*. Washington, DC: GPO, 1975.

U.S. Department of State. *Foreign Relations of the United States: East Asia and the Pacific 1950*, vol. 6. Washington, DC: GPO, 1976.

U.S. Department of State. *United States Relations with China 1944-1950*. Washington, DC: GPO, 1949.

U.S. Embassy, Berlin. *GDR Economic Expansion: First Results and Best Prospects*. East Berlin, May 1990.

U.S. Embassy, Berlin. *Survey of GDR Foreign Commercial Activity*. May 1990.

Yao, Ming-le. *The Conspiracy and Death of Lin Biao*. New York: Knopf, 1983.

Yoder, Amos. *The Conduct of American Foreign Policy Since World War II*. Fairview Park, NY: Pergamon, 1986.

Yoder, Amos. *World Politics and the Causes of War since 1914*. Lanham, MD: University Press, 1986.

Index

ABC Agreement, 58, 106, 240
ABM (Anti-ballistic Missile) Treaty, 63–67, 70, 238
Acheson, Dean, 59
Afghanistan, 13, 47–48, 65, 66, 75, 83, 166, **195–203**,* 213, 230, 238, 239, 241, 243, 249, 254
Albania, 43, 59, 110, 112, 114, **121–123**, 126, 127, 221, 223
Alia Ramiz, 122
Amin, 196–197
Andropov, Yuri, 30, 52, 221, 227
Antal, Joseph, 85
Angola, 212, 213, 247
Armenia, 40–48, 52, 71
Amur River, 15
ASEAN (*see* Association of Southeast Asian Nations)
Association of Southeast Asian Nations (ASEAN), 191, 193
Austria, 16, 81, 85, 104
Austrian Treaty, 61
Australia, 159, 172, 173, 193
Austro-Hungarian Empire, 78, 109
Azerbaijan, 39, 40–48, 52, 69, 71, 231

Baker, James, 69, 70–71, 73, 105
Baltic republics, 35, 73, 239
    (*See also* Latvia, Estonia, and Lithuania)
Bao Dai, Emperor, 179
Batista, 247
Bay of Pigs, 207–208, 211, 214, 247
Belarus (*see* Byelorussia)
Belgium, 55
Benes, Edward, 95

*Entries in bold are covered extensively in text.

Beria, 28
Berlin, 58, 62, 102, 210
Berlin Blockade, 58, 101
Berlin Wall, 72, 85, 98, 102, 106, 120, 128, 148, 229, 238
Bessarabia, 116
Biao, Lin, 224
Big Bang (*see* Market Systems and Reforms)
Bolivia, 212
Boat people, 140, 186
Bolsheviks, 8, 15–18
Borah, William, 152
Borodin, Michael, 154, 178
Bosnia-Herzegovina, 109, 112, 114, 115, 231
Boutros-Ghali, Boutros, 115
Boxer Rebellion, 102
Brandt, Willy, 64, 102
Brezhnev, 24, 26, 30, 52, 57, 59, 63, 96–97, 162, 197, 226, 229
Brezhnev Doctrine, 96–97, 241
Britain (*see* United Kingdom)
Broz, Josip (*see* Tito)
Brussels Treaty, 58
Bucovina, 116
Buddhists, 174, 183, 193
Bulgaria, 43, 54, 96, 100, 109, **119–121**, 120, 127, 221
Burma, 173, 193
Bush, George, 39, 59, 69, 72, 85, 91, 165–167, 201, 239, 244
Byelorussia (Belarus), 28, **40–49**, 69, 71, 230

Cambodia, 1, 47–48, 68, 162–164, 172–173, **186–191**, 202, 203, 221, 243, 249, 252, 254
Capitalism, 9, 10, 13, 18, 55, 75, 137, 139, 159, 182, 213, 215, 232, 243
Carrillo, Santiago, 65

267

About the Author

Amos Yoder is Borah Distinguished Professor Emeritus of Political Science from the University of Idaho. He taught international relations courses there from 1974 to 1991. Before then, he was in the diplomatic service of the Department of State for 25 years, assigned to United Nations, Chinese, German, and politico-military affairs in Washington, DC; to U.S. embassies in Thailand and Israel; and to international conferences. In 1986–1987 he taught at the Foreign Affairs College in Beijing, China, as a Fulbright professor, and in 1991 he taught at the L. Kossuth University at Debrecen, Hungary, as a Fulbright professor. He has published articles and books, including *The Conduct of American Foreign Policy since World War II, World Politics and the Causes of War since 1914, International Politics and Policymakers' Ideas, The Evolution of the United Nations System*, and *Communist Systems and Challenges*.